LOVE YOUR SELF:
NO MORE SELLING OUT

by

J. SPENCER WENDT

ISBN:
Print: 978-1-5356-1571-6
Hardcover: 978-1-5356-1572-3

Dedication

**To all the incredibly brave people
who trusted me and shared their self
and their life story.**

Thank you!

*"Your visions will become clear
only when you can look into your own heart.
Who looks outside, dreams;
who looks inside, awakes."*
— C. G. Jung

Contents

This Work: Overview

This work is my initial foray into the world of "writing a book." It seems appropriate here that I give you an idea of where the book is taking you and the path you will be on.

What follows this explanation and is still within the front matter is my "Prologue," subtitled "Making a Difference." It opens with a montage about to set the table and give you a sense of my writing style. For which, I would appreciate no judgment. Hopefully, my work becomes easier to consume with time and more work.

In case you may ask the question "Who is this guy?" I address "me" in the "Introduction," the last section of which is titled "My Biases and Opinions," which opens with a few words about my biases. We all have them (even BoldAirians). Daniel Kahneman has a fabulous read on the subject of biases and what influences our decisions.[1] He provides very compelling discussions on the biases we have, even when we are giving our best effort *not* to have biases. I have mine, and I share some of the more relevant ones in this section.

But before that section is a random rambling exposé that covers a bit about my background. The "thud" at the end of the rambling is the sound of me landing "here," as a relationship counselor. There is a brief trip down "What Happened Avenue," and you are riding shotgun. I choose the music. The title is "Who I Was, I Am Now" (followed by a short summary, "Who Am I?"). My intention is to set the tone of our conversation. I am direct and have resolved some definitive conclusions about people, life, and relationships. A taste of my conclusive style is served up with summarizing lines near the end: "Life is about choices.

Life is a succession of learning experiences. Mining the gold from your life reveals the hidden wisdom for you. We are all alike. We each have a life, and we each have our story."

I put some thought into whom I am writing to as well. Every business has a "target market" for its "product." When I started putting my thoughts together for the book, I figured out, with my business background, whom I was speaking to and who would most likely benefit from reading this book. The section "My Audience" describes who I believe is my "target audience." I also make an important distinction that this work is *not* for everyone. Maybe I am politically incorrect by profiling the type of person (age, sex, and status) whom I want to address. Maybe that is you, maybe not. I thought a quick heads up might be helpful. It could save you some time and money—especially if you are wondering whether to buy my book or re-up for another month on match.com. Following this section are a few paragraphs about my counseling methodology in case you are interested, "The 360 Model: Full Spectrum."

Speaking of match.com leads me into describing Chapter 1: "Myths versus Truths: Separating Fact from Fiction." Part of the difficulty in becoming healthy (goal number one) and creating and maintaining healthy relationships (goal number two) is that people are operating and making relationship decisions based on some exceptionally poor information. To further compound this error, the wrong information is biased by more bad information. People grow up hearing and being taught that "this is how the world works." But the problem is that people really know that "life" and "it" *doesn't* work this way . . . *from their experience*. Yes, against what they know, they *still believe* that the inaccurate, incorrect information is *correct*, and then they make decisions based the erroneous information.

An example? Maybe you've read this line in a dating profile: "I want 'that weak in the knees chemistry' . . ." and (this time) "I won't settle for less!" Hmmm . . . I suspect the person who wrote this had, in fact, experienced "that chemistry" at the beginning of most, if not all, of their[1] relationships. But those relationships had all "ended prematurely" (that is, "failed" . . . including some epic fails!). But despite the profile writer's knowing that "that chemistry" doesn't lead to successful relationships, instead of doing something different, the same "that chemistry" is still their "criterion" for their *next* relationship as well!!! OK!! Stop the madness. I introduce my first "made-up word": "Mythstake." With the "That Chemistry" myth, we have what is called a classic relationship "Mythstake." These and other myths are "de-myth-stified" in Chapter 1, along with some truth telling about what works and what doesn't. (By the way, although "weak in the knees" is a myth, the truth is you might want to go ahead and introduce your self[2] by saying "Hello" to the one who inspires the knee-weakening response, because if they "feel" what you "feel," that "Hello" will probably result in some seriously hot, passionate sex. However, a warning: It probably won't result in a relationship that lasts . . . FWIW. But you knew that already!)

After the preceding setup for the book is out of the way, it's time to get down to business. Chapter 2, labeled "Your Journey: Discovering 'You,'" draws on a "puzzle" metaphor to set the stage for "your work": being healthy and experiencing healthy relationships. You must "be healthy" to have a chance at experiencing "a healthy relationship." The first pieces of the puzzle are "love and ego," explored at length in Chapter 3 and Chapter 4, respectively. Love (Chapter 3) is pretty much a mystery—before you read these pages, that is. When you are finished with those pages, however, love is a clear, definable concept. When someone asks, "What do you mean when you say, 'I love you'?" you will speak your answer, and it won't be the magazine-rack pablum, such as "You mean so

---

1 For an explanation of my using "they" and "them" and "their" for a genderless third-person singular pronoun (rather than the cumbersome and awkward "he or she" and "him or her" and "his or her" or other barbarisms), please see "My Writing Style Bias" in the Introduction.
2 Also, for an explanation of my using "your self" rather than "yourself" (and "my self" rather than "myself" as well as other "reflexive" forms), again please see "My Writing Style Bias" in the Introduction.

much to me . . ." In your answer, love will be a real, clear, and concrete concept. Hopefully, it will leave your questioner musing something on the order of "Wow! That is the first time I ever knew what 'I love you' meant. . . . Thank you." Chapter 3 is long. How could it not be? Your entire reason for occupying space on the planet is to love.

It's good to know how ego stops love, and that is explored in Chapter 4. The conversation about love and ego brings relationship matters into clear focus. The section in that chapter titled "Two Paths of Life" describes how love is put into practice. The case is made for love but in contrast with "the other side": ego. One or the other is present in all conversations and relationships. No exceptions. Understanding the language of ego is a crucial addition to your relating skills toolset.

With the foundation set, the book moves into "Relationships," Chapter 5, which opens with a view from "fifty thousand feet" and hopefully adds more to your awareness. Relationships are where "you" and an "other" come together. This coming together requires healthy relationship skills, including such elements as "boundaries," "emotions," and "preferences," each element described in its own section in Chapter 5. Then the discussion moves to "conflict resolution," the "multi-tool" in your toolbox, which will help you navigate issues, complete and reconstitute yourself after an "ending," provide a resource to "fill in the gaps" in your past, and more. The case is made for conflict resolution being the "make or break" relating skill that determines the outcome of every relationship. Yes, success or failure is based on this single relationship skill.

Chapter 6, "Healthy Relationships," brings the entire puzzle together. The focus of the chapter is on romantic love relationships. The discussion defines the total universe of "real" relationship prospects. The folks who don't make your list include narcissists, "victims," people with addiction issues, and "the needy" (codependents). Relationships with unhealthy people are "unworkable," and are discussed in Chapter 7, "Unworkable Relationships." Here we add another skill: "loving from a distance." The chemistry of mating is explored in Chapter 8, "Sex: The Drug of Choice"; hopefully, the information provided there explains the manner in which your romantic love relationship is created and gives you insight into what matters most (and it's not "that chemistry"). Chapter 9, "Attachment Styles and Chem-*patibility*," outlines four different relating styles that have been extensively researched, and it suggests ways you can evolve your style of relating toward a secure attachment style. That chapter also describes the chemistry of compatibility, chem-*patibility*, focusing on wiring the elements of attraction that are mostly out of your control to the decision-making aspects of your creating a healthy relationship.

"Standing Where the Road Divides," Chapter 10, completes our conversation. There is no "crescendo" ending. It won't be like squeezing your squeeze during the last bars of Beethoven's Fifth filling a cool Fourth of July evening. No exploding colors and lights in the sky overhead. That's not the ending. With all the skills and wisdom delivered, the challenge is described in the vignette "standing where the road divides." By Chapter 10, you have everything you need. Which, by the way, you always had, but now you will be standing with fewer questions than you had when you opened the book: "What will I do next?" "Can I do my work?" Now the challenges are slightly different: Will you honor your true self? Will you stay aware? Will the temptations to sell out be too much . . . again? "Life is about choices," and hopefully your work has you standing in a place where you choose love. That is my hope.

The body of the book closes with "Epilogue: Afterthoughts and Considerations," introducing the section "Story Has Power: Tell Your Story," which includes a couple of short vignettes, client and friend life stories. There is "gold to mine" in everyone's story . . . for them and for you. There is some gold to mine in these stories, especially if they resonate with you and your response is "Me too . . . I've been there!"

Story has power. Tell your story. The Epilogue wraps up a few loose ends, and then we go our separate ways![3]

Enjoy!

---

3 Of course, after the Epilogue are appendixes, which have additional useful information.

Prologue: Making a Difference

If anyone were really intentional about making a difference in the world, adding a book about love and relationships would seem to be near the bottom of any reasonably constructed bucket list.

So I don't keep you waiting, the focus of my book can be summarized in these words:

> **With regard to people, love, relationships, and intimacy:**
> ***Something is broken.***

Considering all of the man-hours and thought that have attempted to explain, understand, or repair the "broken state" of people, love, relationships, and intimacy, it must leave you wondering: Can another book about how to keep another five-year marriage out of the ditch or help another soul recover from a disastrous relationship really make a difference? Another attempt to address the "brokenness" makes about as much sense as standing at the shore and tossing a beached starfish into the ocean with the belief that would "make a difference." I don't know the answer, but this book is my contribution. I hope it makes a difference for someone.

For as long as I can recall, my desire has been to "make a difference," regardless of the circumstances. After a half century of "learning experience" after "learning experience," I still believe I can make something happen in the world. It's probably an issue I need to bring up with my therapist. But I'll do that later . . . maybe. For now, there is more important work to do.

The details of my story are not that important, nor are they the focus of my book. A decade ago, however, my ego would be reminding me, as it had for most of my life, "*Hey*, your story is important, *you* are important!!" Today, the voice I am attuned to is the "real me," my "true self"—my heart. That is where I choose to live. Yes, there is some ego still hanging out, for sure! But I work at living from my heart and making a difference, in my own way, with my own words and through sharing my experiences.

An important point to make here is that "my story" is the conversation that "I" have with "my self." Yes. There are two distinct voices of "me." One that I work like hell to turn off and rein in. The other I had to dig like crazy to find, deep inside "me." Then to learn it, to hear it. Then to "turn it on," in order to shine my light into the world. "My story" has been the battle of silencing the voice of my ego and finding the voice of my heart. It has been (and always will be) the battle of "I" versus my "true self." This may be something you and I share, too. These contradicting "voices," or forces, are underlying all discussions of love and relationships. Because of their importance, love and ego are covered in detail in this book.

This contest between these two parts of me has been my greatest struggle . . . so far. I share some bits and pieces about me along the way. Hopefully, the result will be that the words, thoughts, and vignettes resonate with you. That is, with your "true self" so that part of you can recognize "the other part."

My purpose in creating and sharing this work is to make a difference in your life. The "size" of the difference is irrelevant. It could be one small insight about the choice of the words you use when someone attacks your heart with *their* angry words. It could be how you look at your child and see *them* for the very first time. How you see and know them as the unique gift that *they* are. Then you tell them, "You are perfectly OK just the way you are." The difference could simply be one small "Ahhhhaaa" moment when you become aware about you, about your past, or about a relationship when you choose either your heart over ego or ego instead of heart. To me, that is making a difference and is my measure of success.

Do I believe you and I connected through this book as a result of some *random* circumstance? No, I don't. Think about it. How many bookstore aisles did you stroll down? How many book jackets did you survey? How many titles did you read with a latte in hand and your head cocked sideways? How many intros or random chapters did you scan before choosing this book? How many workshops did you consider registering for or maybe even attended before you bought this book? How many psych-today profiles did you scroll through but then pass on before you landed on my info or website? Was "our" meeting here on these pages circumstance? Chance? A random event? No. It wasn't random.

That's the way the universe works. Which is good news, because it means there is "something" here for you. I believe that is how life works. I hope you enjoy the time we spend together. I hope what I share and write resonates with you and that whatever the "something" is that you discover makes a difference in your life.

First up . . .

INTRODUCTION

BEFORE DIVING INTO THE SKILLS and practices of healthy relationships, we need to set the table for our time together. This Introduction and Chapter 1 provide some background information for the book. Included here is what you need to know about my perspective, my style, and a few idiosyncrasies that color and flavor my work in a particular way. In keeping with my objective to be open and speak the truth, as I do in my counseling practice, it makes sense that I share a little about my self.[4] Why?

Because you and I are not that different. Of course, I have a life, and you have yours. Mine has had a million great moments, which contain the joy, peace, happiness, and contentment that I know. There have also been many not-so-great moments. Those are where I learned the most about my self and what really matters. But it's my life—and for the most part, I have come out better on the other side of all my life experiences. Yes, I still have work to do. I am and will always be a work in progress.

That is my life, but it's also your life, isn't it? It's in fact everyone's life. We have our experiences and then choose our perspective about "what happened," and that perspective determines the answer to the question "Who am I?" for you, for me, for everyone. These phrases "what happened" and "who am I" occur repeatedly throughout the book, because they are important on your quest to find "truth" about you and your life. They determine how you handle "what's next."

---

4 Again, for an explanation of my using "my self" rather than "myself" (and "your self" rather than "yourself" as well as other "reflexive" forms), please see "My Writing Style Bias" later in this Introduction.

We'll start with some backstory on my life. Obviously, my story has influenced the construction and presentation of the content here. Keep in mind, however, the main focus of the book is how to become healthy and create and maintain healthy relationships.

Who I Was, I Am Now

I have mentioned my quest about figuring out "me." The following is a part of "my story." Its time frame is from high school to my very recent past. It is intended to show that it took me nearly until age fifty before I started putting the pieces of my life together. Somewhere about age fifty is when I wanted to know some really important "whys" and a couple of "whats" in my life, such as:

- What was it about me that successfully crashed all my relationships?
- Why was I never able to love and be loved like I wanted?
- Why was I not able to see my true self?
- Why was I not able to love my self as I knew was possible?
- Why was I attracted to a particular kind of woman?
- Why was that particular kind of woman attracted to me?
- What was it about me that resulted in my relationships always following the same path?

This part of my journey started about eleven years ago. At the age of fifty, I said, "Stop!" followed shortly by, "I want to know the answers!" I had been blessed with some success in business. This allowed me the freedom to dedicate the time and energy to figure out my self and my relationships and to learn why people do what they do in their lives as parents and partners, and how what they do impacts the way they operate in relationships.

When I was young, I bought into a lot of stuff about life—about finding happiness and experiencing joy. Through my experience and observations, though, I learned that most of that stuff simply was not true. Maybe you can relate.

Lots of things were sold to me as being "the right path to follow." But for me, mostly . . . I felt called to go in the other direction. If everyone supposedly "knew" what was on the right path, I was more interested in knowing what was down the other path. If the "right way to do it" took a week, then I wanted to know if it could be done in three days. I guess I finally figured out that I had some measure of intelligence, because, honestly, I cannot remember opening a textbook before getting out of high school. School was not a challenge, but life was.

For my generation, us baby boomers, the paved road to success, happiness, and a great life was the following script: go to college, get a degree, get a job with a big Fortune 1000 company, get married, buy a house, and have kids. Then at age sixty or sixty-five, retire and "enjoy the good life." The daily grind that summed up "the good life" was wake up at 5:00 a.m., go to work, do your job, come home, eat dinner, have a nightcap, and go to bed. That was living "the good life" . . . every day for forty to forty-five years.

As I was growing up in West Houston, the road to success was visible to me every day. It was presented in living color on the long suburban streets of my West Houston neighborhood. The houses were filled with native Texans and a healthy dose of East Coast transfers who were mostly oil company executives and managers. Next door were the intractably boring corporate accountants who probably knew the number of times they smiled or laughed every week. It all looked pretty "samely" and boring to me. All had the same long front porch with the same white bench no one ever sat on. My apologies, I forgot about the corporate attorneys. Tight. Boring.

That was my neighborhood. It was 1960s and 1970s "American Success" personified. June and Ward Cleaver–type perfect. Norman Rockwell must have stood an easel with a fresh canvas in the middle my neighborhood and painted a few masterpieces.

Everything was perfect on the outside . . .

By the time I was forty or forty-five, I saw something different when I went home for the holidays. When I turned into my old street, what I saw wasn't the neatly manicured yards and well-edged driveways or the freshly painted eaves and gutters with the perfectly positioned downspouts. What I saw was the truth. Not one of those houses was any different from the others. Inside, I knew, there were no perfect people.

Every one of the folks inside those exquisitely kept exterior facades was in the fight of their life. Maybe it was their health, their money, their marriage, or their son or daughter who was "four wheels off the road, upside down in the ditch." It was something, and finally I saw and knew the truth.

No one was perfect. There was no such thing as "the good life." No matter the age, the face, the smiles, the new paint, the fancy car, the new pool. . . . There was just "life." It was far from perfect. The same held true about relationships. Some were healthy and vibrant, but mostly the others were broken; just like the one in my house, so was nearly every one on my street. I heard it, but until I became "aware," I didn't *know* it. While I didn't know all of their stories, in the years that had passed since I first ran those streets, I knew more about my self and my story.

"Who Am I?"

I am politically incorrect at times. Some of my jokes are awful. I have things in my life that I have yet to resolve in a healthy manner. I eat red meat. I enjoy bread and pasta, use Splenda instead of sugar, and like smoked ribs. I like one triple-shot latte at 5:30 a.m. I like Newcastle Brown Ale, and I don't drink hard liquor. I drink white wine; red gives me massive headaches. I enjoy a cigar about once a month or so. Rocky Patel Sun Grown (Robusto). Sometimes I enjoy one when I am fly fishing some high mountain stream. I didn't vote for Bill Clinton, but I copied him; I didn't and do not inhale. I work out two or three times a week, mostly spin class and weight machines. I could definitely be more consistent. I believe in God. What other people think or believe is OK. I work at being nonjudgmental, and sometimes I am. I enjoy people and engage with people I meet daily. I love my self.

I have two children and two grandkids, twice made and lost a million dollars, twice married and twice divorced, own two vintage Fender Stratocaster guitars, own two houses, and own two cars. I have had cancer once and filed for bankruptcy once, and I survived both. I play blues guitar and love Hendrix, Kenny Wayne Shepherd, and Stevie Ray Vaughan. Catholic Guilt used to kick in hard that I was "stuck in a rut" with my music. I jettisoned that lie. I love to play the music I like to play. I like things simple, and I believe in being real and speaking the truth in love.

To this end, I believe:

Life is about choices.
Life is a succession of learning experiences.
Mining the gold from your life reveals
the hidden wisdom for you.

This short diversion about me is intended to make one point:

We are all alike.
We each have a life, and we each have our story.

My life has provided many, many learning experiences. Along with immense joy, there have been many pain-filled times resulting in heartache. Sharing any wisdom, insights, perspectives, and introspective thoughts is for a purpose: for you to become a healthier, more aware adult; to experience more love; and to gain the skills you need to create and maintain healthy relationships.

All of these thoughts, ideas, and practices are integral parts of the foundation for the work I do in my relationship counseling practice. Everything shared in these pages has been applied to clients, family members, friends, and my self and my relationships. The results have been real, measurable increases in a client's personal awareness, personal growth, improved interpersonal relating strategies, and altered behavior. When clients choose to develop and refine their relating skills, their intimate relationships are more fulfilling. They enjoy healthier, more joy-filled, more satisfying relationships. This includes partners, parents, coworkers, mentors, friends, children, siblings, and the people they meet along their journey.

After you have finished reading and completed the exercises, but you feel you did not get your money's worth, please write me at spencer.wendt@gmail.com, tell me your experience, and I'll send you a refund. You gave this work your best effort.

Another note for this Introduction: I write like I talk. This is my first book. Thank you in advance for cutting me some slack on my style and the book's format, how it's laid out or structured. I hope you will "mine the gold" here. There is some gold in these pages, for you.

My Audience

There are millions of words produced every day about relating and relationships. The hope behind those words is to help or encourage someone to deal with or manage through a situation. Or to help that person make sense out of the circumstances of their life and their past relationships. There are a lot of great thinkers sharing insightful, well-reasoned work about people and their relationships. The subject headings are endless too. Given the technology available for distribution, whether it is in 140 characters, a blog, online, or print, getting information and ideas into the marketplace has never been easier. In many ways, this is a blessing for people seeking answers. The other side of that coin is that this vast, diverse, nearly infinite stream of thoughts and ideas can seem like information overload. How does anyone figure out what to spend their precious time consuming? Then, even if they spend their time and money, will this book or that workshop help? Will it address or work in *their* circumstances?

Consuming and dissecting means spending valuable time. Time: the asset we value most carries the greatest uncertainty, too. We don't know how much we have left. To this end, this book is not intended for everyone. I am writing to a specific audience. It is the audience that I am most confident will find something of value.

I am sharing this up front so that you can determine if an investment of your most precious resource is likely to have a payoff, for you. Knowing who my target is means that I have an excellent idea who is *likely* to gain something from spending money or time on my book.

Four Targets

Who is my audience? Who is most likely to benefit from taking in my thoughts? I have four broad categories that I think fit.

- The first audience comprises men and women between the ages of eighteen and thirty-five. You may still be single, but you may be in or have experienced a couple of intimate relationships. In either case, you have spent some time thinking about relationships and how to make them work. You have seen both types, too. On the one hand, you want to know what are the attributes of those relationships that "seem to work." These relationships are not perfect. However, the partners seem happy, and they seem to be fulfilled. Theirs is the kind of relationship you want to duplicate. On the other hand, you have looked around and observed way too many train wrecks. Some you've observed are with your family and friends. You want to avoid these train-wreck endings at all cost.

  Now you are trying to figure it all out, considering your relating skills, the various aspects of your self, your past, and how you function in a relationship with a significant other or with family. There are some absolutely critical "must have" skills and awareness to have the relationship you want and to avoid the train wreck. For you, this book is more like a guide. It provides a foundation for how healthy relationships are built, describes the components that must be in place to produce joy and satisfaction, and introduces you to the tools and practices needed to sustain a healthy relationship.

- The second audience is like the first, but this group is "experienced." You have had one or two **successful** relationships, possibly one or two divorces. There are three distinct, very admirable attributes about your true nature and your perspective. The first attribute is that you are holding on to "hope." You hold hope tightly in your soul. For you, whatever happened, your hope is that through perseverance, introspection, commitment, and wisdom, you can experience the love your heart desires. The second attribute is that you want to create a healthy relationship and experience the love your heart desires with a partner. The third attribute is that you are 100-percent, unequivocally "open" to changing. You want to learn, to be accountable, to take responsibility, to do what is possible on your end to facilitate that outcome. You hold on to these three attributes so that just maybe you will experience the love your heart desires. I salute your intentionality and your resolve!

- The third audience is a couple who is "stuck." You "love" each other, but you keep hitting potholes. You love each other and are both committed to looking at your self, individually. You are willing to speak truth about your self and your past. You want to understand your personal issues and how these are affecting your relationship. When these are identified, you are prepared to take action; to change and modify your self, your perspectives, your behaviors, and your communication style—all of this with the objective of bringing joy, life, and love back into your relationship. *Both* you and your partner(s)—that is, your love partner, someone in your family, a friend, whoever—are willing to do what it takes to experience more love with "them" and to make your relationships produce results: more joy, more contentment, more satisfaction, and more shared love.

- The fourth audience is women. Whether you are in a relationship or out of one is not relevant. Women are all about "relating" and "relationships." Generally speaking, women have an innate, genetically wired inclination to be focused on "being in relationship" with all those with whom they are connected or close. However, over the years—with the kids, the struggles, the beginnings, the endings—you notice that things "happened" and that what you expected has not materialized. You are now curious about "what happened." It's as though you had been in a time warp. Suddenly, here you are looking at the debris, watching the smoke clear, and saying to your self, "What happened?" and "Who am I?" These are the two most important questions we all must answer to move forward . . . beyond the wreckage and smoke from the past. These are the answers you are seeking. You know from "once upon a time" to the day when you decided to look, the whole thing *is* your journey, and somewhere along the way you lost your "true self."

Looking in your distant past, you can see the "real you." You are that young girl in the old photos. You knew your "self" then: You were smart, curious, naïve, carefree, fun, funny, laughing, hugging, and full of life. You were the most trusted confidant, the best friend, the closest friend they had. You were adventurous, thoughtful, and brimming with possibility for life. Your future—kids, friends—all lay ahead of you. Today? Not so much so today. But, "she" in the photos is *you*. You want to rediscover your self.

To this end you are resolute at this moment. You want to understand "what happened." Then you want to define or redefine your own "who I am" for your future. It doesn't matter that maybe that hope slipped from your grasp. It only slipped temporarily. Today, you have regained your sense about your self, so tighten your grip and work to regain the hope you hold close to your heart.

So, what about men . . . ?

Men . . . MIA?

Reading the foregoing, you might be wondering, "What about men? You didn't mention men." That is correct. I didn't. Regarding matters of love, heart, and relationships—men, for the most part, are MIA: "missing in action." That is my experience. You've already read my blunt and brutal judgment. I believe it is accurate to say: Men are broken.

That statement may seem like a pretty dark blanket to throw over a large segment of the population. It is a personal observation and is based on what I know, my experience. It's my conclusion. This statement holds a large measure of sadness. Why men are this way is not difficult to understand.

Remember, the movie *It's Complicated*? It provides an excellent, long-form example of why men are broken. Remember Alec Baldwin's character, Jake? His entire relationship strategy and life can be summed up in one sentence: "It's just the way I am, and I cannot change."

For just over two hours, Jake and Jane (played by Meryl Streep) do the dance they have done for years. The bottom line is, it's just not a fit. The reason is, after all the years, he is simply unable to connect with his heart. When Jane needs Jake to find his heart, he never quite gets there. But that is all she wants.

Enter Adam (played by Steve Martin). Jane wants Adam to be Jake in the worst way. But who is Adam? He is *just Adam*. He, too, lost connection with his heart somewhere along his journey. Yes, his heart was crushed, too. However, Adam is not like Jake. He reconstitutes his "self," he realized that he loved himself enough to find his bearings about life, and he began to love his "self." He rediscovers "Adam" and recommits to his passions. He connects to, and begins living from, his heart. What he knows about his self is that he loves his self. He also knows what he will not do is sell out his "true self" again. Even if it means losing a relationship with a possibility of love. Finally, Jane sees the truth about both men.

First with Jake, when they are sitting on the bench swing in the last scene together. Truth: He's just not a fit for her. She realizes he cannot connect with his heart. He's just who he is. She finds acceptance . . . as does Jake. Both are aware; it's not meant to be. He drives away into her past.

Then with Adam, when the day finally arrives to set the stakes for her new addition. She is getting that remodeling she dreamed of having. Yes, with a bathroom with only *one* sink. She sees Adam under the tent, working in the middle of a monsoon. He's happy, content, peaceful even in his "circumstances." This time, for the first time, Jane sees *Adam* for Adam. He is trustworthy, honest, with healthy boundaries, unpretentious, loving, attentive, a good listener, and funny in his odd way. She remembers and longs for the way he makes her laugh and find joy when they're together. Then, she finally sees her self; with her self—her true self—disconnected from the drama and circumstances, she is content, joy-filled, laughing, and at peace. She walks toward the tent . . . in the monsoon.

The power of the story is that together Adam and Jane have found the essence of love. It is their shared attention, acceptance, appreciation, affection, and allowing each other to be OK in any circumstance or seasons of their life. They can give and receive these elements of love. For these are the essence of "love," which they grant with Grace and forgiveness to their selves and to each other. Freedom. Finally, after so many fits and starts, they finally know how to love. **Love.** That is the focus of this book.

If you are a woman and are holding onto hope about a relationship with a certain someone—your partner, your lover, your husband, your mother or father or friend—give them a copy of this book. Maybe it will make a difference. Maybe when they close the cover, that certain someone will see something, discover something about their self, know the relating skills you know—and that will make a difference . . . for you. I hope it does.

Your Work

For those who hold the hope of experiencing the love their heart desires, there is but a single road that can deliver you to that destination. It's valuable to know, in advance, that there is no schedule or calendar. But to reach that destination, and to experience that kind of love for your self and/or with a partner, your journey requires that you do "your work."

Helping you do "your work" and assisting you so that you reach that destination is the focus of this book. At that final stop, when you have unpacked "what happened" and gotten settled in to "who am I," that first new dawn of "what's next" will break, and with it will arrive the warm glow of peace and contentment in experiencing love, the love you wanted all along.

No, it's not complicated. It's about choosing "to love."

You

Even though you are not my client, I want you to know that I derive a tremendous amount of joy and fulfillment working with someone like your self, someone who is willing to take the risk to explore his or her self, because it requires casting aside fears and concerns and holding on to the hope for the possibility of something better. For you, taking risk needs to be recognized as a valuable character trait—along with the rest of "you," of course. So, I want to acknowledge you for the confidence and passion you have for growing. This journey of personal inquiry to find and improve "you," your relating skills, and your relationships will be well worth your effort.

The ongoing gift of living is to discover the depth and beauty you have yet to know about your self. Experiencing your desire to go deeper into your self is just over-the-top energizing. All the foregoing is what makes your journey so intriguing for me.

When I began *my* work, it seemed like an insurmountable task. As time progressed, however, and as I uncovered more of my true self, actually "owned" my self, the benefits became clear. For one thing, I experienced more joy and satisfaction in my life, not only for "me" but also, and especially, in my relationships. The result was well worth whatever risk I took or challenge I faced (and there were many of those). Hopefully, you will experience the same results on your journey.

Another purpose for my writing this book was to realize the immense challenge anyone faces trying to make sense of it all! There is a nearly infinite amount of information available that addresses the subject of "love" and "relationships." Working at this full time, connecting such concepts as love and the ways to communicate to address and resolve issues in relationships, finally started to make sense. As these came together for me, and as I put my perspective into practice, my enhanced understanding began to produce results for my clients (as well as for my friends and family).

My process of "weaving" these elements and getting results is somewhat unconventional, however. Since counseling styles and techniques are different, it seems appropriate that I share a bit about mine. . . .

The 360 Model: Full Spectrum

I mentioned that my counseling style was nontraditional. Why? After I'd evaluated the methodology of "traditional" counselors, something was missing. My first takeaway of my evaluation about what was missing was "humanity": being real and authentic. From a client's perspective, I learned that traditional counseling was hit or miss with regard to producing results. The results that did happen did not strike me as happening in a very timely manner, and timely client results are what matter.

I also realized that my interest was quite narrow. Since the focus of my study and work was more oriented toward the various facets of relationships, that was where I chose to devote my time and energy.

The following describes the methodology and approach that you will find in my work. This relationship counseling method, or counseling model, I like to call the "360," or "full-spectrum," model. You won't be surprised to learn that you are in the middle of this unconventional model.

It's a simple concept to grasp. Here are the basics elements that are brought to a client's awareness and the process to which these are applied:

- Learn the components of love, being healthy, and relationships.
- Understand the big picture of you, your past, and relationships
- Contrast the healthy components with how you know your self.
- Figure out the "gaps" between "you" and "healthy"; this is "your work."
- Put "your work" into practice in your life and your relationships.
- Measure your results against your objectives (more love, more joy, more peace, great sex, or any other measure).
- Refine areas that need additional work or that are not producing the results you are seeking.

If you were in a counseling session with me, the process that produces results follows this basic outline:

- You begin the conversation with:
  - A unique set of relationship experiences and results.
    - Focus on what happened.
    - What was your experience?
    - Reveal your unique set of relating skills.
- You gain an awareness about:
  - The healthy adult components you already possess, *and*
  - The relating skills that need to be added or refined.

- ■ The goal is to become healthier *and*
- ■ Create and maintain healthy relationships.
- You learn:
  - ◆ Where you are in your current relationships and circumstances,
  - ◆ In contrast with or relative to the model for healthy skills and practices.
  - ◆ The "gaps" are your "work"
  - ◆ Conversations focus on your "work" to:
    - ■ Develop awareness *and*
    - ■ Refine relating skills.
- Ongoing sessions evaluate against your measure for progress:
  - ◆ What is working:
    - ■ Support, reinforce progress and/or success.
  - ◆ What needs refinement:
    - ■ Revisit skills and practices for current circumstances.
  - ◆ Address new issues that surface in your life:
    - ■ Identify what is missing or needed to handle the event.
    - ■ Integrate what is missing using elements of the "360" components and process.
    - ■ "Wash, rinse, and repeat."

From a high level, this process moves you from where you are to where you want to be. You learn how you make results happen in the circumstances of your life and your relationships.

Starting now, as you move through these pages, begin to focus your attention on you and your relationships—your perspective on love; your personality traits; your communication style; your past relationship conflicts ("what happened"); your conflict resolution strategies; your personal preferences for your self, your partner, and relationships in general; and how you determine your boundaries.

Throughout this book, you are going to read a reference to the "components" of "a healthy adult." The components required to become healthy are consistent. It doesn't matter whether you are a male or a female, single, divorced, or separated. Some of the components of a healthy adult are in the following list. Take notes, because these are "must haves" if your goal is to become a healthy or healthier self and to experience joy-filled, loving, deeply connected, intimate relationships.

Becoming healthy is gaining awareness of and understanding the following items:

- **Love.** You will take a deep dive into what "love" means and explore "how" do you love; you will find definitions that provide clarity and dispel myths and misconceptions.

- **Ego.** Just as important as gaining awareness and understand and knowing love is understanding the source or manifestations of ego, how ego interjects itself into everyday life, and the impact of ego on your self and others. The language and actions of ego have derailed every failed relationship in the sixteen-billion-year history of the planet Earth. Ego probably needs to be in the "good to know" list.

- **Your past.** What happened? What were your models for love, for relationships, for communication, for bonding and attachment, for conflict resolution, for experiencing your emotional life? What skills do you have? What skills are missing?

- **Healthy emotions.** What are they? How do the occur? What are your triggers? How are emotions expressed in an unhealthy manner? How do you express emotions in a healthy way?

- **Preferences.** What are yours? How do you figure out how you want/need to be loved in your life, regarding your partners, your children, your family at large?

- **Conflict resolution.** The APR method is explained: address, process, and resolve.[5] How can you implement the method?

---

5   The APR procedure (address, process, and resolve) is explained in the subsection "Resolving Conflicts between Heart and Ego with APR" within the main section "Conflict Resolution" in Chapter 5.

Examine sample conversations in the context of your current circumstances. Understand the role of love, Grace, and forgiveness. Accept the circumstances of people and relationships as they exist rather than how you think they *should be* (fantasy thinking). Understand the importance of keeping all your relationships "current" (resolved).

- **Healthy relating skills.** Examine the contrast between a life of abundance, joy, gratitude, openness, and welcoming and where you are in your present circumstances. Notice the difference between relating from the heart and relating from ego. Also examine the differences between vulnerable (open) and invulnerable (closed), between freedom and fearfulness, between responding and reacting. Understand the "gaps," also known as "your work."

- **Sex.** Understand the "real" chemistry of sex, the timing of intimacy, the impact on decisions, healthy relating, and the risks and rewards of sexual intimacy before and after commitments.

- **Chemistry.** Dispel the number-one myth about chemistry and lasting healthy relationships. Understand the definition of "chemistry." What is your chemistry? Find "chem-*patibility*" with prospective partners.

- **Attachment styles.** Everyone has an attachment style. What is yours? How did you learn yours? What role does attachment style play in attraction and mate selection? How do attachment styles impact intimate relationships?

Being aware of and understanding the foregoing items is necessary for becoming a "healthy adult." The process opens by dissecting them in the context of whatever circumstances are present for you—whether you are starting a relationship or are already in one, whether you are recovering from a relationship ending, whether you are addressing a loss or an intense emotional experience, and so on. Once a foundation of awareness is in place for these components, then comes the hard part, which is adding the most important elements: "You" and "what's next."

. . .

A quick note about language, which may help you avoid any confusion about terminology: Throughout the book, you may notice references to *skills, tools, pieces, parts, awareness, knowledge, wisdom*, and so on. These terms all fall under the catchphrase *components of being healthy* or *becoming healthier*. These terms are used interchangeably. Whenever you encounter one of these terms in this book, the most important thing for you to understand is that "it" is something you need. So, whatever "it" is called in a particular context, when you read "it," know that you need "it."

Stay hungry, my friends! For our big discussion about love and relationship, this Introduction is merely "setting the table." It's important that you understand that in society's conversation about "what's the right way" and "how life is supposed to work," there are a boatload of common myths and misinformation about you and relationships.

In Chapter 1 our conversation will be focused on truth by getting some the lies and myths out of the way. But first we need to address some biases and opinions of mine . . .

My Biases and Opinions

Yep, a flawed human is typing away over here. I have biases. These are rather pronounced, particularly concerning men, women, and relationships. My goal is to consistently speak truth about all matters, including me, life, love relationships, and *you*, even though we have yet to meet. Some of my views may or may not sit well with you and your beliefs or values. That's OK. I do not want to catch you off-guard, so addressing a few of these up front makes sense.

My "Politically Incorrect" Bias

As I shared in the "Who Am I?" section earlier, I am politically incorrect . . . with no regrets and no shame. Maybe there is a skosh of Catholic Guilt, but mostly, no—no regrets. As a forty-year recovering Catholic, I am doing well on that front! The culture of "PC" along with social media are two of the biggest cancers infecting our social fabric. "PC" is a substitute for "honestly sharing *my* beliefs is not allowed, because *you* may be offended by my opinions." What a sick state of affairs that breeds!

I am a First Amendment Absolutist, one hundred percent. Everyone is entitled to have and speak their views. Period. Everyone has the right to have whatever opinion they have. Period. No one has the right to say or tell someone what to believe or what opinion is "correct," nor can anyone say there are opinions that are *not* allowed.

In this regard, I am so committed to political incorrectness, I've decided to hijack the title of Bill Maher's show. It is stamped on my forehead, with pride: "I Am Politically Incorrect." There is a ton of freedom in those four words! The honesty feels damn good!!!

The PC mandate imposed in conversations by one person or group arbitrarily devalues people on the other end. More directly, it says one is "better than" the other. That is wrong. It says it's OK to discriminate against people for their right and their choice to be different. Political correctness is the absolute pinnacle of hypocrisy. It's what some of the worst offenders of humanity imposed on oppressed people. It's wrong, and I want no part of it. Say what you think and do so freely.

My Writing Style Bias

This will be brief. I make up words and use them. I put punctuation in the wrong place or not at all. I begin statements of declaration with words of inquiry. Some of my sentences are really long, run-on affairs, which made a lot of sense to me when I was typing them out. I use gender-specific terms such as "he" and "she," rather than the nonsexist assignment of nongender: either "it" or "they." But I use these sometimes too. And I suppose my use is "incorrect," when it's perfectly clear that the "it" is a "he" and the collection of "she's" are actually a single "they."

Also, you may have been startled by my use of "my self," "your self," "his self," "her self," and "their self" rather than the usual "myself" (and "yourself," "himself," "herself," and "themselves"). This is deliberate. I am emphasizing throughout the importance of your finding and loving your "true self" (note the title of this book), and the best way to emphasize that importance is to employ this unusual usage throughout the book.

My Client Discrimination Bias

The first of several relationship biases in this section that are worth mentioning is about "clients." There are people with whom I will work and those with whom I will *not* work. This bias is very clear for me. If you are willing to do "your work," then I am "all in." I am with you on your journey for as long as it takes. But if someone is not willing to do their work, is unwilling or unable to be introspective about "their stuff" and their role in matters, these folks I refer to a colleague. Figuring this out is the goal of our first conversation. The unwillingness to be introspective usually reveals its presence quickly. How so?

Say someone calls and says, "I think I am depressed." As I listen to their story, if I sense that they have not dealt with the issue of their mother abandoning them, my response is direct: "It sounds as if you may be angry." Another response might be "It sounds as if you may not love your self." Suppose they cut me off mid-sentence with a loud proclamation, "Of course, I love my self!" OK! It is the first call, so I sense I need more info.

So, we talk some more. But suppose my sense is the same. I will repeat, "I wonder if you love your self." If this suggestion is met with more resistance, or if my request to "take a moment and consider it" is met with total rejection, it is clear that this person is not interested in "looking," and that is OK. Some people don't want to. But this person would be better served working with another counselor. My goal is to get to the heart of the matter quickly. That is the way to make progress on the road to become healthy. I realize my sense is not always correct, but I trust my skills and follow my instincts.

My "Women Do Their Work" Bias

This bias is interesting, because sometimes it is met with a claim that I am being sexist. Which is not the case. It may be politically incorrect to state this as a bias, but it is my experience.

This bias deals with the contrast between women doing their "work" in relationships and men not doing their "work." A portion of this bias originates from my personal experience of having relationships with females. For whatever reason, most of my clients are women, and most of my work is with women. Whether this is the case for other counselors, I have no clue. In my experience, women are more interested in their "work"; they feel a stronger need or desire to figure stuff out—about their selves, about their parents, about their relationships, about their love life, and so on. Women seem more willing to listen and to contemplate on various observations and inquiries. They put in the effort to gain some measure of objectivity about these matters. That is fabulous because the essential ingredient for successful counseling is you "doing your work," and women are *much* more likely to actually do their "work." That is pretty cool if you ask me.

There is a flip side, however: Mostly, men are not like women in this regard. It doesn't make sense to me, but men just aren't as interested. A man should be interested if he has any intentions of being in a relationship with a woman. Often, I hear some old tired refrains: "You can't teach an old dog new tricks" or "It's just the way I was born." These are misguided lies. The more accurate statement would be "I choose not to change" or "The world will have to conform to me" (also known as "I am the God of my life"). That, my friends, is ego, which is discussed in detail in Chapter 4. Oh, yes, some women are like that, too; they'll say, "It's just the way I am." But, women seem to focus on finding answers. I find this refreshing. My generalization about women dovetails nicely to a blanket judgment, which is shared next. . . .

My "Men Are Broken" Bias

My clients have heard me state, with conviction: "Men are broken." This is very direct, judgmental, and critical, but in my experience, it is accurate. Yes, there are exceptions. But this is my experience, and after I am finished with this work, "men are broken" is still on my plate to figure out.

Here's what I have observed: Typically, when men are moving through life, they do what men "are supposed to do"—or so this is the message society has given them, which may be a myth, because it never works out. Maybe that is the key. Anyway, what they "do" is (attempt to) be successful, to make money, to be a leader, to be head of the family, to create more success, to make more money, to win at the "office" game or the "big boat" game or the "more gold chains and Rolex watches" game, then to earn more money and to be crowned world champion of the Wednesday night "45 Plus" softball league . . . and on and on and on. But what's the truth? Men don't discover their "heart" (that is, "love"). They love a bunch of stuff that is worthless, in hopes that what they want most, "love," will "automagically" appear because everyone will "Ooh" and "Ahh" over their stuff and love them. But it never happens. And if it appears to happen, it's not real.

When a man finally realizes he is on the far back half of his life, near its end, then he may understand everything he has worked to "possess" ultimately falls short in delivering the satisfaction that he *expected* (a characteristic of ego) would happen because of all his "stuff." Then he dies, everyone takes his stuff, and no one remembers him. Upon his recognition or awareness that this is what happens, then, *maybe*, this guy will look at his self and say, "Stop . . ." Maybe he will ask his self, "What is missing?"

The answer will always be the same. What he is missing is "heart" and the "satisfaction of loving." These will never be found in acquiring or possessing any material items on the planet . . . ever. Not sure why men have never figured this one out. They die, and their "stuff" stays until it breaks or stops working.

Enough on that. Men are broken. I'll stick with my judgment. On this introspective front, where a woman may begin to look at her "self" as early as twenty-eight to thirty-five years old, it's amazing that men do not start looking at their selves until well into their fifties and beyond. The sad part is most men don't look until it's way too late to do anything about all the love they missed in their life. Then "The End" happens, and that is sad. But that's life . . . and "life is about choices."

My Gender Bias

So, you know about my gender bias already. It's not a mystery, right? I generally write to, address, and speak to women. Oh, don't be misled; what I talk about *absolutely* applies to men. But in my experience, women are way more interested in listening, contemplating, and doing their work. I think it's because women are all about relationships. Relationships live actively in their everyday consciousness. Their satisfaction is derived from relating and having vibrant relationships. Whereas men are about being independent and "winning" (that is, success . . . making money). Men ride solo with their selves riding shotgun, and they are not aware of, or they choose not to be connected at, the level of their "vulnerability"—that is, the part of their selves that is below the facade. Too risky. That is typically their "fear"; fear is a manifestation of ego. Fear of what? Being unlovable, being rejected, being less than or not good enough. This, ultimately, points to the heart of the matter—thus the title: *Love Your Self.* So, they choose not to go there. The heart appears to be a scary place.

Women own the experience of their feelings and emotions. Men tend to deny theirs. You are welcome to judge me or condemn me for my bias here. I am good with you having your opinion. I am not concerned if you agree with me or not. I stated before that my interest is in reaching people and "making a difference." If what I write makes a difference for both men and women, or for only women or for only men, or for turtles but not whales, that works for me. For me, that is a success.

Sharing up front that I tend to write and speak with a bias *to* women is sort of an FYI. This way when you notice a "gender slant" in my style, the tone, the descriptions, and the stories and vignettes, it does not come as a surprise to you. This bias is consistent with my upholding my personal integrity, because by declaring I have a gender bias is taking ownership of being 100-percent politically incorrect. That works for me—almost perfectly. There is more about my "women" bias in Chapter 5. Stay tuned.

My "Not Being Right" Bias

Finally, I am heavily biased about "being on to something" in my approach and strategy; whatever "it" (that "something") is, it is working. To be clear "being on to something" is distinct from "I am right." I don't care about right or wrong. I do care about making a difference. A lot of my past decade has been spent studying and understanding people, relationships, various theories, scientific studies, well-structured survey/questionnaire results, and me. This work represents my personal contemplation in an attempt to figure out "things" about people and how they act in relationships and why. First, and very responsibly, I set out to understand "me" and my past. Next, I worked to understand "me" in my relationships. Finally, I work to understand others and their relationships. I've noticed that my perspective about counseling was different from that of the "pros." My counseling practices seemed to resonate with people, especially when they were struggling or in a crisis.

That is a large part of the reason I've chosen to pen this work. My thinking was that if I can make a difference for "live" clients, maybe I can communicate what is working by writing about it. Yes, writing for you.

Honestly, the money doesn't matter. Writers don't make money. Right and wrong are of no consequence, either; there are a ton of great ideas from thinker's way more intelligent and thoughtful than my self.

What matters to me is helping one person see something and become aware of some behavior or relating skill, watching how that awareness changes the direction of their life, how they become healthier and experience more love—maybe experience the love their heart desires. That matters to me.

Chapter 1.

MYTHS VERSUS TRUTHS: SEPARATING FACT FROM FICTION

MY INSPIRATION FOR SETTING THIS premise of "truth" in the first chapter came from two of the greatest thinkers on the subject of "how we choose" and "how we decide." These two men changed the world of medicine, government, private industry, compensation, hiring, and so many other sectors of your life. It makes sense for me to share their findings. Their work is focused on human decision making and choices. In the matter of biases and mistakes, what they uncovered is frighteningly consistent in the choices and decisions people make about partners and relationships. Even more alarming, their findings are consistent when applied specifically to romantic love relationships.

Their names are Amos Tversky and Daniel Kahneman. Their bios and publications can be found on Google and Amazon. To my knowledge, they have not written or studied relationships or love. That would have been incredibly fascinating!! They were psychologists, and their interest was in why humans make the choices they make.[2] What influences human decision making? What determines the process of making those decisions? What factors are considered or not considered in decision making? What did they find?

Against what people know to be true from their *own experience*, they many times choose options that do not produce the desired results. In effect, even when they know option A will not produce the results they want but because they have chosen A in the past, perhaps multiple times, they choose . . . option A. Applying Tversky and Kahneman's theories about decision making to the realm of relationships and romantic love, we see that any choices that are based on bad information contrary to personal experience render results that stand out like a black swan on a snow-covered pond. Why would people do that?

The work of Tversky and Kahneman shows how the nature of decision making is biased in several different and quite fascinating ways. How it applies here is this: Is it human nature to bias decisions about who is the right partner for you? Or, how do you create a successful relationship? What's the correct process?

Another interesting aspect of their work shows that elements you do not consider as impacting your thought become the very reference points you use to make a decision. How crazy is that? In other words, you think you are making a choice based on one piece of information. But information you are not thinking about or are unaware of is guiding you to make the choice. You can apply this concept to how you choose romantic love partners.

One decision bias Tversky and Kahneman studied was *inbound information bias*, which works like this: Whenever you make a decision, you have "inside" information (which is what you know from your personal experience) and "outside" information (which are data points and findings from such outside sources as media, family, friends, magazines, and so forth). Here is how this external, inbound, outside information impacts your perspective and your decisions. Even when you know from your personal (inside) experience that the outside information is incorrect, inaccurate, irrelevant, or blatantly false, you tend to make choices based on the bad inbound information.

OK, it would be best to explain this using an entirely insane example: Say you are in the checkout aisle. The headline on one of the tabloids reads: "Research shows hitting your finger with a hammer does not hurt."

That's BS. You know it's not true. *But*, you go home, open the toolbox, pull out the hammer, hit your finger, and scream bloody murder!!

The worst part? While you are in the ER, you see the same tabloid on the waiting room table, with the same headline: "Research shows hitting your finger with a hammer does not hurt." Upon arriving home, with your hand neatly bandaged, you grab your hammer, and again you smack your hand. *Ho. Lee. Snap!!* It hurts like crap!!! Nuts, huh?

That is how people make choices and decision about love partners and what to do in their relationships! Choices are made based on erroneous, inbound outside information, even though people do not to get the results they are seeking.

Why? You chose to believe that "they" were correct and that you must be wrong in your personal experience. You know what happens when you hit your finger with a hammer, but "they" said it doesn't hurt. But it does! And you knew that before you embarked on this bizarre experiment.

So, who has the problem here? You do. You knew *before* your experiment that "they" were wrong. You knew better than to believe the false information coming at you (inbound)—what "they" told you. The truth is that you knew what was true and what was false. "Their" information was way off base; it was incorrect. You knew from your experience what the outcome was going to be. But somehow you doubled down by believing your personal knowledge was wrong, that somehow what you had experience about wasn't the truth.

This remedial exercise in decision bias has a purpose, which can be found in asking this simple question:

How does the inbound information bias impact you and your decisions about relationships?

Luckily for me, there are many examples, and several of these stand out as myths. The first myth we investigate is "chemistry" as it is used (or misused) in matters of romantic love and relationships.

The "That Chemistry" Myth

One of the most common pronouncements you hear in conversations about dating, mating, finding partners, ideal partners, intimacy, and intimate relationships is some version of "You must have that chemistry." How many times in dating profiles have you read "If that chemistry isn't there within five minutes, I know we're not a good fit." Or you find a simple proclamation "I want 'that chemistry.'"

These pronouncements are quite interesting, because when a connection that began based on "that chemistry" fails to materialize into a long-term relationship, the cause for the premature ending is often summarized as:

- "I just didn't feel 'that chemistry,'" or
- "The chemistry I felt 'when we met' disappeared," or
- "Our chemistry was so 'passionate' early on, but we lost it."

Do these sound familiar? Nearly every relationship book or blog published has made the claim that "chemistry" is a requirement for strong romantic love. But there is a problem. Is that true? Is "that chemistry" what makes a relationship successful? Is "that chemistry" what you must have in order to have a successful relationship, the kind that endures "till death do us part"? If "that chemistry" is not there, then the relationship does not have a chance to endure "till death do us part"? Really?? Hmmmm. . . .

One question you need to ask your self is, "Are my decisions biased when it comes to this magical 'chemistry' requirement?" Let's test it out by asking your self a much more relevant question: "What is *my* truth?"

It's a safe bet you have personally experienced "that chemistry." Was some form of "that chemistry" present at the start of any of your past relationships? I suspect your answer is yes. In fact, you experienced "that chemistry" whether it was a relationship that lasted three hours on a flight or three years in a penthouse in Manhattan! Here's the catch: All those relationships *ended.* Probably with a healthy dose of heartache attached to the final "see ya later!"

So, based on your experience, what do you *know* about "that chemistry"?

The fact is "that chemistry" seems to have no bearing on creating a successful relationship. No one must tell you because you've experienced it, and the relationship ended. You have proven, with 100-percent certainty, that "that chemistry" *is not* the foundation for a successful relationship. In fact, if you were partnered with our two research scientists, Tversky and Kahneman, *your* conclusion, based on the facts and findings of *your* relationship life, would render a different finding, on the other end of the spectrum from what the "outside" information claimed. Your conclusion would be:

> **When you feel "that chemistry," *look out!!!*
> A relationship with that person . . . is *not* going to end well!**

Which means that healthy adult chemistry is *not* the butterflies that knocked you over when they pushed open the door and strolled into Starbucks as though they stepped off the page of some mag. Nope! That is *not* the chemistry of healthy adult relating. It is definitely not the foundation upon which anyone would attempt to build a two- or ten- or twenty-five-year relationship. Would you risk your entire social, family, financial, and emotional life on such a *long-proven, well-documented, false indicator?* Especially when your own personal experience provides you ample evidence that the information is false? You *know* this information is incorrect!

What's the truth? It is proven all the time. It's been proven a thousand times since you started reading today. "That chemistry" is a mirage, at best. It is a false indicator. It is *not* the chemistry you need to build a healthy relationship.

The "That Chemistry" myth is the number-one piece of misinformation about relating and relationships. It may be the "hot" social conversation about finding love, but it is 100-percent wrong. The myth of "that chemistry" is the number-one reason for the mistakes people make in selecting a mate or picking a partner . . . and most are aware but nonetheless choose to believe that this time they are right.

What's the truth about "that chemistry"?

"That chemistry" you "felt" was the engagement of *all* your primal mating instincts. All "that chemistry" you were jiving on, that "feeling," can be stated bluntly and very accurately as: "I want to have sex with you."

Yes. That is it. The "feelings" overwhelming your senses are the result of the actual chemical elements released into your system, which are prompting your animal instincts to "go mate." Your base-level mating instincts, your natural drive to procreate, is an explosive cocktail of chemicals. Yes, "chemistry" is indeed what is happening.

"What happened" is your mating instincts were triggered by the sights, scents, and sounds of a suitable mating prospect. This intoxicating mix was "automagically" being poured into your system. You didn't have to do anything. All you had to "do" was be in the right place at the right time—when "this high-valued mating prospect" entered your "territory." They had all the preferences and characteristics hard-wired in your genes and mixing yours with theirs was how you advanced the gene pool of humanity. You saw, smelled, heard, and sensed the "gene match" and *Bammmmm!!!* You were "full tilt" in the "Let's mate *now*" mode.

The chemical cocktail flushed into your system put you in "go" mode to start the procreation process. This is also commonly referred to as "let's have sex." The prerecorded message playing in your head might as well have been playing on the public-address system of the venue where the "chemistry" was taking place. Your personal PA system announcement would sound something like the following:

Pardon me! Over there, in the white shirt with the chiseled abs and cut jaw line! My sex drive chemistry is surging through my veins. Could you please take me to the nearest location TBD? I would like to engage with you in some wildly passionate "gene pool forwarding" activities!!!

Safe to say, given what was going on with you, there would probably be a lot of mating activity. But how about on the long-term-relating side of the equation? That would be questionable, at best. But you knew that already!

The myth consists of the misconception about what is happening and what is the truth about "that chemistry." Your entire experience is simply you are experiencing your primal mating instincts. These are completely natural and can occur with random people, anywhere, as they often do. These may occur many times in a day or a week and certainly once or twice in your lifetime. Sometimes, your mating instincts happen without you even knowing. It's part of being an animal.

The disconnect regarding relationships is the misunderstanding about a "mating response," which is incorrectly fantasized as a positive indicator for finding a well-suited relationship partner—that is, a partner who is a good fit for a long-term romantic love relationship. "That chemistry" makes for fabulous sex. The problem is "that chemistry" does not make a strong, long-term, intimately connected relationship successful. So, when "healthy chemistry" stands in the brighter light of creating and maintaining a healthy relationship, relationship chemistry is infinitely more expansive and relevant than the feelings of those "butterflies" signaling that you want to have sex with a complete stranger. Does that make sense? We'll dissect this at length further along in the conversation.

Back to our friends Tversky and Kahneman. What do you know already? You know you have experienced an overwhelming attraction and primal lust to mate with Mr. GQ or Ms. Maxim. It's probably happened to you many times. Maybe a few of those times you took a risk. You chose to start and be in a relationship with that person for a period. The "mating" (that is, the passionate hot sex) was fabulous, but the relationship ultimately wasn't.

In summary, you know "that chemistry" is about great sex and that it is not a key or a solid foundation to create a great relationship. The truth is, based on what you know, it is much more likely "that chemistry" indicates that your finding love in a relationship with this person is almost guaranteed *not* to happen!

"How about them apples?" (Thank you, Matt Damon!) It's OK. File that one in the "good to know" section of your notes. There will be a lot of those, too.

Next up, a communication error commonly found, which is . . .

The ESP Myth

For some unknown reason, there is an assumption in relationships (and in life) that when you merely think about something, your thoughts are projected throughout the universe. Your thought is automagically distributed as wisdom to all other humans on the planet. Once thought happens, everyone knows what has been thought. This concept of "Vulcan mind meld" is called *extrasensory perception*, or *ESP*. How does ESP work?

For instance, suppose you think to your self, "Blue is my favorite color." If you believe in the ESP myth, when you decide to start a relationship, *all* the prospects you meet will know your favorite color *without your having to tell them*!!! Is that the silliest notion you have ever heard of? I hope it is. However, it happens *all the time* in relationships. Let's look at an example.

Say you like to hold hands. Because your partner has ESP, you don't need to tell them. Nor do you need to ask if *they* like to hold hands. You know . . . because? Because you have ESP. So, you go on a few dates, hold hands a few times, and reach four definite conclusions:

- "I have ESP."

- "They have ESP."
- "I *know* they like to hold hands."
- "They *know* I like to hold hands."

What if it was just cold outside on the first couple of dates? What if they wanted to warm their hand with yours? What if they were "just being nice" and didn't really like holding hands? Are any of these possible? No. You both have ESP. Uh huh . . . how's that working out for you?

The ESP myth is one of the early critical Mythstakes made in the date-mate-procreate game. Making assumptions others will "just know" leads to huge issues later on. The ESP Mythstakes will be discussed more in Chapter 6. For now (and forevermore), if you don't speak your thoughts aloud and get confirmation they heard you, assume that they do not have ESP, and they do not know what you are thinking or what you like or want.

Second critical point, if they do not tell you or ask you, assume that you cannot read their mind and you do not know what they are thinking or what they want. Yeah!! It's a Big Deal.

"The One" Myth

Another infamous declaration made by people who are dating–mating–sexing–relating is "I want to find 'the One.'" That descriptor is used almost as often as "chemistry." "The One" criterion sounds good, right? Nope, it is also a myth. That will likely make more sense later than it does now. But a couple of points are worth your consideration before you whisper, "He's wrong." (Blowing up this myth is something you will greatly appreciate and thank me for later, BTW.)

"The One" myth is a setup for failure from the get-go. When used in dating profiles, many authors—but mostly "authorettes"—state with absolute clarity that there is a singular copy of the perfect mate match who is named "the One." Accurately measured in the universe of prospects, this would imply, "There is *exactly one* out of 3.75 billion who is perfectly 'right for me.'" Geeeez, those odds are flat out terrible. Do you want to bet your happiness, your peace, contentment in your relationship life, on those odds? The answer is no. "The One" is a myth, and that fact will make total sense before you close the book. The following is some insight into why:

For one thing, of course, just as with the "chemistry" that you have experienced many times, my bet is you have called your BFF on more than one occasion to announce that you found (another) "One." But set aside the facts and truth for just a second. Let's dig in on what we are here to do (besides kill off some terribly bad information).

The focus of your work is to become healthy (or healthier). Next is to go about the task of finding a prospect. *Then*, and only then, you work on creating a healthy relationship. Hopefully, your partnership blooms into a healthy romantic love relationship. Here is a piece of the relationship puzzle:

Healthy people build healthy relationships.

Yes, two healthy people share lots of love. They have even more great sex with extra doses of fun, joy, and a better life experience!! Healthy people *attract* other healthy people. Healthy people are more attractive than unhealthy people. Unhealthy people have unhealthy relationships. That changes the "end game" for you.

"The One" you *should* be looking for is more accurately stated as:

- "The One" who is a healthy partner who shares your attraction (yes, including the "weak in the knees" part).
- "The One" who can give and receive love.
- "The One" who can together with you resolve your conflicts, thereby making your relationship a deeper, richer love connection.
- "The One" with whom you each share the experience of joy and fulfillment of being together.

The best way to increase your odds of snagging "the One who is a great fit for *you*" is discovering and then refining your relating tools and skills. That process will result in you upping your dating–mating–sexing–relating game, which is what you have needed to do all along. More awareness, a better understanding about "you," and the awareness of what to look for in a partner is how to get the results you want. That is the best way to ensure that the next one you choose as "the One" is not "just another one."

What if you do happen to be lucky? Then you must be aware of . . .

The "Commitment" Myth

The "Commitment" myth is yet another example of incorrect information. This myth concerns the misguided information about the correct sequence of steps you must follow to create a successful romantic love relationship.

What "they" told you is that the path to finding the love of your life goes something like this:

- You start with hot and passionate attraction ("chemistry," said in jest).
- Then comes the romance part, and it may last weeks or years.
- But when you are "comfortably connected," you and your lover make a commitment and enjoy bliss until you die. And, oh, by the way,
- If "anything comes up," such as a problem or an issue, you handle whatever the "stuff" is and
- Go on about your happy life together.

In other words, "they" told you that the process you should follow—the process that will give you the best chance at long-term relationship success—is:

The "Commitment" Myth:
Romance, commitment, *then* conflict resolution

You already know from experience: *Not!* My guess is you tried and failed to make "their" process work, more than a few times. Even though this is how "they" say romantic relationships are created, it has never worked *for you*. You know the drill.

You meet someone. You are attracted to each other. That "chemistry" thing happens. Its natural course moves into the "romance" phase. Somewhere in the romance phase, you decide to be sexually intimate. If the sex and connection are good, *then* you both agree to make a "commitment." After the commitment has been in place for some length of time, maybe you choose to get married. What happens next?

The truth is often that suddenly "something happens." Your bliss is blindsided. Suddenly, completely unexpected and seemingly from out of nowhere, issues begin to surface. There is tension between you. You have disagreements. But then what always happens?

You resolve these conflicts, return to your state of blissful contentment, and you live happily ever after! Really????

No. What do you *know* is your experience? What have you seen in your family, with your BFF, with your sisters' or brothers' relationships? How about the neighbor of your friends in your Bible study group? Here is what *really* happens:

After you make a commitment, you choose to get married. After you commit and are married, issues arise. You attempt to resolve these conflicts, but something doesn't work. In fact, the biggest conflicts never get resolved. As the list of unresolved issues grows, so does the tension. Anger festers. Then, more unresolved issues are layered in. The unresolved issues build and build and build.

Then one day, seemingly out of nowhere, one or the other of you walks into the kitchen. The entire dumpster of unresolved problems is unceremoniously dumped in the middle of the kitchen floor, and either you or your partner screams, "I want a divorce!"

Now, what do "you" know?

"Their" model of the "path to find true love," the one "they" pounded into your head for years: It's broken! The fact is "they" are wrong. "Their" model has yet to deliver what you want in your relationships. Not only that, *you* know "they" are wrong. You know, for your self, because your experience is that their model is broken. The only logical conclusion is the following:

**After an attraction that leads to romance,
the next step is *not* commitment.**

We don't have to call on our friends Tversky and Kahneman to reach the proper conclusion. If conflict ends relationships and if conflicts happen after commitment, these need to be rearranged.

Today, what you don't want to hear is "happily ever after." No. What you need and what you want to hear is truth. The truth is that "their" model is broken. With regard to relationship models, you know which model does *not* work. You must find a better way, a better model. It's clear there is "something" that is way more important than commitment to "being together."

What you need to ask is a question, which needs an answer before you get very far down the road. The question is:

**Do you and your partner have
the capacity and ability to *resolve conflicts*?**

Once you know that issues which surface can be addressed and resolved, *then* you are ready to make a commitment. Given what you *know*, this seems a more prudent way to create a relationship that will stand the test of time. And issues are always going to surface; it's only a matter of time. At the very least, a model that addresses the reasons relationships end will get you closer to creating the relationship you want.

So, yes, there is a better model. Don't go thumbing forward because the "relationship model that works" is covered in Chapter 2. The current chapter, though, is focused on highlighting and blowing up the myths.

The "Commitment" myth is destroyed, but there is one more to go. Shall we?

The "Relationships Are Complicated" Myth

Love, romance, romantic love, and relationships are very obscure and specious concepts. In fact, these are basically "undefined" concepts. Instead of "knowing" what the definitions are and what these concepts are, people rationalize their lack of clarity. In place of "knowing" what "love" or "romantic love" is, people substitute rationalizations for *not* knowing.

For example, regarding "love," you often hear someone say, "Oh, I *just know* 'it' when 'it' happens." The truth is they don't know what it is. But they will "tell you" when they have it in their grasp. Is it any wonder that experiencing "love" and a "romantic love relationship" is "complicated"? Hey, the reason these concepts are so *complicated* is because they are *not* defined!

The complication is not about all the options, variables, considerations, and circumstances. No. The complication comes from believing myths and misinformation. That is *further* complicated when you do not trust what you *know* about these matters.

In summary, the complication about relationships happens because of the following:

First, myths and misinformation are fed to you from outside sources. You believe and act on these. Second, you choose *not* to believe what you know, which is your personal experience. You discount, dismiss, or decide not to acknowledge your personal truth about your preferences, your likes and dislikes, and your experience about relationships. You choose not to believe what you know is right for your self. Not to believe the information you know from your life experience about love and relationships, about people, about men, and about women. You know all this firsthand, but you dismiss what you know as false or untrustworthy.

In other words, "relationships are complicated" when you choose to believe outside information that is fiction. You choose to believe the fantasy rather than believing or trusting your own factual, known experiences, intuitive sense, and personal observations. You know what is true for you about life, relationships, sex, money, and power. Most importantly, what you know and your awareness about your true self. When you use what you know, what you know to be "truth," and dismiss external information that is false and doesn't work (myths), this reduces the "complications" . . . tremendously.

Relationships have many parts and pieces, but so does your car. You know what must be on that car to get you to the gym. If you walk outside and the wheels are missing, you probably won't burn many calories at your workout. But you'll know why. It won't be a mystery. Cars are complicated—but not really. Wheels, engine, cup holders, DVD.

Relationships are the same way; when everything is in place, relationships become a lot less complicated. That is what we are doing here. Our work here will put the pieces in place. When you learn to trust what you know, when you know the parts and pieces of relationships that must be present, the myths are destroyed, and then relationships will be much less complicated . . . by several orders of magnitude. Trust me on this one.

Now we move from myths to truths . . .

The Truth about "Awareness"

The objective of laying all of this out is to save someone somewhere some heartache and pain in their life, their love, or their relationship(s).

Ideally, someone somewhere will read a line, then reread it. You, perhaps? Maybe it will trigger a thought, so you dog-ear a page or "yellow-line" a chapter. Then, after a short pause, the book softly comes to rest in your lap. You gaze with a "thousand-yard stare," looking at the vignettes of your life . . . and suddenly, *Bammmmm!!!* It hits you. You snap back to the present.

With you, then, arrives a new insight or perspective. You "see something" about your self or your past for the first time; it is in a new light. Maybe this "something" is an insight about your self, your partner, a past relationship, or your childhood. This "new" insight alters the course of your relationship and even changes your life . . . *forever*. That is usually the way "it" happens.

"It" is called "awareness." Holding that new insight, you are now "aware." You "see" something about your self, and what you have gained is a new perspective. That process of contemplation, then experiencing a new revelation, is part of "your work."

When you do your work, you gain insights into facts about your self and your behavior that you were not aware were there. Once you have the insight in your possession, it becomes a new awareness. Your effort to pay attention to this newly found knowledge could result in your making a different choice—a "new choice" that enables you to avoid one of those "potholes" you experienced in a previous relationship; maybe you experienced it more than once.

For instance, before this awareness you were driving along the same relationship road. The one you always chose to take . . . then . . . suddenly: *Boooom!!* Flat tire. Same "road" you've traveled in your relationships for your entire life. Maybe you picked the same partner, or you attracted a certain personality, or you hit the same communication issues repeatedly in your relationships. This is "hitting the same pothole," because you experience the same result: "flat tire," just like all those other times. Now, however, with your new awareness, something you did not see or know before, you have the opportunity to make a different choice.

In fact, you have a choice now. You may choose to take a different road or the same one. The difference is now you have this awareness; the same pothole is visible to you from a mile away. This time you choose something else. Rather than hitting the pothole, you swerve, or stop, or turn around, or slow down. Being aware creates the opportunity for you to miss the pothole completely. That is what awareness does for you (for all of us, in fact). In love and relationships, becoming aware of your self happens when you take the time to understand "what happened." You "see" something new about your self. You contemplate the real cost of hitting that pothole over and over and over again. You learn. You gain insight. You are aware. You choose a different path or make different choices.

For instance, maybe in your relationships the pothole you seemed to hit was giving in or conceding some aspect of your self that you held as valuable or important. This could have been one of your nonnegotiable boundaries. When your partner dismissed it or stepped over it, you didn't say anything but just continued on—*as though your boundary did not matter.* But your boundary does matter, and when this happened, you were hurt and in pain; in other words, if your boundary doesn't matter to your partner, *you* don't matter either. So, your boundary violation issue went unresolved and unaddressed because you said nothing. Nothing changed in the pattern of your relating. "What happened" is that you chose to accept a measure of love and a relationship that was less than what you wanted or what worked *for you* in your relationship. The cost to you? This relationship wasn't providing you the love your heart desired.

When you become aware of "what happened," however, you know that boundaries are nonnegotiable, because they *do* matter, and the cost is borne by your suffering. That *is* important. With your newfound awareness, the next time your boundaries are violated, you choose to speak to address and resolve the issue.

Here is the hard truth: Your choosing not to speak up in relationship after relationship is costly. Hitting the same potholes causes heartache, wrecks lives, and does damage to your family, your kids, and *you*. It can drain your bank account, stress you out, make you angry, and leave you with sadness. If unresolved, the sadness may linger for years. It hurts those you love and forever splits friendships that had been solid. Then, finally, you realize (gain "awareness") that you must do something different. And you do.

I get it. I understand. I'm like you and have hit the same "potholes" many times. The purpose of my sharing these thoughts is to save you from paying another round of "relationship education tax." That is the reason you picked up this book.

Hopefully, you'll read a word or a line or a thought summary and find an awareness that has eluded you. You see more clearly and choose to take a different route. If that happens *just one time*, then I will consider this effort to be a total success. Every missed pothole beyond that one you missed is a bonus.

The Truth about "Your Work."

To have a chance at creating a successful relationship requires a deeper understanding of the dynamics behind the choices you make, including how behavior was/is modeled by parents, families, and childhood events, plus the effects of circumstances you were challenged with overcoming in the past. These experiences and circumstances impact whether you choose to be vulnerable or hide your true self, whether you choose to engage from either heart (true self) or ego (fears and insecurities). Once you understand the nature of these elements and their impact, *then* you can begin to do "your work."

Your work starts when you choose to dig in and unpack your "stuff." I imagine you have already ventured into some of those waters of your self and your past. The next part of your work is developing and refining your relating and interpersonal skills and practices. These skills and practices must be present for you to become healthy. Once you have them in your possession (that is, in your "awareness"), you can live wholeheartedly, love from your heart, and go about creating, maintaining, and experiencing healthy, vibrant, intimate relationships . . . with everyone along your life journey.

Make a note of this term: *your work.* It is important. This is a term you will come across many times in the pages that follow. Your work means:

- To become aware and to be present to aspects of your "self"—your thought patterns, behaviors, activities, choices, and relating skills; some are complete, and others are incomplete or missing.
- To take action and make changes where needed:
  - You do whatever it takes for you to accomplish the action or change you must do.
- To acquire, develop, and refine the relating skills discussed in this book.
- Then, to put these skills into practice, which moves you forward
  - To become a healthier adult, *and*
  - To create and maintain healthier relationships.

That describes the process of doing your work. Completing your work is how you get your money's worth from your investment of time and money in this book. Your work is both necessary and invaluable. That is how you get the results you want: experiencing more intimacy, more love, and more joy; making deeper connections with people; and having better relationships.

By the way, if your list of expected results in your relationship life includes "more sex"? That may or may not happen. But when you do your work, "better sex" is virtually assured. (That should be motivation enough to get started . . . and to make it to the end! huh! ☺)

J. Spencer Wendt

The Truth about "Love"

Experiencing more love in your life is the purpose of your work. That is everyone's work, by the way. The chapters that follow explore, discuss, and focus on love . . . a lot.

Anthropologist Helen Fisher is one of the great minds to have studied this baffling topic called "love." Her personal quest to understand love has produced a number of great books. One is titled *Why Him? Why Her? Finding Real Love by Understanding Your Personality Type.*[3] She has gathered over thirty years of clinical and laboratory research data. She has administered surveys to millions of people about the study of one subject: love, romantic love, and relationships.

According to Fisher, love is like an addiction. It consumes us, we sacrifice for it, and we pursue it relentlessly. Experiencing it brings us ultimate joy, and when it is missing, we suffer great pain. And we still want more.

Outside of food, water, and air, our lives are consumed with love—finding it, being in it, giving it or receiving it, missing it, avoiding it, fearing it, nurturing it, and (best of all) making it. Humans are consumed with love.

Look around. Look at magazine ads, commercials on television. What are they selling? Read the words in song titles. Listen to the lyrics we hum all day. "Love makes the world go round." "All you need is love, love. Love is all you need." "Love hurts." "Let me love you." "I hate you, I love you." "In the name of love." Are we totally consumed? Yes!

We should be. "To love" is our purpose for being on the planet. We'll talk more about that purpose, too. Maybe the unconvinced can be convinced. We will see. It took me nearly five decades to figure it out, but my mind is made up. With 100-percent certainty,

Life is about "love."

Somewhere there is a saying "Love is never enough." I'm pretty sure that is not true. I assert that these pages present sufficient evidence to make the case that "love is enough." In the end, of course, you get to decide. If the construct of love, strong adult skills, and practices of healthy relationships and awareness about love discussed here makes sense to you, then you may conclude, as I have: "Love *is* all you need."

The Truth about "Failed Relationships"

Seems like anytime someone is in a difficult season with a partner, it brings out an oft-repeated lament: "Relationships are complicated." The truth of this statement would be exponentially more accurate if it were changed to read: "Relationships are infinitely complicated." But, maybe they are not!

Relationships are people-to-people interactions consisting of intimate interpersonal communication and shared life events or experiences. Yes, these *two people* are complicated, but maybe the relating aspect is not. What you will learn are the components necessary to create and maintain healthy adult relationships can be understood by anyone who is intentional about experiencing healthy love, healthy self, and healthy relational intimacy. That is the purpose of this book.

To this end, there are some well-defined skills required to create and maintain healthy communication, connection, and intimacy in any relationship. Whether it is with your children, coworkers, parents, in-laws, siblings, or friends, by using the skills covered in these pages, you can advance your ability to "relate" in a healthy manner. That much is guaranteed. That is not an idle musing, either.

Mary Ellen Goggin, noted relationship expert, spoke on a panel with Helen Fisher. She observed that

> there are a million reason why relationships fail, and . . .
> probably the biggest relationship failure has to do with people
> who don't have the tools. Some people, for some reason, . . .

are lucky enough to have the tools, and they're able to get through the complicated issues that they face and the tangled web that sometimes gets woven. But the people who are ill-equipped to work on their relationship together—those are the ones who fail. . . . If they don't come and ask for help, then sometimes the relationship is doomed!![4]

Having the tools and interpersonal relating strategies is required. But not everyone has these tools and competencies *going into* relationships. Some do, yes. Based on surveys and divorce statistics, those people are the fortunate few. For those in the majority, the answer for them is: "Get the skills," and then "Put them into practice." When this happens, the possibility of creating and maintaining a successful relationship increases exponentially. Why should you acquire these skills? A better question might be: "What is the reason for *not* acquiring these skills?" If your end game is to experience the "love your heart desires," there is no other path. Book it.

The Truth about "Your Past"

Regarding your experience and how you know "love," your relationship models, and your ability to make relationships choices, where did you get all this stuff? Answer: These have all been "gifted" to you. Your models were set up long ago. Those "what the hell was I thinking?!" choices you made about partners or relationship—those are also from your past. Yes. The truth is you probably were *not* thinking.

Instead, you were just acting out a well-rehearsed "script," which you never knew existed. The script is the one you have indelibly etched into the deepest recesses of your being, deeper than the marrow in your bones. "What happened" is you were operating on autopilot with a broken "navigation system." Your relationship was on course to crash and burn, but since you were not aware of this script for relationships and love, you didn't have much choice in the matter.

Maybe that description is a bit tasteless for your tastes. Yeah, the use of a bit of drama and hyperbole because it helps make *crucial* points stick. So, the reference to "you" being "on autopilot" . . . and the relationships(s) "crashing" seems appropriate. That reference to a crash will make sense as you work through this process. About that script, though.

Unknown to you, you memorized your script down to the last punctuation mark. It was modeled for you for years during the most impressionable time in your life as a child. If your script was not based on a strong model of relating and healthy love and you did not learn a model of healthy communication and expression of emotions, this is the starting point for you to figure out "what happened." Once you know "what happened," then you can do something about it; you can acquire skills, change behavior, make different and hopefully better choices, and so on.

When you acted out your script, you were just like your favorite movie hero or heroine. You played your part to perfection. You performed flawlessly in relationship after relationship after relationship. And "they" did too, by the way. Healthy and dysfunctional relationships take at least two parties. Our concern is *you.* That other person, they have their work too, but it is up to them. Hopefully, the changes you make and awareness you gain will make a difference in whom you pick to be that "somebody" next time. With any luck (and lots of work), you will make better selections going forward.

In your previous relationships, your destination was dialed into "happily ever after." You were expecting endless bouquets of roses and hearing chants of "Bravo" along the way. But the final curtain fell early. The ending was not the fairy tale ending you dreamed about as a child or young adult. The next line here is obvious: *"It's my mother's fault!"*

Yep. To some degree, that is accurate (if your circumstances were different, though, you can substitute "father" or "caregiver"). Early childhood caregivers "write" most of your script. The way they modeled love and relationships ultimately contributed, heavily, to how and why you make the choices you make and operate in relationships in the manner you do.

We'll dive into those choices you made and the underlying reasoning. We will figure out if your motivations were conscious or unconscious, as well. You need to understand that it's OK. Had you known your "self" better, or received better modeling, your relationships would have taken radically different paths. That is a given.

But your circumstances are yours. That is what you have to work with today. Understanding your past is part of your work. Providing the skills to do this work is one of my purposes for writing this book.

The Truth about "Your Story"

Believe it or not, every experience in your life fits together neatly and is there for a purpose. It's "your story" and yours alone; uniquely yours. Nothing is left out or put in that is not meant to be specifically for you and your purpose for being on Earth. Your story includes everything: growing up, your parents, your family, your relationships, your choices, your heartbreaks—literally everything!! Since this is what you have to work with, I would strongly suggest that you embrace it—*all* of it— because in the nooks and crannies of your past lies the key to making "what's next" for you more like what you want. To realize your dreams rather than another experience of "more of the same." When you make that embrace, life gets pretty exciting . . . pretty quickly!! It's not about the past, because *the past is the past.* When your past finally *becomes* the past, that is when you begin to live for your future. Sweet, huh!!

Once you have a big-picture perspective about your story, getting it right next time or making your current relationship work better (that is, with more love, more joy, . . . better sex) is within your power to experience. The things you discover about your self, your behaviors, your choices, and your "learning experiences" from "what happened" are yours to transform into wisdom. This wisdom you gain you can use for your self. Then "pay forward" by sharing it with your children, your friends, your family . . . everyone in your life.

How does that "pay forward" thing work?

Remember the closing scene from the movie *Saving Private Ryan*? The "wisdom" that Captain Miller (played by Tom Hanks) shared on that bridge? What happened when he grabbed Private Ryan (played by Matt Damon) by the collar? That scene is about "you paying your wisdom forward." Remember the gaze of their eyes meeting in Miller's final moments? The captain passed to Ryan the wisdom that they had gained on that journey. The journey had everything: joy, peace, terror, sadness, jubilation, perseverance, failure, loss . . . everything. The message was "Earn this." In other words, remember the journey, and don't forget the lessons of life we shared along the way. That is the moment which Ryan relives as he and his family stroll into the cemetery some fifty years later. He sees the gravestone of the "teacher" he met on that bridge.

As we move forward, I ask you to do the same with your "self." Gaze into your life, your past, your heart, and your soul, because *you* have "earned" all that wisdom. Take yours into your future. Share it. Give it away. Speak the truth in love, as the Bible recommends (Ephesians 4:15). Abundantly. Give it to your children, your family, your coworkers, everyone

Closing Thoughts

My hope is that these words or thoughts save you, your loved one, or a friend from experiencing the excruciating pain and sorrow of a failed relationship venture. Maybe that happens because of insight into a skill needed to traverse the pitted landscape of a current relationship. Maybe it will be the awakening of awareness about your self from your past. You gain an understanding of what words and actions trigger certain responses that you know all too well. Or, as you journey to find real intimacy and experience joy in relationships—all your relationships—you change a behavior that, without the awareness gained, would have derailed you . . . again.

Some of this relationship and healthy skills stuff is hard to follow. I get it. Trust me. Connecting the dots about people and relationships was and remains a monumental task for me. Part of the decision I made was to speak the truth. That is what clients want. Deep down, my sense is people are tired of being sold and buying the "pablum." They want direct, honest, and real. For me, I've chosen to have integrity for my self. It requires speaking the truth, about my self and what I have learned about people and relationships—based on the stories of people in my private life, the people I have worked with in business, those I have counseled as clients, and my friends and family, as well as my own stories. "Story has power."

It would be helpful if you can find some room to excuse my style of writing. It can seem random at times. That is how my mind works. Please trust that the process is going to "connect the dots," even if the parts and pieces seem randomly assembled. Each chapter communicates a valuable thought or concept. These are advanced so the ones that fit for you can be adopted and embraced as "yours." Each one is a part or piece of your puzzle. You need to have these in your tool set to become healthy. You need to become healthy to create and maintain healthy relationships. Being healthy opens the possibility for you to experience a fabulous romantic love relationship.

While "you" and relationships *are* complicated, the complication becomes less complicated when you know how the pieces fit and become aware of what you have that works and what doesn't. You need to know what information is relevant as well as what is not. You'll get that distinction.

Hopefully, when you read the last line and close the cover, you are farther along your journey. You have refined something in you and taken in a new skill or concept. You have gained an understanding or discovered an awareness of your self. Maybe what you take with you brings you an *additional* measure of Grace and forgiveness in your life, and you find healing for a hurt you carried in your heart.

> **Grace is the blessing of life**
> **that moves you forward**
> **so you *can* experience the love your heart desires.**

Chapter 2.

YOUR JOURNEY: DISCOVERING "YOU"

MAYBE YOU ARE JUST GETTING started or maybe you have been trying for a while to get a handle on how you and your relationships work. As you browsed the aisles or paged through the selections of reading materials available online, you wanted to or hoped to discover the mother of all relationship books.

Thank you for buying this book. I'm not sure what you believe, but I believe everything happens in your life for a reason and with purpose. We've never met, but you are reading my work. So there is probably a reason you put down your credit card and walked out with this book!

My goal for writing this book was to transform the scattered volumes of information into a single "process," or a way to see the pieces more clearly. Then to put the pieces of puzzle together about people and their relationships so it makes sense. To communicate this process in a way that can be easily consumed, so that when you put it into practice, it produces tangible results in your life. That is the process and the goal. The following happens to be at the top of the Big Deal list:

Spoiler Alert

The entire premise of this book, every thought process, every conclusion rendered henceforth about people, relationships,

---

marriage, divorce, infidelity, trust, integrity, values, parenting, dysfunctional individuals and families, business, war and peace, sex, intimacy, emotions, fears, anger, sadness, ecstasy, attraction, chemistry, codependency, narcissism, abandonment, anxiety—and about you, your true self, your heart, your ego, your choices, your relationships, your entire life—without exception is based on the following premise:

A healthy life is a **Life Of Vulnerable Experiences.**
Life is about L. O. V. E.
L. O. V. E. makes the world go round.

"To love at all is to be vulnerable.
Love anything and your heart
will be wrung and possibly broken.
If you want to make sure of keeping it intact
you must give it to no one, not even an animal.
Wrap it carefully round with hobbies
and little luxuries;
avoid all entanglements.
Lock it up safe in the casket
or coffin of your selfishness.
But in that casket, safe, dark, motionless, airless,
it will change.

It will not be broken; it will become unbreakable,
impenetrable, irredeemable."[5]
— C. S. Lewis

It all starts "in the beginning . . ."

The Relationship Puzzle

Under the single word descriptor *relationships* is a very long list of subject headings. Not only is this list of relevant subjects great in number, but these subjects are circuitously intertwined and interrelated.

How does your relationship puzzle fit together? Certainly, there is no "one size fits all" solution. You are completely unique. There is no other you.

However, being a healthy adult—becoming healthier and creating and maintaining healthy relationships—begins with having a toolbox filled with relating skills. First, you must acquire the tools, understand how to use them, and then store them. When "something happens," you decipher what is going on and then grab one of your tools from your toolbox and go to work . . . until whatever needed your attention is back in good working order.

You may have some tools and not others. Some of yours may be rusty or broken. It's OK. You will have a full set of healthy adult relating tools when you are finished.

Think about what you know about relationships. Here is a list of relationship elements. Some you may be familiar with and some not. These are the core pieces of the relationship puzzle we explore in the coming chapters (here arranged in alphabetical order):

- Attachment styles
- Bonding
- Boundaries
- Chemistry
- Conflict resolution
- Emotions
- Fears
- Healthy interactions
- Interpersonal relating strategies
- Intimacy

- Love (the biggest piece)
- Preferences
- Unhealthy interactions
- Vulnerability

This seems like a great place to start! There are a few more elements, and all of them are interlaced into your relationships.

In fact, these elements are present in every relationship. Each of them is an individual piece of your puzzle. The elements do not change from person to person or from relationship to relationship. All of them—except fears and unhealthy interactions, of course—are required items. It is much like a car. To drive your car, it *must have* tires and an engine. For relationships to work, these elements (except the two negative ones) must be present *and* in a healthy manner.

Think about you and your relationships for a moment. You have certain personality traits. You have a style and look you prefer. You have a communication style. You have a method of addressing conflicts. You have an attachment style. You have personal preferences. You prefer a certain type of partner. You have a unique way of being loved. You have boundaries (maybe they are healthy, maybe unhealthy). You consistently choose one type of partner. You attract a certain personality type. You bring certain issues, concerns, and fears into your relationships.

Of course, relationships seem complicated . . . because you have a lot of "moving parts." But then you add in an "other"—another human. They have all their traits, preferences, issues, attachments, phobias, and fears as well. Relationships almost have to be complicated!! Here's what makes all this manageable:

No matter the diverse elements you bring to your relationships, and no matter what any partner brings to the table,

> **All relationship "puzzles" have the same set
> of well-defined "parts" and "pieces."**

This statement is the first of the "simplifying" measures designed to dispense with the "complicated" aspect of relationships. These measures are intended to move relationships from complicated to "not as complicated." The pieces of a healthy relationship are the same for everyone. If the parts are all the same, then what is it about people and their relationships that is different?

Relationship expert Mary Ellen Goggin, whom I quoted in Chapter 1, asserts that successful relationships are created by the people who have the skills. Skills are what makes the difference. From here on out, "having the skills" is referred to as "being healthy." The more relating skills expertise you have, the "healthier" you become. These two terms, *skills* and *healthy*, are used many times going forward. Make a note.

In the context of becoming a healthy (or healthier) adult and creating healthy relationships, the truth is that some of your pieces work fabulously well. They don't need much work or attention. You simply need to be aware of their presence. For instance, maybe you were taught to express your emotions in a healthy manner. You express your anger in a way that communicates your upset. You are aware of the sadness you are holding from whatever injustice happened (to you or to someone else). You have the skills to experience and manage your emotional life in a healthy manner. No work is needed here, because you already have what you need.

What if the "skills" you learned were not healthy, however? For example, suppose you were not given ("shown") a healthy model for managing your anger. Today, when you feel anger, you handle it by screaming profanities, hitting walls, getting up in people's faces, or running away. If you are a "screamer" or a "run away" person, you have some work to do in this area. That particular part of your work is acquiring the skill called handling your emotions in a healthy manner. For you, that skill is missing (and the "skill" you have for handling emotions is not healthy). Without the healthy skill, you are unaware, and being unaware, you cause damage.

As these contrasts show, some of your puzzle pieces are healthy and some simply do not fit in a healthy model. Unhealthy "skills" don't work in relationships and do not bring you more joy, love, and fulfillment. In fact, most often these "skills" are barriers or impediments to your experiencing joy, love, and fulfillment. But that is OK. The good news is you can do something about it.

So, your responsibility is figuring out which of your parts work in a healthy way and which ones are not functioning (not healthy). For the ones that do not work, you need to apply what you learn here, so you can refine or change them. When you do, all the pieces of your puzzle will fit together nicely, and the benefit is a healthier you and the possibility of healthy relationships. That is what this book is all about, too!

No matter where you are now with respect to skills, awareness, or health, what is very important for you to understand is:

You are perfect, *just the way you are.*

There is nothing wrong. There is nothing about you that is "less than." You are not "supposed to be some other way" from the way you are now. You are where you are meant to be. You are good enough. You are whole and complete. Where you are is gaining awareness about your self today. "What's next" is knowing *more* about your self. Focusing on improving your self and expanding your awareness. Adding to and refining personal and relationships skills. You have a purpose, too: You are seeking to enhance the possibility of experiencing more *love* in your life.

No matter where you are on your journey, you are OK. *You* are exactly who you are supposed to be, exactly where you are meant to be, with all your past, your history, your experience of joy and lessons learned, wisdom gained. You are perfect just the way you are. (How many times did Billy Joel tell Christie Brinkley that before he memorialized it by writing a song to remind her? Answer: a bunch! Book it.)

Expanding your awareness about your true self enables you to "see" and become aware of all the things you bring to your relationships. "All of you" is your heart, your love, your emotions, your preferences, your dislikes, your ego, your thought life, your boundaries, your insecurities, and more. When you know these things about you, *then* you know your true self. Awareness provides *you* with an unvarnished perspective of your true self (your whole being: "all of you").

When you know your "true self," you will know your "heart." There you will discover your deepest needs and wishes. From the vantage point of knowing your true self, you can clearly distinguish what you want in your relationship life. Then you contrast the wants and desires of your true self with any actions and choices that are misaligned with your true self and your heart.

So, let's keep going with the puzzle metaphor . . .

All these "true self" references you see mentioned here are pieces of you: your heart, your preferences, your love, your dreams, your ego, and so on—many of the items on the big list presented at the beginning of this section. Those are inside pieces of the puzzle.

Edge and Corner Pieces

In this section, each piece of the puzzle (that is, the parts of a healthy adult and healthy relationships) is identified, dissected, and discussed as an individual element. There are quite a few pieces to your puzzle, as mentioned earlier. The first step is to create clear distinctions about each piece. As with the one-thousand-piece jigsaw puzzles you are familiar with, the pieces to your puzzle don't always go together in a linear fashion. Some you need to know and understand in the beginning. That is why you start with the edges and corners. These are the foundation, and they provide you with a guide to solve the puzzle.

The important pieces are like the corner pieces in the thousand-piece jigsaw puzzle. You must understand these first. They are connected to or interrelated to all the pieces in the center. There is no need for worry, either.

Only, trust your self for now. What you are going to do is understand your "self," each of the pieces of "you." These are the pieces you must have, that you must identify and assemble first to create a healthy "you." Once these are tightly joined, *then* creating and maintaining healthy relationships is 100-percent possible.

So, what exactly are the "pieces" of a healthy adult? What are the components and skills necessary to create and maintain a healthy relationship? The following list includes a few of the items you need, items that will be covered in the ensuing chapters:

- Love, the anchor of life and self
- Ego, the absence of love
- Interpersonal relating strategies: selling out, "victim," "pleasing," and so on
- Emotions: healthy expression of sadness, anger, fear, and exuberance (encapsulated by the acronym *SAFE*)
- Vulnerability
- Preferences: relationship likes and dislikes
- Conflict resolution: address, process, and resolve[6]
- Bonding: intimacy and attachment styles
- Fears: insecurity, abandonment, intimacy, connection, and so on
- Boundaries: setting healthy ones, identifying unhealthy ones
- Chemistry: Chem-*patibility*, not lust or attraction

Making sense of the pieces is well within your capacity. The work is to identify the pieces and see how they "live" in you and in your life.

Different People, Same Puzzle

So, are relationships complicated? The answer is part yes, part no, and part myth. The "complicated" aspect refers to the number of pieces to the puzzle. Although your puzzle is unique, the individual pieces are

---

6 The APR procedure (address, process, and resolve) is explained in the subsection "Resolving Conflicts between Heart and Ego with APR" within the main section "Conflict Resolution" in Chapter 5.

pretty much the same for all of us. A thousand-piece coffee table jigsaw puzzle is an apt metaphor.

Those unusual little cardboard shapes are cut by the same die machine using the same pattern. Every puzzle is essentially the same. Cut from the same die means that every solution is the same. Yet, each puzzle is different, because the picture on the front is different. The cardboard pieces are the same, but they are a small part of a different picture.

We ask once more: Are all the puzzles the same? Or is each puzzle unique? The answer is yes and no. That's how people, relationships, and being healthy work. Go back to the foregoing list: now things should make sense or at least be a bit clearer. The pieces that come together in a relationship are all the same, but the "picture on the outside"—you and the "other" person—is different.

You have preferences, they have preferences. You have fears and insecurities, they have fears and insecurities. They have a heart, you have a heart. They have an ego, you have an ego. Here's the good news: When you "know" your self and develop healthy relating practices, you will know what "unhealthy" is, and you will be able to "see" it and "hear" it in others. The more you know about how the pieces fit together, the better equipped you will be to put the pieces of a relationship puzzle together.

Chapter 3.

Love

This chapter is focused on that which is the purpose of *your life*:

To love is to live.

This chapter, focusing on "love," is somewhat long. That should not be a surprise if you read the Introduction and Chapter 1. It is essential for you to know and understand love. The goal of this chapter is for you to thoroughly distinguish the "concept" of love. Its definition and its application need to become as familiar as your name. Seriously. It's that important. Once that task is completed, we will look at "love and you" and then "love and relationships."

The Beatles said:

All you need is love.

What about a job? A home? Kids? Travel? Companionship? A car? Mehhhh. There are some essentials such as food. Check. How about clothing? Check. Money? Check. But aren't these more about survival? Without a few of these, life in the twenty-first century would be next to impossible—for me at least. But our topic is a *subset* of life. Specifically, the focus here is on relationships and on being a healthy adult.

In that context, the Beatles were 100-percent right. Spot on. A strong case can be made:

> *If* we just "loved" with more passion, more vulnerability, more authentically, more deeply, more compassionately, more intimately . . .
>
> *Then* . . . we would experience more peace, more joy, more happiness, and a more satisfying and fulfilling life.

But . . . *Love?*

It seems as though love and our pursuit of it is more often the source of many of the problems in life and not the solutions. Heck, we have a tough time defining *love* much less agreeing on what *love* means. Including how the word *love* is supposed to be used. Is *love* a verb? A noun? A four-letter word? A thought? A decision? A feeling? The answers to these questions are addressed here. Hopefully, by the end of this chapter, the context created for "love" will result in a healthy perspective. For you, creating clarity about love is the first requirement to move down the path to more healthy relationships.

Why Love?

After all, much of your life energy is spent in pursuit of this mysterious concept called *love*. The truth is you really don't have a sound basis for what *love* is, exactly. That begs the question "Why do you pursue it with such relentless focus and don't really 'know' what *it is* that you are seeking?" Yes, you sort of know what *it* is. You definitely know you want to "make love" as often as possible—right?

When you look, you find many ways "love" lives for you:

- You *love* your kids,
- You *love* your dog,
- You *love* flowers,
- You *love* pizza.
- You *love* Bach or Hendrix or Bruno,

- You learned that there are "five love languages,"[6]
- You learned you need to "love your neighbor the same as you love your self," *and*
- You are instructed to "love your enemy."

But each of these seems like a different kind of *love*.

You tell your spouse that you "love" your mother-in-law. This version of love looks more like a negotiated family peace agreement. The family "affectionately" calls her "Train Wreck" Joan (TWJ). She literally has no boundaries. Not with her mouth with her opinions, not in your house, and not with "her grandbabies"—your fourteen-, seventeen-, and twenty-year-old "kids." She sticks her nose into everyone's business. She says she "never has a care in the world" and "my life is just so perfect, it's beautiful." Yet, the truth is she is one of the most anxious, fearful, controlling, scattered people on the planet. You don't love her self-anointed "Master Chef" cooking skills (or lack thereof). Oh, yes, she is the first to brag about her mastery in the kitchen. She religiously overcooks the broccoli. TWJ can do more damage in three minutes carving the Thanksgiving turkey than a grizzly bear that stumbles onto an elk carcass in the wild.

She is a 100-percent total train wreck . . . and you "love" her? What you know is proclaiming love for TWJ makes for better relations with your spouse's family, the grandkids, and all the in-laws on that side of the family tree. But, how does this concept of *love* work exactly? For example, you "love" Miranda . . . maybe more than TWJ.

Miranda is your two-year-old, 125-pound female malamute puppy. You "love" her. Even though in two years she has eaten a sofa and a half, three one-hundred-dollar yoga mats, and every round object in your house. Yet, she is one big lovable love ball of fur . . . and feet . . . and slobbery tongue. She's all love.

The reason for putting a humorous light on *love*? Because, when someone says, "I love you," do you (or they) really know what it means? From my experience, I have my doubts. Yet, saying these three words leads to making life-altering choices. The words impact your family as well as your personal well-being. They can have a huge impact on your mental and emotional health. Joy and happiness are at stake! As well as years of your life. And all these outcomes are based on three words: "I love you."

The *truth* is we don't know *exactly* what *love* is!! That's a problem. If that doesn't raise an eyebrow, this may: Think about the last part of the "I love you" equation, *you*.

If you don't know exactly what *love* is, how do you know how much of *it* you need? How much of *it* you can give? What if you get too much of *it?* What if you need more or less than your partner or family or "other" can give? What if the kind of *love* you need is different from that needed by everyone around you? How do you want to be loved?

You know already that your relationship is with an imperfect person. Do you plan, in advance, to be "OK" with getting less than 100 percent of the love you want and need? That would mean you would have to *settle* for "less than." If that would be the case, to be in "that" relationship, you have no other choice but to settle. Those seem like pretty important considerations.

Looking at it in this light, what becomes abundantly clear is that with much of your life and future at stake, the concept of *love* needs to be very well defined. Ultimately, how love is defined significantly impacts your experience of fulfillment, connection, intimacy, happiness, and joy. Literally, your life depends on love . . . so being really clear about *love* is a Big Deal.

I've heard that right about here, you may be finding your self wandering off the page a few times—mostly because of asking this question: "What on God's green Earth was I thinking?"

The "wandering off" is your recalling "what happened" somewhere back there in your life:

> About ten or twenty or thirty years ago . . . I sort of remember
> the date . . . I stood up in front of a bunch of people, most

I barely knew. Then I promised that I would "love" him "till death do us part." Then, over twelve long years, it was not him that died, or me, but "the love," which—I realize today—I still can't really define very well . . . *it* died.

But, wait . . . it was like "wash, rinse, repeat"!!

Just like a scene out of *Groundhog Day*, in less than three years after I divorced "the One," I met "The One II." And I did it over *again*. I said the exact same "till death do us part."

Neither he nor I died. But the love? *It died! Again!!*

Sorry to be the bearer of the surprising news: You probably were not thinking! The good news is you're a few pages away from clearing this up once and for all. To gain insight into your self and your ability and capacity to create healthy relationships, you must firmly establish a context for the concept of *love*. It must be able to apply universally—to love your self, to love your partner, to love your kids, to love your friends, to love everyone!

To render this as universal truth, you must approach the discussion of love from several perspectives:

- What is love?
- What is *not* love?
- What is "perfect love"?
- What is "unconditional love"?
- What is self-love?

You tackle each of these as you work through the following pages.

Describing and Defining Love

By creating a universally applicable context for *love*, you transform the concept. It is no longer an imprecise, indescribable, unclear, colloquial term used and applied to nearly everything that someone finds appealing or fulfilling. Love becomes clear, concise, and well defined—as it needs to be. Love then becomes easier to understand and to communicate.

For you, this transformation makes it possible for love to have universal application in your life.

Your firsthand experience tells you that it is no longer acceptable to operate your life in the pursuit of something that is so ill defined. You need a clear context, which can be communicated with precision. The truth is "I love you" needs to be as clear as "I am pregnant." Think about some of the "familiar," or commonplace, phrases people use to describe what *love* is.

Here are descriptions from a random collection of interviews and surveys:

- Love is caring for someone else deeply and unconditionally.
- Love is being motivated to be the best version of your self that you can possibly be.
- Love means finding someone who brings out the best version of your self
- Love is when someone knows you inside and out.
- Love means knowing that no matter what, you have someone to count on.
- Love makes you feel good inside.
- Love never hurts or makes you cry your eyes out.
- Love is very gentle and warm.
- Love is the feeling that something is missing when you are apart and the realization that everything seems so much better when you are together.

No question, these descriptions are very sweet and nice sentiments. They are "thoughtful." They seem like things that are "critical." The truth is these are generalizations. Do any of them—or even all of them—define what love is? They describe some of the ways people "feel," and they highlight some shared values or experiences. I am sorry, but planning your life, your future, and your prospects for kids on such flimsy notions is not exactly a good idea, in my opinion.

So, you may ask, "What *is* this 'perfect definition' of love, then?" Of course, the answer here is easy. There *is* no perfect definition, because humans are imperfect. What is certain is the definition of love can be exponentially more precise than "how" it is used and randomly applied as shown in the foregoing quotes.

Is the definition adopted in this presentation 100-percent universally applicable to all people in all relationships with anyone? For the most part, the answer is yes. But what matters is: Will your definition of *love* work in your life? That is what counts. This is about *you* and your relating skills. That is *your* focus at the moment. For you, a clear, concise definition of love opens the door to experience life and people in a way you never imagined was possible. After all, since that is your reason you are doing your work, that *would* be the best of all outcomes.

Is Love a Feeling (an Emotion[7])?

When you say, "I love you," what you are expressing needs a context that can be clearly delineated. Especially, it must be clear for the person who may ask, "What do you mean when you tell me you 'love' me?" Wouldn't that be fabulous?! Instead of beating around the bush with a stream of trite sayings, dry adjectives, and inane descriptors, you can share what you *actually* mean. And this may turn out to be a piece of wisdom that could be life changing for this someone in your life.

Look closely at these examples. These are exact quotes from clients:
- "It *feels so good* when I love you."
- "I can't really explain it, I *just know it.*"
- "I just *love* their laugh."

---

7   There is a distinction between feelings and emotions, though they are highly interconnected. Emotions are essentially lower-level physical responses that trigger biochemical reactions in your body that alter your physical state. Feelings, on the other hand, are mental associations influenced by memories, beliefs, and personal experiences. Nonetheless, in the context of what this book is about—loving your self—the distinction is not particularly germane, and I have been using the two terms more or less interchangeably. For more on this topic, see https://www.thebestbrainpossible.com/whats-the-difference-between-feelings-and-emotions/.

- "I *love* their smile . . ."
- "Their hair is so *lovely* . . ."
- "I *love* how my BMW hugs the curves."
- "I *love* how *I feel* when I hold/see/smell/hear/am with [Fill in the blank]. . . ."

Notice, these examples basically describe sensory perceptions. They represent the *bodily senses* someone experiences when "loving" something or someone. Look carefully. It appears that each of these examples of what people "know what love is" fall into one of two classifications:

*". . . it **feels** . . ."*

or

*". . . I just **know** . . ."*

No wonder when the descriptions or definitions of love are something you "feel," "love" is very confusing! It is confusing because most people have a difficult time identifying what they are feeling. Even if they can identify the feeling (emotion) in a general sense, once they do, it is often more difficult for them to describe precisely *what* they are feeling.

Herein lies the problem: Declaring "love" as something you "feel" is simply another way of saying that love is a physical experience. "Feel" is a physical experience, and what you "feel" is how you experience different emotions. That is what I conclude when I read the meanings of the words in nearly all these descriptions. "Feelings" are what each speaker is communicating. They are describing what *love* is by describing "how they feel."

Here's the catch, though: love is clearly not an emotion. There is ample evidence to undermine the notion of love being an emotion. For you, love needs to be clear. Are emotions (feelings) precise? Well defined? Universally understood? No.

What is true is this: You may "experience" very pleasurable physical sensations and attach emotional experiences to times when you *love* someone or something and when you are with *loved* ones or when you are being *loved*. But, the concept of *love* in the sense of "healthy adult love" is not the feelings, the physical sensations, or a random collection of emotional experiences.

Yes, in the "love" state, these *sensations* are often present. These are what you may experience. Just to be clear, there is definitely a "feeling" aspect of "love," and this will be covered in the chapter focused on relationships. For now, however, your focus is on *defining* love.

Staying focused on defining what "love" is, go back and take a look at the description that says: "I can't really explain it, I *just know it.*"

This description is different from the others. While most of the others described love in terms of a "feeling" (that is, a sensory experience), this person is describing a cognitive process; *to know*. Here is what "to know" means, according to the dictionary:

> to be aware of through observation, inquiry, or information; to
> comprehend, understand; to infer, being aware of meanings;
> to perceive directly: to have direct cognition of; to grasp in the
> mind with clarity or certainty.

Immediately you can observe that "to know" and "to feel" are distinct; they are apples and oranges. You "know" something because of thinking, observing, inquiring, or processing information; *know*ledge is the result of your contemplation and thought. Defining love with *clarity and certainty* is your criterion.

Whereas the experience of love has "feeling" components, emotions (feelings) are different from *know*ledge (also known as "thoughts" or "thought processes" or "thinking"). When you experience "emotions," what you "feel" are the tactile sensations of your bodily experience. Emotions (feelings) generate a sensory experience, which can vary in intensity. What is happening is not clear. The source is definitely not something about which you have much certainty.

This connection between "thought" and "feeling" may be a large part of the confusion. Thoughts often do trigger feelings (emotions) in your physical self. "Think about" losing your job. Your body may respond by chest tightening, or your stomach may become unsettled, queasy. How about when you round a corner and see a large dog. You are stuck in your tracks. You are immobilized with fear that you are going to be attacked. This is "thought" (that is, is this big dog going to bite me?) and "feeling" (that is, you are unable to move) happening, inside you, at the same time.

The purpose of using these two examples and doing this exercise is to clearly establish "thinking" and "feeling" as distinct concepts. Understanding this difference is critical for exploring the dimensions of love.

With these two perspectives differentiating feelings (emotions) and thinking, what love is *not* can be stated with 100-percent certainty:

Love is *not* an emotion.

At this point, what "love is not" has been partially addressed—hold on to the notion that love is not a feeling (an emotion). If love is not a feeling (an emotion)—then what is love? Consider once more that person's observation about "love": he "just knows" it. A long description of "I *just know* it" might read something like this:

> After evaluating all the inputs and information that are available for me to process about this thing or person, the result of my logical, cognitive process renders my conclusion, "it is 'love'"! That statement comes about without my knowing exactly what "it" is; thus, the statement of certainty I have about the uncertainty is: I *just know* it.

He knows "it" *is* "love." What is unclear is what exactly did he evaluate or measure? What are the elements he processed or contemplated in his mind to reach his conclusion? One thing is indisputable: Whatever "it" is, "love" must be the things he considered. It's almost like he had a list of criteria or measures with checkboxes. What he was checking off must be present. Because if those "items" that he was looking for or "knows about it" were *not* present, then, obviously "it" would not be "love." Since he "thought" about it, the things he considered must be clear and definitive—tangible, maybe?

Love being a "thought process" eliminates "feelings" ("emotions"), a conclusion that necessarily rules out love as something that happens in your physical self. So, the question is: Does "love" happen in your brain unit? Is "love" something you can control? Is love something you "think" about doing? Is "love" something you "choose" or not "choose"? Is "love" or "loving" something decided by "yes" or "no," as in "I will or will not love you"?

Let's revisit the notion you are holding about love not being a feeling (an emotion). We need to state clearly that "love" creates or causes sensory experiences. These were what the foregoing examples proved. People expressed that they felt it, and so if or when "love" is present, it certainly causes us to feel physical sensations. What follows establishes with a high degree of certainty: "love," "to love," and "loving" happen in your brain. If you find your self either confused or doubtful, hold these as well in an open mind.

You think with your brain. You do not feel with your brain. So, love must be the result of conscious thought processes. You know the thinking part of your brain is a "decision machine." Could this mean that "to love" is the result of a decision between "to love" and "*not* to love"? That seems to be a highly relevant question and is, in fact, the answer. What is unknown is precisely the criteria you choose (or not choose) regarding love. The revelation that love is a choice brings with it many implications.

The revelation simplifies the concept of love, and it becomes very manageable. Since love is a choice, then "to love" and "loving" become clear, well-defined actions; you manifest love as your "choice." There is no mystery. Although you can choose to love, you also can choose not to love.

Yes, this long, tedious process purposefully brought about the single logical and accurate conclusion: Love is a choice. The concept of "love" is the act of "loving," which is the result of a conscious decision you make.

The answer to the question posed at the beginning: "What is "love"?

Love Is a Choice

Saying, "I love you," is saying, "I am choosing to love you." In this section, the discussion investigates what "criteria," or *elements*, are you considering in your choice. "What's next" is to identify "love" by the elements you are choosing. Once this is complete, the result will be that your saying, "I love you" will *mean* something tangible.

Healthy love is a choice. You make it. You choose to love. Love is *not* a feeling (an emotion). Love is a result of a mental or cognitive process in which you choose "to love." Yes, you also choose "not to love." With the nature of "love" being a choice, once you know what you "choose," it will become clear when you are choosing "not to love." Choosing not to love is neither good nor bad; it is neither right nor wrong. It's a choice. It's OK.

However, the fact that love *is* a choice makes it a bit harder for a healthy adult to choose "not to love." Knowing what you know about people and relationships, you may conclude, "No, there are people who are very easy for me not to love." Hold that thought. This statement will make sense as we move along.

For now, what needs further clarity is to understand the context of "love" at its extreme. Where the choice to love is beyond the realm of you, or any human, to do or practice. Humans are (perfectly) imperfect creatures. Perfect love seems out of the question. However, for our discussion, the concept of perfect love is important to investigate. Is there is a foundation or framework for love that would be "ideal"—also known as "perfect"? This "absolute love" can be framed with a question: Is there a context of "love" that is *perfect love?*

The closest sense of that context can be expressed as "unconditional love." A simple concept, and very easy to understand: Love without conditions. For "perfect love," there are two excellent points of reference.

The first reference consists of the writings and teaching that have been passed on for generations. These have been adopted by cultures and societies. They are the foundations for spirituality and are used as the basis for creating community. The sources vary. These include the Bible, the works of such famous thinkers as Aristotle and Plato, as well as the wisdom shared by Buddha and others—too many to reference. With few exceptions, they all point to a similar context for perfect love, and that meaning rests well beyond the capacity of humans to execute with perfection.

One of the most widely recognized descriptions of "perfect love" is from the Bible. This "version" you may know or have heard often. It is recited at weddings and landmark marriage anniversaries. This is the description of "perfect love" from 1 Corinthians 13:4–7:[8]

> Love is patient, love is kind. It does not envy, it does not boast,
> it is not proud. It does not dishonor others, it is not self-
> seeking, it is not easily angered, it keeps no record of wrongs.
> Love does not delight in evil but rejoices with the truth. It
> always protects, always trusts, always hopes, always perseveres.

This list represents the "perfect" characteristics of behavior and thought about how to love. Beautiful, simple, and self-explanatory. In this regard, it defines the "attributes" that are to be present when one is "loving" toward an "other." These attributes of love are directed toward a person, a place, or a thing. For our purposes, the focus is on people, and with this description of "perfect" love, *the* problem arises. When someone proclaims, "I love," it means each of the items on this list must be present. Since humans are imperfect, they are unable to execute the practice of love to perfection. "Keep no record of wrongs" . . . "always protects"—these injunctions make for a very short discussion. But, it's

OK, because we are looking for a framework for love, and defining the perfect "tense" is important for that end game.

The second reference we have for love is your personal experience. That is the original context of love which you know. Your model was given to you and imprinted early in your life. How you "know" love is how it was given to you in your childhood—from mothers, fathers, family members, and caregivers. Your "model of love" is indelibly etched in your bones. This imprint of love is carried throughout your life. When you create relationships, you arrive with your original model. Your model becomes particularly important in romantic love relationships. This is interesting, because your parents are yours and no one else's. So, your imprint for "love" is guaranteed to be different from anyone else's. Even if you have siblings, your imprint of love is uniquely yours.

From these two sources, the Bible and teachings plus your imprint, it is now possible for you to develop a framework for healthy love. This model moves you toward healthy ways to express love and create and maintain healthy loving relationships throughout your life. The model of healthy "love" is one that can stand the test of time and navigate all your life circumstances as well.

At the beginning of this discussion about "perfect love," the term *unconditional love* was introduced. This seems to be an appropriate place to examine this concept in more detail. Beginning with the question . . .

What Is Unconditional Love?

The last two words are the focus here. The "unconditional" part means that this is the ultimate measure of love. Recall the statement that "unconditional love" is simply "love without conditions." This kind of love just "exists." It exists without bounds, is limitless, is in infinite abundance. It does not fluctuate or change with circumstances. Unconditional love does not expand ("more") or contract, ("less") over time. It is available in abundant quantities always. The supply is always more than the measure of love needed or required at any moment. The case can be made that these parameters define a "kind" of love that would be the "ultimate experience" of love. A love that is dependent on nothing. It, *love*, simply exists for us or anyone to give or receive. "Unconditional" seems to be a pretty high bar, much like "perfect love." It would be difficult to practice unconditional love flawlessly. Perfect love and unconditional love are beyond any human's capacity to "give" or "offer" to an "other." As it should be.

Humans are finite. Unconditional love is *infinite*. People impose conditions. Unconditional love has "no conditions." You know from your experience, there are those times you choose to withhold love based on merit (condition). You judge worth or assign value. These are conditions, your conditions. The worth of others cannot be measured by an imperfect human standard. These brief examples are intended to show unconditional love is "beyond the realm" of humans.

We need to put unconditional love "in the realm" of God, or "the source of all creation." (There is no need to digress about God here; see Appendix A for more reading.) Even if there is no god in your reality, the logic still holds. Unconditional love would require the capacity "to love" all humans without conditions. This task is one that people fall short of executing. One that they cannot deliver. There is only one conclusion to be drawn:

The measure of perfect love, love without conditions, renders this measure of "love" impossible for humans to gift or practice.

(You are welcome to, and invited to, email me directly if you're thinking renders a different conclusion, or if you wish to engage in a debate about the possibility of perfection being achievable by your self or by someone you know. . . .)

Having defined (through this very long discussion) the relevant contexts for love, and having processed any exclusions to eliminate any uncertainty, I have laid the foundation for a model of healthy love that you can apply to your self, your life, and your relationships, definitively expressed as . . .

A Healthy Model of Love

Most of our lives seem to mirror the journey of Indiana Jones. He was relentlessly pursuing the Ark. He was drawn to the search from a place deep within his being. He couldn't explain it when asked. He was "just called to pursue this quest." This is what C. S. Lewis shares in one of his writings:[9]

> If I find in myself desires which nothing in this world can satisfy, the only logical explanation is that I was made for another world.

It is like we are here in the present, but our constant longing is for something that is indefinable. Yet this is what we search for our entire lifetime.

Jones has two things to work with in his quest for the Ark. The historical accounts of others found in the bits and pieces of a map. Along with his burning desire to experience the mystery of what he knows from his soul. The ultimate experience of possessing the Holy Grail: The Ark of the Covenant. He fantasizes about his journey—discovering, opening, holding, and sharing it. As you watch his relentless pursuit, something inside of you is completely captivated. You can identify with the inexplicable desire that consumes him. You share his "want" to experience this discovery, which seems to continually elude his grasp.

Jones's experience is one you know well. It is familiar. The quest consumes Harrison Ford's character for what seems like his lifetime. As you watch, you have a strong sense of his journey. You feel his struggles. You understand his relentless pursuit. Because you identify his pursuit as yours. His journey is a metaphor for your quest to find love; it resonates deeply in your soul.

Your journey is not to find the treasure of the Ark. Your journey is to find the meaning of life. To discover the essence of your being, the reason you exist. Yours is the discovery of "what is your purpose" for occupying this space, at this time, with your circumstances. The great thinkers of the past and present spanning all the way back to the Creator of All Things, to C. S. Lewis, and now in contemporary times to David Richo, Tara Brach, Brené Brown, Helen Fisher, and others. Their conclusion is that your journey, my journey—"our journey"—is to experience "love." With the meaning of life hanging in the balance, it only stands to reason that you must have the full awareness of this mystery of love.

Now that the context of love is sufficiently framed, you are "choosing" to love. So, the elements must be concrete and definable. What are these "elements" of love that you choose?

The answer comes from one of the great thinkers on the subject of love, healthy adult relating skills, and healthy relationships. The fellow's name is David Richo.

When I first stumbled upon Richo's work,[10] his descriptions and well-constructed thoughts hit me like a ton of bricks. His writing style is not complicated. He is all about simplicity. Not as difficult to follow as some authors' works. He presents complex concepts about people and behaviors and assembles them in a way that is easy to understand. His descriptions and presentation make sense. His thoughts make sense and when put into practice, whether applied in personal relationships or used in client consultations, his work produces results. It is appropriate to acknowledge Richo and his contributions. He is a gifted human being. Of all the workshops, seminars, books, and papers included in this field, Richo's work stands out as exemplary.

What makes Richo's work so valuable and so unique?

First, his definition captures the "essence" of love in a clear, concise, and easy-to-comprehend manner. He uses associations that are presented as personal experiences. They are easy to visualize, which makes them easy to communicate to others. His work is "plus one"; it can be shared beyond the person who reads his work. That is special. He has taken this previously indescribable, foggy concept of love and translated it into a very simple concept made up of five words. That's it. That is the genius. His genius may not be apparent in this early introduction, but as we move forward, hopefully, his talent will settle into your being . . . as it has into mine.

Second, his "five-word context" for love is totally inclusive. These five words denote elements that touch all the "indescribable," nuanced vagaries that bring a pause when we are asked, 'Tell me what love is" or "Tell me what love means" or "What do you mean when you say, 'I love you'?" Richo provides a solid foundation for anyone who finds their self being asked these questions. His five elements are "the choices" when you "choose" to love. They are the essence of *love* . . .

Richo's Model of Love: The Five A's

Richo's "5A" model of love is an extraordinary addition to the study of relationships and people. Going forward you will read the "five A's" often. Make a note (add it to your skills).

He successfully refined the concept of "love" and "unconditional love" into one that can be integrated into your life with ease. The five A's provide the first and largest piece in your model for being a healthy adult and creating and maintaining healthy relationships. The five A's provide an interesting perspective about your past as well. This model can be a guide for you to better understand "what happened"—early on and as a relationship develops. Also, the five A's address the following questions:

- How did you learn "love"?
- What model were you presented with as a child?
- Was it healthy? Unhealthy?
- What model did you carry forward into your adult years?
- What aspects of love were given which worked?
- What didn't work?
- Most importantly, what was missing?

The five A's are *your foundation* for becoming healthy. Answering the foregoing questions is an ideal starting point for understanding "your story." The five A's provide insight into each of these questions. The five A's tell "your story" about "what happened" and "who am I." You have been seeking, searching, and longing to experience love your entire life.

Richo gives a simple construct of love, which fills the void that was created when you eliminated feelings or emotions as the source of love or an explanation of it. Love is a choice, and to this end, Richo's model of "unconditional love" is the most critical addition to your skill set. Richo begins by framing love:

> ***Love is not a feeling but is a choice . . .***
> ***a way of being present.***

Here are Richo's five A's, the five elements you choose when you "choose to love":

> ***Love is a sustained and active presence with the***
> ***unconditional** giving of these five A's:*
> ***Attention*** *to others by hearing what they are saying and noticing what they are feeling*
> ***Acceptance*** *of others just as they are—with all their light and shadow, too*
> ***Appreciation*** *of others' gifts, limits, and uniquely poignant predicaments*
> ***Affection*** *that is shown in holding and touching in respectful ways*
> ***Allowance***—*allowing others to make their own choices rather than the ones I think best for them*

Going forward, your working definition of love, in the context of your life, healthy relating, and healthy relationships is:

> *Love is the presence of five A's:*
> *Attention,*
> *Acceptance,*
> *Appreciation,*
> *Affection, and*
> *Allowance.*

The easiest way to understand the five A's is to observe how it is modeled. Where? By observing the most fundamental of all human love relationships: the relationship between a mother and a child—specifically, during those first, formative years of the child (from birth to seven or eight years old). This relationship is where the most representative example of "unconditional love" is found.

The "healthy installation" of each component of Richo's five A's is described in the following discussion. Visualize each element in the context of an infant or a child in their early years with their mother. (Typically, the mother is the child's primary caregiver, but the model could be any other healthy adult-to-child relationship. The context in the following discussion refers to the mother as the primary caregiver, but feel free to substitute whatever fits a circumstance you may recall.)

Here is how the five A's are modeled and installed, each from the point of view of you, the one being given the model:

Attention: An "other" has an engaged and undivided focus on you—your needs and feelings are noticed, the expression of your understanding and meaning is heard, your verbal and nonverbal cues are taken into account, and the "other" has a keen interest in who you are and what you are experiencing, past or present.

The healthy installation of attention occurs when the mother gives her attention to the baby with "undivided focus." At such an early age, a baby has little awareness of its actual location in the universe. The first and most important reference point is provided by the mother (or caregivers). The baby "sees" (literally) and begins to have a sense (feels, hears, smells) that it exists. All of its early "sense of being" is learned and known by the baby when it is being given *attention* by its mother. The attention begins to instill the baby's sense of "being connected," it gains a sense of belonging. In this "new place," where everything seems bigger and is outside and beyond its self, with *attention* the baby begins to know it "exists."

The focused attention of the mother is a "mirror" to the child. With cue after cue from the "outside in," the mother confirms *to the child* what the child is feeling and sensing. As a "mirror," the mother reveals, reflects, and confirms (that is, models) that the actions of the child either generate a positive response of encouragement or determine what actions are negative and discouraged. The child begins to learn the difference between approval and disapproval from the sounds and activities that come in response to how they operate in the world. Also, they notice if there is comfort coming their way when life "hurts" or when some critical need is not being met.

Mirroring is a vital tool for the installation of love. The child learns and "knows" the experience of attention and associates attention with being "loved." As with all five of the elements in Richo's model, the child's experience during the first few years of their life is carried forward in their memory. What was given? Was it too much? Was it too little? Was it ill-timed? Was it given when needed? Was it given the measure that was wanted or needed? In the end, what was correctly installed, as well as what was missing, are "known" by the child. Attention is the first element of "love" installed in the child's heart, soul, and being.

Acceptance: *The acknowledgment of your unique existence in the universe as a whole and complete being, that you are "perfect . . . just the way you are," without judgment of value or worth, that nothing is missing and that no part of you needs modification or to be changed.*

The healthy installation of acceptance begins and is most visible in the moments following birth. Acceptance begins when the baby is presented to the mother (or parents). In this moment, the baby is fully embraced as "whole and complete." The caretaker's looks, words, and thoughts confirm the baby's "acceptance." In these moments and then for months (possibly years) that follow, 100 percent of the child's self is accepted. Nothing they do is "not OK." All the positive and endearing features such as those eyes, those feet, that smile, the gurgle when they laugh out of control—those are all absolutely unique aspects of the child. They are treasured. There is no request to change them or suggestions that there is something about the child which could "be improved." The child's whole being is uniquely given by God of the Universe. Full acceptance is granted even for those endless nights of waking up at 11:00 p.m., 1:00 a.m., 3:00 a.m., 5:00 a.m. . . . for months. It's OK; the child's waking up is accepted. Spitting up the whipped bananas . . . at every taste? It's accepted, it's OK. Biting the dog's ear till it bleeds? It's OK. As is the perfectly ill-timed ear-piercing scream in the middle of the Sunday sermon? That is also OK.

In other words, acceptance is 100 percent; all the "goodies" are unique and cherished. But so are those things that are "not your personal preferences" and/or "not what you would have chosen" and/or "not how you would have made them if you were God." This 100-percent acceptance is "given" to the child, and it instills the profound sense of "I am OK." One-hundred-percent acceptance requires dispensing with any notions of comparison, critiques, and judgments. Or that there is something "missing." Or that what is "there" is somehow "less than" or "not good enough."

Acceptance does not require many words or well-articulated explanation. In matters of love and intimate relationships, acceptance exists only in an "all-inclusive state." Acceptance means full, unconditional. When your acceptance differentiates between the "perfectly imperfect, human being" and the actions, peculiarities, or nuances of their behaviors and even their "choices," it becomes abundantly clear:

**One-hundred-percent, complete,
unconditional acceptance
is the minimum standard of choosing to love.**

This "100-percent acceptance" is readily given to children, especially in their early, formative years. Maybe not so much later, when 100-percent acceptance becomes more challenging for the ones doing the "giving" . . . ?

In summary, healthy acceptance is the *absence of judgment: Nothing requires modification or qualification.* The declaration of "I accept you" is precisely the description Billy Joel sang to Christie Brinkley:

> Don't go changing . . .
>
> Don't go trying some new fashion . . .
>
> Don't change the color of your hair . . .
>
> I took the good times; I'll take the bad times
>
> I'll take you just the way you are

If you have a sense of uneasiness when you read these descriptions, it will serve you well to hold on to those feelings. These five A's are the components of the unconditional love which we were all designed to experience. "A 100-percent experience" of unconditional love is not likely what you remember as your experience. On this road to "health," you will revisit each component and your experience as you progress. As you work your way through, pay attention to your self. Begin to construct your model of your installation: "How was acceptance gifted to me? Did they want me to change? Was I told I was not good enough, that something needed to be 'added' to me for them to accept me?" These are the questions to ask.

Appreciation: Being acknowledged that you are valued and are valuable. That you possess unique gifts and talents. That you have essential goodness and that you matter. That you possess unconditional worth that cannot be diminished or damaged by choices, or by success or failures or history or behavior, that you are worthy, and that you are to be cherished and to be held, dear in your special uniqueness.

The healthy installation of appreciation occurs when a caregiver recognizes and verbally expresses to the child that they have "value." Recognition is essential for the healthy development of a child's sense of worth. As with each component of the five A's, the caregiver expresses to the child that which makes them unique and valuable. Expression of value and goodness is a necessary action to model the words of recognition and appreciation for the child's self-worth. These conversations the child will hear as the "voice in their head," and they will carry these words throughout their life.

Language, the choice of words, is essential to help the child to "hear" and to "know" their value. These words shape how they experience their self. Speaking the description of their gifts and uniqueness installs in the child's core being the words and descriptions confirming they have worth. Equally important are the caregiver's reactions and responses to the child when they explore their self's functioning in the world around them.

The language used when giving affirmations provides the child with verbal reference points about who they are on their own and who they are as a separate "self" in the world. However, the caregiver's language that deals with negative choices must be carefully selected. It is imperative to neatly and crisply separate the child's choice and behavior from the child's innate "worth" and value, their "true self."

As is often the case in one's personal journey through life, a child's discovery of their "gifts and talents" is not linear. It is a random sequence of trials and "learning experiences." There are always hits and misses. It is incumbent upon a caregiver to allow plenty of space for the child's journey of self-discovery. The words that encourage exploration and taking risks without too many excessively restrictive boundaries are critical. All the child's efforts need to be recognized and acknowledged. These are essential for the child to develop a clear understanding of their value independently, which is *their own personal experience* of their self. Upon the discovery of each unique gift or talent, it is incumbent on the caregiver to express enthusiastic, authentic words of appreciation, so the child's sense of their gifts and talents (their uniqueness) is firmly installed in their core, in their "true self."

When trial exploration produces less than desirable results, the caregiver's words need to provide the child with a perspective of that experience being transformed to a "learning experience." Each learning experience has valuable information to be collected—their activity, their thought process, their expectations—but mostly the transformation creates an internal model of how to capture the value of any experience. The best lessons in life rarely arrive attached to a trophy or ribbon. Instead, the wisdom in life is found in the pieces that lie scattered at one's feet. Learning how to sift through the wreckage of one's personal experiences is life's most valuable teacher. It is the language that makes the difference . . . in both achievement and "mining the gold" when the desired outcome was not achieved.

Affection: *Expressing the value of your physical presence, touching in a nonsexual manner is necessary and cherished. Bonding through touch is the earliest experience of the awareness that your being is separate . . . and alone. Affection confirms your physical connection with your surroundings and others, and it is welcomed. Affection says, "It is OK to be in the presence of you." Touch provides pleasure, comfort, and reassurance, but it is comfortable, not clingy, smothering, or intrusive. Healthy affection establishes your physical boundaries for your self and others: "I am here, you are over there."*

Like appreciation, the healthy installation of affection happens immediately "upon arrival" as well. When the baby is cuddled against the mother's skin, it experiences being welcomed into the world. The instant message is "warmth and safety," and this communicates that "touching is welcome," that "touching provides comfort," that touching provides the connection with what is around you. It is a healthy way to connect to those with whom you are closest. The sense of closeness, warmth, and comfort is the memory that is installed early . . . and often.

Affectionate touching is nonsexual in nature. There is an invisible boundary between touching to connect and touching for erotic pleasure. Caregivers establish the distinct boundary for healthy affection, where the physical connection starts and stops; it never ventures over the line to sensual touching.

Connecting physically is a fundamental element for partner and parental bonding. The parent dispenses hugs on all occasions—as a greeting and at any departure, to celebrate and console—and this happens in conjunction with attention. Affection is often the unspoken, physical "giving" of love from one to another. It is often a stand-alone act without the offering of or requirement for words. Affection is gender-agnostic and does not discriminate by age. Your caregiver's example of caressing your face and hands, of holding hands, of walking arm in arm, of letting you sit in their lap, of sitting next to each other, of lying beside each other, of spooning, and of sitting face to face. You learn all manners of affection from your caregivers as you move through your adolescent years. You learn the measure, style, and types of affection that you like, prefer, and desire—as well as the measure and kinds of affections you do not need. For the healthy human experience, affection is as fundamental and essential as breathing or taking a drink.

Allowance (Allowing): *Being granted the freedom to pursue your personal desires, your deepest needs and wishes, with no consideration or concern for there being a "right time"—but rather "whatever time you need." You can pursue your dreams without restrictions, life's lessons happen when they happen, you experience life without an arbitrary or mandatory timeline or calendar. "It's OK to be where you are . . . stuck in an inquiry . . . soaring . . . it's OK for you to be where you are and for as long as you need to be there."*

The healthy installation of allowing is "granting the right" for the pursuit of one's deepest needs and wishes. The difference between acceptance and allowance is revealed by opposites; the opposite of acceptance is rejection, whereas the opposite of allowance is controlling. Allowing doesn't always include accepting, but acceptance *always includes* allowing.

The context for allowing provides the challenge of "letting the circumstances of life" be "OK" for the child to experience. Whether things are going well, or a situation is a struggle, allowing the child to experience what each circumstance holds provides valuable life lessons. The biggest lesson is in permitting the child to experience the disassembling of their personal situation and *then* to experience the challenge of mustering their internal resources and reconstituting their self back to a place of personal harmony and peace.

Parents often intervene during these times and this, significantly, reduces the value of the experience for the child. This is understandable, because the child is likely in pain, or is holding sadness or feelings that are disconcerting and painful. But the experience of these feelings and emotions are part of life. Experiencing them *is* the full experience of the child's true self. Allowing the entire experience builds resiliency and gives the child confidence in their ability to handle life as it comes, whatever comes. These are critical skills required later in life when there is little or no support from caregivers. They will need to gather their self, in the circumstances of their life, when *they* are the parent and the responsibility of navigating difficult times through to recovery is solely in *their* hands.

Contemplating the Five A's

Your work is to know the perspective of each for the five A's. Contemplate them. The five A's must become an active awareness, held in the forefront of your consciousness. These need to be "how you operate" in your daily life. They are the cornerstone of your becoming healthy. These perspectives model the essential elements of life and love; they are invaluable.

Additionally, it is important to have two perspectives. The first perspective is for you to perceive through the eyes of the child and the caregiver (each side). The second perspective—addressed in the next section, "You and Your Model of Love"—is for you to be aware of "you": how the five A's occur from your perspective, through your eyes, in relation to you and your love "outbound" to the world as well as to the love coming "inbound" to you.

First is the perspective of the child and a caregiver. This view shows "the installation of love," modeled by the caregiver and based on what the caregiver experienced as a child. It is important to note that whatever the caregiver is modeling is impacted by *their* past and *their* circumstances. This is a critical point. It is unlikely that what the caregiver received was "unconditional." So, for the child, the model they get will be the "best the caregiver has to offer," given the circumstances of the caregiver's own childhood. The way the caregiver models the five A's is dependent on how healthy they are and the relating skills they possess. If love is modeled and installed as defined in Richo's model, the child will know love as close to "unconditional" as possible. Think about unconditional love in contrast with what "you know." Observe what you know in your life and what you know about the lives of those closest to you. This brings a sobering realization: It is highly likely that most "installations of love" fell short.

Your new awareness is in understanding love and how love is installed or modeled. That provides clues about "what happened" in and around your life. When you carry this beyond your self, you begin to understand "what happened" to partners in relationships, to "those kids next door," and to your friends from school. Your awareness reveals some staggering truths about "installations of love" and "how love was modeled" in the world. That truth is that most installations of love were incomplete, that something was missing. The results are exposed in the dysfunctional relationships you have been witness to. This fact brings with it a measure of sadness because those installations and models were not "loving." The elements of love that were incomplete, were missing, or were intentionally not given—these caused deep wounds and pain in each and every instance.

The model of love in families is almost like the gene pool. Family genes are passed from generation to generation. If a caregiver falls short in their capacity to model and instill love, what was missing is what had never been passed to them. The caregiver may have been the last of five or six kids, for example. Did they receive the attention they needed? As a child, were they measured against a bar of expectations that was always being raised? Were expectations set above what they could accomplish? Or—worse yet—beyond their natural ability? Perhaps, they were not shown appreciation for their natural gifts and talents. They learned over and over again that they were "not good enough." What they needed was to be appreciated and valued. What they needed was permission and encouragement to be their true self, instead of being held to the expectation of "you should be a doctor" or "you want to play the piano, don't you?!" These expectations were inappropriate, since they were *not* the child's true nature; the expectations were *placed* on them.

Maybe in a family of "real men," the boy loved drawing, music, and reading. His love for the things he enjoyed was not accepted. Instead, his model of love was being told "you're off base," "you need to grow up," "get out and play ball *like the other boys*." He learned he was "incomplete." He was told something was missing. But nothing was missing except that "he" was being missed. He was not fully *accepted*. "Some" of his self was OK, but the rest was "not OK."

How about "her"? Things weren't going well at school, and things were not well at home or with friends. She was not allowed the room to be sad or hurt. Furthermore, there was no time to pause to figure it all out. Her "state of being" was "not OK." She never experienced "being allowed to be." She learned that she needed to "pick her self up and move on" or to "get over it." All without attending to the feelings and emotions that she was experiencing—her experience of sadness, her sense of being anxious. There was no compassion for her fears of not being accepted and about being judged. In her life, she felt alone and disconnected. The injustice was her being told it was "not OK" to be how she was; she needed to "get over it." That is sad.

These vignettes may summon your memories of examples of "love," which you know and understand now, how these were indeed "incomplete." The truth is that stories like these are almost endless—your family, your cousins, your neighbors, people from church, or people at work. Richo's model gives you a new perspective about love. Your experience and the experience of those you have known throughout your life. These models of love "fell short." The sad fact is very few of us experienced a "complete," full measure of love.

When the model of love that was installed was incomplete, that becomes how you carry love in your heart, soul, and memory. Your model *today* is likely to be incomplete, woefully incomplete in some instances. When you allow your self to stand in the shoes of others, you understand how the messages of "not good enough" or "don't feel like that" felt and sounded. This is the love imprinted on their heart. Knowing this today stirs compassion in your soul. It is accompanied by deep sadness in your heart because what was installed was *not* love.

This brings about the next part of our discussion, the perspective of you to be aware of "you" . . .

You and Your Model of Love

Your story may be completely different from those described in the preceding section. Yours may be one in which the model of love, loving relationships, and installation of love was "nearly complete." For you, almost nothing is "missing." You got everything you needed: attention, acceptance, appreciation, affection, and allowance. This is your blessing—especially as you recall those you know who were not so fortunate.

However, maybe some of those stories resonated with you because you experienced some "shortfalls" from your caregivers. Here is an important item to file away: No matter the circumstances, yours or theirs, there is hope for gaining back what was missed. There is a way to recover what was denied you by the circumstances of your life. Second in line behind the skill of "knowing love" is the way you, by your own resources, give your self what your caregivers failed to provide.

To become a healthy adult, any "shortfall" must be "discovered" before it can be recovered. As you move through understanding all the dimensions of "love," your task is to identify the unique way you want/need to be loved. With this understanding, you will learn the skill of how to recapture, reconcile, and "fill in the blanks" for your self. That is "your work." It is, in fact, all our work—for you, for me, and for others. We all have "our work" finding and filling in the gaps to become healthy adults. There are very few lucky ones. For the rest of us, our work is what lies ahead to recover the missing pieces.

For each of the components—attention, acceptance, appreciation, affection, and allowing—your task is to add in "you." "Your work" is implementing the five A's from your perspective *about your self.* The exercise of practicing the five A's in every relationship of your life is the first step in developing and refining your skill of "choosing to love."

You have probably already figured out that maintaining a constant awareness about love and choosing to love is an ongoing exercise. It requires you to contemplate and recognize each element as it occurs in your life on a moment-by-moment basis. Yes, really, that much awareness.

As you move through your day, the end game is to know, exactly, precisely, how the elements of love live for you in your life. You want to *know* where and how you experience the elements "being present." Your work is to become aware of how these are your experience. In other words, how do you give each of these elements to your "self"? How do you give them to others? Do you notice them in your relationships with others? Do others give you these elements, and how so? Do you find you are getting these in the amount you want or need? Do you give them to others unconditionally . . . or with conditions? Are you able to give only measured amounts to some people in your life?

When you review Richo's five words, they are "actionable" for you in your daily life:

> *Love is a choice . . . a way of being present.*
> *Love is a sustained and active presence with an*
> **unconditional** *giving of these five A's.*

Another perspective for you to think about is to understand that the five A's are like a filter. Your "filter" clearly distinguishes love in your past from love in the present.

In the present, notice the five A's being present; for your self, your current relationships, and personal encounters throughout your day. Filtering the conversations of your life through "love" opens your awareness to the presence of love. You begin to experience the presence of love in your self and in the world around you. Being aware of attention, acceptance, appreciation, affection, and allowing makes it almost effortless for you to give these back to the world. When you experience your self in the context of the five A's, you can easily observe when love is missing. If this concept seems a bit hazy, recognizing when love is missing will make more sense after the discussion about those who choose "not to love."

The distinction of choosing "not to love" is going to be added to your skill set. Why? Because those moments when you notice love is missing is your opportunity to "add" love. That is how you make a difference in your life, because adding love matters. Love matters.

Hopefully, the discussion of the five A's has created a new dimension for you. It has opened a new way to experience love in your life. If you take nothing else from this work except this new perspective and awareness about "love," the five A's, then mission accomplished. Everything else is a bonus!! Before we

"contrast" the choice "to love" with the choice "not to love,"
however, it's important to examine installations and modeling
love in more depth.

Love Installed and Modeled

In the introduction of Richo's 5A model for love, many of the descriptions and examples were focused on the relationship between a mother and a child. Ages zero to eight is when the bulk of original installations and modeling occurs in the child. This span is a critical juncture in the child's life in these matters of love and relationship modeling.

In an ideal world, love is modeled to a child by a healthy adult. The child's parent is "healthy" because that parent has done their "work"—most of it anyway. The parent's work is the same "work" each of us has to do to become healthy; they do their work to understand "what happened" and have resolved their past. They are aware of and have addressed their issues and fears. They have grieved their losses. They "know" their true self. They developed their capacity to give each element of the five A's to their self and others. These are the steps and process when they have done "their work."

As mentioned earlier, a caregiver's own childhood "circumstances" have an enormous impact on how they model love *to* their child. That makes sense. If this new parent, in their own childhood, had circumstances that were ideal, it's safe to assume they receive a reasonably healthy model of love from their parents. Since installations of love are "generational," healthy models are passed down the family tree. Your parents gave you your model, and you will give your model to your children. So, what would some "ideal" circumstances look like for a caregiver?

One would assume the caregiver's parents' jobs were mostly secure. They provided sufficient food, shelter, and clothing needs. Home life was in reasonably good order. The caregiver's parents' intimate relationship was on solid ground. They possessed most, if not all, the relating skills needed to be healthy. The caregiver's parents' lives and the caregiver's home life was not sidetracked by excessive fears, anxiety, insecurities, abandonment, emotional trauma, and other issues. Emotions were expressed in a healthy manner. When "issues" surfaced between the caregiver's parents *or* in the home, the parents resolved any conflicts in a healthy manner. The caregiver witnessed their parents move "closer," and they loved more deeply *after conflicts were resolved*. Their achieving a healthy resolution meant that the caregiver's home life returned to a stable environment after conflicts; joy, peace, and love were again present in the home. In this example of the caregiver's background, this soon-to-be parent received as a child a completely healthy model of love and relationships. As soon as the caregiver welcomes their own newborn, then, the "next generation" of modeling begins.

While the healthy model just described is fresh in your mind, let's spend a few minutes looking at "the other way" installations and modeling happen—specifically, models that are "lacking." The circumstances are not "ideal," and the installation of love fell short or was missing entirely. What would be an example of these circumstances?

Perhaps the caregiver's mother carried issues of abandonment or fear of intimacy. These matters she never processed, grieved, and resolved. Maybe the caregiver suffered sexual abuse as a child, and now as a mother she may have difficulty expressing affection. The attention she gives is either too much or too little. Perhaps she was the child of a narcissistic parent who came downhill at her with words and actions. In her experience, her caregiver "never did enough," or "she never felt connected." Now she is needy and insecure in her relationships. What if providing for basic needs was an issue because of an unstable job situation? Or because of divorce or death, the caregiver's parent had no partner to provide support, comfort, or financial assistance. The caregiver's parents were ill equipped with healthy skills and violated the child's boundaries during child-rearing. They encroached into her personal life. This is an example of how a caregiver's own circumstances impact the model of love and relationships she transfers as a mother to her own children.

Unfortunately, the consequences of what she is missing show up. What she is missing will be the source of the issues that arise in her intimate partnerships; this is almost a guarantee. Keep this generational context in mind. It is a valuable perspective for in the sections that follow.

So, while a caregiver is "giving" a child the five A's, the child is "learning" love. These two experiences—"giving" and "learning"— happen simultaneously. That is how the process of imprinting happens. The mother "giving love" is how this model of love gets "installed" in the baby.

The concept of modeling is the fundamental understanding you need to develop strong relating skills and healthy relationships. It applies to many areas, such as communication, managing emotions, expressing emotions in a healthy manner, resolving conflicts, and more.

Modeling Healthy Love

The application of each of the five elements in Richo's model is self-explanatory. The following is a simple description showing how the five A's are imprinted.

A baby arrives in the world with nothing. All its senses are like sponges absorbing every sensory input which is "inbound": touch, taste, noise—everything. The world the baby knows is what it begins to take in even before it becomes visually aware.

First, you observe how the mother is constantly attuned to the presence of her baby. She continually glances over her shoulder in the kitchen, keeping the carrier with her and checking in to notice the baby: its color, its facial expressions, its breathing, the tracking of its eyes as they take in her face and its surroundings. At feeding time, the mother positions her self directly into the gaze of her child. She does the same when bathing, changing diapers, or preparing for an outing. The mother's **attention** is *rarely off* the newborn.

The mother begins to install **affection** the instant she gives birth. She holds the newborn close. The affection between the mother and child is almost constant during the first several years of the child's life. "Touch" and "closeness" are installed as the most natural part of "healthy love." In fact, "no touching" and "no closeness" would seem impossible. Sadly, there are examples of inappropriate touching. As a result, unhealthy "affection" is installed for some children. In these cases, the concept of healthy affection is misunderstood.

The installation of **appreciation** is gifted in abundance, as well. The mother holds her newborn, making copious observations of the miracle of this new life. She begins to appreciate all the beautiful features and nuances that make "her miracle" unique. As the baby grows, it begins to reveal the behaviors and preferences of its true self. The parents express to the child their appreciation of the child's worth and value. The "learning" aspect is happening simultaneously as the child sees and hears appreciation being given from the parents. The child learns what sets them apart from all others. The child learns that they have a combination of gifts and talents that no else has.

The caregiver's robust model for love **allows** the child's exploration of life and the world by their self. When the child takes a different direction from what the caregiver anticipated or encouraged, the caregiver **accepts** that journey as the child's own unique path. Healthy allowance supports the child's journey to be a self-determined course—with guidance, of course. The caregiver enables the child to experience both joy or pain from *the child's choices*. The caregiver permits learning when setbacks occur. These valuable lessons come from the child's *freedom to explore*. The caregiver may not have chosen this leg of the child's path but accepts that the child has their unique path in life. Supporting the child's direction encourages independence and self-reliance, and both are requirements for becoming a healthy adult.

When love is placed in the context of the mother-child relationship, each element of Richo's 5A model can be discerned; these are the characteristics of "love." In these interactions between the mother and the child, the presence of these five A's exemplifies the presence of love. "Love" defined by the five A's renders love rather easy to see and even easier to understand. You observe the activities taking place between a mother and a child, and they fit neatly into Richo's model. The beauty is in the simplicity, because the language defining love is precise: attention, acceptance, appreciation, affection, and allowance.

Richo's work provides the true "language of love" and reveals how "love in action" can be observed. The A's are given and received (learned) as a complete sensory experience: hearing, seeing, feeling, and the closeness of affection engages the senses of smell and taste.

Love is *known*. The experience of the five A's is the observable, tangible, "real" experience of

- "love,"
- "to love,"
- "to be loved,"
- "to give love," and
- "to receive love" . . .

The mother-child relationship shows how love is transferred; it is not a mystery. As a concept, the "installation of love" makes sense. The actions and activities of the caregiver are the five elements of Richo's model. Caring for a child in a healthy manner exemplify each of the "choices" to love. This process is how love was installed for you as well.

In Closing, Love . . .

We have reached the conclusion of our discussion on how "love" is modeled and installed. You are aware of the distinction of love being a choice. You have the precise language for identifying the elements. Before you were aware, "love" was a murky, hazy, unclear concept. It lacked consistency. It did not have the same meaning from one person to the next or among a group of perfect strangers or even friends. The more people you asked to define love, the broader the definition became.

You heard love was "something everyone knows," but the truth was that no one knew what everyone "knows." It didn't seem like a problem, but it was.

This severe lack of clarity was and remains a problem. It is a big problem . . . especially when you consider the sobering statistics about the number of relationships that do not end "till death do us part." Each one of those failed relationships was supposed to be based on a "foundation of love." How solid was this foundation, since the concept was such an unclear, undefined mystery? The truth is that a "mystery" definition of love does not work for anyone intent on being or becoming a healthy adult. A mystery cannot make a relationship work.

We opened our conversation about love with the task of defining it, with the intention of removing the mystery. This task has been accomplished. You are now aware and possess a concrete, workable, sensible definition of love. You also have a clear, precise understanding of how love "looks" as an actionable, observable part of life. You can easily extend the "work-ability" of Richo's definition into every realm of your world, including your past life, your relationship life, and your parenting life. The benefit is you can "pay it forward" by applying it to any relationship in your future. Love is no longer a messy, uncertain, ethereal concept, which is slathered onto anything you like or for which you have a particular fondness.

What is healthy love?

- Love is defined in the framework of Richo's five A's.
- A healthy installation of love happens when love is modeled in a healthy manner by a healthy adult.
- A healthy model of love requires the five A's to be represented by a healthy adult.

Richo's model reorients your thinking about the concept of "love." Using his framework opens a new world of thought about your self with respect to your partner, your friends, your family members, your coworkers, and other intimate relationships. When positioned against your life's "purpose," the model immediately recasts your self into the world. Most importantly, this perspective of love removes the barriers between your self and any "other" person: the homeless, neighbors, estranged friends, former partners, service providers, and complete strangers.

You have clarity and are aware . . . that when you *choose to love* . . .

- You give your undivided, focused attention.
- You grant acceptance without conditions.
- You appreciate the unique value, gifts, and talents.
- You are open to being affectionate—respectfully, to make a physical connection with touch, inviting close proximity, welcoming to "being in the physical presence of."
- You allow others to experience *their journey*; you grant the allowance for others to "be OK" in all the circumstances they encounter along the way.

One final note about this "complete" definition of love. Notice that it encompasses many of the familiar concepts and phrases adopted through the ages that have been used to describe "love." These are common terms people use to define "love": compassion, empathy, caring, comforting, respect, trust, and so on. This is a short list, but after a quick inspection, you will find that compassion, sympathy, and empathy are covered by attention, acceptance, and allowing.

The same applies to the hurt or pain experienced by others. There is more clarity about what you are doing when you love them by allowing them to experience their feelings: hurt, pain, sadness—whatever. You are gifting allowance by the act of being empathetic. Another description of loving is showing respect. You show respect in the *action* of giving your acceptance and your allowance to the "other" to "be OK where they are."

As you move to the following pages of this book, you expand your perspective on the installation of love. This expanded perspective incorporates your self and the role love plays in intimate relationships. Also, the ensuing discussion covers how life and relationships are affected when love is absent. When the five A's are missing, the void is filled by something. This is typically where relationships become disconnected and signal the beginning of "The End."

Now, let's talk about you . . .

Love: The Purpose of Life

As you look at "love" and your "self," it's important to keep two thoughts in mind. First, your work along with the examples and exercises are all laser-focused on your path to being a healthy adult. Doing your work moves you forward along the path to become healthier. Second, all the concepts, tenets, skills, and awareness are based on the single premise outlined at the beginning:

The purpose for life is Love. You are here *"to love."*

"Love" is the all-encompassing, unequivocal, sole purpose for your human "experience." Humans are hard-wired to experience love. It is in your being, your heart, and your soul. You purposefully look for it, seek it, see it, discover it, give it, receive it. . . . You are here to *love in each moment of your life.*

Life becomes uncomplicated when the simplicity of your existence is winnowed down to a single, four-letter word: Love. This is not original thinking, however. A cursory study of any spiritual literature reveals that "to love" is *the* founding principle of these works. Love is the message of Buddha, Allah, Yahweh, Jesus Christ, Abraham, Muhammad, and so on. "Love" is what you are here to do.

The foregoing summary statement usually generates a lot of debate and discourse. Why? Because it leaves "everything else" out. All the "things you are supposed to do." The "things" that seem to be required for "living." However, such things as work, creating wealth, making money, travel, having kids, contributing to social causes, play, sex, and so on are all diversion and irrelevant distractions if they are not done for the purpose of "love" or acted on with the intention of choosing "to love." While these "things" consume most of your time, the truth is they provide little if any genuine joy or satisfaction.

Maybe that is a new thought, or it is an awareness that comes as a surprise to you at some level. Or, maybe it is a huge wake-up call.

It is an easy proof, which you can administer for your self. The test takes about four seconds. Let's do that now.

What brings you more joy:

Closing a business deal?

or

Buying a new pair of shoes?

or

Jumping up and down with joy on
the sideline of your kid's ball game?

Any questions? I didn't think there would be. Yes! "Love" is *your* key to *your* self-fulfillment.

In "love" is found your joy, peace, contentment, and satisfaction in all the circumstances of your life. The bottom line is that "love"—whether used as a verb, a noun, an adjective, or a four-letter word—defines your journey.

Inside your new context of love, the journey to experience love is about your capacity to give (and receive) attention, acceptance, appreciation, affection, and allowing. On paper it appears that "to love" would be a rather easy choice to make and just as easy to act on. Choosing "to love" is surely not difficult to apply in your everyday life. But, given your experience and what you have learned about "life" probably means you have some doubts. Maybe with a healthy dose of skepticism. No problem.

Part of these exercises are to work through the logic and thought process, so it makes sense. This is done with a purpose: What you are investigating and seeking—as well as the purpose of your journey through this book—is done with the hope of improving your self and your relationships. In this context, "love," "choosing to love," is your single most valuable asset. As your awareness expands and you use your skills by putting the five A's into practice, your experience of love in your self and in the world around you will be profound. It changes your life.

Some of the concepts and thoughts about love may seem contradictory to how you "know life works" or have been told how it works. I get it. Hopefully, these discussions about love and being healthy enable you to comfortably alter your perspective. That is the goal and, of course, the challenge. But the end game remains the same: for you to become a healthier adult and experience more love and joy in your relationships.

Next up is to contrast the healthy love versus your model. How love was modeled and installed for you. The question we begin with is *how* do you, *how well* do you, or *do* you love yourself.

Love *and* Your "Self"

To complete your puzzle requires taking the newly defined context of "love" and adding the most important element: "You."

In this section, each component of the five A's is dissected. We begin with a positive statement, describing each of the elements in Richo's model. The narrative that follows illustrates the simplicity of what giving each element "looks like" in practice.

You "choose to love" by experiencing each of these in an unlimited, healthy, unconditional, and compassionate manner. From the previous discussion, which defined the five A's, you understand how to give them to others. It's instructive to listen to these conversations as you might speak to others. *But* pay very close attention to listen how you would give these to your self as well.

You love by giving your undivided attention . . . :

Of course, I pay attention to someone when I am speaking to them, or when they are speaking to me. It would be disrespectful to be in the presence of someone I cared about, and I ignored them, either on purpose or unconsciously! For the brief time we are together, giving each other our focused attention is not much to ask. . . .

You love by accepting people and circumstances 100 percent:
> Of course! Who am I to judge? I am not perfect. I make mistakes. Generally, I believe people do their best, and, yes, they fall short, just like I do. Sometimes they will bring me joy, but they will also disappoint. So "acceptance" is the *least* I can do—no judgment, no slathering on *my* expectations. I want others to accept me "just the way I am"—that is, warts and all! I want others to know I accept them, just the way they are, too!

You love by appreciating the value of people and things . . . :
> We are all the same—equal. No one is better or worse, more valuable or less valuable, than I am. We all have a purpose, and this is unique to each of us. There is value in our individuality and our uniqueness. What each person has no one else possesses in that unique combination. When I recognize and acknowledge this, it becomes a "no brainer" task to appreciate the value of others, to appreciate their uniqueness, their gifts, and their talents. I know my self, and I know I have unique gifts and talents!! The grant of "appreciation" demands that I acknowledge the value of my self and the value of others. . . .

You love by "an affectionate embrace" of closeness and by welcoming the presence of others in a respectful manner . . . :
> We each have our quirks and idiosyncratic behaviors, but don't we all! I am OK being in your own presence, being in close physical proximity to others. Being close communicates that you are "OK to be around," too. I honor you and my self by sharing "space" together. I express my affection by making it comfortable for others to be close. Closeness is the most basic human-to-human connection. When I choose closeness,

my message is "you are welcome, your presence is welcome, you're enough."

We'll unpack "affection" more later, since there are some individuals whom we would not welcome, because they are "unsafe" to let in or to be close to. . . . Set this aside for a moment. . . .

You love by allowing others the "room" to be OK where they are . . . :

> Life is great at times, life is difficult at times. One day I may be stuck, and then just as quickly I am on top of the world. I know this about people: People are not always in the same place, everyone "goes through stuff." Sometimes "where they are" can be very messy. I know: Parts of my life are really disordered, too. In my past, there were times when things were unsettled, messy, but that is life. To this end, with the same compassion I grant to my self, I allow others the same "room" I give my self. I let them know, "I have stood in your shoes, I understand where you are, and *you are A-OK.*" I express allowance (to love) when I grant others the right to be "in whatever place or season or trial or triumph they are in, at that moment" in the same manner I give this to my self. . . .

When you hear "the choice to love" described in these narratives, hopefully choosing "to love" makes more sense. Loving is not complicated.

Those individual conversations describe what you do when you "love" (that is, when you "choose love"). These conversations translate love into "actions." Borrowing terminology from Daniel Kahneman, the "action" is the System 2 conscious thought that you do when you "choose." The manner in which you give love to others is definitive, concrete, and tangible. You love (your self or others) by the "action" you take "to love": giving attention, acceptance, appreciation, affection, and allowing.

When you give your *self* love, love becomes a powerful, energetic force that is alive in you. It creates energy for life, for your self and for others. Love grows as you give love freely. The freedom comes because love is a choice. No longer are you a "victim of love," nor does love *just happen.* It never overwhelms you. Why?

Because you *choose to love.* No superhuman effort is required. "To love" only requires your awareness that *you choose to love* and *what you are choosing* is **attention, acceptance, appreciation, affection, and allowance.** The more the simplicity of "love" settles in, the more you begin to realize the true power of love. The power lies in the fact that love is 100 percent a choice. "To love" is totally within your power, capacity, and ability.

Look at the title of this section again, "Love *and* Your Self." Consider for a moment that "Love" and "Your Self" are not two distinct parts or separate pieces. It is impossible to separate the two; love is "in" you. Loving is a choice you make; you hold love and choose to give it, or not. This is a critical awareness for you because the source of love resides in you. Your work is to know love for your self.

Consider what happens when the words in the title are arranged to read:

"Love Your Self"

The power of these words is profound. The impact and importance of "Love Your Self" cannot be overstated.

**You can become healthy and experience life
as intended *only if* and *only when*
you choose to "love your self."**

Conversely, you cannot become healthy or experience healthy relationships if you do not "love your self." When you choose to love your self, *then* you can experience giving love to others and receiving love from others. Embrace the wisdom of these words, "Love Your Self."

These words hold the key to a healthy life and healthy relationships. The universal truth of *love and you* can be stated like this:

**To become a healthy adult, to create and maintain
healthy relationships, you must *first*:
"Love Your Self."**

Every word, every concept, every narrative that brings you to this page has been laser-focused on that statement. The entirety of the work over these first hundred pages can be summarized in these three concepts:

"Know love"

"Choose to love"

"Love your self"

"What's next" is "your work" . . .

How to Love Your Self

From the definitions, descriptions, and exercises in the previous section, you have the basics of the healthy model of love. As you take your awareness and observe your daily interactions with others, you begin to distinguish how love shows up in your life. You also begin to observe your self and how the presence of love lives inside and around you. Particularly, you are becoming highly attuned to the presence of attention, acceptance, appreciation, affection, and allowance. Soon, your awareness becomes so "tuned in" it is effortless for you to pick out the five A's in conversations happening around you. Whether you are standing in the checkout line, seeing the interaction between a mother and a child, are at school, eavesdropping on the couple at the table next to yours, or are at work, you will notice the presence (or not) of love.

Additionally, you have begun the task of figuring out how love was modeled for you by your mother, your father, your siblings, your family, and/or your caregivers. The model was imprinted in your brain, in your heart, and in your being. This is also a critical awareness, because this is *your* model, which you have *today*.

Knowing your past is the bridge to how you "love your self." Where do you start to figure out how love was installed in you and how love was modeled for you? Begin by considering your childhood experience in the context of the five A's.

The following narrative illustrates how the five A's may have been installed or how love was modeled. The narrative provides a way to process your past, so you can see and make sense of "what happened." The inquiry that you undertake requires you to look and speak *your* truth. This is an example of a "self"-examination that describes the narrative of someone's childhood:

> My father was self-employed. During my childhood, he was the sole breadwinner for our home. Mostly I recall he worked . . . a lot. I did not see him in the stands at my games. When I would run inside to tell him the score and all my best plays, he did not really have the time to hear me: "Great! Tell me later. . . . I'm working." Saturdays, he was in the office early, too. He didn't spend time helping me with my swing or shooting free throws. When I went off to college, we rarely spoke, and it was usually my mother who kept in touch. Sometimes, too much! I remember times when she would call two or three—maybe four—times a day. She never seemed to let me grow up and "do my own thing."

This is a simple exercise. How do the five A's show up in the narrative? How these show up is what was modeled. It may take some time to figure out yours. As you do your work, remember what you are doing is contrasting your actual experience of love as a child (installation and modeling of the five A's) with Richo's healthy model. You want to know the truth about how love was modeled for you early on. The model of love installed by your mother, father, or caregivers is measured or contrasted with each of the elements of Richo's 5A model.

You may have experienced a very healthy installation. It may not have been so healthy. Your work is to discover how each element was given to you and how each one lives for you today. Maybe yours was "not so healthy"? Good news! Whatever model "they" gave you is what you have: it's OK. Not regarding "right" or "wrong" or if it was or wasn't installed correctly or in a healthy manner. Your work is to discover "what happened." How was love modeled for you, and how do you know the five A's today?

This section on "your work" to "love your self" is relatively long. The end game here is to guide you toward giving your "self" a full, complete, healthy installation of attention, acceptance, appreciation, affection, and allowance in the measure you require (a measure that fills your want and need). When you are finished, the objective is for you to authentically "love your self" in a manner that is more closely aligned with the healthy model you have learned. The process of how you "fill in the gaps," those areas that were "short" or "missing," is covered in the next section.

So, what is the "conversation" you have with your self about how you love your self? In the context of the five A's, listen to the following example of a healthy "love your self" conversation. Pay very close attention to the words. You may want to literally put these words in your voice by speaking them to "your self." In each narrative, take ownership of each "I" or "me" as it lives for you. These narratives describe the installation of each element of the 5A model of love in the context of this inquiry:

"How do you love your self . . . ?"

"How do you pay attention to your 'self' . . . ?"

> I pay attention to my self when I focus on my needs, my personal care, my mental and physical state, my relationships, my struggles, and all other aspects of my self. I pay attention to my self a lot during the day: "Am I hungry?" "Am I thirsty?" "Am

I rested or tired?" "How can I resolve this issue?" "How is this issue affecting my mood?" It makes sense for me to say, "When I pay attention to my self, I am expressing love for my self."

"How do you appreciate and accept your 'self' . . . ?"

I appreciate my uniqueness. I have individual gifts and talents. I am not perfect and have things that I am "working on." I am whole as I am, however. I am complete. I am not all one way or all the other way. I accept my self just the way I am. Yes, I am not perfect. There are some things that I am excellent at, things I cherish and admire about me . . . and I have some things that I am aware of that don't work. But all of it makes up "me," and I accept my self as I am. I accept my life as it has unfolded, and though I made some choices that cost me, or hurt others, I accept that I made those choices. I chose.

I gained wisdom and knowledge about "me" from all my choices. I learned about life and others from my choices. I have worth. I have value. I appreciate my self, by my self. I know the value I have, I know my value my self. My value is known to me. I do not need to meet the expectations of others to have value. I do not need the approval of others to have worth. I appreciate my value, and I accept my self as I am.

"How do you show your 'self' affection . . . ?"

I like my self. I enjoy "being with my self." When I am with my self, I like my time and choose activities that enhance my life. Spending time with my self, provides an opportunity to know my self, my preferences, my thought life. "Me" time gives me a chance to process my world and my life, to reflect on events that have happened and circumstances in my life, to meditate, to exercise, to create, to read, to experience quiet, to relax and slow down.

Being with me lets me better understand what I enjoy most about my self and explore what my interests are, the things that bring me joy and fulfillment. I am never alone when I am "with my self." I notice the more comfortable I am with my self, the richer my life is when I am with others. Over time, I have become very comfortable being with my self. How could someone want to spend time with me, if I were unable to spend time with my "self"? I enjoy my "self" in the world.

"How do you grant your 'self' allowance . . . ?"

I know there are times when I have life figured out and things just work. But there are times when I am challenged by circumstances, and I am in the midst of making sense out of what happened or what I need to do or say to move on. I am "OK" to be struggling with life or soaring and growing. I allow my self to be "wherever I am" and to be "OK" in all the circumstances of my life. I do not need to be somewhere else. I allow my self space and time to experience all the events and emotions that happen in my life. And, I am OK allowing my self to experience my life fully.

This is the conversation of *a healthy adult* who can say, with conviction, "I love my self." "Love your self" is not an idle concept, and it may be worth spending time on those narratives. Read each one several times. These words and their perspective are the voice of a person who has done "their work." This is a person whose life is experiencing love, and their foundation is "love your self." They are solid and grounded—in other words, *healthy*!

From whatever age this person started their work—no matter if it began ten, twenty, forty years ago; no matter how well or how poorly love was modeled for them or how love was installed; no matter what was missing in the beginning—*today* this is a healthy adult. They have done their work and are still working.

There is clarity in what they know about their true self. In what is in their heart (love). In how they operate in the world (love). There is humanity in their voice for being human and for being A-OK imperfectly perfect as they are. They are doing their best to navigate life by choosing "to love."

Just imagine the journey they followed to becoming healthy. They have taken inventory of the choices they made; they have contemplated their caregiver relationships and how "to love" had been installed for them. They wanted to know their true self and their heart by noticing what measure of the five A's they possessed. In whatever measure, those are their foundation for love. Then they reflected, investigating their self and their past to figure out what was missing or hadn't been installed. What elements of love were not installed or not in a healthy manner— this was their work.

They became "aware" of "what happened" in their life: Who were they, really? And how did they get "here"? Then they chose to "do something different," to chart a new course with a clear, definitive destination and purpose for their life: "To love" and "love my self." The choice they made was to become a healthy adult.

Time? Time is irrelevant. Whatever time it takes is the time required. Since their purpose "here" is "love," this renders time irrelevant, as it is and should be.

This individual was committed to doing "their work" of restoration. It began by addressing all that happened. Their work meant processing any pain, any suffering, and the injustices that were held in their heart unresolved. Resolving these had to be addressed for them to love their self. How did they "add" the elements of love—attention, acceptance, appreciation, affection, and allowance—that were missing? This was their work; it is your work, too.

Here is how you begin to put "love" into practice: You start with your self. It is the conversation about "loving your self" you have with your self. Accepting that your caregivers did the best they could under their circumstances. Appreciating their value and worth, independent of others' opinions, claim *your* worth in the universe. Reconstitute love in your life by gifting *to* your self a full measure of healthy, vibrant, unconditional love *for your self!* A healthy model of love *is* the choice to "love your self."

Love Your Self: The End Game

The End Game: Find your voice that speaks the words of love to your self. You must *know* the experience of "I Love My Self!" Speaking "love" to your self is a critical step on your journey to becoming healthy.

The discussion in this section is spoken from "where love resides": your heart. The healthy conversation you have with your self is spoken *from your heart to your "self."* Your heart is your "true" voice. "Your work" is to identify the voice of your heart. Your heart speaks your wants and needs for each of the five A's. This conversation begins the process of refining the model of love you were given. This "original model" with all its deficits will be *replaced with a healthy model of love,* which defines how you love your self today.

Yes! Some elements may have been modeled well. You choose to keep them as yours. You begin to "fill in the gaps" with a new conversation, which jettisons the elements that are not healthy, and you "add" what you did not get, what you want and need, from your heart. Your work is to figure out the ones that were not what you wanted and needed. You can find these in all of those "you should" or "you shouldn't" or "if only you had [fill in the blank]" scoldings. Or whenever you hear a voice that tells you to be some way other than how you *know* your self to be, *today.* How do you "know your self to be"? Whole and complete. Missing nothing. Working on your self. Choosing love. That is who you *are.*

Your end game is to "love your self." This mandates that you begin "filling in the gaps" between what you were given and what you know is the model and installation of love in a healthy manner. How do you replace what is missing, the "gaps"? You marshal your resources, the infinite love that you have always had in your self and you give your self what you need and want.

To investigate this further, look at some examples and narratives that show this work from a more focused perspective, showing how you go about . . .

Filling In the Gaps: Love Your Self

Thinking about these conversations about love, you have a broader understanding of what it means to "love your self." So, how do you find the truth about how love was modeled? What do you need or want to truly love your self? This short exercise focuses on each element with questions that reveal how love was given to you and how your model matches up with the healthy model. What is exactly the correct amount which you need or want is what *you* determine it to be.

The following questions (in the bullet-point outline) are intended to help you contrast the healthy model with what you were modeled. When you notice there is a difference, the "high mark" indicates the love you need to give to your self—that is, this is "what you need."

A slightly different perspective is you taking an inventory of what you hold today as the model of love that you know. Then you are asking, what do you want and need? The answer will be: "I need [*fill in the blank of what is missing or in deficit*] to experience 'I love my self.'"

What do you know about your wants and needs, as described in the context of each of the five A's?

> You may prefer some attention. But you have no desire to always be in the spotlight in groups or at parties. You are comfortable in the middle rows, not the front row, but you do not want to be "invisible" and sit in the back row either. You are perfectly comfortable being with your self and reading a book one evening. You have some friends whose need for attention is extreme. They are resolute about planning to be (needing to be) with friends or out on the town every night and every weekend. That's nice, but it's not you; it's not what you need or want. You are OK with your self in this regard.

You know you are valuable, too. You have confidence in your abilities. You do not need anyone to tell you that you are valuable. However, in a relationship or at work, you like to know you are appreciated by others when you accomplish a challenging task. It's not like hearing it is required for you to feel whole, but it's more like it's "nice to hear." It gives you a warm sense of connection. You appreciate your self and enjoy when others express your value.

This exercise of creating the contrast takes time and contemplation. A great activity while you are commuting or as part of your meditation or quiet time. To assist in your effort, here is a framework from which you can begin to review and construct your healthy model of love:

- The attention you received?
  - Was it a full measure of attention? or
  - Was it too much or too little?
  - What measure of attention do you want or need to know that you are loved?
- The acceptance you received or were given?
  - Were you accepted completely, as your whole self? or
  - Were some parts of you accepted, but other parts of you were not?
  - What is the measure of acceptance that was missing, and what do you want or need to know that you are loved?
- The measure of appreciation you received or were told?
  - Were you fully appreciated as valuable ("you are good enough")? or
  - Were you told your value was "less than" ("you are not good enough")?
  - What parts of you need to be appreciated and valued so you know fully that you are fully appreciated to know that you are loved?
- The affection you received?

- ◆ Was it a full measure of affection? or
- ◆ Was it too much (you felt smothered) or too little (you felt disconnected or maybe abandoned or alone)?
- ◆ What affection do you want or need to know that you are loved?
- The allowance you received?
  - ◆ Were you allowed to be "OK" in any circumstance? or
  - ◆ Were you told you would be allowed to be only certain ways?
  - ◆ Where you were or what you were dealing with, was it not "OK" ("you shouldn't be 'that way'" or "be some other way")?
  - ◆ What allowance do you want or need to know that you are loved?

These questions are ways of thinking about your "self" and love. Hopefully, they generate some new perspectives for you. After taking these questions in and sitting with them a bit, go ahead and bookmark the page. Then wait. Ponder the questions. What will happen is that your real self, your heart, will reveal your answers. How will you know?

It's funny how this part works. Initially, the words you hear will be almost as though they were a tape recording, and as soon as you inquire, it begins to play. It is as though the voice were "right there," almost as though it required no thought. That is not your heart, though. That is what Kahneman named your old System 1. You need an answer, *now*, and it's ready and spoon-feeds you something "comfortable" that it knows. That's not your heart.

The voice of your heart and your true self is different. It's softer. It's not demanding to be heard. It's like a faint echo, but your sense about it will be that you notice the strength and purpose when it speaks. Your response will be without reservations or doubt: "That is truth." Sure, you may have some doubts, especially if you have never heard your heart speak, but it's OK . . . your heart will speak to you as often as you need reassurance. Doubt comes from another place, which we will discuss later.

In the context of Richo's five A's, your heart knows, exactly, who you are, the essence of your being, and what your deepest needs and wishes are. Your heart is distinctly clear, because *love* is all that is there. That is the only language your heart knows. The words your heart speaks are love. To hear this soft voice of love, you must be still and pay close, careful attention. Then . . . it happens. You hear. You know. That is where you find truth, and the truth is how you "fill in the gaps." It takes some time if you are not in the practice of listening to your heart. But, get in the practice . . . it's the reason for your being.

Love: You Can Give . . . What You Have!

Another key perspective about love is understanding the following:

> **You cannot give to anyone something**
> **that you do not have.**

Stated differently:

> **You can give only that which**
> **you have in your possession.**

Here you can connect the dots on the importance of "love your self." If you do not possess something, you cannot give it to someone else. That makes sense, right? A crude example would be about riding a bicycle.

Can you give a child wisdom about riding a bike if you have never ridden a bike? Sort of. What you give them surely won't be something you "know." Riding a bike is something you have never actually experienced. You can describe what others say it may feel like or what it looks like when someone is riding. But that is about someone else riding; certainly, it is not you. You may be an astute observer and communicate what you observe spectacularly well. So much so that the person (in other words, your child) may "get it." But the cold, hard truth is you do not "know" how to ride a bike. You do not have the "experience" of riding a bicycle. You share what you have observed of others, but you do not "know." The analogy is identical for "love" and "love your self."

Giving love is knowing the experience of giving your "self" love. When you "choose" to love your "self," you are likely to face some of the same challenges as you would when choosing to love others. Being human, you know more about you, so loving your "self" mandates acceptance of your whole self. You know your life story and the choices you've made in the past. Some people you hurt when your circumstances were "nearly too much," but you accept that you made those choices even though you recognize the choices were unloving. These are aspects you are "working" on; you are working to resolve them and put them in your past. Doing this, "your work" is with the intention to "love your self."

Some choices created difficulty for you, even though when you made them, you did so with the best of intentions. Maybe the consequences altered your life, significantly in some cases. But you give your self "room" (allowance) and accept your self in light of your choices. You "love your self" and are working to be "a better you."

As you are challenged to "choose" to love your "self," the choice to love others will bring similar challenges. When you know how you accept your self, give your self focused attention, appreciate your value, and can give this love to your self, you know what is required to give this love to others. Part of this reconciliation of your past brings you to the place where you must extend to your self Grace and forgiveness for the choices and actions in your past. This, too, will be called upon when you choose to love someone else.

When you love your self, you are connected to the Infinite Love of the Universe. Here is where you discover the love you need, the measure that is "just right" for you. You become aware of experiencing each element of the five A's daily. When you love your self, you recognize the truth: you are missing *nothing*. As you step out in the world, you are not looking for, or in desperate need to find, an extra portion of love from someone else to be "whole" in your self. You are already whole and complete.

In fact, being whole and complete, you are free to give love to anyone and everyone. You can love in whatever abundance someone else may need. You are free to show others the love that resides in their true self as well. For many, your gifts of attention or acceptance or appreciation or respectful affection may be the first experience of love they have had that day or in many days.

Love is the divine gift, which you can embrace with your "whole self." You can take it in with joy and gratitude. It is how you can love others.

Your Work: Love Your Self

Your work is to hear the narrative in your self, which speaks the healthy "love your self" conversation. You began with the questions outlined in the section "Filling In the Gaps: Love Yourself," which prompted you to identify the five A's as they live for you. This work provides the framework for reinstalling and creating your unique healthy model of self-love. When you do your work, you create your model of healthy love. These are the action steps you must complete to love your self; in the process you "create your narrative," using your own voice. Speaking the words of how you want to *give your self* each element of the five A's.

> **How do you need to give your self attention, acceptance, appreciation, affection, and allowance to experience loving your self?**

Having this conversation identifies the ways you want to be loved, how you want to love your self, *and* where love may have been shortchanged. The hints of what is missing lie in the words of doubt that spring out of nowhere; these are your indicators.

For example, maybe you hear your self say, "You always want attention!" Is that your truth? If it is, that's OK—being outgoing and the center of attention is *you*. You love your self by accepting this aspect of your self. The inquiry is to discover the ways you do *not* grant your self the full measure of any or all the five A's. As you do your work, remember this: These clues and hints about what is missing are very important in your relationships.

What is the purpose here? When you reconcile your past, you identify what is missing and what you need. Today, you determine the appropriate portions of love you need and grant the full measure of love to your self, with your resources (the love you have always had in your self). This is the process whereby you are healing your wounded heart. You are giving your self love, which is doing the work that "they" should have done but did not. You give your self love in ways that were missed. Though you can heal your wounded heart, sadly, the scars do not go away. These injuries tend to resurface in your intimate relationships. This is another "good to know" item for you. Remember this:

**Those scars from old wounds are the first place to look
when relationship issues arise
or when the love between partners is "interrupted."**

Your work to love your self requires being objective. You are viewing the healthy model versus your experience, and you are determining what you *want*—how you want to experience each of the five A's. To bring this into focus, the following questions are a guide. These are how you find your answers:

Regarding attention:

How do you like to be shown attention?

How were you taught attention as a child?

How do you pay attention to your self today?

How do you *not* pay attention to your self?

Do you need to pay more or less attention to you?

Regarding acceptance:

How did "they" show you acceptance? Full measure?

50 percent?

How do you know you are accepted?

How do you want to be shown acceptance?

What ways were not accepted?

Regarding appreciation:

Were you shown your value (appreciation) as a child?

How were you not appreciated?

What are the unique gifts and talent you know about your self?

How do you want to be appreciated today?

How do you want to be shown appreciation?

Regarding affection:

How were shown affection as a child?

Were you shown more than you wanted?

Were you shown less than you needed?

How do you want to experience affection today from others?

How do you want to show your affection to others?

Regarding allowance/allowing:

Were you allowed to be OK in your struggles?

Were you not allowed, were told to "be some other way"?

How will you speak when you give your self allowance to be "in the circumstances" of your life?

How do you know, from others, that you're "OK" to be in those circumstances?

What words speak this allowance to you?

Yes, all of this is probably sounding like a broken record at this point. Yeah, maybe so. But you were warned! If it were not so important, the chapter would have been much more condensed. But it is very important.

A few words to close the conversation. The central theme of this exercise is to differentiate Richo's healthy love and to understand "what happened" in your early childhood. There are more detailed discussions and exercises in Chapter 5 on how you address, process, and resolve[8] the shortfalls. There are parts that need to be added to your skills before we tackle relationships.

> The final note here is an example of an unhealthy installation of love. It's mine. My thought here is to show you what an inquiry into your past might look and sound like. It's very helpful to keep those five A's in the forefront as you are reading. This will help to show you where "the gaps" are, and these are where "the work" is. Yes, that is correct: my work.

Unhealthy Installation Example: Me

The truth is that my installation wasn't all that healthy or well installed. I would say, "about average"; some of it was, but some was not. For me, to "love my self" in a healthy adult manner didn't happen until I reached nearly fifty-five years of age. "My work" is what provided the freedom to share my story. After all, like you, I know me, and my story better than I will ever know anyone else's story.

The model of love I carried into my adult life was somewhere between 6 and 7 on the "10" scale. My family story includes three brothers. My mother was from rural Louisiana and endured an unhealthy dose of abandonment, emotional suffering, and abuse in her childhood. Most of her story is a bit cloudy, because, in our home, you didn't "talk about those things." What I do know is that at an early age, she was abandoned by her parents, raised by her grandmother, and was a Catholic. As a mother, she was a truly fabulous homemaker, great cook, and a very talented botanical artist. My father was the oldest of five children. He grew up on a farm, had an "old school work ethic," and paid his way through college by waiting tables. He earned two degrees in four years,

---

8   The APR procedure (address, process, and resolve) is explained in the subsection "Resolving Conflicts between Heart and Ego with APR" within the main section "Conflict Resolution" in Chapter 5.

one of which was in petroleum engineering. His professional career spanned thirty-five years, during which time he rose to the top echelon of a big oil company as a successful senior executive. That puts some light on the previous vignette about "my street," which you read in the Introduction. I loved both my parents. From my journey to discover my self, what I know is that my parents did the best they could, especially considering the circumstances of their own lives.

Applying Richo's model to the model of love that I was given and shown in childhood was quite revealing to say the least. On the big question, Did "I" love "Me"? Hmmmm . . . not really. Was my love for my self "healthy" in the context of this book? No. First, I never really thought about "love your self." That was something you were *not supposed to think about*, much less something you *wanted or needed.* You can guess that with my Catholic upbringing, when I did think about "me," that nauseous twinge of guilt was always close by. Ready to remind "me" of how selfish I was to think about me. It was worse to think about me *before* thinking about someone else (that is, "everyone else").

My appreciation for my value was from low to the middle on the scale. The voice in my head mostly spoke in terms of "not good enough" and "you *should* be better or faster or stronger or smarter or more." How would I express appreciation to my self growing up and into my mid-fifties? Exactly like it was modeled to me by me. I spoke to my self exactly as I heard me in my world: "Wow, Spence, you are very good at that . . . *but* . . . if only . . . you 'should have.' . . ." Frankly, looking back . . . that sucks!!! Since we lived in an upper-middle-class neighborhood, "comparisons" were always present, too. This meant the language of "measuring" and "judging" were in most conversations: "who is better than who," "who is less than who," "you want to keep up with 'so and so', don't you?" These and other similar comparisons were the normal utterances of everyday conversations.

Once I learned what "appreciation" is for my self, you know what? I was *good enough.* There was nothing about me that needed to be added, changed, taken away, or anything. I began to see my self in the light of "good enough." Today I appreciate my gifts: a pretty good blues guitar player, a healthy dedicated parent, an innovator in business, good with money and finances, and more. These were a few of the insights I gained when I looked at "what happened" and how love had been installed for me in contrast with a healthy installation.

Richo's insight about "unconditional" and "love" was a real eye opener. Learning what it meant to love my self—the actual *choices that I could make*—this was a Big Deal. Understanding "how" I could love me—by the gifts of attention, acceptance, appreciation, affection, and allowance—was freedom!

What was even bigger? This will make more sense after the next chapter, but I want to add it in here for my story. When I could distinctly "hear" the language of ego. It occurred in so many conversations I was in and that were spoken around me. I had no clue. Judgment, critique, comparisons (more on this in the next chapter) was everywhere. It was inescapable. Today it takes *zero* effort for me to distinguish the presence of "love" and "ego." My filter for them is always on. The words *fear, anger, assessment, judgment, critique, control, commands, expectation, entitlement,* and *comparison* stand out. It was as though I had been deaf all my life and suddenly I could hear. Not just hear but hear with laser focus. I could distinguish all the notes in the scale perfectly.

Being aware makes it all so much easier to understand. For a long time, I asked my self what had made it so difficult to figure out? Why had I missed what is now so clear? The answer was simple. The language of ego used around my house was never direct. Instead, it was couched in subtle hints sprinkled in like fine dust. Often it was hidden neatly behind passive-aggressive suggestions. The most direct words were, of course, the mother of all Catholic Guilt phraseology: my favorite "add-ons"—the "shoulda, coulda, woulda's." Insidious words. If you can relate to my story, make a special note to listen for these gems.

Looking at "me" back then, then looking at "me" today, I'm clear: I love my self. I experience a lot of joy in my life. I have gotten much better, better equipped would be more accurate in navigating the storms in my life. I seem to enjoy much more peace and calm.

I share this about me and my work because I *do* know my story better than anyone else's. My challenge was the same as yours: "bridge the gaps" between the ideal installation of love, the model of healthy love, and "what happened" in my story. Figuring out what I did have, what I was missing, or what fell short. It took quite a bit of time and a lot of "work"! And it was all worth it.

I would be remiss if I did not say one more thing about my story: I love my mother and father. They taught me many things about my self. From them, I gained valuable wisdom and knowledge about my self, the world, and life. Both have passed, but there was not much that was left unspoken. There is peace in having that as my memory.

Life Reconciled to Love

You have arrived at an excellent way station when both sides of your life are revealed by the light of your awareness. The truth is that some choices benefited your life, and some choices were costly. All choices provided wisdom and insight about your true self. Your awareness and your work reconcile your life to the present, which can be stated as follows:

> **"I love my self,**
> **I am whole and complete.**
> **I have worth and value.**
> **I love being with my self.**
> **I can see my self clearly.**
> **I am not always at my best, and it's OK to be 'here' . . .**
> **I love my self."**

This is a beautiful model: you love your self. After all, whom do you really know in this life? Whom can you really know? Answer: Your self. Reconciliation with your past often arrives with a healthy measure of humility and compassion, too.

The question is no longer "Do I love my self?" but, rather, a declaration with conviction and certainty. This is mine:

Yes, this is *how* I love my self:

> I love *all* of my self. I love all that "works" about me, *and* I see the things that do not "work." I accept these, because they all are part of me, as my whole self. I can integrate all aspects of my self as a whole, complete adult. I appreciate my life, my talents, my skills, and I have "value." I am valuable, I have worth, I am *good enough*.
>
> I have learned to be OK when I am "with my self." I have the conviction that I am never "alone" but rather there are times I choose to be with my self. I like my self, and I know that if I can be with my self, someone else can be with me, too. I am comfortable anywhere.
>
> My awareness encompasses my whole self. Loving my self is essential to my being a healthy adult. My awareness knows about what does not work. These things are with me and are what I am working on to become healthier.
>
> I am always a "work in progress," but today, even as I "work" on me, I love my self with attention, acceptance, appreciation, affection, and allowing my self to be "OK" whatever season I am in.

As you hear in this voice, healthy love is not "self-help" pablum. These words speak about the tangible components of a healthy adult. They are available to all of us. "Love your self" is available to everyone who commits to doing their work. How? Evaluate their self, their life, their past, their choices, all through the lens of love.

Love is the language of the "choice" you make to "love your self." You know the language: Pay attention to your self; accept your self just the way you are; appreciate your value, worth, gifts, and talents, which are unique in the world; enjoy your physical self when you are "with your self" and when you are with "others" out in the world; and finally, allow your self the room to be "OK" both when you are at your best and when you are not at your best.

With the chapter on Love complete, it is time to wade into the "other side" of love. . . .

Chapter 4.

Ego

Since you know you have the power to choose love, now you must face "the other side of love." This means addressing some interesting, quite perplexing questions.

- Why would someone "choose" not to love?
- What is in the constitution of a person who would choose not to love?
- Are there individuals who are unlovable?
- What happens in the moments when you choose not to love your self?
- What about those times when you chose "not to love" others?
- Are there skills and practices that can move you away from ego back to heart?

In the previous chapter, you learned about the most common path relationships follow. Most romantic relationships start with an "I have butterflies" event and that couples who "commit" to marriage agree to choose love "till death do us part." Observing these beginnings, is it safe to conclude that all these people wanted "love"? Since these relationships started with choosing "to love" but (most) ended somewhere along the way, we know "something happened." What happened?

The simplest, most reasonable, logical conclusion is that they were choosing "something else," something other than "to love". In other words, they chose love in the beginning, but as time passed, they began to choose "something else." Had they continued to choose to love each other, then there would be no ending before death, right?

How do people go from "choosing love" to "choosing something else"? It must be that "choosing not to love" is as distinct and clear as "choosing to love."

Choosing "Not to Love" Is Choosing Ego

The next part of your work is to understand ego as the opposite of love. The conversations will ultimately address when heart faces ego. The following pronouncement can be placed on your mantle of awareness right next to "Your purpose in life is to love." The pronouncement is also a truth about life. To establish the context for the dynamic between heart and ego begins with this pronouncement:

> **In every conversation with each person you meet in your life,**
> **you are choosing to engage from**
> ***either***
> **your heart (choosing to love)**
> ***or***
> **your ego (choosing *not* to love).**
> **There is no "in between."**

This may take a while to understand. When you to have this awareness and understanding, *then* you can become a healthy adult. In other words, in the context of your work, this awareness about heart versus ego is a requirement. It is mandatory. Furthermore, understanding this dynamic about *all* your conversations is a crucial relationship dynamic.

It may be that this awareness comes easy for you. Good! If not, it may help for you to contemplate "The End" of a romantic love relationship.

Consider what you experienced in the months, maybe years, leading up to "The End":

- Perhaps you experienced judgment, comparison, criticism, anger, fears . . .
    - What was "operating here" . . . Heart? or ego?
- Maybe in the face of sadness from an ending, you experienced appreciation and focused attention *even though* the relationship ended . . .
    - Did your experience come out of . . . Heart? or ego?
- How about the guy climbing up your bumper on the Interstate? Is he accepting your choice to go the speed limit? Or is he entitled to break the law and is expecting you to yield to his demands?
    - What are you witnessing . . . Heart? or ego?
- Were you ever "that guy" in someone else's rearview mirror?
    - What were you engaging with . . . Heart? or ego?

Distinguishing heart and ego is a black-or-white concept. There is no "gray." There is no "middle ground." You choose either to love or not to love; you choose either heart or ego.

In an intimate relationship, the presence of heart in conflict with the continued presence of ego makes for a toxic mix. The two, heart (love) and ego (not love), cannot coexist. The conflict of a heart with an ego damages relationships and damages the people in them.

We begin to explore "the other side of love." . . .

FACED by Ego

We can move right to the meat here (or Brussels sprouts if you are not into meat . . . you choose!). To further ground your understanding of ego, there is another tool you can add to your skill set. It is an acronym describing the words and actions of ego: When you distinguish ego, you identify its elements using the acronym *FACED*.

When ego surfaces and confronts the heart, it is easily distinguished from the heart (love). Ego speaks "at you." Ego comes at you "downhill." Heart, in contrast, speaks "with you" or "to you." Ego speaks at you with sharp, off-key notes in any conversation. The phrases land on you and create anxious feelings in your stomach. Your chest tightens as though it were being compressed. The sharp angle of the words of ego makes you want to "back away" and distance your self. These are especially true in your relationship when your heart is FACED by an ego.

The following are the words and actions of the FACED acronym. These are the most common responses by an ego, and the most common ways ego shows up in relationships, conversations, and life are the following:

- **F**ear of abandonment, of intimacy, of connection, of trust, of being vulnerable, of becoming invisible, of not being good enough, of being worthless, of being unlovable and more . . .
- **A**rrogance, anxiety, anger, attachment, argumentativeness, avoidance, addictions (to drugs, to work, to pornography, to sex, or to money)
- **C**ondescending, controlling, commanding, critiquing, criticizing, comparing, and correcting
- **E**ntitlement and expectations (theirs about you, your life, and your choices)
- **D**emanding, defending, distancing, distracting, disappointing, disrespect, displeasing, dismissing, diminishing, demeaning, degrading, discounting, diverting, and disgust.

Understanding ego happens naturally when you know "love." It may help to think about each element of the five A's and then to notice that ego has one or several direct contrasts to each of the five A's. "Affection" is opposed by distancing; "attention" is opposed by avoidance and distracted. You will find your awareness becomes acutely attuned to hear ego surface in any conversation, because ego speaks clearly. As you read the language it uses, you realize you have heard it before, probably many times. Think about your life experiences. Was there a situation when you knew you entered the conversation from the perspective of "love" (granting one or all the five A's), but the reply from the "other" was "not love"? What happened? Your love spoken from your heart was "FACED by an ego"!

What came at you was one or more instances of being FACED by ego, as just listed. Hopefully, this is a fabulous revelation for you. You wondered "what happened." You were loving and choosing love, only to find your love confronted by nothing like what you anticipated. Your love was stopped abruptly. The words and actions left you hurt or angry. It was almost as though the intention was to drown your love. That is how ego works. That is what ego does. Now you understand the pronouncement that opened this chapter, distinguishing between love (heart) and ego; there is no middle ground: Heart and ego are mutually exclusive. Love and "not love" cannot exist in the same space, and only one will be left standing.

How do you know that love provides a solid foundation to distinguish ego when it is present? Consider again the elements of love in contrast with how ego shows up:

- Love's attention is undivided.
  - There are no distractions when there is undivided attention.
- Acceptance is 100 percent, not 88 percent or 97 percent.
  - Granting acceptance has no conditions.
- Love grants appreciation in an unbounded measure.
  - There is no comparison or judgment when there is appreciation.
- Love's affection desires to make a connection and remove distance.
  - There is "less distance" when leaning in with affection.
- Love's allowance is with Grace.
  - Love has no need or desire to control.

The simple examples that follow show the contrast between living from the heart (choosing to love) and living from ego (choosing "not to love"). They show the clear, definitive difference between the two. The mutual exclusivity of "to love" and "not to love" is elementary logic. The examples are virtually unlimited. Referring to any element of ego's language reveals the void where love has been pushed aside.

As you become more aware, you witness heart FACED by ego all around you—at work, in the checkout line, when couples argue in public. You hear ego when parents speak to children and spouses to each other. The situations you are most aware of is in the conversations with those with whom you have the most intimate, close, loving relationship: your parents, your children, your partner, and your extended family. It doesn't seem as though that is the way life is supposed to work, but it happens—way too often.

In your life experience, you have many examples in which you can clearly distinguish heart versus ego. The following situations, considered from the perspective of a "global" third-party observer, juxtapose heart and ego. Let these responses, arranged in the order of the five A's, frame your understanding more completely:

- Love is giving your attention to the "other" and receiving attention from them.
  - Ego responds with anger, impatience, distancing, and dismissing, and it is distracted.
- The gift of loving acceptance with an embrace says to the other: "You're OK, just the way you are. You are enough."
  - Ego responds with critiques, comparisons, and judging, declaring that changes are needed.
  - "You are not OK, just the way you are; you are not enough!"
  - "In order to be OK, you need to be different."
- You acknowledge the other's gifts and talents, expressing appreciation for their uniqueness; you make it known to them the following: "You are valuable."
  - Ego responds with condescension, criticizes effort and output, and diminishes worth and value.

- ◆ Ego degrades and slathers on expectations with projections.
- ◆ "You should be [some other way] to have value, to be good enough, to have worth."
- You enjoy being close, being in the company of the other, sharing space and often with a loving embrace.
  - ◆ Ego responds with distance; being close is uncomfortable.
  - ◆ Ego is distracted, anxiously wanting to be "somewhere else," with "someone else."
  - ◆ Ego often adds a touch of arrogance, such as "I am too good to be here" or "These are not good enough for me."
- You lovingly "allow" the humanity of the other's circumstances, express compassion, and understanding about their experience, grant them Grace and forgiveness if and when needed. "It's OK to be where you are in this season of your life."
  - ◆ Ego responds with little or no compassion or understanding.
  - ◆ Circumstances are judged "less than."
  - ◆ Ego has no allowance to be out of sorts.
  - ◆ "You apparently do not have your life together."
  - ◆ "You 'should' be some other place in your life."
  - ◆ "You are *not* OK, to be in this season of your life."

These short responses provide the two sides of the battle between heart and ego. The heart reaches out, embraces, and draws near. The ego responds with a counterstrike to destroy the choice to love. Have these two perspectives played out in your past? How have you experienced the interplay of heart and ego in your relationships?

Your work entails reflection and contemplation. Your work requires you to look back at your personal relationships. Almost all relationships have provided the experience of the heart being FACED by ego. Were there times you were "living from the heart" and the response to your choice to love was FACED by ego? What was your experience when the words and actions of ego came inbound, "at you"?

Often these instances can be identified as those times when you experienced pain and hurt. The sad part is these experiences often happened with those people in your life who were "not supposed" to treat you that way. Yet the truth is you know today what they chose was "not to love" you.

Most of the preceding conversations have been focused on "them." But there are always two sides of any conversation. Your work is to understand when *you* have chosen "the opposite of love" as well. The times when "they" choose to love, but you didn't. You chose to live from your ego; you chose "not to love."

Those times when you offered a harsh critique instead of granting acceptance. They needed your focused, undivided attention. Instead, you chose a dismissive tone or chose distractions or tacked on an insult of arrogance or condescension or entitlement. Maybe you were preoccupied and decided they weren't worth your time (arrogance).

"Being aware" requires that you look "outbound," and look at "what happened *to me*." Having full awareness requires you take a "360-degree view." Looking at your story, the impact that you had on others when you chose not to love, is insightful. These are the places you also learn from. These are places you grow and become more aware and healthier. Your work requires that you be an "impartial observer" about you and your relationships. By the way, none of us are immune from choosing "not to love." And, it's OK. We are all human, a minor stat that we can never forget!!

In the big picture, the hope is by your raising your awareness in the matter of loving your self more fully and maintaining your commitment to live from the heart, you can stay grounded in even the most stressful situations. After all, it is possible for you to hit your "pause button" before any situation craters into the abyss of "not love." That is the "end game" of this part of your work. Ego does the most damage in relationships that are closest to your heart. With your awareness, you will catch your self before you respond to others from your ego. Hopefully, over time, with clear distinctions about both sides, your choice to love will become easier and easier.

Why? Your purpose in life is "to love." Choosing "not to love" is the same as wanting to lose what is most precious in this life. When love is lost, life is lost, too.

So now the relationship dynamics have been framed in a very simple context: to love versus not to love. In the next chapter, the conversation of your heart heads into the deep waters of "creating and maintaining healthy relationships." As previously discussed, there are several key components to be added to your skills and awareness. Here, you begin the practice of applying your healthy skills into the complexity of relationships. Hopefully, at the end of the chapter the conversation about the heart-versus-ego dynamic resonates with you, and which path you choose is a choice: your choice.

To Love or Not to Love

The landscape of your life is shown under a new light of awareness about love and about loving your self. Choosing love brings "you" and "what happened" to a more comfortable place. Hopefully, your experience of your self in the present moment is with a sense of peace, which replaces any anxiety and uncertainty. You have accepted and embraced Grace for all the circumstances that allow you to "be here." With the perspective you have now, when love is present, you "know" it. You hear it. You see it. Knowing love entails the active presence of attention, acceptance, appreciation, affection, and allowing. You are fully present to love being given and received. The source of love is within you.

Choosing to Love

In case you missed it, being aware of the choice to love or not to love removes any cover or excuses, such as "I didn't know" or "I wasn't aware."

Yes, you are aware, and you do know. Being authentic makes you very uncomfortable when you choose "not to love." That is how your heart works; your heart is never fooled. Could you depart from this awareness and "go backward"? How is that possible? That would be like "unlearning" how to ride a bicycle. Not happening.

Regardless of the model you started with, from this point forward, you have a new, different, and a complete model of love. This new, different model is virtually unlimited. It is boundless. This whole measure of love you can give "inbound" to your self or give "outbound" in abundance.

This brings us to an ideal place to extend our discussion of love by posing the following question and answer:

> **Question:**
> **Where, within you, does the choice to love originate?**
> *Answer:* **Your heart.**

That makes sense, right? It certainly fits with what you know from your past and what you have always been told. After all, when you look around you, what is the universal symbol of love? Heart. What do the great spiritual works tell you where the source of your being, the place inside you where you find "love"? Your Heart. A quick survey of the Bible in Galatians 5:22[11] reveals that the gifts that you are given ("the fruit of the Spirit") are placed in your heart. These gifts are "***love***, joy, peace, patience, kindness, goodness, faithfulness, gentleness, and self-control." First on the list? "Love." Where does "love" reside? Heart.

Brené Brown writes about the concept of living from the heart, which she describes as "Whole*heart*ed living,"[12] about which there are many tenets for sharing all your self, sharing your whole story, with your whole heart. She goes on to say,

> **"Connection is why we're here;**
> **it is what gives purpose and meaning to our lives."[13]**

The purpose here is not to debate the metaphysical, ethereal mysteries and mysterious powers of the heart. The purpose here is to proclaim the heart as the source of and the "resting place" of love in you. In the context of love, "the heart" is a metaphor for how you operate in life and relationships. This is important, because your purpose, the focus of your work, is to become healthier and to create and maintain healthy relationships.

"Being healthy" means "I am choosing to live from a healthy place" (it is a "healthy place," because to the best of your ability, you are choosing to love).

Choosing to love, and choosing to "live from a healthy place," you can add a new awareness. Your choice to love means that you are choosing to live from your heart.

This section is titled "To Love or Not To Love," and we have just identified the first portion of the question. That portion is stated like this:

When you choose to love, *you are living from your heart.*

Perhaps you experienced an "Aahhhhh" moment here, which may have also happened as you became aware that love is a choice. There is a sense of freedom knowing you have the power to choose the greatest of all gifts. You find the same freedom in your ability to choose "living from your heart." "Choosing love," "loving," and "living from the heart" are seamlessly connected. The truth is you possessed these well before you began your journey to being healthy. You were born with a sense of your "self," which always knew that love was placed inside you. The "universal truth" that you are born with is:

Your Heart = Love.

Your "love" and "heart" are "known to you." This is the reason the heart and love connection resonates so deeply in you, in all of us. You *are aware in your bones, in the deepest part of your soul:*

You love from your heart.

"Love" and "living from the heart" are part of your divine nature. The infinite source of love is beyond you, and you know it. Yet, love is your, my, our "Holy Grail"; it is what we spend our life seeking. There is a very uneasy peace in knowing you choose to live from your heart. As it should be.

With the first choice known, what remains unclear is the second. When you (or I or we) choose "not to love" . . .

Choosing Not to Love

This second portion of the question is interesting. You may experience that "*not* to love" resonates deeply within you, too. Maybe being aware of that is a rather sobering thought. In a balanced universe, "not to love" means that this is the choice that leads *away from* love! How could this awareness not bring just a slight bit of uneasiness? "Not to love" immediately begins to move your thoughts "away from the light." In fact, "not to love" can be a place far removed from the light. "Not love" brings you close to the extremes of darkness—where the "sinister" parts, or the "morbid" side, of humanity exists. In its darkest place, no humanity lives.

Looking back, you can find morbid darkness in Columbine, 9/11, Aurora, Sandy Hook, and Charleston. Without much effort, you see the clear evidence of how the choice "not to love" leads to the darkness parts of a human. In these places, the light is undetectable. There is no love. These memories serve to exemplify the contrasts. The choice not to love is diametrically opposed to the choice to love. Is there a middle ground?

No. As evidenced by a nearly unlimited number of acts, the contrast of love and not love is known; they are mutually exclusive.

One of the most famous recitations about love was cited in Chapter 3. It is a biblical reference, and it is one of the most important readings about love. You know it well, because it is often the citation exchanged when two people have made a choice to love and seal their love with a commitment to each other in marriage. This biblical reference is used to describe "love" in its purest form (that is, "unconditional love").

It is a description of the perfect practice of love. The citation is 1 Corinthians 13: 4-7,[14] which reads (from a slightly different translation than that in Chapter 3):

> Love is patient and kind. Love is not jealous or boastful or proud or rude. It does not demand its own way. It is not irritable, and it keeps no record of being wronged. It does not rejoice about injustice but rejoices whenever the truth wins out. Love never gives up, never loses faith, is always hopeful, and endures through every circumstance.

This citation provides the adjectives and descriptions of what love is. We know what love is, so this reference makes getting to "the other side of love" an easy trek. Applying very simple linguistic math is all that is needed to describe what "not to love" looks like.

More appropriately, the words and actions when the choice is *not to love* are as follows:

- Impatient
- Unkind
- Jealous
- Conceited
- Arrogant
- Rude
- Demanding
- Easily irritated
- Keeping score

- Delighted in the suffering of others
- Enjoying injustice
- Avoiding the truth
- Faithless
- Hopeless
- Giving up easily

These are the opposite of love. The truth is these are a nasty collection of personality traits. The saddest part is some people have them all. But mostly, I hope, the people in your life are those who are "lovable." They, or you, may show these traits or choose these actions sometimes. . . . We all do. But it doesn't change the choice being made, does it? No. These adjectives and descriptions manifest the choice not to love.

Part of becoming healthier is understanding when you choose to love and "they" choose not to love. You can recall situations in your life, past and present, when you have chosen one or the other. In fact, you probably have way more experience than you ever want to admit when you chose to be loving but did not have love returned. It happens. Sadly, for some, this describes the story of nearly all their close family and "romantic love" relationships.

Look hard enough and long enough, and you find that every relationship provides examples when one person is loving, and the other person is not loving. No surprise here. Humans aren't loving and loyal all the time.[15] With a clear understanding of the choice to love and the components that define this choice, what we need is a clear understanding about "what is happening" when the decision is made not to love.

On the surface, choosing not to love seems especially odd, given the simplicity and beautiful construct of Richo's 5A model. Choosing to love those with whom you have the closest, most intimate relationships would seem to be the "always" choice. Love would continuously flow— paying attention to the "other," giving them complete acceptance, acknowledging your appreciation, expressing affection, and allowing them the "experience" of their life whatever their journey. Love would be exchanged in abundance. Seamlessly. Ever-present. Effortlessly. The most arduous task would seem to be incorporating all the superlatives that would be needed to describe these bliss-filled and joy-filled most loving relationships.

However, more often than not, describing your most loving relationships with the storybook descriptions about real love are the exception, not the rule. Why? Here is number five of David Richo's list of five things in life[16] that you cannot change:

"People are not loving and loyal all the time."

Our experience of life confirms, "No, they certainly are not!" In fact, you know this your self. Even when completely aware and focused on being the best you can be . . . *you* are not loving and loyal all the time. When these unloving behaviors and choices show up, they usually arrive in small doses. It's perfectly understandable, too. Maybe you are in a hurry; you have a commitment to be somewhere at a particular time. You glance at the time and realize you are going to be late. You may be impatient with someone. They don't hold the elevator for you. You are irritated at the driver who missed the light. In any moment, your choosing not to love just "happens." It doesn't make it OK, however. It doesn't magically excuse your choice, enabling you to brush it off—"Oh well, life happens"—endowing you with a "free pass" to respond without thinking. No. You own what you did, you *chose* not to love.

You are, in fact, *human* all the time. However, the observation "people are not loving and loyal all the time" has multiple dimensions, and a couple of these are worth your time here. Critical questions such as: What is it about people when they choose not to love? What are people choosing instead of love? What is happening with them? Since the conversation is focused on you, the questions can be framed with you as the subject: What are *you* choosing when you choose not to love?

Also, since the case has been made that love originates from your heart, then "not love" must come from within your self as well Why would you "choose" not to love? What is in your nature that you would choose not to love? Our attempt to figure out the other side of love is a very crucial aspect of our conversation, because if there were only one side of love, the love side of love, you would have spent your money on another latte . . . not this book!

When you look back to the beginning of relationships, the answers begin to emerge. You know that most relationships started with the "butterfly effect." Couples "committed" to marriage and vowed to choose to love "till death do us part." In each of these relationships, in the beginning, each couple chose love (*even if they didn't really know "what" they were choosing*). They begin by choosing love, but something happened. Eventually, many chose to end their relationship. The logical conclusion is: Somewhere along the way, they must have begun choosing "something else." So, how do people go from "love" to "something else"? For your journey to health, you likely know the answer already. They are clearly choosing their ego over their heart.

All these endings are 100 percent the result of choosing "the other side of love." Recall FACED as the words and actions of ego, and see if you notice something about the list of ego words and actions that described the opposite of "perfect love" in that list:

- Impatient
- Unkind
- Jealous
- Conceited
- Arrogant
- Rude
- Demanding
- Easily irritated
- Keeping score
- Delighted in the suffering of others

- Enjoying injustice
- Avoiding the truth
- Faithless
- Hopeless
- Giving up easily

These attributes do not come from the heart, and they do not seem like they are anything associated with love or loving. They are, in fact, the manifestations of ego in action; they describe what ego says and does.

In the same way that "heart" is to love, ego is not actually a "physical" part of your body, yet it does reside "in you" in the same manner that love resides in your "heart." Yes, you have a physical heart inside you, but you know *that* heart is a working organ, a muscle. For our purpose here, in the context of love, however, the "heart" we are referring to *is the* "heart" as a symbol. For the time being, just accept that ego is also "in you." It may help to say that ego comes from your "head."

Doing this gives two visual reference points for love and not love. Love is "heart," and ego is "head." Love versus not love is the same as "heart" versus "head." We like things easy around here, so "heart versus head" should be easy to remember.

Now, the second choice is coming into focus. What is needed is a statement like the one that declared that to choose love meant that you were "living from the heart." For the second choice, then, the description is the exact opposite of the first. Choosing not to love can be stated like this:

> **When you choose *not to love*,
> you are *not living from your heart*.**

However, you need to go one step further. To be consistent and create some much-needed accuracy and clarity, you need to add "ego," because it is the opposite of heart. Then the choice "not to love" reads:

When you choose not to love,
you are living from your ego.

Now you have the full context for your two choices of life. The two choices are about a single choice, and that can be stated in the following nine words. In each moment, conversation, and engagement with life and others, you choose to:

Either
live from your heart
or
live from your head.

I hope you can see all this clearly now. And that it all makes sense. Your heart or your ego are the two places from which you choose "to live":

When you choose love,
you are living from your heart.
When you choose not to love,
you are living from your ego.

Yes. You, your self, your life, your relationships with your children, your boss, your mother-in-law, your aunt, your nasty mean neighbor, your brother, your rabbi, your wife or lover, your ex-wife, and anyone and everyone you will ever engage with either face to face, in an email or text message, Snapchat, group chat, or WebEx . . .

This line in the sand, unfortunately, leaves *no* wiggle room or gray area. The choice for how you "live" is either one or the other:

You choose either to love or not to love.

Your choice is either one or the other:

> ***Either***
> **you live from your heart (love)**
> *or*
> **you live from your ego (not love).**

The simplicity of this contrast is infinitely beautiful. It is clean. It is concise. It leaves no gray area. It is universally applicable. It is truth. Yours. Mine. Everyone's. This contrast supports the original premise about your purpose in life, in its entirety:

> **Your purpose in life is to love.**

And so, it is. When you choose to love, to live from your heart, you are love. It follows, then, if you are *not* living from your heart, you are living from your ego and *you are choosing not to love.*

In Closing . . . Love and Ego

The objective of Chapter 2, Chapter 3, and this chapter has been to provide a solid foundation and understanding about the most important concepts of being healthy in your self: love, the five A's, ego, FACED, and choosing either to love or not to love. Your knowing these concepts are a prerequisite for your figuring out "what happened" in your life *and* for you to choose to do "something different" (that is, "your work"). The goal of these three chapters has been for you to understand that whatever you do next, this time your choices reflect who you are as your true self. Know that healthy choices made from a place of understanding and awareness produce the results you want to experience in your self and in your relationships.

While everyone is unique, each of us begins life with the same purpose: to love. "What happens," how you get off track from love, can cause you to slowly drift from your purpose as the years pass. The focus of your life can become clouded by the circumstances of your life. But if you are so blessed, you reach the place in your life where whatever it is you are doing becomes "too much." "Too much" may look different to each of us, but that day of realization comes nonetheless. You realize that are not your self, that you are not living from the heart, and that you are sideways in the ditch, no longer focused on your purpose for being here. When "that place" and "that time" arrives, the decision you make is to consciously reflect and declare, "I must do something."

That "something" begins with your making sense out of "what happened." With your gathering up what is left and starting to reassemble "who am I." Today, you know this is your work: the task of figuring out what *you* must do to change, refine, learn, and adopt as a practice and to do life, your life, differently going forward.

As the sands of time continue to diminish in the upper portion of the hourglass of life, you tend to become more purposeful in your quest. The challenge of your work that must be done is more firmly embraced. You seek the "answers" in a more resolute, expeditious, manner; in fact, they cannot arrive fast enough. These early chapters about love and the other aspects related to becoming healthy all speak to that end.

In this matter of love, what is the conclusion of the most famous, most published works in recorded human history regarding relationships, interpersonal communication, self-awareness, personality, relating skills, and the realms of spirituality? What do you find when you study the greatest priests, thinkers, and writers—those with such names as Buddha, A. W. Tozer, Tara Brach, Brené Brown, C. S. Lewis, the Apostles, Ellen Langer, Erich Fromm, Helen Fisher, Susan Forward, Pia Mellody, Charles Whitfield, John Piper, Rick Warren, John Gottman, Larry Crabb, Robert Firestone, and Jesus Christ?

In the totality, the works of these men and women can be synthesized into a single four-letter word: *Love.*

Their collective thoughts can be summarized in two statements:

Your purpose is to love, your self and others.
Your ability and capacity to love is unlimited.

It is appropriate to assemble the ground you have covered up to this point. The following short list summarizes these early chapters:

- You learned that your purpose in life is to love.
- You explored what love is and what love is not.
- Love is a choice; each of the five A's is "actionable."
- Love resides in and originates from the heart.
- Ego is defined in its words and its actions; it is the antithesis of heart.
- You live from the heart *or* from the ego—in every moment.
- Life is a series of encounters, of one-on-one relationships.
- All relationships are engaged from:
  - Either the heart, "to love,"
  - Or from the ego, "*not* to love."
- You choose how you engage every moment of your life with every person who crosses your path.

The foregoing considerations are the foundation for you being healthy in your self, and they need to be marked in red highlighter. They are universal "constants." They don't change. There is no shortcut, or way around them. To reach your goals for your self and your relationships, your work is to grab onto them with a vengeance. They are no longer "missing," because you are now aware. Your task now is to develop and refine them, so they become *your* constants.

Becoming more aware of the presence of love and not love in your life is a constant practice. Your objective is to know when you are operating "from your heart" and to recognize when you hear a response that is "being FACED by ego." You need to pay close attention to your self as well. When do you respond to love from your ego? These occasions need to be instantaneously recognizable and to become seamlessly integrated in your being—just like your breathing or your beating heart.

Your "listening" needs to become attuned to the one true love language: attention, acceptance, appreciation, affection, and allowance. At the same time, your early warning systems need to be "always on" so you can discern the presence of the words, phrases, vocal tones, and downhill conversations that come from "the other side of love"; these are fear, condescension, critiques, control, expectations, entitlement, anger, arrogance, and judgment—in other words, ego. And, of course, you need to know whether these are coming from others or from your self.

You are now way down the road toward living from your true self. You are now aware. Your awareness began when you stopped in your tracks and chose to live life differently. With these early chapters now complete, hopefully your awareness or knowledge has been greatly expanded, or at least the content has stimulated new thoughts and ideas for you to contemplate.

Now the discussion is expanded, and these concepts are put into practice. The next chapter is titled "Relationships." The context here begins from the inside out. The relationship with your self is the starting point, and we will explore how your past relationships are viewed from your new perspective being aware and having new skills to work with as you engage with others.

Chapter 5.

Relationships

At this point in our conversation, the essential components of being healthy have been presented. The following is a quick recap:

- **Love**: You are now aware that love is a choice. Love is not a feeling (an emotion), though feelings (emotions) are part of the mix. The important discussion of how love (or not love) triggers emotions and the interplay of love and emotions is still on the back burner.

- **The model of healthy love**: The choice to love entails the presence of the David Richo's five A's. No list is needed here, since the five A's have been overexposed to this point; they are (hopefully) engraved on your soul. Yes, if you need a cheat sheet, or if a tattoo would help, do it!

- **Love your self**: The first and most important love you must have to be, or to become, a healthy adult is: Love Your Self. I prefer to say, "love your self" rather than "self-love." "Love your self" is a call to action. It's a call "to love," and since love is a choice, this calling to love your self is actionable and clear. The narrative in the preceding chapters describes a comprehensive outline on how to love your self.

- **The voice of your heart**: The voice speaking love is the voice of your heart. Your heart literally speaks the words of love to your self. You are in a constant conversation to confirm and validate your experience of giving your self attention, acceptance, appreciation, affection, and allowance. The narratives in Chapter 3 are important. Read them as many times as necessary. The embedding exercise requires that you read the descriptions and make the words speak your voice from your heart. Yes, the words your heart speaks is about you—your unique model of love, which is yours.

- **Hearing the voice of your heart:** This practice is invaluable. Your need to marshal the voice of your heart develops your skill to find that voice. "Developing" means "clearly discerning the voice of your heart." Your work is to raise your awareness in the discernment of your voice of love to your self. Your heart, your "true self," is the source of love within you. The voice of your heart speaks the love in you. Why must you develop a keen listening ability for the voice of your heart? Because that voice may have been drowned out for much or all of your lifetime. The more you hear the voice of your heart in your journey through life, the more grounded "love your self" becomes in you. When you cannot hear the voice of your heart, love is missing; what you hear instead of heart is the "other voice"—the voice of ego, either your own ego or the ego of someone else.

- **Ego:** Ego speaks and acts using the acronym FACED. Anytime you hear the FACED words and descriptions coming at you, coming downhill on you, at you either from inside your self or from someone else, you are experiencing a heart being FACED by an ego. The skill and ability to distinguish heart (love) versus ego (not love) cannot be emphasized strongly enough. Know it. Learn it. Get it instilled in your self in the same way that blood flows through you.

- **Love versus ego:** Choosing to "love your self" identifies the elements of love and the dispatch of ego. There are choices of words and actions that have been playing in you *not* to love your self. Recall that in each moment of your life, in every encounter with another and in your contemplations about the choices you face, you are choosing either to "live from your heart" (love) or to "live from your ego" (not love). It is one or the other.

(In this chapter, on relationships, other essentials will be covered, including boundaries, preferences, potential prospects, your unique way to be loved, and more . . .)

Piecing Together the Relationship Puzzle

The elements just discussed are your foundation for "what's next." The compilation of these skills and your awareness about their interplay have prepared you for the ensuing conversation about relationships. The attempt here is to neatly weave these into the first layer of relationship matters, including boundaries, your unique love style, preferences, conflict resolution, love from a distance, and healthy chemistry. Other aspects of relationships are covered as well: attachment styles, fears, bonding, sexual intimacy, independence, and interdependence. The discussion examines the broken model for relationships that is propagated in our society and introduces instead a model that works.

The last item in the foregoing introduction summary is "Love versus ego." A good amount of time was spent on this in Chapter 4. These diametrically opposing forces impose their will in nearly every facet of a healthy relationship. As our relationship conversation begins, the contrasting natures of love and ego need to be put in the proper context regarding your relationships:

> **These two enemies, love versus ego, stand toe to toe**
> **at the base of every mountain**
> **that started out as a mole hill.**

**The conflict turns peaceful sunsets into raging storms.
When conflict is left unresolved,
the casualty is always love lost.
These ongoing battles are the red-flag warning
marking the beginning of
"The End."**

The purpose of posting this warning at the beginning of this chapter's discussion is to establish, in concrete terms and without equivocation, the sole reason for relationships ending "before death do us part." And don't get hung up on the quote there, trying to divert the conversation. Though a relationship starts, with the intentionality of experiencing love, "The End" can be traced back to all the battles between heart (love) and ego. And the loser? Love. If this may not make sense to you right now, I get it. But the foundation for you has been set.

These components of a relationship are "the essentials." Maintaining the integrity of each is how you stay "healthy" as you navigate the challenges of creating a healthy relationship with an "other" . . . and all their "unique" stuff.

So, we begin . . .

Boundaries: Keeping Your Love Safe

You have a just learned about creating a distinction for the "two sides" of people, your self, and conversations—the side of heart and the side of ego. There is living from the heart (love), and there is living from ego. The choice is always one *or* the other. When you are choosing heart—"to love" and to live from your heart—you are making an important statement. This choice you are making is "I love my self" and "I am complete and whole." In other words, you as an individual are physically, intellectually, socially, and sexually separate and distinct for anyone and everyone.

Regardless of whom your relationship is with, you are one, "by your self," whether the relationship includes you and your lover, you and your partner, you and your child, you and your parent, you and your boss, you and your sibling, or you and anyone else. Why does this matter?

Because, when you love your self, you have established that you occupy a certain place in the universe. You have granted your self the right to "choose" love, whom you love, whom you relate to, and how you relate to them. More importantly, you have established *if, when, and how* others relate to you. You have declared your self to be a whole and independent human being. You have set up the distinction about your self and your heart. You are unique and separate from others.

In essence, you have established your place. You have drawn a line in the sand—not a physical line but a conceptual line. This "line" is the clear division between you and any "other." This line is called "your boundaries."

Boundaries are essential for being healthy. Setting your boundaries is an essential part of your work. Your boundaries establish "I am over here." This is where "all of my self exists in the universe." More importantly, these boundaries are your indication to others that inside this invisible line in the universe, this firm, well-established boundary line, others may not encroach without your permission or invitation.

When you look back at "what happened," you realize that you may have had unhealthy or "loose" boundaries, that you did not establish them clearly in your communication, or that you were not resolute in your effort to maintain healthy boundaries. "What happened," you discover, is you "sold out" your boundaries. A short exercise works through some examples of "selling out" and may help bring clarity to healthy boundaries and the real cost of "selling out."

At this point another component of your healthy self can be introduced: "preferences." Your preferences and your boundaries go hand in hand. Reflect for a moment what you know about preferences. Preferences are those certain ways of relating or things you want to be present in your relationship; these are the unique ways you experience love. The list of preferences is lengthy; it includes holding hands, giving or receiving flowers, maintaining friendships, independence, enjoying date night, travel, sexual play, managing money, eating and exercise habits, parenting styles, and so on. Preferences are what you want to experience in your relationship. Preferences are necessary for you to understand the concept of boundaries. This is the area where people allow others to encroach "over the line" of their boundaries.

For example, let's say one of your preferences is that you are particularly uncomfortable with excessive public displays of affection (PDA). Specifically, unappealing is getting a "deep throat" French kiss in a public place. During your dating–mating–sexing–relating together, you have communicated your preferences. You have made clear to your partner (or partner prospect) your preference about PDA, and your preference about PDA is "your boundary."

In theory, once you have communicated your preference, you establish this as a boundary; this is "how I want to be treated." When you are with someone, you know they respect you (that is, "value" you) if they acknowledge how you want to be treated and *then* treat you in this manner. They are "aligned" with you. They "respect your boundary"—in this case, your preference for tasteful PDA. In your relationship, they respect your desire to have tasteful displays of affection when in public.

Another example of preferences is sexual intimacy. Early on, as you have begun to share about your "true self," you share your preference to be in an exclusive dating relationship for at least four months before being sexually intimate. You indicated that your sexual intimacy preference is high on your list of nonnegotiable preferences. Let's assume for this example that you have shared it early on, more than one time. However, just three weeks in, you are being pressured with the expectation for sexual intimacy in the first month. This person's expectation (also known as "ego") is "crossing your boundary."

It is important to note what is happening here. Any *demand* or *expectation* coming *downhill at you* early in a romantic adventure is a red flag. Your preferences *and* your boundaries are being *discounted* and *dismissed.* Your partner is not *accepting* you, your choice, your preferences, and they are not *appreciating* and valuing you!! Do you recognize the "language" here? What are these actions? These words? Do you see where "heart" is missing here? What is clearly present? Answer: ego.

Boundaries establish your self, separate from any other. Your boundaries are how you have chosen to "love your self" *in a relationship.* A healthy partner acknowledges and reciprocates by loving you in the unique way you want to experience love: *accepting, appreciating,* and *allowing* you to be OK with whatever circumstance you are in. In the second example, you communicated your preference, you set your boundary, and then "what happened"? Keep this in mind going forward.

In all your relationships, you set your boundaries, and others set their boundaries. No one has the right to change or challenge any boundaries you have established. Likewise, by living from your heart you accept and appreciate others' boundaries. You love others by giving love in the unique manner they want to experience it. Accepting and appreciating them means accepting and appreciating their boundaries.

Several points need to be highlighted regarding boundaries.

First, your work is to be vigilant and aware of where *your* boundaries are in relation to the world and others. Boundaries establish the unique way you want to experience being loved. If you do not declare your boundaries, no one will know where you are in relation to them. How would they know where the "line" is that defines "you" separate from "them"? You set your boundaries to establish what is acceptable for you and what is unacceptable. People with codependency issues typically have no boundaries. Or the boundaries they do have change with the flow of emotions of guilt and shame carried forward from their past. Respecting your boundaries means there is a line between you and others, a line that *only you can invite* them to cross. The critical awareness note here is that you set your boundaries. Then, you need to *respect* your own boundaries . . . or no one else will, literally.

Second, your work is to communicate effectively. Specifically, when you are in the dating–mating–sexing–relating phase with a prospective partner. They will not *know* your boundaries unless you speak up clearly and tell them. If you do not communicate with them, you are "at risk" for having your boundaries violated. If you do not communicate effectively, that is your issue, and the sad part is, you, not your partner, will suffer the consequences.

Third, your work is to communicate each and every time someone violates any of your boundaries. No exceptions. This is the way you established how you want to be loved and in the unique manner that works for you. In a healthy relationship, when a boundary is violated, there is a conflict; an encroachment has occurred by one of the partner's ego, which is in conflict with the heart of the other. Conflicts occur when heart is FACED by ego. That is the nature of boundary issues. The full details of the healthy method to resolve conflict is shared in the next chapter. For now, know that when a boundary has been established (that is, "communicated") and then is crossed or violated, the issue must be addressed. You address the issue by speaking up; only then can the issue be resolved.

Finally, and this is a biggie:

Boundary violations happen in all relationships.

Sometimes you don't know other people's boundaries. They didn't communicate them, and sometimes you don't communicate yours well, either. Perhaps you rely on "ESP" or make incorrect assumptions about others' boundaries. When you don't communicate, others may make incorrect assumptions about your boundaries. These things happen. Resolving boundary issues can be handled by simple, direct, honest communication. In a romantic love relationship, boundaries and preferences are what you want to know about each other. You and your partner are always learning about each other as the relationship becomes more connected and more intimate. Knowing more, sooner, is always a benefit, because determining if you are compatible or incompatible is *very* good to know.

Make a note here. Your work is to clearly state your preferences and boundaries several times. *Any* ongoing boundary encroachment is an early warning sign that something is off about this prospective partner. Any and every violation is a red flag . . . for *you*. Take notice and respond.

Red flags being raised and waved repeatedly are the audible shrill of grinding metal of the train as it begins to leave the track. Your relationship is heading for life support. Your choice to not speak about this is "selling out." Whom are you selling out? Your true self.

Every time a client discusses with me their train-wreck relationship, they look back and bring up those "red flag" incidents that signaled the train wreck in progress. Their relationship was in trouble, the warning signs were there, they *heard* it . . . but they chose to do nothing.

> *FACT:*
> **Saying nothing,**
> **resolving nothing,**
> **is *choosing* to sell out.**

Important? Certainly. The following is the crisply worded cross-examination of the witness to *their* train-wreck ending:

Q: What happened?

A: My boundaries were violated, repeatedly. I chose not to love my self by not speaking up for my own value and worth, regardless of the circumstance. What I did was I "sold out."

Q: Looking back, what do you know about what happened?

A: What I did was chose their ego over my heart, my love—
my love for my self, my love for them, and my love between
us in our relationship.

"That's all, your honor." Case closed!

That brutally honest assessment is intended to emphasize:

Boundaries are critically important.

They are woven deeply into the tapestry of "you" to become healthy. They are essential. You choose how you set them for your self and your relationships. It is your responsibility to communicate and protect them. Boundary violations are *your* warning sign that a relationship is heading off the tracks. When a relationship's autopsy has been performed, boundary issues—"I sold out . . . on my self"—are second only to "I did not love my self" as the cause for the relationship to die before "till death do us part."

With the critical nature of preferences and boundaries now in your awareness, another element of healthy relating is moved into focus . . .

Emotions

Emotions are one of the more difficult subjects to be addressed in the conversation about being healthy. The volume of research and writings are well beyond anyone's capacity to consume in one lifetime. There a number of modern theories that have evolved the "science" of emotions, including that by William James and Carl Lange, by Robert Plutchik, by Walter Cannon and Philip Bard, and by others. This section contextualizes emotions as they apply to your work.

In this matter, Robert Plutchik's work is quite interesting. He makes the case for eight categories of emotions, which are arranged in a circle.[17] Contrasting emotions are positioned on the opposite sides of the circle. Complementary emotions are located side by side. Rather than add few thousand words trying to describe the circle, I provide an explanation, including an easy-to-comprehend graphic representation, in Appendix D.

I should note that some variations of Plutchik's model include "love" as an emotion, but I do not share this opinion. The inclusion of love is "*allowed*" and "*accepted*" as an alternative perspective, but I do not share or adopt it. In any event, Plutchik is worth mentioning since his research presents a well-thought-out examination of emotions.

Some readers may find this section lacks depth or may conclude it is far too "simplistic." Such observations fall into the category of "missing the point." Emotions are, or can be, confusing, but my goal here is not to create a Pulitzer-level work. Rather, this effort is an attempt to remove some of the confusion and create clarity—not regarding the entire science of emotions but specifically for your purpose in the context of the goal: becoming healthier.

With regard to emotions, your work is to make the experience and expression of emotions a healthy relating skill for you. What follows aligns with that purpose.

Your Emotional Life

For the most part, most women do not need encouragement regarding experiencing their emotional life or to expressing their emotions. However, for the rest of us, healthy expression of emotions may be not quite so well developed. Regardless of your current state, the skill needed for managing your emotional life is required for healthy relating. How to manage and express emotions is the focus of this section. You can refine this skill with practice throughout the day.

Emotions (feelings) are conditions that are experienced when they occur. But the experience dissipates as you move forward in time. You leave the actual circumstances that were present when you experienced the emotion (feeling) in your past. What you remember are the feelings, or the physical sensations, associated with that past event (the "triggering" circumstances). The experience, however, becomes a Post-it note in your memory of something in your past life. The circumstances of a situation or event that caused you to experience certain feelings (emotions) will never happen again in the same manner at any point in your life.

The interesting aspect of emotions is how you remember them, the feelings and/or the physical sensations that remain with you, forever. The emotions are indelibly etched in your memory; they are stashed away in your subconscious mind. They are also stored in your physical being, your body. Both the circumstances triggering the emotion and the physical experience of your response (the physical sensations, your emotion) are, in fact, held indefinitely in your memory.

The feelings (emotions) you experience in the present (today or tomorrow) come upon you and then dissipate.[9] They are also added to your memory. The memory of *all* your emotional experiences is infinite. It is with you always. This is a critical fact that must be considered as part of your work regarding relationships and being healthy. Why?

Emotions are complicated. They are difficult to deconstruct and understand. Often, we do not know the source: Where do they originate? Where are they coming from? What is "in the present" and what is being recalled from memory about the "present"? Why are we experiencing them now?

Most often, emotions arrive out of nowhere. They are upon you in an instant, then . . . *poooof* . . . just as quickly they seem to vanish. Some do not vanish, of course. The experience of certain very intense emotions may linger for days or weeks or months . . . or years. These will "be present" until the necessary action is taken to address, process, and resolve them so they *become* your past. It is often the case that putting

---

9   There is a distinction between feelings and emotions, though they are highly interconnected. Emotions are essentially lower-level physical responses that trigger biochemical reactions in your body that alter your physical state. Feelings, on the other hand, are mental associations influenced by memories, beliefs, and personal experiences. Nonetheless, in the context of what this book is about—loving your self—the distinction is not particularly germane, and I have been using the two terms more or less interchangeably. For more on this topic, see https://www.thebestbrainpossible.com/whats-the-difference-between-feelings-and-emotions/.

the emotions into your past is a large part of your work. Therefore, this particular skill is one you must have in your tool kit.

On the one hand, emotions are a lot like any other bodily sensations you experience—for instance, your experience of an upset stomach. What you "feel" grips you in the moment and requires your focused attention to address and process what is happening:

"Why is my stomach hurting?"

"Am I coming down with something?"

"Is something really wrong with me?"

The feeling triggers a logical, cognitive response to inquire "what is happening" in your body. Your System 2 thinking brain goes into overdrive to figure out the source and the solution. It tells you the most expeditious action to take to handle the situation. You choose the best option presented by System 2 and execute that solution. This processing, which happens in your brain, may sound something like the following examples:

". . . Was it something I ate?

Yes, it was that spicy food I ate at lunch today!"

". . . Is it a virus?

Oh, I feel a bit of a fever;

then I must be getting a bug."

". . . I've never had my appendix removed,

If this pain lasts more than a day or two,

then I'll see my doctor."

In each sequence, you "address, process, and resolve" (more on this procedure later[10]) the physical ailment when your body is out of sorts. Rarely do you simply ignore it. At least, not past what you can tolerate as your pain threshold. You can handle your emotional life in much the same manner.

---

10 The APR procedure (address, process, and resolve) is explained in the subsection "Resolving Conflicts between Heart and Ego with APR" within the main section "Conflict Resolution" later in this chapter.

An example of an emotion you experience might be when you suddenly sense a tightening in your chest and lung area, or when you notice an anxious agitation beginning to grip your midsection or in and around your chest. Your heart feels compressed and constricted. When your physical state is irregular, and it is not associated with a physical ailment, these sensations signal that you are *highly likely* experiencing something associated with some aspect of your emotional life.

What might this look like? Say infidelity sideswipes your life. This causes a deep "emotional" wound. Much like a physical wound: For example, if you break your arm, you experience all the pain associated with your injured limb. The pain you experience usually lasts for a while even as the broken bone is healing. The wound of infidelity, an emotional wound, causes a bodily experience as well. Your experience could be literally that a sharp object is stabbing or poking into your heart. Sometimes this deep emotional wound "feels like" the pain of a crushing weight on your chest or your heart. Other times your heart feels as though it were being compressed. It needs more space to function normally. The pain you feel is real. No question. Your heart hurts. You are physically hurting. What you feel is actual, real, authentic hurting. You feel the physical sensation of pain. The emotion is real; it is not something you imagine.

Like a physical wound, an emotional wound can heal, but the healing takes time. Usually, sometime after the event, you begin to process what you are feeling in order to understand the cause. In the same manner as you would when you are physically out of sorts, when you are experiencing an emotion, you attempt to understand the source, then process and resolve what it is you are feeling.

You may or may not figure out the source of the "heart ache" (or the "queasy stomach"). The important aspect to note first is the healthy adult response. You always allow your self to experience the *full measure* of what you are feeling. Allowing is how you love your self. Experiencing your emotions is how you love your self. You need to experience the emotion for as long as it is present "in" you.

My purpose here is to define the healthy response: that you experience your emotions. Experiencing them, fully, is how you begin to address, process, and resolve any changes in your emotional life.

(*This discussion substantiates the premise that emotions are completely distinct from the concept of love, which is something you choose.*)

A play-by-play description of experiencing your emotions in their entirety would go something like this:

- Your emotions are triggered
  - by some externality (an event or action by another person) or
  - by your conscious or unconscious thoughts (a memory or mental projection of fear or worry).

Then

- Your physical being responds
  - by a stimulation of some area of your body (chest constriction, eye twitch, and so on) or
  - in an internal organ (heart, stomach, neck, and so on).

And

- You experience whatever emotion has been triggered

when

- You actively notice and observe the changes in your physical state

And

- You allow your self to experience the physical response of your "emotional life."

The first step of handling emotional experiences in a healthy way is to *experience* what you are feeling! This may sound a bit silly, but the fact is many of us go through life denying the physical experience of our emotions. Once you allow your self to experience the emotion, *then* it is possible to take the next step: "processing your emotions." The general sequence of how "processing" occurs is described as follows:

- First, it is critical that you consciously focus your attention on the area in your body where sensations are being triggered.

Then

- Consciously contemplate the source without regard to your ability to resolve "why" or "what is causing me to feel this way." You need to be focused on being aware of the sensations with the purposeful intention to experience fully whatever physical sensation the emotion triggered in your physical being . . . for as long as the sensation is present.

Then

- The next step is take an inventory of the sensations from the context of the four basic emotions—SAFE: sadness, anger, fear, or exuberance. These four emotions (described in detail in the next section) will be the source of your emotional experience. There is nothing to "fix" or "change" when you identify the source. Processing emotions is not about fixing anything. You are perfect just the way you are, experiencing the emotions that occur. Knowing you are "sad" or "angry," or that you are experiencing a "fear," is the objective. When the emotion is from a "fear," for example, bringing this to your awareness is your objective: "I am feeling abandoned" or "I am feeling insecure." With anger or sadness, the identification is "about what" or "who": "I am sad about the loss" or "I am angry about being treated in such a callous manner." These are covered in depth shortly, but locating what is underneath the feeling is your goal.

- The final step is to take inventory of your self in the context of the healthy model of love (the five A's), seeing what is required of you to love your self by granting your self the full measure of each of the five A's. The steps of addressing "what happened" will be discussed in detail later. An abbreviated example of the final step is presented here so you are familiar with this skill. It can be illustrated using the "I am sad about the loss" of a long-term relationship. You pay *attention* to your self, your physical pain, and your needs for expressing sadness (tears, crying, and so on) in the moment. You *accept* your circumstances as they are. Yes, you could have done some things differently, but you did the best you could with the tools and skills you had. Things do not always end as want them to. You *appreciate* the good times, the memories, the valuable lessons, the experiences, and the wisdom you gained from this relationship, even though it ended. You are comfortable being *with your self (affection)*. Yes, the physical connection with a partner will be missed, but you are whole and complete and "love your self" with someone or without them. Finally, you *allow* your self the opportunity to be OK in this circumstance, to feel your sadness, to experience your loss, for whatever time it takes. You are OK in this season of your life.

You now have this skill of experiencing your emotions (the working model), and processing your emotions is another instance of putting into practice a skill you have learned.

The amount of work and time required to reconstitute your self to the state where you "love your self" (fully) is commensurate with the emotional impact of whatever event happened. Being angry at a minor injustice you experience from a random person in a store is one you handle rather expeditiously. By addressing, processing, and resolving— and then granting forgiveness and moving on—you love your self.

However, when the event that rocks your world is from someone with whom you have a close intimate love relationship—for example, maybe a trust has been breached or there has been a devastating loss— the emotional experience is greater, has a bigger impact, and lasts longer. These events require more work to address, process, and resolve.[11] Your healthy response is to "execute" the steps to address, process, and resolve

---

11 The APR procedure (address, process, and resolve) is explained in the subsection "Resolving Conflicts between Heart and Ego with APR" within the main section "Conflict Resolution" later in this chapter.

the conflict. The focus of this section is to make you aware of the need to fully experience your emotions. The skill to resolve "what happened" is covered in more depth in the sections that follow.

In summary, your emotional life is a fairly random experience. You don't know when "an event" is going occur. Why something has been triggered is not always known "in the moment." Nor do you know how long the emotional experience will last. You have little or no control over your emotions. Sometimes you figure things out quickly, and sometimes you don't. But the key to a healthy emotional life is allowing your self to experience each emotion, fully. Remember, love is not an emotion, because your "free will" and cognitive ability to choose gives you total control over your capacity and ability to love. Emotions? Not so much. What are the types or categories of emotions you experience and must process? Let's start with a simple methodology to add to your collection.

SAFE Emotions

The "wheel of emotions" in Appendix D is a great resource. I encourage you to spend some time with it. It is a great tool to use as a reference when events happen and you are having difficulty figuring out what exactly you are feeling. For this conversation, the "range of emotions" can be simplified further by reducing the relevant categories. The objective is to create a more manageable set of categories with an easy way to add them to your skill set. A "thank you" goes out to Mr. Richo. His strategy places emotions in one of four distinct headings.[18]

The acronym is *SAFE*, which represents

Sadness

Anger

Fear

Exuberance

In these categories are found the most common emotions humans experience in relationships. Of course, the actual "experience" itself is not uniform. All humans experience each of these in varying degrees of intensity. In other words, your emotional experience is unique to you.

The next paragraph will address the first of the SAFE emotions, sadness. The second emotion, anger, requires an extended discussion, and two sections of their own, "Righteous Anger" and "Other Anger," will explore this emotion in depth, and the discussion will delve considerably deeper into sadness, the first emotion. The third emotion, fear, will be covered in its own section, "Fears: Handle with Care!" The fourth emotion, exuberance (also known as exhilaration or ecstasy), will receive a few words in a brief section, "Exuberance."

In terms of duration, **sadness** is the emotion that is most often experienced for the longest time. This one you likely know well. Especially, if you have invested your heart and soul in a relationship and there was an "ending." Experiencing the sadness of a loss may stay with you for a long time; all losses bring sadness. It is inevitable. Every loss must be grieved, and there is no measure of time which "should be enough." Your unique manner of grieving a loss takes whatever work you must do and last whatever time *you* require.12

The other end of the "duration spectrum" is the second SAFE emotion, **anger**. Anger tends to be the emotion that comes on the quickest with the highest intensity. Yet, the feelings associated with anger dissipate the quickest. Consider, for example, a short burst of road rage, when "that idiot" didn't signal and cut you off. This burst lasts only for a brief period because your "attention" moves away after a few moments. In this case, the event happens and you react by hitting your steering wheel (rather than signaling their IQ with your middle finger). But you quickly *must* refocus as you realize you are traveling "three wide" NASCAR style on a strip of concrete eighty feet wide in a four-thousand-pound car with five hundred of your closest friends you've never met in their bigger cars, going faster or slower than you. When your quick glance notices some

---

12 Sadness and its relation to anger is covered in more detail in the section "Experiencing and Expressing Emotions," later in this chapter.

are texting or putting on eyeliner, at seventy-five miles per hour, your anger dissipates fairly quickly, in most cases.

But anger is a bit more complex than the other emotions. Not only does anger have different dimensions of "depth," the "source" of anger is widely misunderstood. In the foregoing example, your anger is superficial, because the event didn't cause any emotional harm. There was nothing "inside" your self that "was hurt or damaged." That is not always the case.

Righteous Anger

"Real anger" occurs when it is related to an "injustice." The anger that surfaces as a result of an injustice is **righteous anger**. The "source" of this anger is your "protective" instincts, and it emerges from deep within you. You may sense the source is near the place "in or around" where you experience the source of "love" (your heart).

You see a parent yank a crying four-year-old's arm in the grocery store, or you hear a conversation that is loaded with the downhill language of ego: "You are worthless! You will never amount to anything!" A visceral reaction rises from within you, which is your self responding to the injustice being perpetrated. Even when the injustice is not directed at you, when you witness it, your emotional response is righteous anger. Obviously, however, the target of an injustice *can* be you.

When the injustice *is* aimed at you, the eruption of righteous anger is your reaction of your self going into primal protection mode. You experience anger, because your healthy boundaries have been violated, egregiously! You respond with anger in an effort to keep your heart, your source of love, safe and out of harm's way; verbal damage does the most damage to your self.

Regarding relationships, when "The End" comes, often anger follows. The ending is seen as an injustice, regardless of the circumstances. You made an investment of your heart and soul into this connection, and when "The End" happens, you experience authentic pain. Your heart hurts. Your heart and soul feel the devastation as though you had been struck by a large object to your chest. Getting hit causes pain. It hurts. Your experience is "This is an injustice that I never asked for. This has been done *to me.*"

You experience anger, but as you process, you begin to notice that as the anger subsides, it seems to be accompanied by even stronger feelings. It is as though the anger is sitting on top of residual fear (the third of the SAFE emotions) and deep sadness (the first of the SAFE emotions) for this "loss." However long it takes for the anger to dissipate, what remains afterward is the sadness.

Sadness is the true emotion that lies beneath all righteous anger. Yes, endings may make you angry, but the true impact of "The End" is sadness for your loss. You have lost something or someone that you cherished. What is "lost" is the dream, and with the dream the possibility of a "happily ever after" outcome has vanished as well. The expectations of happiness, of connection, of true love—all gone. You invested and now have "lost" a part of your heart. Maybe the loss was the passing (death) of someone with whom you were closely, intimately connected; it could be family or friend or partner. The sadness in these losses is a much deeper emotional experience, but with less anger.

For whatever reason, it is "our design" that anger serves another purpose. Anger is your "ally," which jumps in forcefully to protect you. An odd concept? No. Think of how anger (first) covers over sadness (the true feeling underneath); when anger comes on strongly, what is it doing? It is, in fact, keeping you "away from" having to experience "what is next." The deep sadness is "what's next." This is particularly true in a relationship. You know the ending is bringing sadness. The sadness of what you have lost carries with it an immense measure of pain. Your "senses," your preprogrammed System 1, is "on guard," so it works desperately to avoid the emotional suffering, the heartache of what it knows is coming: "The End."

You know what your automatic systems are doing, but your task is to have the full emotional experience. You accomplish this by "allowing" your self the experience, which is at hand. First, you experience any anger associated with the lost hope or dream that this ending has denied you. Your anger is real. The healthy expression of righteous anger is *to experience* the sensations that are present *but not to act out.* Speaking the injustice is the complementary expression of *experiencing* righteous anger. This may sound like "I am angry about how the child is being treated." This is a simplistic summary of a healthy expression of righteous anger. Notice there is no blame, shame, or slathering of guilt but simply the statement about *your experience* of the event you are witness to.

But second, it is paramount that you "find" the sadness about what will not be realized: the joy, peace, happiness, exhilaration, connection, and possibly the love that your heart desires. These are the "things" that have been lost, and this loss brings you sadness.

As is often the case, you may choose to hold on to your anger in an attempt to avoid having to face "what is coming," which is the sadness of what is lost. Your true self knows the sadness is in you, just below the anger. You will do almost anything to avoid having to experience it. Anything.

When people choose to deny their emotional experience, the most familiar and comfortable refuge is to choose to live from ego. You can *dismiss or avoid* the coming experience of sadness and instead hold onto your anger! It's OK. No one wants or seeks to experience deep heartfelt pain. No one. It's not what you are designed for; you are designed to love, to experience exhilaration and joy!

So, the truth here has two story lines, one from ego (your head), the other from love (your heart). First, denying and dismissing with your ego is completely understandable. Who wants to experience pain and sadness? Who would want to intentionally step into the path of hurt and pain hurtling at them from their loss?

The second story line is your being aware: You recognize the truth from your heart; you love your self, and by choosing this, you allow your self to experience your full range of emotions. The truth from your heart are the words highlighted in *italics* in the following text. These words reveal the contrast between the choice of living from ego (the head) and the choice of living from love (the heart) when you experience a loss.

Denying your emotional experience, the experience of your sadness, involves your choosing at least three of the letters in the FACED acronym: *F* (fear), *A* (anger), *D* (dismissing)

What is the takeaway here? As a healthy adult, you choose love:

- You *allow* your self the full experience of all of your emotional life by *accepting* your self and paying *attention* to what is happening in the moment, to what you are feeling.
- You "embrace your physical self" by *affectionately allowing* the tears, the doubling over in pain, and the sounds of loss.
- You *appreciate* (*value*) this part of your journey; like other times in the past, this "means something."
- You *appreciate the value* of your ability and capacity to experience your full life . . . especially the sadness (grief).
- You choose to love . . .

Love

is a

Life Of* Vulnerable *Experiences

Almost no other experience in your life exposes your vulnerability than when you "choose" to love your self by *allowing* your self to experience your full range of emotions. This is particularly true when you experience an "ending," a loss. You take whatever time is required.

Often the reservation about experiencing sadness (the first of the SAFE emotions) is held in the fear (the third of the SAFE emotions, the first of the FACED ego attributes) about what might be "on the other side" of your anger (the second of the SAFE emotions, the second of the FACED ego attributes). But, the question must be "What is happening?" What purpose does it serve for you to be fearful? Is "to fear" your "purpose"? Are these "fears" a manifestation of some part or parts of your self that you do not fully embrace, fully love? Is there something that you don't accept or appreciate about your self?

In this context, your reservation resolves itself neatly, does it not? Yes, you know your purpose! It is to love. The purpose of your life is to love.

Choosing love, choosing to love your self, reconciles the fear because fully experiencing your life, living a life of vulnerable experiences (LOVE), creates a deeper sense of love, *within you!* The conflict within your self is the following: Do you choose to love, or do you hold on to fear. While it may not have been apparent when the journey of experiencing a loss began, this contrast is another example of the classic conflict we face in life: the conflict of love versus ego, heart versus head. This time the conflict is within you. These two cannot coexist.

> **Choosing to love is choosing to
> cast out your fear for the experience
> of *more love* in your life!**

Choosing to become healthier, you *already* made your choice to live from your heart. You embrace your true self by loving your self, allowing your self to be worthy of experiencing the hand that life has dealt you. Life has *given you the privilege* of experiencing sadness, because it deepens and expands your capacity to love!!!

Yes, there is a ton of gold for you when you embrace this counterintuitive perspective. We will get into this in more detail later. For now, choose to love your self, by *choosing* to experience the complete sadness of any and every loss.

Other Anger

So, now we look at what is the "other" anger. Five hundred points and a trip to the Bonus Round if you already know the answer! If anger is not a matter of the heart, as righteous anger is, then what is the source of anger if it is not "injustice"?

The "other anger" is solely about ego. (Of course, righteous anger has an ego component, too, but in this instance ego is acting as a cover to protect against sadness. With "other" anger, the other elements of FACED come into play: arrogance, argumentativeness, condescension, controlling, expectations, pure defensiveness, dismissing, demanding, and all the rest of the nasty attributes. In fact, you can refer to it as "ego" anger.)

Anger solely from ego sounds different, because it comes from a different place than from your heart, than from love. This anger is purely defensive in its nature. "What happened" is that somewhere, somehow, ego (yours or another's) has been bruised or damaged. Most often, "what happened" involves a person who is living from their ego getting caught in the act of . . . (*wait for it*) . . . living from their ego. Someone has called them out. The actions or words of ego were put in their place or were rejected. The ego has been confronted.

When "something happens" in a relationship or in a conversation—maybe words are misinterpreted or have unintentionally caused damage—the healthy response from the heart is wrapped up in humility and ownership, with an apology or a resolution following shortly.

When ego is expressing its anger, however, you hear:

- "How dare you!!"
- "I told you!!"
- "You can't say [fill in the blank]!"
- "How could you even *think* that?!"
- "I'll put you in *your place*!"
- "I'll show you."

Listen closely, and you recognize the anger spoken here is about protecting ego:

- **Defending**, insisting on being "right,"
- **Controlling** another's thoughts or feelings,
- **Arrogance** and **dismissing**,
- **Declaring** its territory or possession,
- Making **demands**, and so on.

The distinction between righteous anger and "ego" anger needs to be clear. Is it possible there is sadness under anger from ego as it is with righteous anger? No. Well, yes, but the sadness is purposely being well hidden.

Look again at those examples of "ego" anger. There is no "wrong" from an injustice. That anger is from an ego that is suffering because the person speaking is disconnected from their heart. They have chosen "not to live from the heart," which is the choice not to love. None of those statements exemplify the elements of the five A's. A life without love is an existence of suffering. The person speaking is suffering. That much is guaranteed. You many need to ponder this, but people who choose to live from their ego are in deep pain, which they are choosing (ego) to avoid, choosing not to experience.

In other words, ego's anger masks the sadness from choosing not to love. There is sadness when the choice is not to love, whether someone is aware of the sadness or not. This is the explanation of unjustified anger from ego. It is easier to choose anger (ego) than to experience their sadness (heart, Love). They are afraid of experiencing love. They are afraid to "love their self." It is that simple. How so? Love means allowance and acceptance. One-hundred percent.

Here is the key takeaway about anger for you: Begin to distinguish anger from injustice, on the one hand, from anger from ego, on the other hand. Both have sadness, but the sadness underneath the anger from ego is "unknown" and stays hidden. If the angry person had been living from their heart, being aware how sadness lies beneath the anger, even "ego" anger, then they would have responded differently—from their heart. Be aware of this distinction whenever anger strikes you.[13]

Fears: Handle with Care!

F in the acronym *SAFE* stands for **fear**, the third of the SAFE emotions (and the first of the FACED ego attributes). Fears are by far the most complicated and the widest-ranging category of emotions. Fear is different in a number of ways. First, notice that the other SAFE emotions—sadness, anger, and exuberance (also referred to as ecstasy or exhilaration)—are common, or shared, emotional experiences. Most people know of or can relate to sadness, anger, and exuberance. However, with respect to fear, this is not the case. The fears that you experience may be "unknown" to someone else.

Say you have a fear of flying, which produces anxiety in you. Another person, who has no fear of flying, does not know the experience of anxiety from flying. In fact, as part of their nature, they may not feel anxious or experience anxiety in *any* situation. In fact, it could be the complete opposite. When they fly, they experience a feeling of complete, unbridled ecstasy. Joy, happiness, and peace is their emotional experience of flying. That is one example, but there are many just like it. To this end, fears must be considered a unique, personal experience.

There is another aspect about fear to understand and be aware of. Fears may be carried forward from childhood, *or* fears may be "newly acquired." As is the case when "what happened" in a previous relationship generated a fear that had not been present before the relationship. Some of these fears are much more common than others. Both childhood and newly acquired fears can leave deep scars. Especially when they are not processed and resolved. Often, before you begin to investigate "what happened," these fears may be lying dormant, stuck off in some distant

---

13 The connection of anger with sadness, and the distinction between righteous anger and "ego" anger, will be further discussed in the section "Experiencing and Expressing Emotions," later in this chapter.

part of your memory. The fear is waiting to be triggered and cast upon you in the present. When this happens, these unknown and unresolved fears can have a tremendous impact on you in your relationships.

Fear is a complex emotion. There is much to learn about fears that you must add to your awareness. First is the source of the fear. Second is how it "shows up," or surfaces, in the relationship. Finally, is how you handle fear when it has been triggered and surfaces, whether in you, in your partner, or in others.

In the context of becoming healthy and having a healthy romantic love relationship, here are some fears that are quite common (each of which will be dealt with in turn):

Fear of . . .

- Abandonment
- Rejection
- Being unlovable
- Being hurt
- Connection/closeness
- Intimacy/vulnerability
- Failure/trust

As a general rule, these fears can be mapped back to the installation and model for love, which you were provided in Chapter 3. In that chapter, you learned to focus your work on reassembling and resolving that which was missing by choosing to love your self. In summary, you give your self the love you need to heal the wounds from any "shortfall" that occurred from caregivers. When you love your self, the wounds are healed, even though the scars remain. The resolution work you do in that process moves you toward being healthy. Then, going forward, you are vigilant to do any remaining work when issues arise.

You do all this work to bring your healthiest self into your romantic love relationships. Why? Because being healthy offers you the best chance to experience the love your heart desires. Remember, the purpose of relationships is to experience the love your heart desires.

Your quick review of these concepts sets the stage for your understanding how fears surface in romantic love relationships. In fact, your most significant fears surface in a romantic love relationship. They will surface even when both you and your partner are well down the road toward becoming healthy. You might think this seems a bit odd: Shouldn't two healthy partners be on top of their game (their awareness) and catch these fears *before* they impact the relationship? That is unfortunately not the case, but there is a divine purpose at work here.

Those "scars" from previous hurts are actually very tender spots in your "heart" now. Weren't they healed? Yes. But in a romantic love relationship, the connection you share brings closeness, and this calls forth vulnerability to deepen your love connection (which is how you experience more love). The more you expose your heart (and your partner exposes theirs), the more vulnerable you are in revealing your true self, the more love you experience. Yes, when you are most intimately connected, your heart is the most vulnerable.

Vulnerability is defined as "the state of being exposed to the possibility of being harmed, either physically or emotionally." The word *vulnerable* is derived from the Latin noun *vulnus* ("wound"), and the Latin verb *vulnerare* means "to wound."

In a way it is almost as though you place your heart in the hands of your partner. In a sense, you have chosen to take the ultimate risk to experience love. This is where the expression "you are completely vulnerable" comes from. You are risking the most precious and valuable thing in your life, "your heart," "your love."

What is being exposed is the essence of your being—including those tender places in your heart. This makes more sense when you think back: Who caused the "pain" you know in your deepest self? When were you at your most vulnerable? When were you completely exposed earlier in your life? Yes, the hurt and wounds you hold, your experience of these wounds which you "know"—these came from the people (your caregivers) who were supposed to love you the most, unconditionally.

But what happened? Back then, your heart was exposed, was made vulnerable, and those people, the ones who were supposed to "love you the most," hurt you—whether intentionally or unintentionally is of no consequence. You did not make a "choice" about whom you exposed your heart to. You "got" your parents; you didn't have a choice. But now you chose "your love" partner, and you choose to hand them your heart. In a way, choosing raises the stakes; it makes you even more vulnerable. So, it follows that, in romantic love, you find your self in the same place.

Conversations and your "sense" about a romantic partner often "feels so familiar," because there is a sense about them that authentically feels as though they were *family*! Remember when your sense was that this person is "the One"? You connect with your partner based on the model of "love" you bring with you to the relationship. It is relevant to ask, "the One for what purpose?" The answer—whether you are conscious of it or not—is "the One who will help you restore what was missing from those who were *supposed* to love you unconditionally early on." That is a very big "get" for you. This is an awareness that you *must not miss*.

In this manner, you have a certain sense that you will experience the love that you *know*. Both the love you received *and* that which was missing are etched in your bones. You hold *both* of these in your memory. You now expose your heart with the same trust as you did before, early on. What happens next is that "something happens" between you and your "love" partner. This "something" triggers a memory of how you suffered the wounds of your childhood. What is triggered is often a memory of an event in which they were supposed to grant you the five A's, but *that love was missing*.

Romantic love . . . always happens this way. In fact, that is the "divine purpose" I referred to a little earlier. When this aspect of the nature of romantic love is known by both partners, the results are extraordinary. The experience of love that then happens when both partners are aware of the "divine purpose" is beyond any experience of love either one of you imagined. But to get there requires going for the "end game," which is always . . . what? Address *all* issues and resolve *all* issues back to love.

Let's connect the dots here. Recall that, for your self, you resolved what was missing by choosing to love your self when you addressed, processed, and resolved your circumstances, your past, and what was missing.[14] Your whole self is restored, and any love that was "missing" or modeled in a manner that fell short of a healthy installation is reinstalled, so you regain the healthy love for your self. You did that work to heal your self, but the scars remain. Now, in your romantic love relationship, "something happens" that is completely unexpected; you hear a word, or a phrase, you remember an event . . .

That "something" triggers one of those embedded memories of an old wound. Think of it this way: The "scar" of a wound on your heart is being poked again. The emotional experience you have in this moment "feels" like it is the same as the wound you have been carrying. Your present experience speaks to you: "Oh, no!! It's happening *again!*" What surfaces is the fear that you are reliving that "old wound." It is completely real for you as an emotional experience. The fear you are experiencing *is* the same emotion as what you experienced with the original pain or hurt.

You know that when you resolved your own issues, you moved closer to love. The love you experienced *in your self* was richer and deeper than before, when the issues had been unresolved. This is representative of what happens when issues surface in your romantic love relationship. In this case, a fear surfaces that begins to move you *away from* the love that is shared between you and your partner. You are moving away from love. How do you reconstitute and strengthen the love you have been sharing? Address, process, and resolve the issue (fear), which has moved you and

---

14 The APR procedure (address, process, and resolve) is explained in the subsection "Resolving Conflicts between Heart and Ego with APR" within the main section "Conflict Resolution" later in this chapter.

your partner away from love. This is a very significant "connecting of the dots" about love and relationships.

Does the way to experience the love your heart desires go through these old wounds? Must you deal with old conflicts between heart (love) and ego (not love)? Yes and yes. It didn't seem as though that would be the case way back when you experienced those butterflies! Logical thought seems to indicate that all the "remembered pain" was set up to make relationships *not* work. Not true.

It is true that the butterflies have gone away, and issues have come up that move you away from love. I conclude, however, that this is the "hidden genius" in the design of romantic love relationships. Relationships work this way precisely so that you and your partner will experience the love your heart desires. Precisely so you have another path to regain or heal the elements of love which were missing from early on. This shared experience of *more love* is the result of healing, which you do together.

The conclusion highlights three significant points:

1. **Romantic love relationships are designed to connect hearts to a shared love, which creates vulnerability.**
2. **Vulnerability exposes old wounds and residual or latent fears as "issues." These issues (fears), using the elements of ego, challenge the strength of the love bond between the partners.**
3. **The partners must resolve the issues together. Resolving the issues restores the elements of love, which have been missing in one (or both) of the partners, and restores and deepens the love they share.**

It may take some time to digest these points. Maybe it will require a couple of readings to fully absorb them. If your first takeaway from the points is very contrary to "what you know" from your relationships, understand that the difference is you are now journeying toward becoming a healthy partner. That journey is different from your previous relationships; now you love your self, you know love, you are selecting a healthy partner (hopefully), and you are prepared, going in, with knowledge and awareness that you did not possess before. Your sense about "resolving back to love" in all circumstances is new, and the three significant points just presented flip the concept of "issues" in a relationship on its head. Do issues arise and move you and your partner away from love? Yes. Do issues arise for the purpose of creating distance? *No!* Issues arise for healing, and they open the possibility for a deeper bond, a richer shared experience of love through reconciliation *back to love*. When two people are working *together* to find deeper love, then the resolution back to love makes total sense. Does this require *both partners* to be in the practice of living from the heart? Absolutely. All it takes to kill the relationship is the presence of one "ego." These points are worth some contemplation. When practiced, they will produce results. Love always wins. That is the key.

In the sections that follow, the most common fears that surface in relationships are briefly discussed. In many instances, these fears can be very complex. The idea here is to raise your awareness. In this context, the presentations are not as in depth as some may like; more information is readily available online. Yes, this is a lot to take in. However, you must; your relationships, your love, depend on you gaining the skill to recognize these fears when they surface. You have the capacity and are gaining the skills to handle it—to address, process, and resolve the fears. This is just another piece of your work.

Let's examine some of the common fear-based issues that you are likely to encounter in relationships:

Fear of abandonment: The source of this fear is multifaceted. Maybe your parents worked, and they left you at home—a latchkey child. Perhaps when you needed them the most, they were consumed with "their stuff" and left you to figure life out on your own. Maybe your caregivers were consumed with an addiction, and you were always alone, even when they were "there" with you. If they were consumed with themselves—that is, if they were narcissists—then you were always "second." You never knew when they would show up, and, not surprising, they often didn't. Or when they did show up, you received momentary, overwhelming attention: "Disneyland Dad" or "sMothering." The truth is, you realize now: It was all about them, not about you. Then, just as fast they appeared, their attention disappeared, and then they disappeared. They abandoned you. The wound inflicted on your heart is the "fear of abandonment." What you know is "those who love you . . . will leave you."

When triggered, the voice of abandonment speaks these phrases:
- "You are leaving me!"
- "Are you abandoning me?"
- "You are leaving me alone!"
- "You are leaving me because you don't love me!"
- "You are leaving me because I am unlovable."
- "People who love me always leave me."
- "I can't count on the people who love me most."
- "No one is there when I need them."
- When you said, "I love you," you mean, eventually, "I am leaving you."
- "I am alone . . . again."

When you hear these words and phrases spoken *in you*, or *from your partner*, these are the verbal cues that your (or your partner's) scar of abandonment has been triggered. The cue being triggered by your partner is felt as a physical sensation in you; you sense that you are being left, "again!" It could be a tightness in your chest, an elevated temperature in your forehead, a queasy stomach, or an overall agitated, anxious state.

Note: Most often all these sensations occur *before* your mental processes are engaged to investigate the matter. The skill that needs ongoing refinement here is your awareness. When you feel the emotional cue(s), then what you need to ask as your healthy response is "Something is up! What is going on?" Remember how you are "wired." Does your "thinking" (System 2) engage first? No. Not usually, because System 1 is in full-blown protection mode; it responds to the perceived "danger" (that is, the eminent fear of abandonment it knows) well before *any* analyzing can take place.

Often what happens first in relationships are the instinctual responses from the ego: distancing, dismissing, defending, critiquing, and so on. This is what System 1 does. The feeling of being abandoned comes over you, and you want to react from ego. However, the healthy response is to hold your ego response in abeyance. So, you need to pause!!

Your proper response is waiting in the background. This response you create well in advance, because from your work, you know already "what happened," "they left you!" This you have carried with you since early on. In fact, it is how you handle all the fear-based issues that are going to arrive "out of nowhere" . . . but as you know now, these are never out of "nowhere." The fears are etched in your soul. So, you have your healthy response waiting in the background.

The healthy response, the proper sequence and conversation *with your self*, sounds something like this:

> **"Hold on! Yes, something is happening.**
>
> ***Before* I do anything (such as lash out, shrink away, run, attack, blame, shame, vanish, become invisible, become unlovable . . .),**
>
> **I must *sit with this feeling*.**
>
> **I need to *investigate* and *understand* what is happening!"**

Wow! What if that were your response? A fear derails the moment, and you immediately respond with calm and introspection. That sounds like Nirvana, doesn't it? You have the capacity to do that! It comes from being well down the road toward becoming healthy. It is yours when you choose to "love your self!"

When an old wound has been gashed open—seemingly, from out of nowhere!!—what do you do first? Answer: *nothing*. You pause and experience what you are feeling, *then* . . .

Always "move in" toward your partner.

Always "close the gap," resisting the temptation to move away and create distance. Distance is ego. Ego makes you and your partner become *more* disconnected. Understand that ego is really strong in these moments. You must summon your healthy self. Summon your healthy self to take control. Here is where you engage your self to live from your heart. How? *You always move toward your partner.* You can accomplish this simply by speaking what you are observing, thereby creating a shared awareness . . .

> Gosh, something is up over here. You said you were going on your trip and would be leaving in an hour. I heard "I am leaving . . . you." I noticed that something is happening over here with me. I am suddenly gripped with fear or anxiety or something about your leaving.

Let's you and I hit Pause here . . .

If you're anticipating a "happily ever after" soliloquy that delivers the perfect resolution in words more suited for a gift card attached to one of those powder blue Tiffany & Co. gift boxes with the famous white satin ribbon around it and a bow on top, sorry. Penning that ending did get a few moments of contemplation over here. But, no.

This is, however, the perfect moment to reflect and make another couple of points; there may be some dots to connect *after* you read these questions. I hope so:

- How important is it for you to do your work?

- How important is it to let the froth of another steamy, lusty, attraction melt into the "Grande cup" of reality, which means making sure you know "who is this person whose clothes I want to rip off?"
- How important is it to find a real, authentic, genuine, healthy "match"—or said more simply: a *real* relationship partner?
- How important is it that *you* find and *choose* a partner who is also on their journey, just as you are, to become healthier and to figure "stuff" out?

"What's happens next" in this example of the fear (abandonment) surfacing between you and your partner will be the difference between connection and disconnection, more love or more pain, opening hearts versus closing them, and so on:

> **What you do next, *together*,**
> **to resolve this or any other issue,**
> **ultimately determines whether or not**
> **you experience the love your heart desires.**

I hope that point is now crystal clear. I hope some of the random dots that have been scattered throughout these pages just snapped into place as though they were being pulled by some incredibly strong magnetic force. Your clarity about love? Love your self? Being healthy? Chemistry? Picking the *right* "One"? Conflict resolution? Installations? Models of love? Relationships? Your purpose? These are all the dots so that you have the skills, the awareness, and the knowhow to create and *maintain* a romantic love relationship, in which you experience the love your heart desires.

It would be a good exercise for you to work through the resolution here on abandonment, using your words, not mine. You know what needs to be said, what needs to happen . . . so do that. Make that exercise be the "what's next" for you . . . now. Reread it and construct the scenario. Conflict resolution is covered in great detail in a section later in this chapter. But this exercise is intended for you to gather your healthy self and work through the conversation. The mental practice for you is to develop and refine your skill of *addressing the issue*. So, please take the suggestion and finish each discussion of fear in this manner. Speak from your self in a conversation with "them," a conversation that addresses the issue. This is a good practice; yes, it is your work.

Returning to the list of fears . . .

Fear of rejection: This fear can be sourced from both early childhood *and* from past relationships. The situations are consistent in that the wound is the same in both: you are "less than" or "not good enough." The conversation around this fear mostly happens inside your head. What is the source? Ego, and it pulls *no* punches: "Of course you're not good enough." "You have never been good enough." "You always come up short." "You *know* you are not good enough."

Which voice and action do you need to mobilize here? First, immediately: "I love my self." When you are with someone and you hear the words that bring up the fear of rejection, your conversation and your action needs to "move closer," to close the gap. How? Just as you have learned, express what is happening *in you,* and address the issue:

> I don't know where this feeling is coming from, but when I shared my opinion, I had a strong reaction that you didn't take my advice seriously. Suddenly I felt less than or not good enough. It was more than just my words or ideas being rejected; it was like *I* was being rejected or discounted. Like I didn't matter.

The missing component of love in this instance is *acceptance* and *appreciation*. Neither of these had been confirmed and installed early on. Yes, maybe in your work, you regained these, but remember the scar? It has been poked. Perhaps it is more than just a memory, though. If in a past relationship you experienced rejection, this wound was inflicted by an unhealthy soul. You can't do much about that former partner. But you can be more diligent about your next choice of partners (*which I am confident you will be, because it's been drilled into you repeatedly in these pages!*).

Fear of being unlovable*:* This fear is almost identical to the fear of rejection, because the missing components are *appreciation, acceptance,* and being *allowed* to be OK in the circumstances that you find your self in. The fear of being unlovable is the interpretation of an inbound message through the filter of your past. Maybe the following was spoken directly to you:

If you don't stop crying, I am not going to love you.

Wow! Can you imagine a tender four-year-old taking in that nasty comment? But it happens. More examples? Sure:

If you don't change your attitude and get a smile on your face,
I'm taking all your brothers and sisters and *leaving you* by
your self.
Who do you think you are? *You don't deserve* a toy! You think
someone like *you* is *worth* the cost of that toy? Think again.
That toy is *worth more than you will ever be!*

In the context of love, these examples are woeful "shortfalls." Or, said more bluntly, they reflect miserable parenting. They are, in fact, completely thoughtless. When the half-muted tones of these words are heard in relationships, the fear of unlovable strikes . . . again. Your answer, your response, is? Move closer. Share your observation of the experience. (Then APR.[15]) By the way, if these words are spoken to you by a "partner," your choice needs to be completely revisited: Do those words sound healthy? Loving? Living from the heart? What is the long-term prospect for you to experience the love your heart desires with this partner? You may ask, "Are such contemplations really necessary?" I believe they are.

---

15 The APR procedure (address, process, and resolve) is explained in the subsection "Resolving Conflicts between Heart and Ego with APR" within the main section "Conflict Resolution" later in this chapter.

Fear of being hurt: This fear is usually expressed as an ongoing action to "maintain distance." You want to make a connection and open your heart. For whatever reason, the risk of exposure and being hurt is a possibility that you simply choose to avoid. So, you don't go there. You are "nice" and "kind" and "thoughtful" and all the other superficial ways of "being with them." But the truth is you won't allow your self to get close enough, or open your heart, because of your fear of being hurt. You actively work to keep the hurt from happening, which means you keep your distance to avoid being vulnerable. It's totally understandable; you feel safer "at a distance." Oh, yes, you may have sexual intimacy, but even then, you are always holding something back.

The source of this fear could have been early on, or it could have been your more recent experience with someone who was supposed to love you consistently ending up hurting you. The one you thought you could trust failed to be trustworthy. It could have happened recently if a relationship partner violated your boundaries; you simply wanted to "be loved," and so you didn't say anything. You may have been afraid: "If I say something, they may hurt me . . . more." That relationship reached "The End," but the hurt you carried with you.

What did you commit to after you were hurt? "I will never let that happen again." Unprocessed, this wound lies just beneath the surface of all your relationships. It is even more likely to show up in your intimately connected love relationship. Why? Recall the "divine purpose" of relationships. Your fear of being hurt will be one that you confront until it is resolved. That is the design, and that is a good thing. "Resolved back to love" means what? . . .More. Deeper. Love.

A quick note is in order. All of this conversation about fears, leaning in, addressing issues, and resolving back to love may seem counterintuitive at this point. I get it. I ask that you "trust the process"—the *whole* process. There are parts and pieces yet to come, and when you are finished, I believe it will all make sense. Trust me here.

Fear of connection/closeness: It is important to see this fear as different from the fear of intimacy and of being vulnerable, which is discussed next. The experience of this fear is about "physical" more than emotional or heart. The source here is about *affection*. In a healthy state, this is the ability and the desire to be physically close. Touching and physical contact in a *respectful manner.* Those last two words are the focus point.

Some caregivers had boundary issues themselves. Along with a toxic mix of insecurities and the inability to give allowance to and acceptance of your individuality, even as a child. They were "in your face" a lot. They were uncomfortably close. Your experience was that you "never had room to breathe." They were always hovering over you. Never taking their eyes off you. Never letting you out of their sight. Was this respectful? No.

Was theirs the healthy expression of love, which allowed you the freedom to explore and have your life experience? Did you have your life be *your* life experience, or was your experience the one that they "knew" was the right path for you? You had no choice . . . they did not give you a choice. You were never allowed the room or space to "be your self." Because? They were too close. Overwhelmingly close.

In a past relationship, to make up for what was missing, maybe you selected a "control freak" as a partner. You did so in the hope that "this time" your partner would grant you the space, that they would help you reconstitute what was missing from your caregiver. What you wanted most was to "chart" your own course. But you found that was not an option . . . again. As a result, now you are hesitant about letting people get close to you or wanting to get close to people. When it happens in your relationship, your experience is . . . you feel like you are being smothered . . . again. When you sense this, even if it is genuine affection from them to you, the memory of being sMothered is triggered. Your System 1 responds, and you begin to plot your escape route, to create a "safe distance" between you and them. You do everything possible to keep "leaning away" versus experiencing healthy affection leaning in (which is exactly how you want to experience affection).

Fear of intimacy/vulnerability: If there is a consistent theme regarding these fears, it is this: In some way, shape, or form, the source can *almost always* be traced back to a caregiver's installations, and the missing pieces are sourced from those incorrect (that is, unhealthy) installations. Fear of intimacy and fear of vulnerability are vigorously reinforced through the experience of unhealthy relationships. When you have chosen to "love" and your experience has been heartache and heartbreak, each incident results in less and less risk taking with your heart. This fear is another that attempts to "maintain distance"; you do not want to get "too close."

In a romantic love relationship, the fear of intimacy "dances" with the fears of rejection and being unlovable. To reconcile the fear of being unlovable when it becomes present, you must gather your resources that reconnect you to "love your self." Being complete and whole, you have everything you need to do that work; you know how.

As you love your self, you regain love so you can give it in abundance. Then you find and measure your healthy boundaries. As your relationship calls you to "step in further," you choose to live from your heart as much as you are comfortable keeping your self-love alive and your boundaries intact. Then you "go in" a little more over time—more deeply, more open, with measured risk. Using your resources, you choose your boundaries and find your love. When an "uncomfortable" sense rises in you, the solution is, as before and always, to open a conversation from your heart and with your partner—moving closer, maintaining contact and connection with the person whose love you are sharing.[16] The fears of intimacy and vulnerability are unlikely to be overcome if you are with

---

16 The APR procedure (address, process, and resolve) generates an agreement that provides you with "reassurance." When an issue arises and you express fear, what is returned is reassurance and love. APR is explained in the subsection "Resolving Conflicts between Heart and Ego with APR" within the main section "Conflict Resolution" later in this chapter.

an unhealthy partner. They won't have the skills to establish the trust you need in the moment, or over time. Their ego will confront your heart, and you will be sent reeling. This is a warning, more or less. If you know or sense that you are harboring the fear of intimacy or of vulnerability, it is paramount that you choose your partner wisely. If that takes more work up front, so be it. Do the work.

Fear of failure/trust: The fear of failure is another one sourced mostly from experiences with past relationships. It is closely tied to trust-related fears. Fear of trust and fear of failure are slightly more complicated. Depending on your upbringing, you might be the kind of person who grants a healthy portion of trust to others from the beginning. This requires a high degree of confidence in your ability to "know" people intuitively. You must have an accurate sense about who they are early on in your relationship.

This ability could be just an intuitive "feel" that you possess and that has served you well in the past. Or it could be a highly refined skill that you have developed. You are skilled at asking questions that reveal "their" true nature: Are they trustworthy, honest, authentic, and genuine? And do they have integrity—that is, do their words match their actions? If this is the case, you are probably a genuinely healthy person. You love your self. You know your healthy boundaries. You are confident in your resolution skills. You may make a mistake, but you are confident that you have the resources in your self to recover. So, you trust early on rather than later.

You weigh the opportunity for gain (in other words, finding a partner with whom you can enjoy the love your heart desires) against the cost of a potential mistake (heartache or sadness of loss), and you choose to take the risk; you grant the trust. This is a very commendable trait . . . but it is not for everyone to attempt. Knowing your self is the key here.

If in your experience you are not particularly adept at executing this approach, then fear of failure and trust issues are likely to be lurking just below the surface at all times. If this is your experience, then the least risky path *for you* is to build trust slowly—at a rate that is comfortably inside your resources to love, set and maintain your boundaries, and recover from conflicts. Overcoming this fear is really a work that you need to do before getting too intimately connected with *any* partner prospect. Because the nature of romantic love relationships is *all about trust.* If you find you have trust issues, it's OK because you have all the skills to *create* the relationship that works for you. In other words, to create your relationship, you diligently apply the skills you have *in the circumstances of your life*, and you create the relationship that works *for you.* If that means you go slow, you go slow. If you set your boundaries for sexual intimacy at six months, that's your choice. Because? That is how you love your self. And it's OK.

Summary on fears: So, as we close here in our discussion of fears, what are the takeaways? The following points summarize:

- An intimate romantic love relationship opens your heart to love.
- An open-heart exposes prior wounds and scars—from caregivers and from previous relationships.
- Fears are triggered by the memory of the wounds that occurred in the past.
- Fear is the sensation that a past experience of the hurt or pain is going to be "relived" ("It is happening *again!*").
- Resolution begins with awareness, and then you "address" the issue or fear ("Something is going on in me").
- You move toward your partner, creating closeness rather than distance.
- You share your observation of what you are experiencing—no guilt, shame, or blame.

Healthy partners view any "issue" as something between them that they both must take responsibility for "what happened." Both partners take action together, first by "addressing the issue." The following introduces the last two pieces of the complete APR model for conflict resolution (**A**ddress, **P**rocess, and **R**esolve)[17]

- Express ownership and apologies with Grace and forgiveness.

Then

- Create an agreement.

Then

- Make a commitment to keep your agreement.

If the skill of resolving conflict with agreements is very important, then addressing fear-related issues is *very very* important. Because every romantic love relationship, with or without two healthy partners, will experience fear-related issues. The difference between success and heartache is the partners' ability to resolve these issues. But that is one of the beautiful treasures of romantic love.

When the conflicts and issues *are* resolved, the love those partners give and receive grows, and the love in their relationship expands. Their love brings more joy, peace, and contentment. This folds in neatly with the original premise:

> **The purpose of a romantic love relationship is to experience the love your heart desires.**

That is the design of an intimate romantic love relationship.

Exuberance

The last emotion is the easiest to address. The *E* of *SAFE* is **exuberance** (sometimes referred to as "ecstasy" or "exhilaration"). Exuberance is self-explanatory. It includes joy, happiness, contentment, peace, accomplishment, re-creating, renewing, and any other emotional experiences

---

17 There is more discussion of the APR procedure in the subsection "Resolving Conflicts between Heart and Ego with APR" within the main section "Conflict Resolution" later in this chapter.

of success. This is the emotion that is the most anticipated in any event or life experience.

A healthy adult who is choosing to love seeks to find more joy and peace in all aspects of life. Even in the darkest hours, where the measure of joy is the least, your heart seeks to experience joy and peace. How so? Attention. Acceptance. Appreciation. Affection. Allowing. That's how.

Experiencing and Expressing Emotions

You now know the design of an intimate romantic love relationship, but there is more to add regarding emotions. This closing section on emotions contains a few observations about experiencing emotions as well as a discussion about expressing emotions in a healthy manner.

Recall our SAFE theme, which identifies the common emotions of sadness, anger, fear, and exuberance. With regard to experiencing each of these, exuberance and fears can be dispatched quickly. Exuberance needs very few words. In short: "more is better"—more often, more intense, more, more, more! Expressing and experiencing fears was covered sufficiently in its own section as well.

This section focuses on the remaining two emotions: sadness and anger. The experience and expression of these emotions is somewhat unique. Sadness is more of a personal experience, but since anger is rarely directed inward, it must be dealt with very carefully. First, though, is a look at the experience of sadness.

Developing the capacity and ability to experience sadness is a requirement for becoming healthy. When you chose to love your self, you granted your self the *allowance* to experience all that happens to you. "To experience" sadness is paramount to having a complete and full human experience. Experiencing sadness is the process of healing "what happened" in both your childhood and in your current relationships. Experiencing sadness is the practice of healing those early wounds and the heartaches from past relationships.

The practice means that you allow your self the full measure of all your sadness. Rarely is one able to experience this full measure as a single event; more often than not, the experience of sadness is a process, sometimes referred to as "the grieving process."

Note: The process is not a list of "the steps" but rather a "how-to." You can repeat this "how to grieve and experience sadness" as often as necessary in order to experience all the sadness related to an event. Since sadness often is the result of, or in some way related to, a "loss," you have a significant investment of your heart in what has been lost. The greater the investment, the greater the loss and the deeper the sadness.

Again, sometimes things "get in the way" of your experiencing the full measure of your sadness. System 1 goes to work with a defense mechanism designed to postpone or avoid your having to experience the sadness. Why? Sadness hurts. The experience is painful. But you are aware that all endings entail *some* measure of sadness. Your being healthy will mean that you are aware how sadness is in your "self." Even if, in the moment, you don't know "where it is," you know it must be "experienced"—that is, through APR.[18]

Often when you can focus on "what has been lost," you can initiate the healing process. The loss is usually associated with an event that is the source: Is it an ending of a love relationship? Is it some other lost connection? Is it the loss of a favorite pet? Is it the loss of a beloved figure with whom you had a strong emotional connection? Something has been lost, and the sadness lies in you. So, the process begins when you bring into your awareness that the "ending" has indeed occurred.

As the first bodily sensation arrives, indicating that the sadness is surfacing, it is a good idea to do whatever it takes to find a location where you can "be with your self." This could be anywhere—your car, a sofa, a room, out in nature. It is helpful that this place is free from

---

18 The APR procedure (address, process, and resolve) is explained in the subsection "Resolving Conflicts between Heart and Ego with APR" within the main section "Conflict Resolution" later in this chapter.

distractions and/or interruptions. When you are situated comfortably, you begin to narrow the focus of your attention.

Your goal here is to locate where you sense the sadness surfacing in your physical body. Relationship pains usually reside in your chest, specifically in the area around your heart. A traumatic ending often causes a physical pain in your heart. Literally, your heart feels a "puncture," like being stuck by a needle. Or the space where your heart resides inside your chest feels as though it were under compression. Your objective here is to "be with the sadness."

Your focus on the location where you are feeling the sadness enables the emotional experience, what you feel, to become more present to you, more in the moment. The feelings you experience can be very intense. There is no "thinking" here. Your mental concentration is on the loss and the pain of the loss, which is gripping a part of your body. *That* is the sadness. You may experience many tears arriving with the sadness. Focus your attention on letting your tears pour out; crying is the experience of your sadness.

Through a "divine purpose," your tears are healing. More tears, more healing. Many people can experience their sadness with hardly any effort. But for others, specifically for those who were told to deny their emotions, the practice is one that must be learned.

The process of resolving all the sadness you hold does not have a time clock or a calendar. What is certain is when the sadness has been fully experienced in your being, you will know. Because when the sensations of the sadness have been exhausted, you feel as though the sadness had been washed away, and in its place your work is to return to love.

How? Find each of the five A's inside what you have lost. Finding these begin with your focused *attention* to experience your loss. You *accept* the loss as a part of your life. You may not have ordered life this way, but it happened, and you accept it. You *appreciate* the value of everything you have gained from the person or the relationship experience before the loss. And the lessons about your self, which the loss has revealed;

these are what you have gained about your self because of the loss. In the process, you *allowed* your self to experience the sadness of this loss; your physical being hurt, you experienced the hurt, you felt tears, and you allowed your self to cry.

Arriving on the "other side," you find that you are intact; you are more whole and complete. With your experience, you are more connected to your self and life, to your heart and love. While the experience of sadness happens in you, it can be a shared experience (in the case of death). With love relationships, your personal emotional experience and the process that is your work is our focus.

There is a final piece to processing sadness, and that deals with Grace and forgiveness. This may or may not apply to all losses. For instance, if your loss is the death of someone beloved, there is usually no requirement for forgiveness. However, the loss of a romantic love relationship, where the ending was combative and where words of anger were exchanged, will require forgiveness to complete the cycle back to love.

Grace and forgiveness are covered in more detail later in this chapter. Meanwhile, we have one last emotion to cover after sadness: the experience and expression of anger.

Earlier we noted the difference between righteous, authentic anger from injustice and the "other" anger (sourced solely from ego), which would better be referred to as "ego" anger. Now we will look at how to handle each of them.

The key awareness about expressing righteous anger in a healthy manner is that in expressing this anger, you do not employ blame, shame, or guilt. The words spoken speak truth only about the injustice. The truth about the injustice is your emotional experience, which sounds like this:

> I am angry and saddened about the hurt experienced by your child, who is not being allowed to be "OK" and is being dismissed and distanced, being told they are "not good enough."

Or

> I am deeply saddened by the insensitive words you used to impeach my character. I am valuable, but your words devalued my worth and contribution.

When righteous anger is expressed, the words spoken identify the pain of the injustice. Use the 5A model of love to find the source of that pain—because an act of injustice is *not* delivered from a place of love, nor would it be present if the person delivering the act were "living from the heart."

Injustice is a blatant example of a person making the choice not to love, a choice that defines ego.

These two examples illuminate both the emotion that you experience in terms of your self and the element of love that is missing. Notice the difference in the two examples. The first example speaks anger about an injustice *to someone else*, which you witness. The second example is anger *directed at you*. In both cases, notice there is no blame, shame, or guilt in the expression of anger. The injustice is identified, and the encroachment on love is called out. That is how you express righteous anger. It's a simple concept, but you must be wary of letting *your* ego slide in with words of blame, shame, or guilt. That takes practice . . . and being aware.

What about expressing anger from ego? Well, there is no healthy way to express this anger because it is composed of and sourced from ego.

Look at these examples and see if you notice how the anger is derived from ego:

- "How dare you!!"
  - Arrogance, entitlement, dismissing . . .
- "I told you!!"
  - Arrogance, contempt, control, condescension . . .
- "You can't say that!"
  - Control, entitlement, diminishing worth and value . . .
- "How could you even think that?"
  - Control, arrogance, discounting . . .

These words may be spoken with velocity and rage, but there is no injustice. The examples are common flare-ups of ego. The person is speaking from their ego. Notice the person is fully engaged and is coming "downhill" at their "target." No additional words are worth the effort because there is no healthy way to express anger from ego. Because anger from ego is simply ego expressing *itself* by lashing out, with the tools it knows best: FACED. In this regard, in the same way that you are fine-tuning your "filter" for love and ego, add to your awareness the skill of hearing the anger of an ego, and develop the skill to express righteous anger in a healthy manner.

This brings us to a final note, which carries us beyond emotions. Note the "unanticipated circumstances" of life that brings emotional pain, sadness in loss, hearts being disconnected by words and actions of ego and denial of feelings. All of these can be resolved back to love. It is not by chance that this happens. This is the *essence* of your work. Your work is the *process* of becoming "whole and complete" by choosing . . . what? Yes. L.O.V.E. In all the circumstances of your life, the "resolution" is always to choose to love. Doesn't that simplify things greatly?

Preferences

Since page 1, you have seen or read the word *preferences* thirty-two times. Preferences are a critical part of the mix on your road to becoming healthy. Earlier, we discussed preferences in connection to the "relationship" portion of our conversation. Here is where we reconnect with the concept of preferences.

You may have noticed something curious about your thoughts, especially as you are becoming much more aware about "you." When you are introspective about your self and your past, and when that introspection arises from your loving your self, how you see your self tends to be very honest and objective. There is hardly any guilt or shame or condemnations about "what happened" regarding choices you made and any errors in judgment in your past. That is the way life is supposed to be. "You live and learn." That trite saying is not "You live and shame your self for the rest of your natural-born life," is it? No. You live and learn, because you know that love is acceptance, allowance, and appreciation. That's nice. Pretty damn comfortable, in fact. At least, I find it so.

Hopefully, your honesty and objectivity has revealed some clear distinctions about what you like, what you want, and what you need for your self as you go about life as an independent healthy adult. The work on preferences is to contrast your self ("who am I") with a new perspective about your self in your future relationships. With a focused perspective, you want to clearly identify what works for you and what doesn't work for you. That middle area between the two is a gray area that we'll discuss in a minute.

What works for you, in this case, concerns your preferences—the ways you are, the ways you know your self to be, the things that bring you joy and peace. Your preferences are that which is *from* your true self.

Your preferences probably comprise a very very long list. Here are some ways to look at the conversation about preferences, which might help you figure out yours:

- How often do you like to exercise?
- How often do you go to church?
- What kind of church do you like?
- What do you like to eat?
- How do you like your steak cooked?
- Do you like your potatoes baked or mashed?
- What do you like to wear?
- What colors work for you?
- What colors do not work for you?

As you can imagine, compiling a list of your preferences could take a while and a few legal pads. All my clients must make the list; it is part of their work. You can love your self more fully when you *know* your self.

Listing your preferences is a way to move this knowing your self from a random concept to a tangible set of wants and wishes—your desires. The list takes a sharp turn, though, when the focus narrows to your preferences concerning a romantic love relationship.

Your list of preferences is critically important. Relationship preferences are unique in that they are the most important things you want to have "in" your relationship. Here you are not offered the choice to "opt out." Get out your Big Chief writing tablet and number-2 pencil; listing your preferences is (more of) your work.

Your preferences reveal how you want to experience your deepest needs and wishes in an intimately connected romantic love relationship with a partner. These preferences are your personal declaration of the things for which *you are unwilling to compromise—because*, if you were to compromise them, then you would not experience the love your heart desires inside your romantic love relationship. We all have preferences. That has always been the case; even if you did not make a list before your previous relationships, you have taken your preferences into every romantic love relationship you have ever had.[19]

It's now time for you to know your self better. Make a list of your must-have, nonnegotiable relationship preferences. Remember, there is no right or wrong, good or bad. There are just the ways that you want to experience your self in your relationship. And yeah, it covers all the good stuff—how you want to spend your holidays, how much affection you like, how you like sex, how many times you want it, when would you like to have kids, how many kids would you like to have, how much do you want to engage your family in your life . . .

Yes, the list is really, really long. But it is totally unique to you. These are your preferences. There is no one who knows these better than *you*, and for you to become healthy, you need to *know* them. These are what

---

19 For the balance of this section, when you encounter the word *relationship*, think *romantic love relationship* even if that is not the expression on the page. It is a long expression to type out every time.

you are going to communicate to any and every prospect who is really a prospect!!

In the peace and quiet of your own mind, if you were to speak your list in a conversation, it would sound something like the following (write *yours* down . . . hint, hint):

- I want a kiss hello and goodbye when coming and going.
- I want to hold hands in public.
- I like PDA.
- I want to go on one three-day weekend every quarter.
- I want to save 10 percent of my income.
- I want my partner to be fiscally responsible.
- I want my partner to be "stylish" when we go out.
- I want us to put five hundred dollars each into our travel kitty every month.
- I want us to cook together.
- I want to make love every morning.
- I want a partner who relishes love making.
- I like to dress casually.
- I like short skirts and high heels.
- I sometimes like to wear a coat to dinner.
- I have no great desire to live near the ocean.
- I do not like hot weather.
- I want no more kids, but I love kids.
- I enjoy having friends over for dinner once a month or so.
- I love to have Saturday nights be for one-on-one dates.
- I enjoy movies from Netflix and Redbox and going to theaters.
- I like Jimi Hendrix and '70's rock. Rap? Mix? OK, not my pref.
- I like to spoon when I sleep with my partner.
- I love touching when I sleep.
- I love a rare grilled steak, with S&P the only spices.
- I do not eat tofu or chili with beans.
- I like dogs but do not like dog hair all over my house.

- I want to live in the "burbs" with a yard.
- I also would like to live "uptown" in a high-rise, no maintenance.
- I love to cook.
- I would like a partner who enjoys home-cooked meals.
- I like road bikes.
- I do not like mountain biking.
- I do not like to run (bad knees).
- I smoke a cigar once or twice a month (Rocky Patel Sun Grown).
- I like Newcastle Brown Ale.
- I like white wine.
- I do not drink red wine.
- I have a very, very occasional mixed drink: mojito and marg are favs.
- I don't care about a college degree—nice to have but not a requirement.
- I want a partner who is outgoing and spontaneous like me.
- I want a partner who is quiet and introspective also.
- I want a partner who is financially independent.

That list? It is mine. Those are my preferences. It would be impossible for you to list every preference you have but be sure to get the ones that are "deal breakers" in writing. Yes, get started. Make your list. Take your time. It's important that you develop a complete picture of your preferences.

When you are finished, take out your highlighter. This part is where the rubber meets the road. Some of the items on your list are nonnegotiable. For you to be in a relationship with anyone, these are the items that represent things you are unwilling to compromise on. In other words, say you meet someone and it seems like everything is copacetic. Many of your interests are aligned, but a couple of your nonnegotiable preferences conflict with their preferences. This is something you must know *before* you make any type of commitment. Why? It's simple.

Your preferences are exactly the manner you want to experience the love your heart desires in your relationship. To experience that love, you have things that you are *unwilling to let go of* as a requirement to be with someone. Stated another way, if you let go of just one of your nonnegotiable preferences, you would not experience the full measure of joy and happiness from your relationship. Letting go would mean that you are sacrificing something that is deeply a part of your true self. These nonnegotiable items are things you cherish, and they would connect you more deeply, more intimately, with your partner.

Selling Out Your Preferences; Selling Out Your Self

This brings us to a very critical part of our discussion on relationships, which needs to be stated very bluntly. More directly. Giving up a preference that is part of your true self means that you are *selling out* your true self.

Compromising your preferences = selling out.

You are making a compromise on preferences about which there is no room for compromise. If you give up or let go of any of your nonnegotiable preferences, you are giving up and letting go a part of your heart, your soul, your true self!! Does that come out as too dramatic? *No.*

"Selling out"
is how the foundation of a relationship begins to crumble.

Selling out preferences is not being true to your self. The sad part here is that selling out is often part of the story for many relationships that once held so much promise . . . but then someone chose to sell out, which sounds like the following:

"What happened?"

I want to feel connected to my love mate. I love touch. I love holding hands and feeling his arm around me, especially in a crowd. It makes me feel secure in our connection. It makes me feel safe . . .

When we first started seeing each other, I noticed that he shared my desire to hold hands and put his arm around me. The first couple of times we were sexually intimate, we spooned and held each other after making love. After a few months, though, I noticed that as soon as we finished, he moved away, and we barely touched at night. After a year, we never held hands. And though he used to kiss me when we reconnected at the end of the day or when he returned from a business trip, now there were no kisses . . .

But . . .

I thought, "Well, this is just temporary, and I am sure he misses it, too, and the old pattern will come back someday. Maybe I'll say something, and he will change. I know he loves me, so he will see what I need and start holding my hand, and we'll go back to touching and connecting like I want when we make love and sleep together . . .

We decided to get married.

And twenty-three years later, nothing has changed . . .

No, it hasn't. "What happened" is that this person sold out. Early in the relationship, she gave up a part of her true self. That is how she sold out. She compromised on a part of her self for which there was no room to compromise.

Mostly when people "choose" to sell out, they do so in the area of kids, money, and sex. And make a note: The sellout comes way before the commitment to a long-term relationship.

The requirement to sell out signals a "red flag." The actual sellout happens when this red flag warning is replaced by a hope, or a fantasy:

What they sold out will automagically reappear . . . someday. But that day never comes.

> **When the choice is either to hold on to your true self
> or to give up a part of your true self,
> and you *choose* to let go of a part of your soul,
> *you* have chosen to sell out.**

Applying this to the impact on relationships:

> **When a relationship depends on *you*
> selling out a part of your soul
> to continue in that relationship, A) it is not a healthy
> relationship, and B) the relationship is *over*.**

It is impossible to recount the number of times these two facts are the source of heartbreak and train-wreck endings. The sellouts capture the essence of what clients share about their relationships and "what happened." These situations are particularly sad, yet it happens all the time. More often than not, selling out happens numerous times, a recurrence that ultimately leads to "The End." When this happens, "selling out" becomes the irreversible terminal cancer of romantic love relationships.

What happens is that one of your nonnegotiable preferences conflicts with theirs, or they refuse to accept your preference(s). You have your answer, right? The "red flag" warning has been waved! But you ignore the warning and choose to compromise, to give away part of your self. Or maybe you and your partner *do* address it. But their position is clear: "This is the way I will be. *You* must change!" Again, you have the answer: Their preferences and your preferences are not aligned. Is there but one choice here? Yes. You need to choose to love your self.

Do you choose to love *most* of your self but sell out part of your soul? Not if you have chosen to love your self! In fact, it would be more authentic if you simply said, "I am choosing to sell out so that I do *not* experience the love my heart desires."

**Compromising your preferences
is selling out your love.**

Take, for example, your preference for touching. This is a way that you pay attention to your self, and you want/need to be affectionate to experience love with/from your partner. Early on, you probe, and their answer is: "Sorry, not my preference." What you need to understand is that they are really saying: "No, I will not give you love in the unique manner that your heart desires in this relationship with me." You have their answer. On the matter of affection, they are telling you, "I will not love you in the unique way you want to be loved."

Once you have their answer, it would make a lot of sense for you to acknowledge them for showing up, to thank them for a wonderful time, and to wish them the best of luck in finding the right fit for them. Because for you? This person is not "the One." An astute observer of social matters says it this way: "If the love don't fit, you need to quit." (RIP, Mr. Cochran!)

But the bigger point for you on your journey is this: When staying in the relationship requires that you *dismiss* or *discount* (ego words) or not *appreciate* (a love word) your preferences, you are choosing *not to love* your self. You are choosing to *dismiss* and *not value* how you want to be loved because you do not value your own preference. That's it.

From the work you have done so far, hopefully you understand that selling out is a classic example of a heart-versus-ego conflict. When selling out is required, which one of those is the winner? Ego. Ego has won. Heart (love) has lost. But who is the real loser in this battle? I don't think I need to hint at or even write the answer, because that is the saddest part of this whole situation . . . and it doesn't have to be that way.

It is appropriate, then, to ask these questions:

- How important is it to know your preferences?
- How important is it to know your nonnegotiable preferences, for which there is no room for compromise?"
- How important is it for you to love your self by honoring your choice to hold on to your preferences, which are the foundation of how you love your self?

The answer is simple. Just as critical as setting your boundaries, knowing your preferences and holding firm on them are the way you love your self in your relationships—romantic love relationships, relationships with family, and relationships in the workplace. If it helps, think about your boundaries and preferences as being fixed. No one can change them or has the right to change them except you. No one has the right to encroach on them or tell you where your boundaries *should be* or what your preferences are.

Keep this in mind and open your toolbox. There will be times when your boundaries are violated and when your preferences are not aligned with others. How do you hold fast to loving your self when these occur? Here we introduce the critical skill of conflict resolution.

Conflict Resolution

Conflict resolution is a relating skill you have been exposed to a number of times. It was difficult to figure out where to slot it in, given all the foundation for healthy relating that had to be in place ahead of it. So, here it is. Since redundancy is one of my writing "skills" (or problem), hopefully you will be able to take this concept in and connect any un-connected dots from earlier discussions.

Conflict resolution is the one skill that "weaves everything together"; love, love your self, APR, FACED, etc., etc., etc., all come together in this section. I think that is appropriate, too, because at the end of the day, conflict resolution determines whether any relationship succeeds or fails. Yes, it is just about that simple.

Why? Issues are guaranteed to come up in every relationship. That didn't need to be stated; you knew it already. Since "unresolved issues" are what tanked all relationships that have reached "The End," this is the one skill that must be in place for a relationship to have *any* possibility of succeeding. Here is another way to say that: If you and your partner do not have conflict resolution skills in your bag of tricks, your relationship has *zero* possibility of delivering the love your heart desires. Yes. Zero. Given that somber note, let's dive deeply into this subject.

This section begins with an exploration of how heart and ego play off each other in your self and your relationships. The basics of how these interact and engage is a critical awareness for you. It's very important for you to know the "end game" of this chapter before we get too far in.

The following is a fact:

**Without the skill of conflict resolution,
a healthy romantic love relationship cannot exist.**

My promise has been to speak the truth. You have been reading and hearing myths all your life, so here is another one of those instances where truth is required. Yes, just like love, love your self, preferences, and selling out, conflict resolution is Big.

If conflict resolution was a graduate course, your work would be graded "Pass/fail." There is no C+ or A–. There is no middle ground. If there were, then the title of this "Conflict Resolution" section would be "Mostly/Almost/Partially/Three-Quarters/Best-Efforts-But-Fell-Short Conflict Resolution." It's not. There is no gray area. It is black or white. Conflict. Resolution. Either conflicts "are resolved," or they "are not resolved."

To set the stage for the discussion on conflict resolution, let's deep-dive into the first element . . .

Conflict: Heart Is FACED by Ego

The previous chapters have exhaustively investigated heart and love in contrast to, or with, ego. You know the makeup of each, you know where they come from, and you know the purpose, or agenda, of each one. Hopefully, the case has been made that these two are joined at the hip. It is impossible to discuss these two facets of your life in any sort of disconnected fashion.

The way I prefer to look at heart (love) and ego (not love) is that they are the two sides of a gold coin. You cannot separate them. You are constantly holding this "coin" in your hand. With nearly every thought about your self, those with whom you have a relationship, and even random people whom you meet every day, you choose which side of the coin you are going to show them.

Consider for a moment the following statement, adapted from an earlier chapter:

> **In every conversation you have
> over the course of your entire life,
> you are engaged
> either from your heart (love)
> *or*
> from your ego (not love).**

From what you know now about living from your heart (love) and living from ego (not love), I hope this statement of truth makes more sense than when you read it the first time.

What do you choose when you choose to love? The five A's, right? Attention, acceptance, appreciation, affection, and allowance. These are one side of the coin. They are found in your heart; they are your true self. You choose them when you want to experience joy, peace, and satisfaction . . . in other words, love!

Now let's look at the other side of the "coin": ego. But this time I want you to focus on the elements of ego, and as you read each one, position it *against* the elements of love.

Here is our big list of words and actions of ego:

Fears	Correction
Frustration	Entitlement
Argumentativeness	Expectation
Arrogance	Demands
Anxiety	Defensiveness
Anger	Distancing
Assessment	Disappointment
Condescension	Dismissing
Control	Diminishing
Critiques	Displeasure
Criticizing	Degrading
Comparison	Discounting
Commands	

Maybe, you can bookmark this page. That list contains more harmful toxic elements for mankind than all the CO_2 gases humans have ever spilled into the atmosphere. A bit of humor? Yeah. Truth? Undeniably, 100-percent Truth.

The practice of discerning the sights and sounds of ego is *as important* as knowing what you are choosing when you choose to love. Why the heavy "gravity" here, why the intense focus on developing *your* skill and discernment of ego? The answer is simple:

Until you understand and learn to distinguish the voice, sounds, words, and phrases of ego, and know instantly that the choice being made in that moment is *not to love*, you cannot experience the love your heart desires.

225

This statement describes where many people find themselves at the end of a relationship. Notice the statement reads that the choice is *"not to love."* That is "what happened." They *both* started out choosing to love. Somewhere along the way, something happened, and they chose not to love. "Something happened"? Yes, a conflict between heart (love) and ego (not love) . . . which went unresolved. How can the outcome be different? You are on that journey.

Getting a solid foothold on "love your self" and what love means is raising your awareness into a new realm. You will notice that you begin to hear "love" in the measure of the five A's being spoken everywhere—from the pillow next to you or five rows back in the movie theater.

Distinguishing ego when ego shows up, regardless of the source, needs to be an integral part of your true self. It is already, by the way. You simply did not know it, because it lay dormant in you—or you had fallen "out of practice," failing to "notice" when ego showed up (and slowly suffocated love).

These reminders are intended to emphasize the distinction between the "language" of heart and the "language of ego." The languages are literally the choices, the words and actions you hear in every conversation. The words and actions indicate who's "talking": heart? or ego? Being aware of these words and actions and having the tools ready at hand gives you what you need to develop your "listening," your discernment. It takes time to refine your listening. The good news? Now that you're aware; you know what to listen for and what the source of those downhill conversations are.

From the perspective of a relationship counselor, distinguishing heart from ego is 99 percent of what people and relationships are missing. That is why the distinction is *so* important.

So far, the conversation about ego has been in the context of a relationship with an "other." What is the truth? You need to be objective. There are instances when you were the victim, *and* there were the times you were the perpetrator. You're human. It's OK.

That is why the acronym FACED is such a critical piece to grasp. Those words that ego speaks—the words that are criticizing, commanding, assessing (that is, judging), and manifesting entitlement—are often the words spoken to *you* by *you*. This concept may take some time to understand, especially if this is the first time you have focused on "listening" to the conversations you have with your self in the context of distinguishing your heart speaking or your ego speaking. Your being aware means that you are beginning to hear these internal conversations—by you and to you, about your self.

The following conversations are examples of "by you and to you, about you." These may sound familiar. In the bright light of love, they may trigger some not-so-pleasant memories:

- "Mother was right. You are bad" . . . *or*
- "There is no way you can accept everything about your self and your past and your choices" . . . *or*
- "You have been stuck in a rut for weeks. You should have gotten over it way before now. Get your self together. What is wrong with you?" . . . *or*
- "You don't deserve love and to be happy" . . . *or*
- "You're just lucky someone would have you" . . . *or*
- "Stop asking for what you want" . . . *or*
- "Nothing you do in the next five minutes is going to make those pounds and inches disappear!"

Each of these is a conversational example of the heart-versus-ego dynamic. They represent the *conflict*. Ego is the source and the instigator of conflict. That is what makes your skill of listening and discerning the language of ego so vitally important.

If you didn't know better, you might have concluded, "Oh, that is two people talking to each other." But the more accurate statement is "This is one voice speaking to an 'other.'" And these are examples of how your ego speaks to you, about your self. Can you identify what voice is speaking? Compare those words of ego with the five A's. The two points to gather from this exercise are:

1. Contrast the language of love, which you know, and consider how those statements are the complete opposite of love, how they are the language of ego.
2. These examples could be what someone is thinking, **or** they could represent a conversation spoken between two people.

With that in mind, here's a couple of questions:

- Have you spoken this way to your self?
- Have you heard these words spoken in your voice to your self . . . ever?

For most people the answer is yes. The words may be slightly different, but you have experienced speaking such words as these in conversations in your thoughts about your self. That conversation coming "downhill" on your self? That is your ego. That is *your* voice of *your* ego. Ego is speaking to you any time you choose "not to love" your self. When your ego speaks, it uses the words or phrases of FACED. That's how you identify it versus the language of your heart, which is love, the five A's.

Funny how this sort of makes sense. In every conversation, the "speaker" and the "listener" are choosing to speak either from heart or from ego. That is the nature of all conversations. You are raising your awareness about these two voices, which are *inside* you. These voices are different because the source of each "voice" is distinctly unique. The voice of your heart has as its source love, whereas the voice that ego uses speaks every word, thought, or idea that is *not* love. It's really that simple.

You have a clear distinction about the words and actions of ego. Ego *is* how the choice not to love shows up in the world—in you, in others, and in relationships. Ego is like the jackal prowling around the dark fringes where the shadows mix with the light, waiting for a chance to move in and feast anytime love falters. Ego *always* fills the gaps when love is missing.

How is it possible that ego is still present after you have consciously chosen to "live from your heart" and to love your self? Frankly I don't know, but who cares? The bigger question is what skill do you need when these words are "coming downhill at you"? How does this work exactly? And is it the same when you are resolving inner conflicts between your heart and your ego as it is when you are resolving heart-and-ego conflicts with another person?

Yes. Now it is time to add and address the *resolution* aspect to your skill set . . .

Resolving Conflicts between Heart and Ego with APR

This new task can be more accurately described as "adding a layer" of awareness to skills you have already learned. This layer rests on top of nearly all the things that have been covered so far, such as the choice to love (heart, the five A's) and not to love (ego, FACED). This all-encompassing layer is how you resolve conflicts between heart and ego.

As you move through this section, my hope is that you literally, viscerally, experience your self grow. Seriously. Yes. That you begin to experience your self become healthier as an adult. This is a circumstance where you consciously choose to love your self. Because you are going to speak your conflict resolution from the voice of your heart. The resolution declares to the world your choice to love your self and to live from your heart.

Given the contrasting natures of heart and ego, it should be abundantly clear that they are mutually exclusive. To love and not to love constitute an either-or construct. In heart-versus-ego conflicts, ego's objective is to push love aside. The conflict happens when a previous commitment to "live from the heart" gives way to the words and actions of ego; this is the definition of "living from ego." The *allowance* of this to happen is "selling out." These instances are where you find the conflict that must be resolved "back to love." For whatever reason, the voice of "not to love" has spoken, and the voice of your heart must be found and must respond.

A quick reminder from earlier, to set the context here:

**Every conversation is
either from the heart or from the ego.**

Regarding the skill you use to resolve inner conflicts between your heart and your ego *and* to resolve conflicts between your heart and the ego of others, is the APR method. It was introduced on several occasions, but here is where it will be explained.

The abbreviation stands for: **A**ddress, **P**rocess, and **R**esolve. This section reveals the complete framework of the APR method. Later in this chapter, two more elements that have been mentioned earlier will be added: Grace and forgiveness, on the one hand, and agreements, on the other hand—two critical pieces for healthy conflict resolution skills. Now let's dig into APR.

The elements of the APR method can best be described using short vignettes that are examples of the thought process to keep in mind with each APR element. These examples are intended to "speak the language" of conflict resolution when each element of the APR model is put into practice. Each vignette is constructed as an example of an APR element when an issue has surfaced, and a conflict needs resolution. Authentic conflict resolution requires two hearts to be present and engaged. Conflict resolution is an "ego-free" experience.

Address: The step of addressing acknowledges "what happened" (that is, stating the heart-versus-ego conflict) from "the other side":

- Addressing is a statement of *the heart* "experience," because "what happened" *was the* experience. It happened. The words of the heart share about the experience.
- Heart speaks the words and/or actions that have been presented; the impact of the experience, including emotions, physical

sensations, and innermost thoughts. The words describe how the event lives from the heart's perspective.

- Ego is *not present* when making the statement of address. There is no defending, denying, dismissing, diverting, or redirecting.
- *Address* means *acknowledge* and *own*.

Let's look at two examples. First, when your ego has FACED their heart, your conversation of addressing may sound like this:

> That is what happened. I was judging you, being critical, putting my expectations on you. All those choices I made were not loving or thoughtful. They were mean and vindictive. I said them. I did not honor you in the moment. I didn't pay attention to you and what you needed. I didn't allow or accept you and your circumstances . . .

Second, when your heart is FACED by their ego, your addressing the conflict may sound like this:

> I shared my thoughts about how to spend the holidays as you asked. I said it was important to see my parents, because they are getting up in their years. When you walked away, I felt disrespected, as though my opinion did not count, and my family didn't matter. It left me feeling that my perspective and ideas were irrelevant. It was as though you had said, "I don't care!" I didn't get the sense that you appreciated what I had to say.

Once the issue has been addressed, and once words and actions have been owned, the next part of the work is to identify what was going on that caused the response from ego versus living from the heart with regard to this event. The next step is . . .

Process: The step of processing expresses the emotions and state of being that were present and part of the experience:

- These emotions may not have been realized at the time, but with time and reflection, a healthy adult can render what happened in words.

- The processing element of APR requires unvarnished reflection from a humble, compassionate perspective, because it speaks to the "injustice"—the hurt and pain experienced.

  I didn't realize I was so angry. I was hurt. My heart hurt. I was in pain and did not have any outlet, no one to talk to, no place to go. I felt alone, and I was hurting. But most of all, I was deeply sad, but at that time, I did not have the ability to have the perspective that I have today. I can now see things more clearly. I know now how much my lack of awareness and lashing out hurt you.

This element is not about making "excuses" for behavior; rather, it is to figure out "what happened," what was underneath the choice to move away from love and hide behind ego as this event unfolded. The words are often raw and precise, sharp like the words of ego are *but* as an observation of "what was happening" in the moment. Think of *process* as "the impact" of the words and actions of ego. The observation progresses beyond the "reaction" down to the essence of emotions and lack of awareness (in this example). All being owned by the speaker; the impact of words and actions is the *processing*.

Resolve: The step of resolving generates a commitment to be more aware and to change behavior if and when the issue surfaces in the future (which it most likely will):

- The objective of APR is to be more aware, and sooner next time; to handle things in a healthier manner; to be more consciously attentive, more thoughtful, and more patient.
- Resolving involves:
  - A recommitment to one's life purpose, to love your self and love with abundance, living from the heart.
  - A commitment to change, *and*
  - Making an agreement, *and then*
  - Being accountable to keep the agreement.

Speaking a healthy resolution with an agreement and commitment might sound like:

> It was my responsibility to speak up sooner rather than later. My silence and unilateral decision without checking in with you broke our trust, and it hurts the relationship. Next time, I will commit to speaking up, rather than acting on my own, and to asking your opinion before making a decision of this magnitude.

Or

> I was angry in the moment and acted out of anger. I apologize. I am committed to living from my heart, to loving you with acceptance and appreciation, and to allowing my self to experience my emotions, but to express them in a healthy manner—which I did not do, and that was hurtful. I am truly sorry for the harm I caused and the pain you experience from what I did.

Or

> I am committed to speaking up and to discussing decisions with you. I am human, and I won't be perfect—I will notice any anger or sadness, and I am committed to expressing my emotions in a healthy manner. Hopefully, my doing this will bring us closer and will deepen our connection . . .

These brief vignettes model the language and intent of each element of the APR model. Your task is to understand the purpose of each element, which is summarized in the following discussion.

Processing conflicts with APR: The APR model provides you the opportunity to do your work to restore love and heal hearts.

First is addressing, when you step back and reflect on "what happened." What is the nature of the event that caused the disconnect? Was there an injustice done? What were the words and actions of ego? What was their impact on the heart? This is when you distinguish the event in terms of identifying ego on one side and heart on the other.

Next is processing, which states the impact of the event. This perspective can be stated several ways. What was the cost to your heart? Or theirs? What was the impact of choosing ego in terms of moving "away from" or "disconnecting from" love? How did ego show up? What triggered it? What did ego respond with? What did ego say? What actions did it take against love or your (or the other's) heart? There is always an emotional wound to the heart. This is what you are searching for: What is the "cost" of the conflict in terms of emotional damage or wounding?

In closing, you are bringing the event "full circle" to find resolution. Your commitment is to raise your awareness about what triggered the event. You are making amends about the issue, the words, and actions involved. At this point, commitments are made! To what? Committing to make an agreement to do something *different* in the future, to *make another choice* in the future, and to *not respond from ego* but rather to live from your heart in the moment! This is the agreement you make. You are resolving the issue *with your commitment to keep your agreement.* This concept is absolutely critical, because it represents the outcome that brings you and "them" back to love. The concept of the commitment and agreements are covered in more detail as we progress, but this summary sets the foundation.

Let's dig into issues for a moment. Usually at the source of issues that surface in a relationship are "what happened" incidents, damage or injustice, which have been carried from the past into the present. The scar of an old wound being triggered causes the ego to jump in by attacking, defending, judging, punishing, and so on. These examples show the source of these old items. It is worth noting that even if you have done a good portion of your work, old wounds and scars can be triggered, and the triggering is often unexpected. Listen to these events to hear "what happened"; notice the words in *italics*:

> When I started to do the taxes and asked you a question,
> you jumped in and took over. *They were right.* I can never get

anything right. Even when I try my hardest, *I always come up short.* Now you are telling me *I am not good enough.*

You want me to stop being so emotional! You are telling me I can't feel the way I feel! *My feelings have never mattered.* It's like *I don't matter.* No one cares. It's like *I have been invisible all my life.* I guess in this relationship I don't really matter.

You asked me to look up the address and get directions. That is exactly what I did. When I started to tell you, you didn't want to listen. All I wanted to do was give you what you asked for. All *I want to do is please you* and *make you happy.* But nothing is *ever enough (not good enough). I feel worthless.* I have felt this way my whole life. *When I try to help, it always turns out bad or makes things worse.*

You decided you could make the decision without me. So, what you're saying is *I don't matter.* We are supposed to be together, but you make decision with no consideration about my opinions. *No one thinks I matter*, or that I am smart or that what I say counts for anything.

The "damage," or wound, to heart is set out in *italic* letters. This is what needs to be healed. Conflict resolution is a bridge for the restoration of love. It spans the chasm created when ego perpetrates an injustice or causes damage. The resolution happens when love fills the chasm.

These examples highlight some "old wounds" that have been carried from "early on" as well as new heart-versus-ego conflicts in the current relationship. The APR model is designed to restore love, to make it whole, in both instances. In other words, the APR model restores the love after ego has created distance between partners or when a heart wound held in memory has been triggered by an event in a current relationship.

The APR conflict resolution model has a twofold purpose. First, it creates an opening for healing the sadness that remained from an early wound or love that was lost or missing. The sadness is ultimately what is revealed when an event in the present triggers an old wound. Experiencing the sadness, you have learned is how those wounds and scars are healed. The added benefit in a relationship is that the restoration of love can be a *shared* experience with a partner. How so? When one partner grants the other a measure of the abundant love they possess. They pay attention to you during your experience, they accept your experience as part of your self (your past and you in the present), they appreciate you in your circumstances, and maybe they express loving affection by holding you as you experience the sadness. These actions represent the highest level of conflict resolution: when love pours in to fill the space created by whatever issue surfaced, no matter the source—past or present.

Second, the APR model provides the opening to restore whatever measure of love is needed for repair of *new* relationship-related conflicts (conflicts of heart versus ego that are not associated with a wound or damage from "early on")—by granting acceptance of "what happened," by allowing it to be OK with a shared commitment to be more aware in the future, and by paying closer attention to responses when wounds are triggered. Each partner appreciates the value of the experience, even though it had created a temporary disconnect. Love expands and deepens as a result of the lessons or insights into your self and your past or that of your partner. Each of you exhibits the capacity to handle the sadness, fear, and anger as well as the highs of joy, happiness, and ecstasy of the restoration.

Up to this point, the focus has been to illustrate the full circle of a conflict resolution that returns your relationship to the place where you love your self and each other more completely, more fully.

In a romantic love relationship, when conflicts between heart and ego are addressed, processed, and resolved to completion, here is what happens:

**The APR model deconstructs and dissolves ego,
which had created a void and distance
in the relationship.
The opening is an empty space between the two,
which can be filled by the partners
choosing to restore their shared love.**

Healthy conflict resolution identifies the voice and the language of ego *and* brings the darkness of ego into the bright light of truth, where ego cannot survive. The bright light of truth is love, and when love is present in a relationship, there is no space or place for ego.

With the full APR model in place, we can move to . . .

Healthy Conflict Resolution

Healthy conflict resolution exposes ego to the bright light of truth and defines whether or not the "choice" of the relationship is to "live from the heart": love. This knowledge goes well beyond "good to know." Your capacity for conflict resolution with your partner tells you the direction your relationship is headed. It will take one path (love) or the other (ego). The path of ego is a slow death march to "The End," extinguishing any love that was present. The path of love is vibrant and filled with the possibility for more love and more joy, peace, contentment, and ecstasy in life!

Your work is learning how to respond as events and issues surface. Your challenge is to respond from heart with love. Let's refer again to the "vocabulary list" of ego. Recall any dialog from your personal experience of caregivers or from your past relationships when some or all of ego's vocabulary was used, coming downhill at you. Your work is to clearly distinguish how the ego sounded from people you know or from other relationships. If possible, an excellent exercise is to work through how you would use the APR model to resolve one of these heart-versus-ego conflicts. The conversation you recall may contain some of ego's favorites, such as "you are not good enough" or "you're worthless" or "you are unlovable" or any refrains that were telling you *should, could or would.*

This exercise focuses on listening to your own voice and resolving the conversation of ego back to love. This may seem a bit odd, but it is worth some effort on your part. Why? This is the work of conflict resolution, and given the importance to your self and relationships, it a skill that you need to be adept at using.

One final note that is worth mentioning here: There is one personality type that *only* operates from ego (which you may know). Instead of a heart, there is a "void"—in other words, no love. We'll discuss this situation in the next chapter. There is a strategy for surviving in a relationship with a partner who is heartless and blind to love. If you are married to this type, there is a specific conversation to add to your skills, which is exemplified in a section in Chapter 6. Now let's conclude the discussion of conflict resolution by looking at a healthy model.

Conflict Resolution Modeled

It's useful to put the skill of conflict resolution and the APR method in the overall, big-picture view of the skills and awareness you have gained up to this point. Here is a quick review of what skills and awareness are in place for you today:

- the definition of love and ego;
- the active choices when choosing to love (the five A's);
- to know you choose to "live from the heart" (or not);
- the choice to "love your self" and how you do it;
- the construct of the heart-versus-ego dynamic;
- the mutual exclusivity of heart versus ego;
- knowledge of the words and perspective of ego ("not to love");
- knowledge of the contrasts between the five A's and FACED;
- the healthy experience and expression of emotions;
- the importance of preferences and selling out;

- the importance of conflict resolution skills;

And add the most recently added skill:

- the APR method to dissolve ego with love.

Conflict resolution connects all the dots. Connecting all these dots *is* being a healthy adult. You understand more clearly with each awareness and with each opportunity to practice that *you* are *becoming* healthier. This is "Riding Your Bike 101"; now you are riding the bike!

Since you have gained the awareness of these vital skills, you will find it hard to be witness to a conversation and *not* immediately distinguish attention, acceptance, and appreciation, or *not* hear those sharp off-key notes of control, critiques, judgments, entitlement, or condescension. Being healthy, your observation would probably sound like this:

> **"Wow! That is a conflict between heart and ego.**
> **I know the language of ego and love.**
>
> **There is *no* love and**
> ***no* heart in that conversation . . ."**

The more you pay attention, the more the off-key notes of ego will stand out. When you are in the middle of one of those conversations, the opportunity to share some of your abundant love is created. Now we move forward with . . .

Reconciliation: From the Heart

It should be abundantly clear to you that the voice speaking the words of restoration and reconciliation is the voice of love and heart. The heart initiates the work of resolving conflict. How this materializes is described in the following examples.

The first item to note is this voice could be inside you or spoken at you. The source is not important, the "perspective" of the speaker is. The accusations, judgments, and demeaning phrases are crisp and cutting? All ego. The replies here are spoken from the perspective of the heart, and its response is choosing to love:

(Ego) "Oh my!! You have always been so bad. All those terrible choices in relationships! How could you possibly be OK with *your* past!"

> (Heart) "Yes, I made some choices that were not the best. I know now I was doing the best I could with what I knew at the time, with what I was aware of about my self and how to handle the circumstances at that time. I made those choices, and my choices caused hardships, hurt, heartache, and pain. Today, I choose to love my self, and I accept my self where I am today as a more aware person because of my past. I will pay attention to my needs, my emotions, all of me. Going forward, I will be more diligent to notice when I am backsliding away from love. I will appreciate my self. I love me."

(Ego) "Wow, you have been stuck in a rut for weeks and should have gotten over it by way before now. What is the matter with you? What is wrong?"

> (Heart) "Yes, I have been stuck in this spot for a while. I have been struggling to resolve some issues and am not quite there yet. I know there is nothing wrong with me, and I know that sometimes life is about struggles, difficult circumstances, and being stuck. I accept who I am completely, and I choose to love my self by granting my self the allowance and freedom to be in this struggle at this time in my life. I am OK being here in the middle of it, for as long as it takes, and I choose to love my self 'here.'"

(Ego) "Why do you insist on touching and holding hands every time we are out in public? It's so embarrassing. It's so uncalled for. You 'should' know better, or at least care what other people think about you holding hands!"

(Heart) "Yes, I love touch. I love affection. When I experience touch, I experience love. My holding hands fills my need and desire to love others by being affectionate, and I also enjoy being loved, sharing the affection of others—particularly my partner. Affection and being affectionate is one of my preferences: holding hands, walking arm in arm, cuddling, snuggling. Touching is a way I experience love, and I cherish that part of me."

(Ego) "Why do you take so much time getting ready? You are always late. You should be on time!"

(Heart) "For a long time, I did not pay attention to my self. I was not important. I appreciate my self more when I feel good about how I look, to me! And I want to look my best. Paying attention to what I wear—my hair, my shoes—is one way I love my self. I have not respected others by being late on occasion. Mostly I am on time, but I accept that sometimes I am late. Being on time is important when I have committed to be somewhere. I want to show my appreciation for others and my self by valuing and honoring my commitments. I will work on being on time and keeping my commitments.

These are the "conversations" between heart and ego. These examples have been about you and the conversations of your internal heart-versus-ego conflicts. Their purpose is to distinguish the language of ego (yours) and how it differs from the "action" (that is, choice) to love (your self).

I pointed out earlier that you can give only what you have. That reference was stated in the context of "love your self." You must know "love your self" before you can give love to someone else. The same dynamic applies with conflict resolution. When you know from your personal experience how to resolve the conflicts of your heart and your ego, *then* you can give conflict resolution to others. The beauty of being able to model love and conflict resolution in your life has several dimensions.

First, it calls upon you to raise your awareness and actively choose to love. You are not a "victim of love"; love *is* your choice. Learning to love your self is the first mountain to climb, the first battle you must win: learning to speak from your heart, to "love your self," to resolve your own personal conflicts between heart and ego.

Second, you become healthier in a steady, progressive fashion as you become more and more comfortable speaking the truth of love from your heart. This is when you have love in *abundance.* You can share love, outbound, with anyone, in virtually any circumstance, in whatever measure is needed.

Third, using the APR skills you have gained, you contradict the language and accusations of ego to resolve what is unresolved in your past. You acknowledge what happened (address); you state the impact, the cost, what was lost, and the pain (process); and then you give your self each element of the five A's to fill the "gap" (resolve). It cannot be emphasized enough, but this third item is a critical component of your skills and awareness—doing *your work* to repair and heal from *your past!*

Finally, the practice of addressing, processing, and resolving issues is what you, as a healthy adult, employ when conflicts happen in relationships. So, the stakes are just as high. A few more words about addressing "what happened" in your past and applying the APR model are in order . . .

Reconciling Your Past

When ego speaks, whether it is in your own head or in the conversations around you, it is as though a buzzer or warning signal had sounded. You can immediately pick out the nuanced language that is "not love." Even though you consciously want to love with all your heart, you cannot, nor will you ever, be free from "the voice of the other"—ego. No matter how healthy you become, no matter how much of your work you do, that voice is always lurking to confront you and derail your relationships.

As you develop your "listening," you notice that sometimes the words of ego are laid in softly like a feather, and other times the words of ego land like a sledgehammer. But you notice.

When you dissect a conversation, your work is to call out the lies of ego with the truth, the language of love. To resolve this for your self and your relationships, you use the APR method. Where do you start? Where do you learn? Where do you practice? I suggest with the conversations you know best. You and the conversations in your past and present . . . with your self.

Why is it necessary to address the voice in your head? Because the words you speak to your self create your perspective for your world and shape your experience in life. Yes. If you are focused on love and lovemaking and loving life, the universe will present love to you. You will be open to experience more joy, see more beauty, and notice the magnificence around you. You will be living in a world that is expanding, growing with abundance.

However, the opposite is also true. If you are consistently hearing the limiting, defeated sounds of ego, if your heart is constantly FACED by your ego, guess what? As you journey through your day, your conversations about life will be cloaked in fears, arrogance, anger, condescension, control, expectations, and entitlement. As you can see, it is critical for you to notice your own conversations so that you can hear your self sliding out of the heart conversations and into the dark side of ego. Don't go full on Catholic Guilt on your self because, suddenly, as you become aware, you realize that you slip into that ego mode . . . a lot!! That is the work!! That happens to be where we *all* start. The key is to *begin* to notice. That is the starting point.

The first practice, then, begins with your thought life for resolving the conflicts between your heart and your ego. Early in this practice, it is likely that the conflicts within you originate from your past. These are "items" that you have consciously or unconsciously chosen not to resolve. It's OK. If you could have resolved them before and realized the benefit from doing so, you would have, but you are working on them now.

A common term to describe events of the past is *baggage*, and this word I find appalling and totally inappropriate. It's a pejorative label, which does not fit. If someone never had the skills to address their past or gain awareness, how can their life be baggage? "What happened" in their past is *their life*. Life is not baggage. The phrase to use is *unresolved issues*. The term puts "life" in a different context because it is OK to have unresolved issues (in other words, allowing). You are OK with having these today (acceptance). Why? You start down the road to being healthy where you are standing *right now*; you don't get to "go back." You play the hand you are holding with the cards life has dealt you. That is why you do your work to address "past" issues. And you are OK with the hand you are holding. No worries.

Where do you begin to reconcile your past? You start by simply listening to your self, by being aware of the conversation you have to or with your self. No one else is privy to these conversations. They are your thought life. They sound much like any conversation around you. Because it is guaranteed in your conversation with your self that either heart or ego is speaking. You know these conversations intimately. Which one is speaking is usually dependent on your past and your circumstances. This portion of your work is the process of resolving issues that were left unresolved from your past, which you carry in your heart today. That is how you reconcile your past—so your past *becomes* your past rather than your present.

At this point, you have all the skills and tools to do this work. The skills are "love your self," your awareness of heart versus ego, and the model for conflict resolution—the APR methodology.

How did you arrive at the place where the words of ego, "not love," began to dominate your internal thought life? It's simple. Most stories read something like the following short version of "what happened" from a client:

Once upon a time, I loved my self. Then over time, as the circumstances of my life unfolded, I loved my self less and less. I didn't see what was happening. I just accepted what the voices around me were saying about the conditions and circumstances of my life and me, and these voices diminished the "real" me. I hardly noticed that the real me was fading into the background. Nor did I notice that what was filling in the "gaps" were all the lies and deceptions about me . . . which I bought into!!!

Eventually, I could not hear the voice of my heart. All I heard were "not good enough," "unlovable," "worthless," "can't," "don't try," "quitter." . . . Then, somehow, some way, I "woke up" and realized that "something" was missing. Maybe God stirred my heart [yes, He did, in fact].

Whatever was awakened in me that pushed back against the lies. Something in me said, "That is not the truth about who you are." I realized what was missing was the unconditional love I knew was inside me . . . for my self and others and life. Love in my life was missing. "Love my self" was not what I was experiencing. Love in me had diminished. Love was a rare experience. It was not an "always" or "mostly" experience. Love was supposed to be joy and freedom. I realized I had been missing love in my life. Love *was* missing in my life.

Today, I am committed to finding answers and changing. Now I want to know what love is. Resisting and countering the lies about me is hard; it's difficult to change, but I am committed to becoming aware and becoming healthy. And loving my self is the first step.

I find that vignette moving. That last sentence signals where you entered the "on ramp" on the highway to becoming healthy. The evidence change has begun is that you have chosen to act and have begun to search for answers. Now on to the work of "reconciliation". . .

"What's next" is to address and reconcile all those "what happened" events you experienced. Maybe you won't address all of them, but you will begin to work on the ones that have impacted you the most. All the events and circumstances that undermined the love placed in your heart when you were born. Those things that weakened and diminished love—today you know those were not love; they were ego, the voice of ego. The words were "inbound" at you, and your mistake was to believe "them." You did not know you could listen to your heart. It's OK, because if they didn't show you, then you didn't know how to distinguish the voice of your heart. It's OK. You were never taught that love has always been "in" you. It's OK. Because you are "here" now; you are aware.

Those "events" and "things" that happened need your attention. The effect of the "what happened" events through all the years has slowly and steadily chipped away at the essence of your heart, which *is* your source of and store of love. All the events that caused a hurt or pain impacted your ability and capacity to love your self. They impacted your ability to love your neighbor *as your self*; this was diminished as well.

To reconcile your past and restore love, you must give love to your self. Each time you were hurt or suffered an injustice, a bit of your heart was sliced away. Left unresolved, with each nick or cut, a piece of your heart was left behind. These blows or wounds to your heart have remained locked away in you. They have never been "healed," and that is now the work of reconciling your past.

What are you reconciling? The lies. When the "other" voice in you, the one that speaks the language of ego, speaks *to you* to diminish, condemn, judge, criticize, or any other words that ego speaks about your self, you answer with a statement about each element of the five A's. It's that simple.

As you look back, with your newfound awareness knowing love, you understand the real impact of these hurts and wounds as the years passed. "What happened?" You *appreciated* your self less and didn't *allow* your self to be OK in your seasons of struggle. When life was rockin', you didn't take it all in, because you were told to "temper" your joy and euphoria; so, you did, you cut off the "feel good" so you wouldn't enjoy "joy" too much (*crazy talk!!!*).

You didn't pay *attention* to your self, and you didn't *accept* that you were OK just the way you were, and as a result of "not being OK," you discovered that you were less connected to your self and less willing to connect to others (that is, experience *affection*). All of this you carried with you through the years. How they showed up then is how the "other" voice speaks to you today, in the present.

These wounds resurface as a conflict between your heart and ego. The source of the conflict is the deafening voice of ego. The language of ego speaks all those refrains that were shoved down your throat or relentlessly came at you in a relationship, downhill at you. These words you hear clearly. The purpose of ego is to drown out the voice of your heart: love. You know that those ego words are not love. They are *not* your heart.

Today (and going forward), your work is to address, process, and *resolve . . . your past*. You resolve using the APR method. APR describes the actions (steps) you take to reassemble your self. You are returning your self, by your means, to be a healthy adult who lives from your heart. Only you can do this work for your self. "They" (caregivers, family, past partners) cannot do it for you. If they could have, they would have done it before—back then.

Now the work is up to you. But the good news is you have everything you need. To love your self is within your power, and you can give love to your self. How beautiful is that!! How sweet is it!!

> **FACT:**
> **When you love your self,**
> **you are complete and whole.**
> **You are missing nothing.**
> **You have love in abundance to give.**

Grace, Forgiveness, and Agreements

The work of healing your past is often difficult. Recalling the conversations about how love was installed is painful sometimes. Earlier, you were encouraged to begin looking at how love was modeled for you. You have been shown many examples of "the ideal" installation and the healthy model of love.

You know most installations fell short of "ideal" or "healthy." Some missed by a small measure, others by a lot. It all happened before you could spell the word *damage*. That is "what happened." Unaware, you moved forward through your life, and you carried the "shortfall" of your model and installation of love. That is OK. Today, with your self as your resource, *you* will now fill in the "gaps" of what was missing.

Where do you find what is missing? Where are the "gaps"?

They show up in internal conversations you have to your self. They are the issues that surface in your relationships. Being angry, anxious, distracted, condescending, doubting, and any other examples of the language of ego show you where your "gaps" are, show you how love and relationships were modeled for you. This distinction of conflict you observed between heart and ego has its source *in what you were given early on.*

"What's next" is working with the model of healthy adult love. The gap between "ideal" and what you were given—that difference is your work. The method of filling the gaps, the "how to," has been described in each of the vignettes you have read in this chapter. Every conflict and resolution tells the story about "what happened." Every incident of a preference being sold out or boundary being given up is an example of "what happened." There are more stories in the chapters to come.

You have all the tools, but the truth is that the actual "doing" will take some time. Listening to your inner thought life from the perspective of heart versus ego gives you the answers to where you need to go to restore your heart.

You dismiss the lies and speak the truth about how you love your self. You have the formula as well. With each event or circumstance, you notice where ego comes downhill on your heart. These are what you are challenged to resolve, with love.

The APR model is your guide:

- Identify and address "what happened." You speak the words.

And:

- Process the "lies" and "what is missing," granting to your self any element of love that the lies diminished.

Then:

- Resolve to "the truth," which is *your* truth . . .

> **You love your self, and**
> **you grant your self each of the five A's,**
> **in the measure you need of each one.**

- Accept the infinite Grace granted to you for your life and the circumstances of your unique journey to experience love.

And:

- Find forgiveness for your self and for "them," from the love you have in abundance:
  - giving your self the attention you need for this work,
  - accepting life as it happened,
  - appreciating your gifts and talents and the lessons that the universe has shown you,
  - noticing you have the capacity to weather any storm and experience both sadness and joy (affection),
  - and allowing your self to be OK in any season you find your self in today.

Then:

- Make an agreement to "love your self" in all circumstances you encounter in your future:

- ◆ paying attention to your needs and desires,
- ◆ accepting your self as you are, that you are OK and growing in your awareness,
- ◆ appreciating who you are today as a unique being,
- ◆ embracing the company of others and being OK when you are "with your self,"
- ◆ and allowing your self the full experience of each season and circumstance you are presented with in your future.
- Your commitment is to keep this agreement to love your self in these ways.

And:

- You hold your self accountable when "something happens" and when you do not keep your commitment (*you retrace your steps at that point to APR that event*).

That is the full model of reconciling your past. The truth is you are enough; you are lovable, you are valuable, you are whole and complete. Your resolved past arrives with the words:

"Yes, I love my self."

As this section on reconciling your past is concluded, hopefully, you see the implications here regarding relationships.

Being healthy, loving your self, means you are missing nothing. You have the capacity and ability to love your self, and you are not missing anything. Loving your self means you are stepping into any relationship with nothing missing. You do not need "an other" to give you "something," because you have all the love you need. You have chosen to give it to your self. There is not *any aspect* of love that you must find from someone else.

With your freedom and abundance of love, *now* you are seeking a relationship with an "equal." With your romantic love partner:

- You can give to them "all you have"
  - ◆ in the manner they want to experience love . . . *and*

- You can experience being loved *in the way you want, because*
- They, too, are whole and complete, *and*
- They have an abundant source of love
    - which they give to you.

Does that describe the "Holy Grail" of relationships? Of love relationships? Of romantic love relationships? Absolutely! Before we move deeper into relationships, though, let's take a quick inventory of the journey up to this point. . . . It's important to keep everything we have covered in focus because it is a lot of "stuff" . . .

Where Are You Now?

The journey you have taken to "now" is all part of you "seeing" your self with a new perspective. Before you started this work, each morning when you looked at your self, what you saw was a two-dimensional being: (1) the inside, and (2) the outside. But is that correct? Yes and no. Seeing your self "with perspective" calls on your capacity to understand the depth of your being more completely, with more understanding and more clarity about what *is* inside your self.

If you look closely at you, you discern at least five dimensions to your self. The outside, the inside, your brain unit (your cognitive ability to comprehend and reason logic), your heart, and your ego. Let's review these with a bit more context about each one:

- You have your **external physical body**—your face, limbs and your whole exterior.
- You have all the **internal physical parts**—blood, your lungs and other organs.
- You have your "responding" and "thinking" **brain**. These comprise "System 1" and "System 2," which were described in Chapter 3. I don't know where these are located in your head, but these are nonetheless your "brain," which reacts to the world and thinks and reasons about such problems as what road to take and what

movie you want to watch when you are standing in front of the Redbox.

- You have your **heart**, where **love** resides in you, Love resides in your heart; whether it can be seen on an X ray or not, love is in there.
- You have **ego**, the "other part" inside, which is **not love**. I don't know exactly where ego resides "in" you, but it's in there somewhere (maybe it's in your foot or earlobe).

From this perspective, you are more like a diamond that has many facets.

The truth is for your entire life, you have never been "missing" anything. You have been whole and complete all day, every day, for your entire life. You have been perfect "just the way you are" from "once upon a time" until today. The circumstances around you were changing *while* you were changing. "Now" (that is, today), you have a different perspective, which has arrived with an awareness about your self.

Resolving to Mine Your Gold

Your newfound skills, knowledge, and awareness have given you a new view of "you," which is *your whole self.* You now "see" dimensions of your self that were not clearly visible to you before, and now your view is different.

There is a sentence that often arrives in conversations when all of this new perspective and awareness takes hold, which is this: "Wow, things sure would have been different, *if only* I knew *then* what I know *now!*" This dull refrain is like fingernails dragging down a chalkboard to me. It's not true. It's another lie. It brings to mind several thoughts.

The first thought is MOTO (Master Of The Obvious). Of course, things *could have been different.* But *if* you were different "then," the fact is you would be different *today.*

The fact is—or, more accurately, *how life works* is—you would have encountered "other circumstances" in your life, which you would have needed to experience. The conditions of your life are the learning experiences for your growth—always. You need what the universe gives you to become healthier and love more, wherever you are. Becoming healthy is not a place you arrive "at." It's not like going to San Francisco and landing at SFO: "We're here!!!"

> **Growing and becoming healthier is a "journey."**
> **It not a "destination."**
> **Your destination is "The End."**

On your journey, you observe where you are, what is passing by today, what you reflect on in your past, and what you dream lies ahead. That describes your journey. It happens to have a familiar nickname called: *your life.*

The phrase "if things would have been *different*" is the uncomfortable lament of "*if only . . .*"

These "different" events that are about your past were not acts of love and kindness, people not living from the heart, not giving and receiving love. In summary, those "If only's" and "shoulda, coulda, woulda's" are most often related to people and circumstances that were "not loving." "If only . . ." misses the point, because using your skills and awareness to reconcile your life gives you something valuable:

> **Addressing, processing, and resolving**
> **all the circumstances of your life back to love,**
> **is where and how you "mine *your* gold"**
> **from your life experiences!**

The "gold" you mine paves the way to being healthy *so that you can* create healthy relationships in your future. Reconciling your past is how you mine the gold, which you use for the journey to come. This is "divine purpose." No one is exempt; everyone has the opportunity to mine the gold . . . which brings us to the next thought, the third and final thought about "if only":

> ***No one* has the right or the room to speak the words**
> **"If only *you* [fill in the blank] . . ."**
> **or**
> **"YOU shoulda, coulda, woulda [fill in the blank] . . ."**
> **to *you*, at *you*,**
> **or about *you* or *your life* or *your choices.***

Those words are *their* ego coming downhill with judgment and critique and arrogance *at you.* They are spoken with the intent to shame and guilt you, whether intentionally or unconsciously. Today, you *know* these words and where these words are coming from: Ego. Not love.

If you get nothing else from my book, get that!! These are the most common ways that ego shows its pathetically ugly face. Tragically, these words often come from those to whom you are the closest—your children, your parents, your siblings, your partners. That is just plain sad.

But, wow, it seems to be the truth of your experience. Living from your heart gives you another perspective. When you are FACED with their ego, your healthy response to those who speak at you from their ego is to respond from your heart:

> **You choose to love them**
> **where they are with their ego,**
> **giving them attention, acceptance, appreciation,**
> **affection, and allowing them to be OK,**
> **even in their state of being unaware.**

This perspective on "how to love" those who choose not to live from their heart is addressed more in depth as we look at relationships in the sections ahead.

I hope you gain the full dimension of the truth about "mining your gold." It is a truth you take in just as you take your next breath: a "breath of truth," which stays in you and with you forever. The truth about mining your gold is simple:

**Grab hold of the knowledge you have been given,
apply it to your self and to your life.
Your gold is your awareness about how to
experience more *love* in your life.**

When you mine your gold, "what's next" is your experience of love for your self and others as a deeper, richer, more joyful, and more satisfying experience than before you realized that you needed to figure some things out about you, about love, about life, and about relationships.

All the things you have gained to this point are important. The parts and pieces of you, love, the five A's, choosing to love or to not love, FACED, ego, loving your self—these are all things you need to know and to be aware of. They need to "live" in you as clear distinctions about your self and your life. Yes, if just being aware changes your perspective about your self, that would be a big win in and of itself. There are some more major wins for you, but what you have been made aware of so far is valuable; like discovering diamonds and gold in your self, awareness reveals the hidden treasures of your life.

One of the biggest treasures for you is reconciling your past, to understand "what happened." Next would be with your awareness expanding how you can see "you" more clearly today. Your capacity and ability to love your self means that regardless of what happened, you hold the power of choose love, and you can give your self love, by simply choosing to give love to your self. The power to love is *in you*. You also knew that love is a sharp, two-edged sword.

If you choose not to love your self, you cannot experience the gift of loving others. You just can't, not in the "full measure" of love anyway. But when you choose to love your self, your ability to give love is boundless. Infinite. But loving is an either-or paradox. You can choose to love or not to love. You get to *choose*.

"Choosing" is what free will is all about! Think about it:

Free will is having a choice.
The choice is always:
to live from the heart and love . . .
or not.

Knowing this truth about life and love is invaluable. Love (and life) becomes a richer, more satisfying experience *because you choose*. Now we dig a bit deeper in our conversation about relationships.

Maybe you need more time on the conflict resolution and reconciliation section. That is totally understandable. If you do, thumb back through the pages and take whatever time you need.

Feel free to write me directly and ask any question you may have; maybe it's for clarity or how these skills and practices might relate to you and your circumstances or to life, or maybe you just disagree and want to share your opinion. That works. My direct email is: spencer.wendt@ gmail.com. I am available for you.

Now on to relationships . . . *healthy* relationships!!

Chapter 6.

Healthy Relationships

Figuring out how to lay out and navigate through a discussion on relationships was quite a challenge. You notice the previous chapter was titled "Relationships" and that it introduced several key concepts that are foundations and "must haves," such as boundaries, emotions (defined, experiencing, and expressing), conflict resolution, and reconciling your past (mining your gold). This chapter is titled "Healthy Relationships."

With the "Relationships" foundation set and in place, "what's next" is refining the discussion and layering in some additional skills. On that note, after a few starts and restarts, I have decided to discuss healthy relationships from two perspectives. This seems like the best way to tackle the subject.

The first perspective follows the pattern used in this work up to this point: viewing relationships from the standpoint of "you" being healthy. The conversation is aligned with and stays consistent with the idea of "being/becoming healthy."

The second perspective combines "you being healthy" with the second theme of the book: "creating and maintaining healthy relationships." All the parts, awareness, tricks and tips, and skills that have gone into your "awareness-about-you" tool kit are going to be applied to relationships. Yes, you'll be adding a few new skills as well.

It would be impossible to create a sound presentation that only addressed aspects of "healthy" relationships. Why? Unfortunately, there are far more unhealthy relationships than there are healthy ones. To approach this from a strictly healthy point of view would imply that there are *a lot* of healthy prospects out there. You've been "in the market," or dating, for a while, maybe for a long time. You know the difficulty of having *just one* wholesome conversation, much less getting a date with a healthy person. That is a monumental task, because the pool of healthy prospects is rather thin. A large portion of the conversation will be covering "the other side" of relating: unhealthy people and unhealthy relationships. Remember, this approach of presenting all perspectives is the "360" model: speaking the truth in love!

By the way, it would be a ton easier to talk about the healthy side only!! But, taking a "healthy-only" approach would be failing to deliver. Because the truth is that most of us know far more about the unhealthy side of partners, relationships, and people than we ever thought we would. Why? Because there are *far more* unhealthy people looking for relationships than there are healthy ones. You would like to avoid these people at all cost. Given your active life and your desire to be efficient with your time, you may *choose* to look for a partner using match, "*where broken people agree to meet for coffee before sex*".com. In case you find your self looking for a needle in "the match haystack," I guarantee all your effort taking in this work to become healthy and the added skills will be worth a thousand times the price you paid for my book. Just sayin' . . .

In this "unhealthy light," know in advance that this chapter and Chapter 7 contain a rather large dose of scenarios and vignettes presenting the "dark side" of relationships and the damage to people caught in unhealthy relationships. Some are the shared experience of clients and friends. Some reflect my personal experience. Some of these you may be familiar with as well. Included in the "unhealthy" sections are topics that are commonly found in unhealthy people and relationships: such items as codependency, addiction, narcissistic partners, narcissistic parents (or in-laws), selling out, attachment issues, fantasy bonds, and more.

Presenting a balanced perspective is intended to raise your awareness and provide you with more understanding when "things happen." If you or someone you know is stuck in a situation that is unhealthy, there are some methods laid out to help you "take back your life" as well. These methods explain how to protect your self, recapture your heart, and return you to "love your self" again. Whether you are starting out, are starting over, or are currently in an unhealthy situation, the conversation can help you recover—especially if you have recently exited a particularly unhealthy relationship.

You + Love + Relationships

Didn't we start this section already?!

I sense with all of this "awareness" I have,

the most important relationship I have is

the relationship I have "with my self"!!

Ding, Ding, Ding!! Winner, winner, chicken dinner!! (*Unless you are from BoldAir, you can make the preceding sentence politically correct by scratching out the poultry reference and replacing it with "tofu" or "free range" or "organic free" . . . whatever you need to love you!!*)

You probably guessed by now the answer is "Yes . . ." Your relationship "with your self" is the one that matters most. Discovering that you are 100-percent lovable and that you possess the power to love with an abundance is B.I.G. You have everything you need and can give your self any measure of the five A's to satisfy all your value, worth, and so on. You love your self. You need no one, because you are whole and complete *just the way you are.*

On the relationship front, the romantic love relationship experience is rather simple. It's all about love. In this light, it makes sense to cut to the chase and address the questions "What happened?" and "Why do relationships fail?" We'll knock this one out first. Then the least desirable outcome is known up front. All the effort beyond that will be about avoiding that scenario.

For all that is written and practiced, every relationships success or failure is dependent on one and only one thing:

> **When one partner makes an offer to engage or connect**
> **by living from their heart,**
> **and**
> **the other partner responds with rejection or avoidance**
> **by living from their ego,**
> **then**
> **the relationship is broken**
> **and**
> **will remain broken until the break has been repaired**
> **and love has been restored between the partners.**

In other words:

> **Relationships survive and thrive**
> **or**
> **crash and burn**
> **on**
> **"Conflict Resolution Hill."**

The matter of conflicts has been addressed; conflicts are a heart-versus-ego confrontation. This much is certain. All relationships experience conflict, and the source of that conflict is heart versus ego; people make a choice to love or not to love. The central theme for this chapter is about "you" and "an other" in a relationship.

Like the chapter on love (Chapter 3), this chapter on relating and relationships is "progressive," or "cumulative"; skills are added, and then the dots are connected. The conversation about relationships follows the same sequence. Your work, as before, is to understand each new element and to add it to your awareness. You put the new skills into practice by noticing or distinguishing them, and then by implementing them in your relationships. Raising your awareness along with the practice of each skill moves you closer to experiencing the results you sought when you embarked on your journey.

The Purpose of Relationships

We began with "love" and stated that your purpose in life is love. We are expanding your purpose with the appropriate language to include relationships. The following is the foundational premise on relationships:

> **The purpose for being in a relationship is
> to experience the love your heart desires.**

Recall the focus of the book is (1) *being healthy* and (2) *creating and maintaining healthy relationships*. This statement of two concepts describes a two-phase process. Part one, the first phase, has been focused on you being healthy. Part two addresses creating and maintaining a healthy relationship. What is certain is that relationships are dependent on you being healthy. But not just you. . . . Your partner must be healthy as well. Why?

Because the purpose of relationships leaves no room for those who are not healthy. . .

> **If you are not healthy,
> the probability of your experiencing
> the love your heart desires in a relationship
> is infinitesimally small.**

When stated from the "healthy" perspective, this statement reads:

**If you are healthy,
the possibility of your experiencing
the love your heart desires in a relationship is
exponentially greater.**

Your work has been heading toward the following goal from the beginning of your work:

**The healthier you become,
the better chance you have
of creating and maintaining healthy relationships,
in which you experience joy, satisfaction, peace,
and the love your heart desires.**

You may have noticed the word *relationship* used in different contexts. That is done purposefully. You are *always* in "relationship." No matter if you are with another person or with your self; you are always relating. If you are experiencing the Grace of your next breath, then you are in "relationship."

Types of Relationships

Today, you are in a different season from any other season you have been in since "once upon a time." Why? You are "aware" and are becoming healthy. You have the power of love; you can choose to love . . . or not. When you love your self, the possibilities for experiencing love in relationships with a partner or any "other" are infinite. Because you have chosen to love your self, you have love to give "in abundance," a condition that must be present for any relationship to succeed—that is, for it to be fulfilling, joyful, peaceful, and so on.

The dictionary defines *relationship* as follows:

> The way in which two or more concepts, objects, or people are connected, or *the state of being connected.*

The way in which two or more individuals or organizations *regard and behave toward each other.*

Look at the different types of intimate relationships that are available for your consideration. Here is a short list of some of those possibilities:

- An intimately connected monogamous relationship.
- A physical-and-social-only relationship.
- A spiritually and sexually intimate relationship.
- An intimate relationship with your self (no "other" involved).
- No intimately connected relationships; only social connections.
- And so on . . .

The relationship combinations are virtually unlimited: platonic partners, friendship-only partners, travel partners, life partners, lifestyle partners, tax partners, insurance and retirement partners, friends "with benefits," workout partners, dinner partners, and so on.

People add their preferences as "qualifiers." Some people want to "find a partner" and want to "settle down." Some people want "a relationship but refuse to settle." Some are not going to be in a relationship until they find "the One." (I always find this last one as rather odd; if someone doesn't get in a relationship, how would they know if a specific person is "the One"??? Unless they have ESP, how could they know? Can they know without taking the risk to jump all the way in?) Finally, there are those who want a relationship that is "uncomplicated." They want to find a person "to meet for dinner, maybe travel, and have sex." As choices, any one of these will work—provided it is the choice of both parties.

But no matter the arrangement, human-to-human relationships are dicey propositions. What is interesting is this: For the most part, the further "romantic love" is *removed from* the relationship, the better chance the parties will experience the results they wanted from the relationship. We will investigate this further as we progress. For the moment, we need to make a "hard right turn."

Every day, everywhere, with your self, with others, with your kids—it doesn't matter—you *are* in relationships. Which means that you are experiencing one of several possible situations:

- You are living from the heart and loving, and "they" are loving you right back. *Or*
- You are loving, but they are confronting your love with critiques and judgment (ego). *Or*
- They are giving you love, which you are rejecting with your arrogance, expectations, and entitlement (ego). *Or*
- You and they are living from your ego, volleying back and forth with endless streams of critiques, condescension, anger, fear, expectations, demands, and more; neither of you is choosing to live from the heart.

Yeah. Those examples sum up your day. All day. Every day. Book it. Truth. *And*, it's the summary of "their" day, too. I have found no biblical or luminary reference that states: "Love takes a day off."

If your radar has gone off in the preceding paragraphs, that is a good catch! That nuanced descriptor tossed in, not so subtly, was "romantic love." You mean after the long discussion on "love," there is another aspect of love not covered yet? Yes.

If you look carefully at the list of relationship possibilities, some of those descriptions do not include "romantic love." Romantic love relationships are different. This difference is critical. One way to describe the difference between a "relationship" and a "romantic love relationship" is the following perspective:

If you love rock climbing, you join meetup.com. All the folks who meet you at the base of the "Back Breaker Ledge" at 7:00 on a Saturday morning are going to be giving and receiving "love" to one another. Because everyone is looking up at that 120-foot vertical rock face with *appreciation* and *affection* for touching and giving individual and their collective (seriously focused) *attention* on hard-to-navigate, slippery, vertical surfaces. These "climbing" folks may be very healthy, or not. It doesn't matter. Why? While they all share the "love" of scaling vertical surfaces, there is not much at risk on the "heart" (love) front.

There is likely to be a good deal of "ego" on display, though, in the context of "better than" and "not good enough," as well as critiques on "how to do it right . . . next time" and so on. These people share a love for climbing. For these "relationships," there is no dependency or expectation for "romantic love." It is not necessary for these relationships to be fulfilling, for providing the outcome all participants expected when they entered the relationship.

But it's my guess that if you come flying off that rock and "Joe" breaks your fall, you will probably love the hell out of him because he was "loving you"; he was paying attention to you, accepting your minimal skills, and allowing your full experience of your self, and mostly he appreciated your value by keeping you from breaking your neck in that fall. You will most likely "love" him in return, too. ☺

However, about you and this discussion of relationship: "romantic love" relationships are found elsewhere. If you want to find romantic love, you are likely to join match.com or another dating website. Romance is *the* differentiating factor in these examples. It is the complicating factor, too.

Finding a romantic relationship means flipping through profile after profile, viewing picture after picture. You will notice if "have kids," "no children," "allergic to dogs or kids," "yogurt-free but gluten-tolerant and sugar-free," or "Wednesday not Sunday" is checked or not. Finding your romance, dating, mating, having sex, make-a-life-with-me partner is a difficult task. The truth is when you miss on the romantic love front, your mistakes tend to be way more costly than a small mistake in rock climbing, which has "safety ropes" and "bags" to overcome your mistake.

With this in mind, it is a good idea for you *to know what you are doing* when you want to create a romantic love relationship. The "know what you are doing" reference means that you have a perspective with more "substance" than those early-in-life fantasies of finding a "White

Knight" or a "Princess." For those of us in the "relationship industry," this is the greatest time in history to be in the dating–mating–sexing–relating business. The "Romance Business" is a complicated mess, but it generates a ton of profits. ☺

Lucky for you, you bought this book, and as a result, things (including "you") are a lot less messy. You have everything you need to have a great relationship. You know love, you live from your heart, you love your self, you can hear ego twenty kilometers away in gale-force winds. The fact is, on the relationship front, you really are "good to go."

It's time to deep-dive on finding healthy partners, setting boundaries, how to love the "unlovable," resolving relationship conflict, and more. Also addressed is how to spot and avoid picking a narcissist or getting involved with a drug- or sex- or porn-addicted person. Plus, some insights about some of the challenges of romance and romantic love relationships.

Let's jump in!

Dating–Mating–Sexing–Relating

So far, many of the references about relationships have applied to the generic, platonic, friend and family relationships as well as the romantic ones. The discussion has not been *exclusively* about romantic love relationships. My purpose was to align "love" in those "other kinds of relationships" in the context of "love" as used in the verse "love your neighbor," because "neighbor" covers pretty much everyone you meet in your life.

But "lov*er*" is different from "neighbor." The intent now is to differentiate romantic love relationships from all other types of relationships.

When your focus is specifically on "romantic love relationships," the "population" of prospects is reduced to a select few individuals. These are the ones who are the focus of the next section.

Differentiating Romantic Love

Romance, romantic love, and romantic love relationships have several key features that are distinct from "platonic" or "familial" or casual social relationships. For this discussion, the characteristics of a romantic love relationship involve two people:

- who share an intense physical attraction that is accompanied by obsessive thoughts and desires to connect;
- whose mating instincts are in overdrive (they share a strong desire to have sexual intimacy, sooner rather than later);
- who are open to and desire to experience an intensely intimate connection (socially, intellectually, physically, spiritually and sexually);
- who are willing to explore and expose their deepest, most vulnerable, intimate self with each other, with the hope their vulnerability will be reciprocated; and
- who would like to have this shared experience of romantic love for a period measured in decades rather than hours, weeks or months.

Usually, they share the hope that the relationship will be a long-term engagement because the amount of time, energy, and personal investment required to create a romantic love relationship is significant.

True romantic love is built on authentic vulnerability, shared intimacy, and intimate sexual connection. These result in an attachment and emotional bond forming between the two. The initial physical attraction and intense primal lust typically last for six months to two years. As their appetite for passion dissipates, there is a shift in the quality of the connection. With any luck (*it's all skill*), the shift is to a mutual giving-and-receiving love.

Their hope is that they develop a sense of safety and trust in each other and that they form a more secure attachment (versus insecure attachment). When this "secure bonding" takes hold, the foundation of the relationship is security, support, and vulnerability. These replace lust, attraction, and any fantasy bonds that were the basis for their original connection.

Ultimately, their experience is joy and satisfaction from their shared intimacy, and these sustain the relationship between the partners. That is how the ideal romantic love relationship is built and sustained until "death do [one or the other of] us part."

Of course, there is a caveat! There are many factors that must be present to make that description of romantic love your experience. Let's look at some of the "minor" details.

The Path to Romantic Love

Finding romantic love happens in stages, each successive stage is supposed to build on the previous stage and further cement the bond between the partners. The challenges are numerous, and they are dissected (and resolved) in this section. The place to start is at the beginning: the stage where the first bloom of love emerges.

Many aspects of a romantic love relationship are misunderstood, especially concerning what is happening early on. Specifically, what is happening during the "date-mate-procreate" phase. This is often described as the "romance" stage of the relationship. This where many of those "Mythstakes" are made as well. Some of these can be illustrated using online dating profiles. You may be familiar with these from your experience or from that of a close friend.

The hallmark Mythstake of this stage is the required presence of one particular "partner attribute." Reading about this one is mandatory and, in some cases, an absolute requirement. What is the "must have" that is being referred to?

Revisiting the "That Chemistry" Myth

Yes, welcome back our old friend and longtime nemesis: the "That Chemistry" myth. Anyone familiar with dating profiles has read about the intense expressed desire to make mandatory this experience of the phenomenon called "chemistry." References to "that chemistry" often read like this:

> I want that buckle at the knees, melt in his arms,
>
> sweep me off my feet, take me away forever . . . chemistry!!!

Often this high-bar qualifier is deftly followed by a proclamation that reads more like a declaration warning away any would-be prospects:

BEWARE:

I refuse to settle for anything less . . .

On the surface, one might naturally assume: "Lord have mercy!!! This person knows what they want." One might ever too hastily conclude that this person is very intentional about finding love and is doing so with a keen understanding about explicit nuances that make or break a relationship. Me? Not fooled in the slightest. Not a single doubt over here! Why?

For the person seeking "that chemistry" combined with a claim that they will not "settle," here is what you can bet the house on:

- This person is a seriously passionate partner; they love intimate adult pleasure, in large doses . . .

And

- This person has "settled" before in their life, at least once and probably many times . . .

And

- Because of their misunderstanding of "chemistry" that they claim is mandatory,

Then (fact)

- They will most likely "settle" . . . again.

That "buckle at the knees" thingy in the context of healthy relationships, what they are calling "chemistry"? You already know, "that chemistry" is *not* the *healthy chemistry* of healthy relationship. It won't last, much less sustain a healthy relationship. Not even close. We'll look at that more in a second. What is important is your awareness. You have been fine-tuning your listening and raising your awareness about healthy people and relationships. To that end, you would do well to file the words of this profile neatly in the bottom of your toolbox, especially if you are planning to use a dating site.

FWIW: Anytime you read the word "settle," know that this is a way people are telling you, point blank: "I have sold out in my past relationships." Proclamations stating, "I won't settle" translates to "I have sold out in my past romantic love relationships." The description of "how I sold out" probably sounds something like this:

> In my past relationships, I did not love my self enough to pay attention to my needs and appreciate my value—as a partner or a lover. Piece by piece, what I compromised were my values, preferences, boundaries, and behaviors. In other words, what I did was "sell out" the authentic and unique parts of me, such as my self-worth, my heart, and my soul.
>
> I did all this so that I could stay in a relationship with this person. So, for me to stay in past relationships and to sustain these for any reasonable length of time, what I chose to do was to "sell out"!
>
> The hurt and pain I experienced were devastating. If you and I connect and you are healthy with strong relating skills, you will find out quickly whether I have processed and reconciled this past tendency to "sell out." Because if I have not resolved it, the issues that caused me so much difficulty and distress in those relationships will surface in my relationship with you.
>
> Please know that I seriously want to experience a romantic love relationship in which I can keep my authentic self always present and that I do not have to sell out again to be in a relationship.

Brutally honest? Yeah, yeah it is. And it's darn sad, too. This story strikes with such a crushing blow because the cost of selling out is so high. At "The End," the impact is devastating. Anyone who knows the experience of heartache, and how much it hurts, knows the actual price someone pays when they choose "selling out." Hopefully, speaking the truth here will prevent someone from selling out again. That would be a huge success!

"Selling out" usually starts with the "That Chemistry" Mythstake. That "buckle at the knees" chemistry was covered in Chapter 1. It happens anytime your pure animal mating instincts are triggered. That's it. Nothing more. It is not a sign from the cosmos that you hit the jackpot on the relationship "Wheel of Fortune." Big mistake. That's it. In this date-mate-procreate state, the only presence of love you experience is "I would *love* to have sex . . . now."

Recall that mating "chemistry" is a sudden but fleeting bodily sensation much like any other emotionally charged state you experience. The problem comes from the common belief that this lusty mating chemistry is the Holy Grail, which indicates that you have found a romantic "love" relationship. This Mythstake is compounded even further because it is believed to be the necessary ingredient required to make a romantic love relationship successful. Mythstakes are exactly that: myths that lead to mistakes. The mating "chemistry" Mythstake sits alone at the top of errors in picking partners and understanding healthy relationships. With no peer.

It is time to stop using the term *chemistry* in association with healthy romantic love relationships. Going forward, instead of "chemistry" you will find the word "chem-*patibility*" (see Chapter 9).

Chem-*patibility* describes the presence of healthy attraction, connection, bonding, secure attachment, conflict resolution, agreements, and love being given and received. *That* describes "the mandatory chemistry of compatibility" for anyone with the desire to create and maintain a romantic love relationship. Your work is to be aware of the difference between the chemistry of healthy romantic love and "that chemistry" of your animal mating instinct.

Continuing over the ground to cover romantic love relationships . . .

J. Spencer Wendt

Revisiting the "Commitment" Myth

Commitment was one of the first topics addressed in Chapter 1. The purpose was to highlight the fact that commitments don't seem to make a difference in the longevity of romantic love relationships, and worse, they don't seem to do much in the way of delivering results for the people making the commitments. This is an issue on several fronts; the biggest may not have anything to do with the people but rather with what could be a "design flaw." That is where we start in revisiting the topic of commitments . . .

What do you know? Do you get swept off your feet, "fall in love", make a commitment "till death do us part" and "live happily ever after"? Is that the path you were taught or learned or absorbed by osmosis in the first twenty or thirty years of your life as the way to create a successful romantic, forever-after, love relationship? Does it work? Were you told that "this is the path to follow to create a romantic love relationship"? Really? Wow. How is that working out? Not well?

The ballots are in, the results have been tabulated, and it's not pretty. This path doesn't work. In fact, citing the results renders the opposite conclusion: "'Falling in love' and then making a commitment is not the way to create a lasting love relationship! It is unquestionably not the recipe for success." It is prudent to speak the truth on this matter!

What you do know, with a high degree of certainty, about relationships is the following sequence:

> Two people experience "attraction" and make a connection; this is the beginning of the "romance" phase. Over some period, which is entirely random, they independently and mutually determine that they are "in love." That may result in a decision to be monogamous, "exclusively committed"; the decision may be with the intent to marry.

Their "commitment" may result in starting a family and buying a house. Over time, buying two or three houses, sharing some car notes together, taking some vacations, traveling a bit, and so on.

Then, out of nowhere, the bliss is broken. "Something happens." The "something" is almost *unexpected*. The "something" is described as an "issue." It blew up suddenly, and the issue was so impactful it undermined their trust and halted vulnerability. The sense of safety and bonding they had shared is lost.

The relationship never seems to quite get back to the place it was before the issue happened.

Hit the Pause button here. The "issue" created a disconnect in their shared love and put distance between them. The source of the issue is not relevant. But what might be relevant is the focus of this section, which is the concept of their "commitment." Let's back up a bit.

OK, the sex was great—fabulous, in fact. She was gorgeous, happy, a great mom, and she made a ton of money. He was smart, funny, and charismatic, with an excellent job. They liked each other, a lot. She had a killer forehand, and he was a solid "5 handicap." They declared they were "madly in love." Of course, what we know for sure is: they were "*committed to each other*," right?

But now, this "small issue" surfaced, and it has shaken the foundation of their relationship. "What happened" is that it completely changed their relationship. That brings up an interesting question:

> **Was their commitment to each other**
> **the most important criterion for**
> **making their romantic love relationship work?**
> **TRUTH:**
> **Their commitment *to each other* is**
> **pretty much *irrelevant*.**

What is relevant is what this couple needed to know—well before they had kids, bought the second car, up-sized the house, and doubled their mortgage payment—and well before they bid each their reciprocal promise of "till death do us part." The biggest question about their "commitment" popped up *after they were committed.* The excruciatingly relevant question which appears to be the question that must be addressed is:

> **Were they committed to resolving**
> ***any* conflict or "issue,"**
> **which was *100-percent guaranteed***
> **to surface in their relationship?**

With so much at stake, wouldn't it have made a boatload of sense to figure out *this* "commitment" way earlier? The question they needed to ask each other was:

> **"Do we have the skills necessary to resolve**
> **the conflicts that will come up,**
> ***and* can we address them,**
> **so the resolution of conflicts**
> **brings us closer and deepens our love**
> ***after* we handle the issue?"**

Based on what you know, these two questions would seem to be the *most* relevant questions anyone could ask about a love relationship partner. Don't they?

As shown in this example, the sequence romance–commitment–conflict resolution does not describe the correct path or the right way to create and maintain a romantic love relationship—even though that sequence has been promoted and sold by parents, magazines, digital media, relationship gurus, and religious and social institutions since the beginning of time. The measurable results of this "sage advice" render but one, lone, profoundly obvious conclusion:

> **The romantic love relationship model**
> **that suggests the correct path is:**
> **1. find romance,**
> **2. make a commitment, and then**
> **3. resolve conflicts . . .**
> **is *extremely broken*.**

That model has been the socially acceptable construct for most of the past 120 years. The results are in: That model does *not* lead to "happily ever after." That misconception you must add to your toolbox as something to be keenly aware of in matters of love relationships. The truth is, more directly, that if you want to create a romantic love relationship, then you *must* have a different model. The good news is that it requires only a small tweak to the model to get it right. But this change is a valuable yet difficult-to-achieve tweak, to say the least.

The model that is the correct sequence of phases for creating and maintaining a healthy romantic love relationship, the one that gives you the best chance at long-term success, is:

> **Truth about "Commitment" *revisited*:**
> **The path that provides the greatest probability for**
> **creating a lasting romantic love relationship is:**
> **Romance, conflict resolution, *then* commitment**

That is the correct order and the model that gives the best chance for producing the desired results. Once again, credit for this insight goes to David Richo.[19] His masterful work on love and relationships identifies this commitment Mythstake. Just as you are reading it, your thinking about romantic love relationship almost demands an audible declaration: "How did I miss that?" That may not be your reaction, but it was mine. This model is the correct sequence of phases for anyone whose goal is creating and maintaining a healthy romantic love relationship, one that accommodates the inevitability of "issues" that will surface.

Just how important is this? This awareness is the *most* critical on the list of your relationship skills. Right up there with "love" and "love your self," and the skills you (now) possess to resolve a conflict—which, for you, is some seriously good news.

The benefit for you is that you know the methodology for conflict resolution. You know the APR model for how to restore love. You have used this method to resolve issues in your past. You have used it to fill the "gaps" in your original install of love. With APR, you made up for any deficiencies. Yours may still be a work in progress, but the method of addressing, processing, and resolving is a skill you possess. It works. That APR method works when issues surface in your romantic love relationships as well.

Recall that conflicts happen between heart and ego. That insight applies to romantic love relationships. When an issue surfaces, its source is the heart of one partner being met by the ego of the other. Usually— and this is critical—conflicts happen unexpectedly. They appear "out of nowhere": "I thought everything was copacetic, but suddenly my entire world was turned upside down."

The insight I like to share with my clients is: "An 'issue' is a 'relationship IED (Intimacy Explosion Device)' that has blown your relationship off course." This seems an appropriate comparison, because, in one moment, both are living from the heart, giving and receiving love. Then *Boooom!* "something happens." The "something" is an issue, which is always a conflict between heart and ego. It could be yours with theirs, theirs with yours, or your internal conflict from the past (they are just an innocent bystander when something was triggered from your past). The fine details of what that "something" was has no bearing at all. Understanding that the source is always heart versus ego gives the partners the precise point to investigate and figure out "what happened." Make a note.

FACT:
Conflicts happen in all romantic love relationships.

Here is another benefit for you as a healthy adult: You can pinpoint the source of any issue, because it is going to be found somewhere on that long list that describes the words and actions of ego. This is true 100 percent of the time. With this knowledge, two healthy adults can then set about "their work together" to resolve the conflict by using the APR method. You know this process: Each partner addresses the issue, sharing what happened from their perspective, describing the emotions that were their experience, allowing for each side to share. Then each partner processes their experience and the experience of the other, expressing, with compassion, the damage or hurt. Through shared resolving of the conflict with a firm agreement, the relationship is brought back to love.

And this brings about another critical point:

FACT:
Relationships fail when conflicts are
not resolved in a healthy manner.

That one statement validates Richo's model because it implies the following:

If both parties are not committed to resolve their issues
with an agreement to do something different
in the future
to actively work to change their behavior,
responses, and their words or actions
that were the source of the issue,
then
they are *not* in a committed relationship.

This makes total sense. With no commitment to be more aware or change anything, are they committed to anything more than being together? "Being together" is nice, but what do these people honestly have? What are they actually "committed to"? Stated another way, more bluntly, but truthfully, "speaking the truth in love" (Ephesians 4:15[20]).

> **Without the commitment
> to resolve conflicts in a manner
> that results in a more intimate, deeper love,
> and a closer bond,
> there is *no* "commitment"
> and
> a "healthy committed romantic love relationship"
> does not exist between these two people.**

The implications of this statement are significant. In fact, it creates an interesting set of questions about romantic love relationships. The answers to the following questions should be obvious:

- How many healthy adults are needed to build and *maintain* a healthy romantic love relationship?
- What are the *required skills* that each partner must have to *maintain* a healthy romantic love relationship?
- How important is it for *you* to select a partner who is aware and focused on becoming healthier for *you* to have a chance at creating and *maintaining* a healthy romantic love relationship?
- How important is it for both parties to have a well-developed set of relating skills if their goal is to be in a "committed" relationship?
- What is the most essential and defining characteristic of a "committed" relationship?
- Is it possible to have a committed relationship *without* the capacity, ability, and practice of conflict resolution?

In the light of your previous romantic love relationships or of the relationships you know of in your circle of friends and your family, these are sobering questions. For you, a new light is cast onto the panorama of romantic love relationships.

Your new awareness is the correct sequence of the stages for creating a healthy romantic love relationship.

- First is the "romance" phase. After the lust and attraction, alignment on values, etc., you *must* determine if you and your "partner prospect" possess the skills to resolve issues in a healthy manner to restore the love and deepen your connection.

Then

- Second is the "conflict resolution" phase. If the skills are there to resolve conflicts, this is the phase where they are revealed and put into practice. When issues arise, they are handled, and the result is more love and deeper connection. When issues have been resolved back to love, *then* a commitment to romantic love relationship is possible.

Then

- You and your partner make a commitment.

There are more details about what the commitment looks like, and they are covered later in this chapter. At this point in the relationship discussion, you are aware of another application for your skill of addressing, processing, and resolving a conflict. You are now aware of the model that provides the best opportunity for creating a lasting romantic love relationship. But you cannot be the only partner with relating skills. You are tasked with finding a partner with a well-developed set of relating skills, so it only makes sense to focus on picking a healthy partner, which is "what's next" . . .

The Narrow Door of Prospects

This section continues with the theme of simplicity by providing some direction regarding the task of sorting through prospects and the process of picking partners. Selection skills sit somewhere near the top of the list—right below love, love your self, and conflict resolution in importance of relationship skills that you must develop.

This section's objective is to make romantic love relationships a less complicated puzzle. To structure your thinking and with a perspective that leaves you saying, confidently: "I can pick a healthy partner!!" Yes, you can! Anyone can find a healthy partner if they are aware of what "unhealthy" looks and sounds like, which is the focus of this section.

The place to start is all the way back to Chapter 3 on love, with this statement:

> **All engagements and conversations are from either heart or ego.**

The simplicity here is excellent. Suddenly, all communication is reduced to one of two "languages." You know these two languages already:

- One is heart (the five A's), the language of love.
- One is ego (FACED), the language of "not love."

These are the two languages spoken by the partners in all relationships; this is particularly important to know regarding romantic love relationships. If all conversations are either one or the other, it's a matter of paying attention and listening. That's it. Simple. Personally, I find the simplicity comforting!! The issue comes when you choose not to listen or when you listen but change the meanings of the words. You could try by some fantasy or delusion to make someone "fit." But the truth is they are not a fit for you, a truth they are "telling" you through their words (and actions). The truth is simple: They are not a fit. That "make them fit" scenario happens a lot in the partner selection process.

As you have been working through this book, it may have occurred to you that not everyone is in the same place that you are now on the journey to become healthy—knowing about love, heart, ego, and awareness. Not everyone understands the distinctions about relating and relationships that you now have. Not all people know about or can choose love, nor can they speak and live from the heart, and they cannot resolve conflicts in a healthy manner. That is how life works. It's OK. It is what it is. *(You can always gift them my book to help get them up to speed . . . just sayin'!)*

By your being aware and being in the practice of noticing and choosing the healthy options means that you determine whom you engage with as a potential romantic relationship partner. Regardless of how well you know someone, when their heart speaks or when ego speaks, you know. Recognizing this "polarity" in conversations brings even more simplicity to the dynamics of picking a relationship prospect. The simplicity of the two "languages" also applies to the type of people you want to connect with or bring into your life. Your objective is to identify relationship partners who are healthy and who are a good "fit" for you. That's it.

Whether you realize it or not, we just reduced the entire universe of potential prospects for you. They fall into one of three categories. Stated more precisely:

Every prospect has one of three different capacities regarding awareness about their self, about you, and about relationships.

That probably doesn't make a lot of sense now, but it will shortly. Let's put this into context.

You are one voice in your relationship. The person with whom you are speaking has a capacity and level of awareness just as you have. The question is: Are they at or close to your level of awareness, skills, and so on? Since the goal is for you to select a partner who *also possesses* the capability to create and maintain a healthy romantic love relationship, this is the most important thing you need to know about them. Some will be at or close to your level, some will not be at or close to your level, and some will fall in between. So, we are left with:

QUESTION:
Can the list of potential partners or partner prospects be simplified to *only* "qualified partner prospects"?

The answer is yes, but only if you know what your selection criteria is . . . and that was just identified:

ANSWER:
A person is a partner candidate based on *their* level of awareness and *their* healthy relating skills.

That reduces the universe of prospects to a very select group (*but you have been on match.com, so this was not new news to you!!*). More precisely, there are *exactly* three categories of prospects. Each is distinguished by the levels of awareness and skills they have. Better news? Yes. Every candidate you meet falls into one of the three.

The beauty is that before you make a commitment or begin to share intimately, this three-category prospect model gives you a highly reliable indication of the likelihood you will experience the love your heart desires in a relationship with this person. That's pretty sweet!

(A modicum of humor is tossed in, because the number of legit prospects is so small. It's good to be entertained as you are working your way through the "culls," and since you know "where broken people agree to meet for coffee and have sex . . .," you know about the "work" required to finding a healthy prospect.)

Now, getting down to business. The three prospect categories are:

Category 1: A Healthy Aware Adult (AHAA):
- This individual loves their self. Like you, they are on the road to "healthy" even if it is still a somewhat cloudy concept.

- This person is seeking to become healthier, and they are OK where they are on their journey. It is who they are.
- They are always seeking to grow and learn to "be better" at life, love, and relationships.
- This person is aware of their past and has taken inventory of their relationships, is capable of giving and receiving love, can address, process, and resolve issues in a healthy manner . . . with you.
- This category is pronounced: "Ahhh Haaa,"
  - as in "Ahhh Haaa . . . Yes! I found one!!"
  - Go ahead, bust out the champagne, you may have found a legit prospect.

Category 2: UnHealthy-Healthy Adult (UHH):
- This person is somewhat aware, but mostly they are unaware.
- They may be willing to do their work—to know love, to love their self . . . but maybe not. You must figure out if they will or they won't.
- Sometimes they are actively seeking to learn and become healthier. It's new to them, but they are willing to work, except when it becomes "too much" work or too hard to handle, and they just do what they have always done; "I tried, it didn't work."
- They want to be aware of their past and take inventory of their relationships, but they may be afraid of doing their work with you because it's too "scary" and they can't handle the truth.
- They certainly want to give and receive love (the five A's) and may get excited about learning the skills and practices to address, process, and resolve issues in a healthy manner, but mostly the burden of getting *them* moving, and keeping them moving, to become aware will fall in your lap.
- This category is pronounced: "Uhh,"
  - as in "Uhhh . . . maybe this could work?"

- And if it does or if it doesn't, it will be a lot of work for you, because you will be leading the way for the foreseeable future. Good luck!

Category 3: Not A Healthy Adult (NAH):
- This person has no interest in or concern for love, not for their self and certainly not for you.
- They are not actively seeking to become healthier.
- They could care less about their past or the need to take an inventory of their relationships: "It was his/her fault."
- They have *no* capacity to give and receive love (the five A's).
- They have Kelvin-zero conflict-resolution skills; such skills don't matter. Whoever is in a relationship with them is "lucky to have me."
- They are consciously unaware of the other relating topics. "Who cares?" "No biggie." "I am who I am, take it or leave it."
- Nothing you say, do, suggest, recommend, or demand is going to change them. They can't even change their self and frankly don't see any need to grow or change.
- This category is pronounced: "Nah."
  - Phonetically, this requires no explanation: "Naaaahhhh, *no way*!!" Any questions?
  - For you, you have likely "been there, done that, have the T-shirt, the bumper sticker, the keychain, and the hat . . . never again in my natural-born life . . ."
  - Any questions?
- For those of you who have hooked your shooting star to the energy-sucking, life-suffocating black-hole narcissist, this last one is unmistakably *not for you . . . again*!
  - (We do a deep dive on the "N" types later . . .)

(I hope you appreciate the simplicity and the very long reach to find some comedic humor in each of these prospect category labels: "Ahaa," "Uhh," and "Nah." I did, but I laugh at my own stuff a lot. ☺)

The choice to create phonetic illustrations to define the "desirability" of each category of prospect seemed to make sense. It's easy to remember and you can have some good laughs with your BFFs when you meet up for a glass of wine. Getting back down to the serious business of "love" and "you" . . .

This three-group model includes the entire universe of potential candidates. The implication here should be obvious. There is precisely one category that has all of those much-sought-after prospects who might qualify as "the One." Next you notice one group that contains prospects who might be fun, but you will be doing the work. Then there is the "last group," the "Undatables." These are the train wrecks waiting to happen. If you need some short quips to remember the categories, here is what I tell my clients:

- "Ahhhhhaaaa." Yes, definitely a prospect.
- "Uhh . . ." Maybe. But this one will require some work.
- "Naaaahhhh . . ." No way. Think about waking up in the penthouse suite at the Chernobyl Hotel but in the context of a relationship. Are we crystal clear? Good!!

I suggest you commit these descriptions to memory; your life, your health, your financial future, your security, the future of your kids, and your experiencing the love your heart desires—*all* depend on it. Yes, all of it rests on your ability to determine which type of person you are agreeing to meet for coffee or possibly choose to have as a relationship partner.

A good television drama series always has a "hook" at the end of each episode. The hook is designed to keep your attention and make you want to stay tuned for what is coming. In the spirit of good storytelling (which may be up for debate), the next section does not start with the ideal prospect description. No. The prospects you must avoid like the plague are discussed first.

These are candidates you reply via email with "Thank you, I wish you all the best in your search!" Or, if you are meeting for lunch or dinner, you bid "all the best" as soon as the wait staff clears your tab. You shake their hand and give them a big "Highland Park Hug."

The what? Let me explain . . .

The "Highland Park Hug" is the most insincere embrace in all of humanity. It's the one where you are pulling back on your heels but fake it as though you're "leaning in" to the person you do not want to hug. You have put on your premeditated "I'm doing fine" smile. Your palm sort of touches their shoulder blade and as fast as you move in, you are stepping back. You deftly execute a precision pirouette and exit, stage left, while ever so smoothly delivering a well-rehearsed "Thank you. It was a pleasure to meet you! I was going to suggest getting together again, but after thinking about it [for fifteen nanoseconds], I don't believe that we're a fit. Best of luck." Done. Moving on.

Now that we have added that bit of skills work to your repertoire, and before we look at the "where have you been all my life?" prospects, the discussion focuses on the folks who "fit" in the "unfit" category. First up . . .

Prospect DNQ: Does Not Qualify

When you are tuned into conversations that come from the heart, it's guaranteed that the one who is *not* a prospect, the one in the last of the three categories—Not A Healthy adult, "NAH"—is going to be easy to spot. Not necessarily when you first sit down, though, because they will play a great date-mate-procreate "game." They know they are unfit, and their goal is to not let you know . . . for as long as possible. Truth.

The primary distinction for this person is they are simply not aware of anything. Nothing about choosing to love and being healthy or the foundations of a romantic love relationship is of interest to them. They just aren't concerned. And you will not, nor can you, change them. It will never happen. You cannot rescue them. You cannot save them. You cannot please them. You cannot satisfy them. Most of all (*read this closely*), they cannot love you; they do not have the capacity.

Even if you were to spend your *valuable life energy* and time with them, patiently showing them example after example of your practice of the ideal model of love and relationships, at the end of the day, you are *most likely* wasting your time. If you choose to go down that path, the result is usually heartache, and that heart that will be aching is the one located in your chest. Yes, speaking the truth in love once again.

Having said all that . . . Wow! A NAH can be fun, engaging, adventurous, exciting, successful, worldly, and smart and a great conversationalist and fabulous intimate sex partner! Yes, *and* most *are*! That is part of what makes them so attractive. Toss in some good looks, and some money . . . it appears to be a pretty appealing package. All these aspects draw you in and capture your imagination about "the possibilities." But stop. Think for a minute. If they were "all that," how come they are not already in a romantic love relationship? *Ding Ding Ding.* Because they are *only* "all that." But regarding the stuff that makes relationships work? *No.*

Maybe you met, dated, and even have been in a relationship with a NAH in your past. Good! *Now* you know better than to fall for their facade. That is really, really good news. Back then, you were not aware. Today, you are aware. Back then, you never could understand what was "missing" and the reasons the relationship never seemed to work or move forward (especially after you had such fabulous sex). Maybe you spent years thinking, hoping, waiting for their lights to go "on." But they never did.

Finally, you had enough, or they had enough. The hurt was so much, the damage was so great, and the relationship ended. The fact is the relationship never had a chance from the start. Do you see it now? I hope you know the reasons why. You understand and know what was missing—with your self and about what must be present in both partners to make a relationship work.

Here is the gold you mined from that train wreck . . .

> **FACT:**
> **Unhealthy, unaware people cannot
> create or maintain healthy relationships.
> They just can't.**

Which calls forth the second truism:

> **FACT:**
> **A healthy person (you) cannot create
> a healthy relationship with an unhealthy person.
> You just can't.**

The NAH is not actively seeking to become healthier. They are not like you in this respect. Becoming healthier is *mandatory* for you, but it is of no consequence for them, *so* this is a deal breaker for you. Walking over this nonnegotiable preference is selling out!!! The NAH has no interest in being introspective about their self, nor are they seeking to make changes.

There is a reason the NAH is this way, too. They are totally comfortable living from their ego, because living from their heart is either completely unknown to them or is too big a risk. Being authentic would expose their humanity—their flaws and the stuff that doesn't work. Because of that, they are deathly afraid that no one will love them. They believe they are not good enough and that they are unlovable! Even though this is never true, it is what they believe, so they hide behind their ego.

They are almost the complete opposite of you and what you are up to in your life. For you, living from the heart means vulnerability and intimacy. It means you are willing to be known for your real self. You are ready to let your partner know you in the most intimate ways possible. There is no holding back. Boundaries? Yes, of course, but you lead with your heart while keeping your self safe. But the NAH?

The NAH leads with their ego, which means that for the most part, they are acting from their fears:
- fear of intimacy,
- fear of closeness,
- fear of abandonment,
- fear of being unlovable,
- fear of not being good enough,
- fear of judgment,
- fear of rejection,
- fear of not being accepted,
- fear of experiencing emotions,
- fear of getting hurt . . .

It is highly likely they are completely unaware that their fears are at the source of how they relate. Which should not be a surprise since they are choosing to live from their ego. The NAH presents the most complete presentation of all the descriptions you learned about when a heart is FACED by ego:
- Fears (see the preceding list)
- Frustration
- Anxiety
- Anger
- Argumentativeness
- Arrogance
- Assessment
- Condescension
- Control
- Critiques
- Criticism
- Change
- Comparison
- Commands
- Correction

- Entitlement
- Expectation
- Demands
- Defending
- Distancing
- Disappointment
- Dismissing
- Diminishing
- Displeasure
- Degrading
- Discounting

Bottom line: The NAH does not love their self. The elements of the five A's that you have? They cannot give those A's to their self, and they do not have them in abundance to give to you. Look at the following list of questions to better understand where they are compared with your self.

- Are you good enough?
- Do you accept your self?
- Do have worth?
- Do you appreciate your self?
- Do you allow your self to be OK in your circumstances?
- Do you want affection—that is, closeness?
- Do you love your self?
- Do your circumstances define your self?

Yes, you love your self. Recall that you can *give* only what you *have*.

Now, ask the question. Can an unhealthy adult who does not love their self give *you* love? No. They cannot. That is the reason any individual with no capacity for love and who is not interesting in becoming more aware is *not* a prospect for you.

Obviously, "hanging out" with a NAH could be a load of fun. You certainly can spend time with them *as long as* you are clear about their prospects as a partner. They are *not* a prospective committed romantic love relationship partner candidate.

Now. Let's talk about the dark side of the NAH in relationships.

That can be a relatively touchy subject. It is highly likely you know someone—maybe a friend or sibling—who is in a relationship with a NAH . . . *or* . . . maybe *you* have been in the past . . . or are now. The key points are:

- What are the "characteristics" (in other words, "red flags") of an unhealthy adult?
- What are the "distinctive features" (in other words, "dysfunctional aspects") of a relationship with an unhealthy adult?

The answers you know. The NAH is the "less savory" side of people and relationships. It would consume too many trees to write accounts of their dysfunctional behaviors and the characteristics of their relationships. Rather than stories, some detailed descriptions of the most common types of NAHs complete this section.

The three types of unhealthy adults most frequently encountered are:

- the narcissists,
- people with an addiction issue (substance, sex, porn and—yes—love)
- people with personalities and behaviors frequently described as codependent, bipolar, borderline, emotionally vacant or disconnected.

The following sections discuss each in detail. This discussion is a high-level presentation and is intended to bring certain aspects of their behavior into the light. These you add to your awareness. It seems the appropriate place to start is "the bottom of the abyss."

Shall we . . .?

The Dreaded "N" . . .

The ugliest of the NAHs is the narcissist. The heartbreaking stories here are the most tragic. The stories are the same; only the names, the depth of heartache, and the years spent enduring the pain are different. The stories nearly all have the same "once upon a time." When these stories are revealed, one cannot help but extend tremendous compassion to the "survivors."

"Survivors" of "N" relationships have gone "all in" with 100 percent of their heart and soul in most cases. (Perhaps you are such a survivor, and this narrative will be presented from that perspective.) You bought into what seemed on the surface to be exactly the traits and behaviors of an "ideal" partner. Your anticipation was that you would experience love in a romantic relationship with a partner who was "all in" with you. What you didn't know about was the nature of a narcissist and what the relationship would be like: the opposite of anything you possibly could have imagined.

First, an N's capacity to love their self is almost nonexistent. Their ability to give love (the five A's) to a romantic partner, you, is *zero*; "you cannot give what you do not have." Without the capacity to love their self, they have a void inside their being. To fill the void requires a constant inflow of love and energy from others (from you). Does it sound a lot like one of those cheesy vamp movies? Yeah? Well, it is.

The N has mastered the skills of disguise, trickeration, and manipulation to suck the energy from a lover and partner (you)—as well as family, friends, coworkers, and so on. Their appearance on the outside is a facade to pretend that their demeanor, their presence, and their life is perfect. Their focus is to create the impression they have their stuff 100 percent neatly piled and stacked together. Their stuff doesn't stink (just ask them).

You may also "hear" them wax on about their incredible maturity and well-developed relating skills. How so? Unlike every other person on the planet whom you know—including your self, your friends, your family, your dog sitter—this "dreamboat" supposedly has *zero* unresolved issues. None. Every relationship they have or had, past or present, is in near perfect shape:

- With siblings?
  - *"They're great! So lucky to have them as family!"*

Truth?

  - The sibs have avoided him like the plague, for years . . .
  - They "know" who he is.
- With mother and father?
  - *"Mom is a saint. He was a great dad; God rest his soul."*

Truth?

  - Dad was distant, cold, emotionless, disconnected; "Jr" was never good enough, always failed to meet expectations.
  - Mom was a controlling, passive aggressive, covert narcissist without peer; "Jr" was reminded, daily, that he was going to turn out "just like your father" . . . and for the most part "Jr" did.
- With exes? All eight of them? In three words:
  - *"They were bats**t crazy!"* and
  - *"I couldn't get out of there fast enough!"*

Truth?

  - All the exes figured him out.
  - They had enough and left him.
- With work and job?
  - *"Everyone loves me. I love to come to work. No issues, no tension . . ."*

Truth?

  - They know, too! He's a tyrant, cold and plastic.
  - If he hadn't designed the bonus and 401(k) plans to lock them in for life, they would have left long ago.

Lord knows about their kids! Here, the suggestion is you make a modest inquiry about how long their children have been in counseling. And, how long they have been living with their mother ("the crazy one").

Do you see any red flags? Maybe a better the question is, have you seen anything that is *not* a red flag? Here's the rub . . .

Of course, you saw red flags—tons of them! *But* the N is a highly skilled manipulator. Their best talent is delivering the appearance of the "perfect partner." You, on the way to "going all in," are in a suspended state of "pleasurable sensory overload." The attention, acceptance, appreciation, and affection are all incredible!!!

In fact, it feels like all the "goodies" are going to drown you!! What are you supposed to do? *Of course*, you are "all in"!! You always dreamed of finding "this kind of love" in a package that looks like this. You are certainly not about to let this one "get away," ever. "What happened?" You bought the facade, exactly as you were supposed to do, and like the preceding eight did as well.

Once you are "all in," you begin to attach and bond with your heart and soul, because that is what you do; you know love. You literally pour your heart into this person. You align your life with theirs. You shape your values and preferences to fit them. Once you are committed, you close your eyes, open your heart, and pour every ounce of your soul into them. That is the sad part, because they are a bottomless black hole. There is nothing over there. No love. No heart. No compassion. Nothing. And you? You may not know it yet, but you are committed to a void in space.

(Please feel free to write if you are offended by my callous, very harsh characterization of narcissists. I would love to hear your opinion or feedback . . . but before you do, take the time to read the stories.)

How would it be to describe a relationship with this type of person whom you poured your heart and soul into? Maybe the following narrative will paint the picture more clearly than what has been presented up to here:

> We met at a charity event where I was working. He was a very successful, very well-known doctor . . . and was a dreamboat. Six feet two inches, beautiful eyes, yummy smile with cute dimples and a cut jaw line. He trained for marathons and was always "Miami tan" . . . like a caramel dreamboat. I remember how warm his hand was when he took mine and said, "Hi, I

am John," gazing into my eyes as though he could see my soul. We talked all night. I remember breakfast ended at the Four Seasons with a kiss. . . . He must have caught me from falling when our lips parted. I don't think my feet hit the ground the rest of Sunday. All I could think about was "John . . . give me the matinee and the all-you-can-eat buffet."

I was sitting at my desk the next day, daydreaming, and in walked the FedEx guy with the most staggering array of stargazer lilies, and before I had them sorted and arranged, I got a text. "Sail to the Bahamas Friday? Back by Sunday. Fun. I promise . . . pack light!" I was committed to be at my sister's birthday party and had to decline. "Enjoy . . ." was his reply. How sweet!! He totally understands how important relationships are to me. Wow! This guy gets me. *He sees me!*

For the next month, the relationship was "off the charts" romance. Six weeks in, he invited me to his forty-fifth-floor condo with a spectacular view. Dinner. Wine. We took in the sunset from the balcony. Did I spend the night? Of course! I was in love!!! Yes, we made love all night. Passionate. Connected. Within six months, we were living together. Then he popped the question. We were on a friend's "big boat," and right in the middle of everything, he took the mike from the skipper and called everyone to the bridge. He proposed, and I remember I had to sit down to take it all in.

After a whirlwind nine months, we were married. He suggested I think about "doing something I wanted to do. Something that I had been particularly passionate about . . ." Maybe consider quitting my job. He made well into seven figures, and that was ten times what I was making. A year after meeting, I took him up on his offer. I quit my job and began to volunteer at various charities and art-related organizations. We had talked around the subject of kids. He was forty-eight, and I was thirty-seven, so time was getting short for me. I knew I wanted to be a mother.

All my friends were "on the clock," as I was. It was time to talk about kids. I had moved farther from my friends since I wasn't working, and John was handling everything financially. But I figured if I wanted my kids to know their kids, I could arrange play dates. I could always drive, and my friends and I could spend time together . . . which is kind of what we had talked about before leaving college.

But John and I never got around to planning for children. He would just say, "Enjoy your freedom, Love Kitten." The conversation about kids went back and forth for almost a year. He seemed less and less open to it. But I knew I wanted at least one. My dream was always two. I had always wanted to be living in a house and raising kids in a neighborhood, which John had hinted that he was open to. This high-rise was nice. He seemed to like the convenience of "just page the front desk . . . they'll find it, order it, have it delivered, canceled, exchanged, or picked up for you." That is nice, but kids? Family? Not so much what I had envisioned. I decided to keep quiet and give it some more time.

By nearly three years in, most of the "dream" and "partner" romance was a distant memory. John was working a lot, and we were not going out with my friends or his much anymore. Maybe we had "maintenance sex" once or twice a month. We spent one Thanksgiving with my family, but the travel was "interfering" with his work, he told me. He said he preferred spending holidays with his family; those always seemed like the last meal on the *Titanic*, the one being served as it hit the iceberg.

He always had two or three Scotches on the rocks on the way home or when he walked in the door. I started to hear more conversations about things that I "might like to do" . . . such as another breast job and maybe some face "enhancements" and maybe get back into yoga or meditation. Of course, he would do the "fix me up" work; that *was* his work after all.

Then, one day, the anvil dropped on my head. On the night of his fifty-first birthday, he walked in and announced that in six years, "we would be free to travel the world"—no more worries, no troubles, just fun and freedom. He announced he had had a vasectomy that afternoon. "How happy are you now, babe?!!"

My world crashed in on top of my head. My life was gone. My job was gone. My career was over. My friends were gone. My family was a distant memory. I was totally alone. And the blow to the gut. No kids!! He never even asked me or gave me an answer. . . . My dream of being a mother he totally took away from me. He never said a word!

I realized I had married a selfish, self-interested, self-serving disconnected, dispassionate, monster . . .

I present the Narcissist. The unhealthiest of all forms of the upright, free-will-gifted bipeds walking the planet. This submarginally evolved species is worth your time to understand.

They orchestrate a devilishly masterful facade. In "Phase I", the N gives you attention, gives you appreciation, accepts you (temporarily), is very affectionate, and feigns the allowance you have always wanted, because they are suppressing their desire to change and control you. They know that once you are "all in" . . . you're done! They are on to "Phase II," which is the slow process to methodically, steadily, take it all away and reduce you to nothing except what they desperate need: a "supply" of love and life energy that is missing in their self.

So, the question often comes up: Were the red flags completely missed? That is always a difficult question to answer. Why?

Mainly because an N is *excellent and highly skilled* at "their game." They must be. Without the internal resources to love their self, deception and manipulation are two of the means they use to experience love. Remember, for the N, love must be obtained from external sources— from you and from others. It's not true, of course; love is a choice, but that is not what an N knows about love and about their self.

In the beginning, you are unaware of their facade, and even if they made a few small slips here and there, you didn't notice, or you chose not to acknowledge what you noticed. How to spot the slips, the changes in their behavior, is covered in detail in the following paragraphs.

After you have totally fallen for their game, that is when you start to notice the changes. Once a "target" (you) is "all in," the N slowly and steadily removes each element of the five A's of love. Often, it starts with a "conversation" about how *you* have changed. Suggestions pop up that you need to "fix" something about you. Or they tell you that something is "off about you." It *is* off, but not about you. You know what is true, what your experience is, but you buy in. Remember the conversation about the bias of knowing what you know is true, but believing what they tell you is true, even though you know it is false? That bias is in play here. It is not true, though. Nothing about you is off. You are fine, you are "all in," *and* you have noticed that something is off, too—about them and how they have changed.

The sad part is that over time your real self, the person you love, is lost. You lose all of your self. Often, you have a sense you are "nothing." You have become invisible—to your self, to the world. At that point, you are caught in a most unfortunate situation. It seems hopeless. But, you are not a quitter, and you are not about to quit on "the love of your life". You are prepared to expend whatever energy and resources you can muster in an attempt to recover that "love you shared." You do what you know; you respond with more love and more heart. You continue pouring out your being, hoping the "love," which was never really there, will return.

But it never will, because their "love" was never real; it was always a mirage, a façade, a ruse, a manipulation, a game. How could that be?? Simple. That is the mastery of the N.

How do you deconstruct the nature of an N? Start with love. What do you know about giving and receiving love?

FACT:
They cannot *give* what *they* do not *have.*

Remember, the N begins with little or no ability to choose love or live from the heart. They do not love their self and, thus, do not have the capacity to *give* you love. The N can only take from you. They play on your desire to give and your hope that giving love will be reciprocated. The N has a unique skill, which (until now) you were unaware that they possess. They are the master at figuring out exactly what you need in the way of the five A's. They give you "all that," in abundance . . . until you "commit." Then "game over"; you become their source for love.

In essence, what is happening is that you provided the N with the only love they can experience. They need your attention, your appreciation, your acceptance, and your energy to feel alive. Since they are an empty vessel, your love sustains their being. Once they know you are "all in" and know you are committed, they simply shut down and stop providing the elements. Because? You are committed. That is what they wanted from the beginning. And they know you are highly likely to stay committed, because that is the essence of your true self. The N is extremely skilled at figuring you out. When you go "all in," you are intentional about *staying all in.* They know this about you, too. It's OK. You did not know this about them, but today you do, and you are more aware about your self, too.

When you *choose* to leave, that is when the game is "over." In most cases, "The End" will happen only when the "target" (you) of the N's manipulation decides "enough" and chooses to end the relationship.

Disasters like what has been described here are the saddest of all stories about love and relationships. For the survivors, the wasted years, lost love, and broken hearts are the complete summary of their relationships with N's. The good news is with what you know now, what you can see from these vignettes: A lot of the damage can be avoided with diligent application of healthy relating skills and awareness. At the same time, it would be wrong to imply all the heartaches are avoidable.

The red flags are there, and by exercising patience, a healthy adult can discover these well before "commitment." What are some of the biggest red flags to look for? The biggest warning is hearing a claim that someone's life, their past, is "perfect." This tells you immediately something is *off*. If you do hear this claim, just ask your self, Is something "off" here? Is there something about this person, their past, their family, their relationships that just do not seem to fit? What is their story about their past relationships? Is it possible the issues were always someone else's fault (the ex, the kids) or that they were the "victim" or that they "did everything they could to save it, to make it work"? Really. Everything?

That doesn't make sense, because you *know* what "everything" means for a healthy adult. First and foremost, it means a healthy person is *always looking inward* and owns their side of any issues in a relationship. If a person understands what love is, they have a healthy foundation: They love their self and are aware that conflicts are about heart versus ego. What did you actually hear about their past? Expectations, entitlement, pointing fingers, casting blame, critiques, control, demands? What do you know is the source of this "language"? Heart? Love? No. That is all from ego, and *those are the red flags for you to hear.*

So, you enjoyed all the lavishing of attention and affection, but did you ask about conflict resolution? This is the next red flag. You know how it works. Everyone had conflicts in their past relationships. Did you ask about theirs? Did you say, "Tell me how you addressed and processed the conflicts and issues that happened in [a past] relationship." After all, what you are interested in figuring out is what level of relating skills does this person have. You definitely want to know their capacity for conflict resolution. Does it sound like healthy skills, or do you hear an "it was all their fault" perspective?

You also know that healthy conflict resolution resolves issues, deepens love, and tightens relationship bonds. Yes, maybe their relationship would have ended. But their "story" tells you a lot about whether or not they were speaking the language of the heart and how the ending of that relationship affected them in terms of gaining awareness—about their self and future relationships.

Another red flag is what you know: healthy people grow from "mining the gold" from past events and relationships. They would tell you about their desire to resolve the issues, to figure things out, and to grow closer, not more distant. You would hear Grace and forgiveness, which also comes with healthy resolution. The "ending" of a previous relationship may have been inevitable, but issues would be "resolved"— even if they resolved them only for their self and they would have grieved their loss. (Otherwise, that grieving may be on hold waiting for their *next* relationship . . . with you?) They will be able to recount the gold they mined from their past relationship. Guaranteed.

If they "gave it their best effort" but none of their issues were resolved and they grew further apart, then distancing from their ex is understandable. But how about closeness with their children? Family? Siblings? No closeness? Then, for you, a bell or whistle should be going off here. You have your answer: This person is lacking the skills to address, process, and resolve conflict!

If you take out from consideration the romantic relationships in their life, conflict resolution with other loved ones is a great indicator of what healthy adult skills someone has in their tool kit. In practice, the results won't always be perfect, but will *every* close family or friend relationship a prospect has be perfect? Not likely, at least from my experience. For you, time and patience are key. You are tasked with listening, asking questions, and deciphering. What they told you about their work, their parents, their kids, is not "what happened." Eventually, you learn that this N is all about dysfunctional and disconnected relationships. The red flags are there, and you have your work to do.

The bottom line for you is: Exercise patience and perseverance because the clues show up. The clues are *always* there. Trust your self. You know what relating skills a healthy adult must have to make their relationships work. These are what you have been learning and developing. Putting your skills *into practice* gives you the answer to whether or not you need to be planning a second or third date with the person who has invited you for a dream weekend sail to the Bahamas!

One more item before moving on:

These stories about N relationships are sad, very sad. There is a good chance one of the vignette examples in the book may ring very familiar for you. In fact, you may relive the emotional trauma of an event and an ending from your past. It may bring a lot of sadness back to you. If that is the case, I suggest you take whatever time you need to fully embrace the sadness that comes to you. If you have tears, experience your tears. Feel the complete experience of the sadness you feel. Those tears of sadness are working to heal and repair the part of your heart that is still hurting from that experience in your past.

So, yes, you may have already addressed, processed, and resolved an enormous amount of the pain. But the sadness you experience *at this moment* is sadness that is still with you. That is the "scar." These tears and sadness you feel now are residual damage and unresolved pain. When you experience your emotions and feelings as they occur, you are making progress on your journey to *becoming healthier.* Experiencing your emotions, in the moment they occur is the *healthy experience and expression of your emotional life!*

Your goal is for the day to come when you are daydreaming about your life, and there in your rearview mirror is the vision of "that" relationship. Once again, you "see what happened." But this time, something different occurs. This time you do not experience the tears, the sadness, or the hurt. This time it occurs like you are watching the event play out like a movie. You are somewhat removed as you observe it in your past. What you see and feel is more than "just understanding."

This time you "see," but you are looking through the eyes of compassion and love. You understand "what happened." This time there is no hurt or pain, no shame or guilt. Instead, you find acceptance and appreciation. You did the best you could with the skills and awareness you had then. You have compassion and love your self for who you were then and who you are now. When that day comes, you will have resolved "what happened" in that relationship. Your return to love in that relationship will be complete as well. *Then* it moves into your past. It was your effort to figure out "what happened," which gave you the opportunity to "mine the gold." That "gold" is what you "added" to your self from that life experience. That part of your past is integrated it into your true self; that is "what happened," and because it happened, *this* is who you are now!

Any time your recollection brings back "something" from your past, *your work is to experience it*. Your work of experiencing what comes up *is* part of your healing process. That is your work.

Another quick point: Always remember as you experience life, you are *moving forward* and *looking back*, and these perspectives are from the present in which you are a "healthier" person.

(Have you noticed you are always "working on you"? . . . Yep, when you are healthy and becoming healthier, and attempting to create and/ or maintain a healthy romantic love relationship . . . there is always some work to do. Yes, it is always your work!)

"Hi, My Name Is [F.I.T.B.[20]]. I Am an Addict."

Located just off the bottom of the abyss, not quite as dark as narcissism, are people with addiction issues. There are many similarities between

---

20 Fill In The Blank.

the two, however. At their core, an addict does not love their self. That is what is missing and is the primary catalyst for their addictive choices. Whatever they are addicted to is used to fill the void where love for their true self is missing. This brings up some important questions:

Can a healthy person create and maintain a healthy romantic love relationship with a person with an addiction issue? *No.* Addiction issues are an immediate disqualifier. A person with an addiction issue or issues is *not* a prospect. In this regard, they are just like the N because they are not romantic relationship material. Since this conversation is about you creating a healthy relationship, the discussion could end here. But there is a question that must be asked.

Can you have a healthy relationship with a person who has an addiction? Absolutely, unequivocally, *yes.* However, it is imperative that you firmly establish and maintain *your* healthy boundaries (Chapter 5 introduced the topic of boundaries, but there will be a complete discussion of boundaries, particularly in the context of boundaries with unhealthy people, in Chapter 7). Boundaries are the key to your establishing a relationship. So how would you operate in a relationship with a person who has an addiction issue? It goes without saying: *Be Constantly Aware!!* Since you are healthy, know love, love your self, and are living from the heart, all of that necessarily implies that you *can* love someone with an addiction. How so?

Primarily, because you live from your heart, you are always looking to give love to anyone along your journey. However, when this "anyone" has an addiction issue, the love you give is 100 percent, but it is with 100-percent vigilance about maintaining your healthy boundaries. Meaning, you will not compromise your boundaries at the expense of maintaining the relationship. In other words, you always hold your value for your self; appreciation. You do not stop paying attention to your self, which, unfortunately, often happens. How does such a "slip" occur?

Suddenly, you might begin to feel "drawn in" to the drama, which typically accompanies a person with an addiction issue. Being sucked into the drama is a common way *not* to pay attention to your self. How might that happen? It could be agreeing to give them a ride, but *the cost for you* is arriving late to pick up your kids from school. It could be taking time off from your work to help them handle their business. Agreeing to be a midnight taxi service to rescue them when you do not have a babysitter for your kids. Hopefully, you see that each of these is an example of selling out. In short, you are accountable and responsible for your commitments at work and to your children. Making *new* commitments a priority over your work and your children is selling out. When you are healthy and love your self, you don't make choices to sell out on your responsibilities or on those you are committed to or to your self.

> **Healthy boundaries are at the edge**
> **of where you end**
> **and the other person begins.**

Healthy people do not infringe on the boundaries of others. Healthy boundaries do not overlap into the circumstances of unhealthy individuals and their lives (*note to self!*). Of course, it happens, you're human. But when it does, once you become aware that you have encroached on an other's boundaries, or that they have encroached on yours, what is *always* your next step? Handle the issue. How? APR: address, process, and resolve it. You acknowledge what happened. You own your experience and take responsibility for your oversight. Then there is your commitment to being more aware in the future. Grant your self or others Grace and forgiveness; we all make mistakes. The issue becomes part of "the past." *Then* you "reset" your boundaries, verbally, with your agreement on what the relationship will look like going forward.

A conversation about a boundary issue, which you caused by choosing not to love your self (selling out) and must resolve, might sound something like the following:

Jill, when you called and asked if I could take you to your meeting last night, I made a mistake agreeing to drive you over. I did not have a babysitter for the kids, and I chose to leave them alone, and that was a mistake (*addressed*). I want to support you and maintain our friendship. But the choice I made put me in a very anxious state. I was worried the whole time. It was irresponsible, on my part as a parent. I didn't realize the issue I created for my self until this morning (*processed*). Going forward, my commitment is I will help you if I can. But only if it works for me with my current circumstances and responsibilities. It's not always easy to make things work, and if I cannot make it work. I will let you know. It's important for me to always put my children first. I am committed to doing that (*resolved*—with your implicit agreement with your self).

As a general rule, addiction issues are a "red flag" indicator of missing components of love in their self and of poor (unhealthy) boundaries. That may not be an issue with someone with whom you have a long-standing friendship, but here we are talking about romantic love relationship prospects.

Generally speaking, poor boundaries can be identified in their current and past relationships as well as other parts of their life. Being aware of their circumstances means you are learning about their state of being, and gaining that awareness is your work. You are vetting prospects against a measure of some state of being a healthy adult. Ultimately, the addiction indicates that "something is missing." What they are seeking is "something" that they do not have? They do not love their self.

Perhaps no one paid attention to them as a child. They were invisible. No one saw them. Attention was missing from their addicted parent or caregiver. Or maybe the attention was smothering, suffocating at times. They were not given a healthy model of love (or of relationships); focused attention was, and still is, missing. They might have chosen to pay attention to their needs and wants, but this was not modeled; attention is something they do not "know." Now, they want to fill that void from sources outside their self; that void is filled with the addictive behavior. They may seek it from others in the form of sexual addiction as well.

In many cases, addicted individuals were told as a child, "You are worthless," "you don't matter," or a litany of other phrases that diminished their self-worth. In order to feel "right" and to be "OK," today they fill the void with addictions to money, career, material possessions, and "augmenting" their appearance. All done with the hope that what they possess on the outside will make them feel valuable on the inside. Their "appreciation" of their worth and value was not installed in their heart. It was not "wired in." As a result, what they "know" is not that model. Today they believe they are "not good enough." This is reinforced by their "inner voice"—the "other voice" of their ego.

These are aspects of love that are missing from their past and remain "unresolved" in the present. Their childhood model is carried from their past into their present. Now they are seeking to be valued, validated, and appreciated from sources outside their self. Now that they are an adult, the tools to reconstitute and reassemble their self, to "love their self," are not skills that they know or possess. It is unlikely they possess the ability to reconstitute their true self.

The type of addiction is unimportant. Why? Because whatever form the addiction takes—sex, porn, drugs, alcohol, adrenaline, another compulsion—this is what the addict chooses "to love." They choose to love this above all else, including a romantic partner. A person with an addiction eliminates their self as a prospect. They love their addiction. They cannot love you, which eliminates them as a romantic love prospect.

You can, however, love them "from a distance." In other words, you can have a relationship, but it is not as close or intimate as a romantic love relationship. In either case, it is imperative that you maintain vigilance about *your self* and maintain healthy boundaries.

This exercise is not intended to be a deep dive into addictions. Nor is the purpose to debate the various theories about addictions, since it can be argued, based on the range of definitions, that everyone has some evidence of behavior that could be classified as "an addiction.". Whether it is pot, or sex, or love, or another behavioral choice with adverse consequences, the specific addiction is not relevant. Addiction has its source inside the person with the addictive behavior. It is their choice of behavior. That does not mean that every person with an addiction issue will be unable to move toward love, living from the heart, and loving their true self. Anyone can choose to become healthy and create healthy relationships. But, like you, they must do *their* work. There are many fabulous examples of people with an addiction issue who have "chosen differently," regained their self, and are moving in the direction of being healthy. The focus of this section are the candidates *in your pool* of prospects.

In summary, you are looking for "now" prospects. People who meet your "qualifications" and your preferences *today*! While there are certainly exceptions, in general an individual with an addiction issue is not on your list and is not a prospect.

Healthy versus Unhealthy Dependency

When the term *codependent* is mentioned, often the description carries an unhealthy or negative connotation. That characterization is not entirely accurate. The misunderstanding ignores the fact that in every healthy romantic love relationship and in most other healthy relationships, there is some measure of "co" dependency between the partners.

Take a closer look at the root of "dependency." You find (in verb form) "to depend on," the definition of which is "to rely on." A healthy relationship is the inter*dependence* of two separate, uniquely different individuals. As their relationship moves into a more and more healthier state, it is a very natural progression for the partners to rely (depend) on each other. Not 100 percent. It is often the case that one partner excels in or is more efficient in an area than is the other. The relationship works more smoothly if the partner with the skills handles tasks that they are better suited for or more knowledgeable in—from the mundane, such as shopping or cooking, to the complicated, such as arranging a vacation or financial planning.

These "dependencies" are part of the "fabric" that weaves together a healthy relationship. The dependencies play to the strengths, skills, and talents of one while removing potential stresses, anxiety, and frustration for the other. In a way, healthy dependencies are one-way partners express their love for each other. It is giving love by appreciation, allowing, and paying attention. Appreciating the gifts and talents of each partner inside their relationship happens when one partner says,

> Hey, you are excellent at budgeting. I would **appreciate** you handling money matters.

The other partner replies,

> Thank you. I have a talent for numbers and would enjoy doing this for us.

How sweet is that!! This is an inconsequential matter, but the thoughts here show the value of "dependency" in a relationship.

But . . . "unhealthy dependencies" are the focus of this section.

Codependent people bring their unhealthy and unresolved issues into all their relationships. Unhealthy dependencies are also shown by a person's behaviors or choices. These are red flags. The source is the same as in the discussion on addictions. Whereas "healthy" starts with the foundation of "love your self," the unhealthy codependent reflects something concerning their ability to "love their self." Something is "missing." Not always, but the odds are it is.

The primary piece of love that is missing is a healthy sense of self-worth. This person holds the perspective that *they* are "not good enough" or "worthless." When observing others through the lens of love and "healthy," the "math" is always the same! The equation for determining worth and value is shown in the following logic statement:

Healthy Value Logic
"Worth" = "Value"
"Value" = "Appreciation"
"Value my self" = "I appreciate me."
"I am valuable." +" I appreciate me." = "I love my self."

Unhealthy codependency places a negative operator in each line of this equation—no worth, not valuable, do not appreciate, as shown here:

Codependent Value Logic
"No Worth" = "No Value"
"No Value" = "No Appreciation"
"Do not value my self" = "I do not appreciate my self."
"I am not valuable." + "I do not appreciate my self." =
"I do not love my self."

The codependent perspective of self is the opposite of a narcissist. The N makes it known that they are "worth more than you" or than anyone else. Whereas the codependent's perspective is that they have no worth compared with an other, they are not worthy of love, theirs, yours, or anyone else's.

Codependency is "red-flagged" by the outward expressions that communicate *how* they do not "love their self." A codependent person consistently seeks approval and validation from those around them. The codependency is often spoken in anxious tones and phrases, and at times it even sounds neurotic. A familiar signal is an insatiable need to always be checking in: "How are you doing?" "Are you OK?" "Is everything OK?" "What happened? Are you all right?" That is a very different from the conversation with a healthy partner.

Your partner may seek reassurance from time to time, and they are interested in your well-being also. There is a certain comfort when you hear their attention and concern for your well-being. When the

310

attention and concern is expressed in an "informational" manner, it tightens your bond; "they care, they asked how I was doing, how my day went . . ." Even the healthiest adults can use a few words of reassurance and encouragement now and again. The difference here is that nothing is missing; there is no deficit in the healthy adult. It's "being human" to enjoy confirmations on your journey through life. A healthy person has enough love, but it is reassuring to experience more love by way of attention from those you love—always!

On the other hand, when this constant attention is packaged with a generous dose of anxiety, neediness, and worry, it becomes very uncomfortable very fast. This unhealthy seeking of approval and reassurance is born from a profound sense of doubt and insecurity. That is tied back to a model of love that was installed. The essence of what they are missing is that solid foundation that they "love [their] self." Healthy self-love would have provided a deep-seated sense of their value, their self-worth, their unique place in the universe. But, appreciation for their self is missing. The constant "checking in" is often a measure of reassurance that *they need* to know that everything is OK *with them*!!

As with those with addictions and narcissists, the codependent must gain their fulfillment from sources outside their self. While the addicted person fills their void with their substance or distraction of choice, the codependent (like the N) looks for a more reliable source: *you*. If you let your guard down and become automagically unaware, the result *for you* is the same as what happens when the mistake is made with the N. You become engulfed in the codependency vortex of drama, unhealthy behaviors, and practices. Participating in the vortex requires some manner of selling out; one or more of the 5A's, your boundaries, or your preferences.

Usually with a codependent personality, you notice something is "off" in the early stages. Initially, your sense is that you have found an intense romantic engagement. You find that you can pour out your love to them in abundance. But you are unaware that you are pouring into a mostly empty expanse. The challenge for you is to determine whether you are experiencing authentic elements of "love" in return. The attention is nice at first. Over time, however, you realize that "attention" is not the attention of love but rather of neediness and insecurity. Initially, you "feel" very wanted and needed. You have love in abundance, so you can give them incredible amounts of love. For you, this giving is very satisfying! Undaunted, you respond with *more* attention and affection. You even provide generous acceptance of their unhealthy, clingy, insecure, needy behavior, because you sense that they have a very real need for your love. You allow them to be OK in their constant state of anxiety and ongoing insecurity. You support them with appreciation of their value and share about *your* confidence in them, a confidence that they typically do not have for their self. Knowing love, giving is what you do when you love; you allow others to be OK in their circumstances.

Eventually, though, you discover or become aware that this happens to be their permanent needy, codependent state. Their state of being might be rationalized and dismissed as you say to your self:

> Oh, yes! Certainly, I understand! Of course, you're OK where
>
> you are . . . and I'm right here with you.

Even though you notice their circumstances remain unresolved, you give more acceptance and allowance, anticipating they will "reassemble" their self and move "out of this place." Eventually, however, their "truth" finds its way into your awareness. When it does, you understand they do not have or cannot muster their resources to do something *for their self—* which is to be whole and complete. At this point, you see the intensity of their insecurities and anxiety, which had *felt* like intense romantic love but is their unhealthy self unmasked. You were pouring out your love, and they were lapping it up like a runner who just finished a marathon. You gave in abundance, which felt right, so you kept pouring until you realized the love you need was not coming back in the manner *you* wanted to be loved.

It's a relatively safe bet that the sex was extremely passionate, extremely intense, and extremely pleasurable. Sex is about closeness and being connected: affection, one of the five A's. However, the sexual/physical connection does not strengthen this relationship. Often, it may breed even more insecurity. As you step back into your daily routine and healthy life feeling closer and more connected after sex, they move back into a more doubtful, anxious state. The wildly passionate sex deepens your bond and fosters a deeper desire within you to connect and become attached. That produces *even more* intense romantic *feelings.* For them, the experience produces more anxiety and greater insecurity about the relationship. All of this "seems like" what you were seeking all along. However, it is a facade. The codependent person is clinging to stay attached and "gain" love and respect for their self, a love and respect that they have not yet discovered in their self.

For you, "The End" is the same as it is when you discover the true nature of any N who looked like a prospect. You realize what is "missing" is not what is missing with you. You disconnect and cross them off as a romantic love relationship prospect. "The End" is where you "mine the gold" for you.

Your work starts with reflection, with your asking your self, "What were the 'red flags' way back there?" Sometimes the answers arrive instantly. The red flags are always found in their actions, their choices, and their conversations. Look back from the new perspective you have of becoming healthy, gaining relationships skills, and knowing healthy skills and practices.

In the matter of "what happened," you observe that as you poured out more love, they became needier, and nothing of what you needed was returned. From your new perspective, you realize that you witnessed no commitment or ability to resolve their past issues. Nor were they able to reconstitute their self to the place where they "loved their self." The skill of doing "their work" was not in their possession. Eventually, you saw the direction of the relationship clearly, and you withdrew your self; you chose to end the relationship and let go. As with all endings, your work is to process and resolve any pain and sadness from your investment of your heart. It was an unfortunate outcome.

Keep in mind, you are on your journey to find a partner, your romantic love relationship. You are anticipating "pouring out" love and living from the heart with a healthy partner who can give love back to you. That is what distinguishes a healthy romantic love relationship between two healthy partners and a "relationship connection" with any individual who is "Not A Healthy" adult, the "NAH."

The NAHs Summarized

Hopefully, this major section, "Differentiating Romantic Love," has been highlighting the fact that the codependent, the person with addictions, and the N are *not* like you. Since our focus is creating and sustaining a romantic love relationship, the circumstances about "why" or "what happened" in *their* story is irrelevant. They may or may not become aware of their past, take inventory of their relationships, or, eventually, do their work. Can they change? Sure! It's possible for them to do what you have done. They can become aware, commit to making changes, and become healthy. But for you, today, these folks are not prospects.

This discussion about NAHs is intended to create clarity for you regarding the importance of being diligent about "knowing" them. When you meet someone who might be a potential "candidate," what you are tasked with is to determine the following:

- Have they been introspective about their life, love, and relationships?
- Do they have an understanding of the choice to love, *and*
- Do they have the capacity to give and receive love (the five A's), *and*
- Have they developed the skills to know how to address, process, and resolve issues in a healthy manner?

When you meet and talk, you *will* hear these elements of being healthy *in their conversation and their actions.* Period.

With this summary, the conversation about the types of individuals *who are not* a prospect is complete. Your work is to have the conversations that filter these people *out of your list* of "potential" candidates.

Now, it's time to choose a partner . . .

Prospects: Door 1, Door 2, or Door 3

The importance of screening your prospects has been mentioned early and often. Hopefully, the information provided has refined your thinking and changed your perspective about how you "judge the field." It must be a bit more comforting to know the total universe of prospects is sorted into just three categories. You know me: I like simple. Let's keep working with that theme.

Those who are not "prospects" happen to be an enormous portion of the age-appropriate pool of candidates. Their choices and behaviors eliminate them before they are considered a prospect. Not sure what to call them, but it doesn't matter, because they are not on your list.

Since you want "healthy" prospects, it may be time to celebrate, because the entire universe of *your* dating–mating–sexing–relating prospects is found in only one of the three categories. That means that your selection process about these candidates concerns the answers to some very pertinent questions. Picking a partner comes down to just a few critical data points. These seem to be the essential items you need to know:

- Are they self-aware, or not?
- Do they love their self, or not?
- Have they processed their past and learned from it, or not?
- Have they found their heart, or not?
- Are they aware of ego, or not?
- Are they living from their heart or from their ego?
- Have they healthy boundaries, or not?

- Do their preferences align with yours, or not?
- Do they resolve conflicts in a healthy manner, or not?
- Do they make and keep agreements, or not?

This partner-picking business is not rocket science. It boils down to the preceding ten questions. Ten questions determine if a person is a healthy romantic love relationship partner prospect, or not. That's it. Yes, we need to cover a few of those items a bit more thoroughly, but that's it! Ten answers will tell you everything you need to know. It is simple.

Either someone you meet has begun their work, *or* they have not. That's the truth. You cannot change them. You certainly can "wish" or "hope" or "want" them to be some other way. But the truth, the facts, the reality, is they are who they are *today*. Lots of prospects have chosen to "sit on the sidelines" and age like a clump of moss fermenting in the sun in this season of their life. They may be the most smoking hot, steamy, dreamy love muffin or sex kitten on the outside, but so what? Seriously. You've probably been down that path one too many times. Good! You know from experience about relationships with folks who have chosen to sit on the sidelines.

The simpler, the better:

> **Ten questions.**
> **Ten answers.**
> **"Y" or "N," "heart" or "ego."**
> **Prospect or not.**

The category that holds 100 percent of the folks you want to pick from? Category 1, **A H**ealthy **A**ware **A**dult ("AHAA"), is the one who probably had the most yes, or affirmative, answers to the questions just listed. In fact, these *are* your prospect candidates for a potential romantic love relationship partner. Healthy prospects are your prime targets. You want to have your radar tuned for these people at all times. Yes, including at the vegetable aisle at Half Foods.

I suspect you knew this already, especially if you have been searching for a romantic love relationship partner for a while. It is even more relevant if you have experienced heartbreak from a relationship that didn't work. The "misses" in your relationships were most likely a "selection" issue. You picked a partner from a group that did not contain prospects. You were not quite up to speed on how to qualify a prospect, and you didn't know most or all the important criteria for a partner. But it's OK, you didn't know. But now you know.

Just as important as finding a prospect who is healthy is understanding the ones to avoid like the plague. That includes anyone who is *not* "**A Healthy Aware Adult**" (the "AHAA" group). Your chance of making a successful relationship work with someone not in this group is: There is little or no chance. Besides, why would you even attempt it? It would be a waste of your time since you know the outcome in advance!! Both partners need to have certain relating skills, or the relationship will crash and burn. Train wrecks leave you with more heartache. You know this. What's the point? Accept these people where they are, allow them to be OK in their unhealthy place . . . and move on!

Now let's hit the Pause button on "what's next" for just a minute. Let's look back and figure out more about "what happened" in your past relationships. Today you know that a healthy adult creates and maintains relationships with other healthy people. An unhealthy adult cannot build a healthy relationship with anyone, much less with you. Oil and water do not mix.

In your past or last relationship, maybe you chose someone who was not a healthy prospect because you didn't have the skills and practices that you have now. You chose the ones you chose because you were "less aware" than you are now. Today you are doing your work, and you are processing your past to figure out "what happened." The value in "looking back" is to mine *your* gold. Hopefully, what you discover are some enormous "golden nuggets" for you!!

The biggest "chunk of gold" may be understanding these three categories. Which one have you been attracted to in the past? Which type did you pick for a partner? What was your experience? What was the nature of the issues? Love? Ego? Plus, it is *critical* that you understand or attempt to figure out which group of prospects is *attracted to you.*

It may be time to sit with paper and pen to reflect on your relationships with these specific questions in mind:

- Which category (or categories) described your previous partner (or partners)? Your last partner?
- Which category have you picked more than once?
- Did you marry and divorce one type, and then choose the same type again?
- What was the nature of your conflicts?
- Can you discern the conflicts in terms of heart and ego?
- How were the issues resolved? What was missing in the conflict resolution?
- What agreements did you make after resolving?
- Which one of you could not make agreements?
- Which one of you could not keep your agreements?
- Who chose to end the relationship?
- What were the reasons for ending that were spoken at that time?
- How do those reasons line up with the truth about "what happened" in the context of being healthy?

These answers reveal a lot of pertinent information about your relationship choices. No matter the answers, it's OK. *You* are OK. You love your self today; "stuff" happens. Mostly it happened because you were simply unaware. Join the club. None of us is exempt from this lesson; if we were, we would have been living "happily ever after" instead of trying to figure out "what happened." The purpose of this exercise is to take an unvarnished look back. Be very objective. See what you did, see what they did. There is no right or wrong, shame or guilt.

What you want to identify is this: where was the "heart" in your relationship, and where and how did ego show up? Why is that instructive? Because as you "interview" a prospect, you want to be aware of what you have struggled with in the past, what kind of partner you were involved with when conflicts happened, and why the conflicts were not resolved in a healthy manner. It seems elementary, and it is important to understand your relationship patterns . . . before you chose to do something different. Your goal is to "improve" and experience a more satisfying relationship this time around.

By the way, if you can see *only* "their fault(s)," you have not looked very carefully. Surely, you are not looking objectively. You would do well to go back and figure out your own role. Two parties create relationships, and at "The End," two sides walk away. You want to be clear *about you*: where *you* missed the red flags. At what point did you choose to sell out rather than honoring your self? Or at what point did you not declare your preferences or boundaries clearly? The goal is to have different results in your future relationships. To make better choices about partners and get different results. That requires your understanding "what happened" in those relationships. The exercise in "looking back" is from your *new*, "healthy" perspective! That is how you "mine your gold."

You are focused on making some changes and are choosing differently the next time. With your knowledge of the traits a healthy partner needs, you know the skills and awareness needed to make a healthy relationship work. Equally as important is your understanding the individuals with whom a relationship is unworkable or too difficult.

The big "get" with unworkable people is that *even when* a relationship starts with incredibly intense attraction—all that "weak in the knees" chemistry—your task is to look beyond "all that." The truth is: A healthy romantic love relationship with an unaware, unskilled person is *impossible*—even with the awesome intensity of mating "chemistry." Just because you experience those exceptionally passionate kisses and long afternoons and evenings of deliciously sweet, intimate multi-orgasmic, passionate sexual play that is "off the charts," the truth remains:

**Creating a relationship with an unhealthy prospect is *always* a losing proposition . . .
*for you.***

Just as with past relationships that started so well, after the mating hormones dissipate, the relationships changed. Usually, it began to change when ego showed up where the heart had been present before. You noticed growing tensions and unrest (heart versus ego). Issues went unresolved and started to pile up. You gave up more love, gave up more of your self, and in return, you received less and less. You thought you had a partner, but instead you found you had an adversary: an ego. Communication broke down, which created more and more distance. Suddenly you realized the love was gone and the relationship was fractured.

The truth is "The End" to the relationship was written from the beginning. The only unknown was how long before you (or they) said: "I've had enough." That relationship, in fact, never had a chance. It was set up for major disappointment, incredible heartache, and wasted life energy with a partner who was never going to work . . . from the start. So, with all these discussions and examples, here is an observation that should be plainly obvious at this point:

**Some of the most powerful attractions
you will ever experience in your life are with
some of the most unhealthy souls on the planet.**

Yes! They were charming, attentive, drop-dead gorgeous, generous, successful, engaging, intelligent, funny, highly entertaining, spectacular lovers, great storytellers, and having more friends than the Pope. Yes!

Upon meeting them, you will walk away weak-kneed and in a delusional state of euphoria, maybe even fantasizing about "the One."

What happened? You were consumed by the infamous "the One" Mythstake (*reread Chapter 1*). That error was further compounded by the "That Chemistry" Mythstake, which was layered in with your making a commitment before you knew whether or not you and they could resolve the inevitable conflicts *that were going to surface.* It cannot be stated more clearly than this:

> **If someone is not healthy,**
> **is not working on their self,**
> **is not introspective, does not love their self,**
> **is not committed to resolving conflicts,**
> **cannot make and keep agreements that**
> **bring more love and deepen your connection . . .**
> **they are *not* a romantic love relationship prospect.**

Sorry. They're just not. No matter if they have abs that are an "8 ½ pack" or perfectly toned calves, a killer smile, or a witty wit . . . it doesn't matter. You cannot make them healthy . . . nor will you *ever* change them! What is your "only" choice . . .? *Move on.*

Healthy Partners in a Relationship

The next several sections cover "must have" items for healthy partners and healthy relationships. Before we do, a bit of housekeeping.

As I assembled the outline for the book, my challenge was figuring out how to arrange all the pieces. In this regard, some things may seem out of order. After reading a section, you may wonder why wasn't it slotted in earlier in the book. The reason is simple: There are a good many of these topics that overlap and are connected to multiple perspectives about you and relationships.

Here is what I will promise: When you close the book, you will have everything you need to change your life and get the love you always dreamed of experiencing. Every skill or practice that you need to be healthy/healthier or to create a healthy relationship, you will have. You need it all. Even if it could have been given to you in a different order . . . relax, and go with the flow. And *yes*! Of course, you can love me by accepting and appreciating my effort to organize an impossible subject to organize: Relationships!

Thank you! ☺

Let's dive back in and look at several aspects of healthy partners when they are in relationships . . .

Resolve Conflicts

Conflicts happen. Preferences and boundaries are challenged. Even when your healthy boundaries are set and judiciously communicated, they get "stepped on," "stepped over," and violated. As always, these matters are heart versus ego. You face a dilemma. You must choose: sell out or love your self. What do you do? What choice do you have? You have but one healthy choice: conflict resolution.

Healthy partners resolve conflicts.

The model for employing this skill in the context of an "issue" is provided in the following scenario, which sets up a typical relationship situation regarding preferences and the call for an issue to be resolved:

> You are with a stable partner who seems aligned with you
> in many ways. *And* you are still in the investigation mode,
> holding the "attraction" that you experienced in the beginning.
> In the romance phase, you have steadily revealed your "true
> nature." Over the course of your conversations, you have
> shared many, if not all, of your preferences. In this process,
> you have stated clearly your desire to have a partner who shares

your appreciation for affection (closeness and touch)—both giving and receiving. You have communicated that affection is one of your nonnegotiable preferences, which is your desire for touching, holding hands, cuddling, and closeness before and after intimacy.

In your disclosure, it is incumbent upon *you* to determine *how this prospect views affection.* You share your desire for it, and you listen to theirs. Very shortly in the conversation, you are "highly likely" to know if this prospect's desire for affection is aligned with yours.

Their answer is either "I like affection" or "I do not care for affection." This person will speak one or the other. That is how you know *if* you will be getting what you want and need concerning affection, should you decide to have a relationship with this prospect.

What if their answer is "I like affection"? What's next? Truth!

Their actions will *match their words.* When you are together, what do you notice? When you go out, do you hold hands? When you stream a movie, do you sit close or apart? Do you cuddle according to "your heart's desire"? If they are someone who *in their true self* enjoys being affectionate, then over time, whether it is six months, two years, or thirty-five years, *their* preference will be consistent. They will be affectionate *and* express their affection to you. It doesn't change. It does not diminish.

But what if you notice that after six months, holding hands happens less often. Their arm is not around you as much. There is no snuggling or cuddling when you are watching a movie at home. After sex, you don't feel them wrapping you up tightly as you did early on. *Now their affection is different.* In six short months, their *preference* for affection is "missing"; it is no longer there for you. At that moment you become aware that affection is missing and that your relationship has an "issue." *Here is where the rubber meets the road on "commitment" and "selling out."*

In the classic sense, your relationship (and you) have a conflict. It is important that you notice there are *two* dimensions to this conflict. First, your need or desire for affection from your partner is not being met. Second, which is very important, their behavior has changed. That is a "red flag"!

You know how to resolve conflicts. Because you have a skill called APR: address, process, and resolve. At this point, the "gravity" of the conflict resolution skill and the *need to address the conflict* cannot be stated strongly enough.

FACT:
How you resolve conflicts determines
***if* you have a committed relationship.**

Which necessarily implies:

FACT:
How conflicts are resolved
determines the outcome of the relationship.

In other words, do you have a relationship based on honesty and integrity? Do you see the "real" other person now versus whom you saw early on? (You may see a lot more of the "real" person from now on.) Is who they now are not authentic and sincere? You will find your answer in the way you resolve this conflict with them.

They will address the issue in a healthy manner, or they will not. The following is a crucial narrative, which outlines two perspectives of conflict resolution—one that is "ideal" and one that is not ideal but nonetheless extremely important for you to experience regarding the long-term outlook for this relationship. Here is the flow of addressing, processing, and resolving this example of a relationship conflict:

First, *you* **address** the issue:

Randy, when we first met, we shared so much about our preferences and what we wanted in our relationship. I really appreciated getting to know yours and for the opportunity to share mine with you. One of the things that I shared was that I wanted an affectionate partner in my next relationship. For me being affection was holding hands, cuddling, and being close after sex. This is very important to me. It is something I did not have in my previous relationships. I wanted it, but I "sold out." I gave up on something that was critical to the way I want to be loved.

You and I were very affectionate during the first six months of our relationship. I loved it. I loved being close to you and feeling your touch. I felt safe. It was comfortable. That is what I wanted, too.

Lately, I have noticed that closeness has gone away. I don't hold your hand as much, and we don't cuddle or spoon after making love. Honestly, for me that hurts, and I am sad. I feel I have lost something that made our connection special.

Pause . . .

In a healthy relationship, your responsibility is to "address" exactly what has occurred from your perspective. What happens next is that you "process" what has been addressed together. Something that you must be aware of here is when you "pause," you put the ball in their court.

You have stated the issue and *the emotional impact* that you are experiencing from the loss of affection in your relationship. Explaining the issue without any blame or shame (ego). There are no words of condescension, disparaging comments, or attacks.

Addressing in a healthy manner happens when *you state the issue.* Then you *share the impact to you.* That's it. That is the healthy way to begin to resolve a conflict (any conflict) in a relationship (in any relationship). Your partner now has the "ball." They are "holding the microphone." It's their turn to speak, and you are waiting. The step is important.

One of two things is guaranteed to happen next. This person is going to tell you in no uncertain terms, whether:

> **They have the capacity, ability, and skills
> to resolve conflict in a healthy manner . . .**
> *or*
> **they do not have healthy conflict resolution skills.**

If you hear answer number 2, this is a *huge red flag.* They don't possess the ability to resolve conflicts in a healthy manner. *You* need to know this early on! In their answer, they have revealed who they have been, who they are, and who they will be in *their future* relationships.

This note of caution has been slotted in before the processing step because you need to be aware there *are* two possible outcomes. One that you have been looking for and the other you want to avoid.

The next step is **processing** the issue regarding affection. Your pause after stating your experience is an "opening". Your *heathy, aware* partner acknowledges "what happened" and expresses clearly; *they understand your experience* (that is, the hurt, pain, disconnect, and so on). At this point, *you will hear them own their role* in "what happened."

Healthy processing sounds like this:

> Oh, I am very sorry. You are hurt. You want to be close, and affection is what you want from me. It makes you feel connected and loved. You are not feeling loved because I have not been affectionate in the ways you like and in the ways we shared affection when we first met. I apologize for not showing you affection and for that hurt. I understand you are sad because you are not feeling loved in the way you want and need . . .

Stop. At this point, some people have looked up from this page and declared,

Isn't this being blown out of proportion a bit? Spencer, you are being so dramatic! Holding hands is not that big of a deal.

After all, relationships are built by *two people compromising* . . .

That is 100-percent, totally, and completely dead wrong. Relationships are *not* built on compromise. They are not. Sorry to be so blunt, but that view is entirely incorrect. How so? If you have been doing your work, you probably know the answer already.

Affection was *and is* a nonnegotiable preference. Choosing *not to address* this as an issue would be a problem. How exactly is someone's desire for affection going to be their experience of love in a romantic love relationship if they don't speak up when it is missing or when it goes away? When your preferences or boundaries are ignored or dismissed, you *always* address "what happened."

The reason for your being in this relationship is to *consistently experience your preferences for how you want to be loved.* To make your experience be the love you want requires *you* to do two things:

1. State your preferences about how you want to experience love in your romantic love relationship early on.

If something happens and you discover that is *not* your experience, then,

2. You address *your need*, to ensure that your partner, the one you are spending time with, planning a future with, making financial commitments with, introducing to your mother, having sex with, gives you the unique love you want.

In this example, your preference for affection was present in the beginning, but then the affection you want/need disappeared. That is the *issue*, and that is what must be addressed. Now for the last piece: resolution.

The **resolution** happens when you make an **agreement** with your partner. The resolution is a two-part dialog, an "exchange" between you and your partner.

The first part of the resolution is a statement of agreement how you and your partner *will handle this issue in the future*. This begs the question "You mean it will happen again?" No, not necessarily. But since we are talking about two humans involved and a preference of one of the partners that was missed, the act of making an agreement represents something extremely important. It shows two people handling an issue in a healthy practice of conflict resolution that brings them closer together. This is the *practice* of *the* relating skill, which will ultimately make or break the relationship. Stating the agreement is important.

The sequence of who speaks first or second is not relevant. The substance is what is most critical. In most cases, the person who caused the "disconnect" begins the resolution. They volunteer a course of action to resolve the matter from their perspective, which might sound like the following:

> I want to love you like you have never been loved before, and sometimes I may not be aware of how affectionate we are when we are together. I want to do better and change that. I will work on noticing and reaching out to you. I may not be perfect, and when you feel we are not connected, or not being affectionate in the way you want to experience affection, you have my permission to nudge me. Perhaps, you can walk close, pull my pocket, and say something like "Will you hold my hand or put your arm around me?" I love to be affectionate with you. Please let me know.

You confirm that the agreement is satisfactory and works for you:

> I agree to do that. Thank you! [*followed by a sweet kiss or some seriously passionate lovemaking . . .*]

If your partner does *not* take the lead, then you start the resolution conversation:

> Thank you for seeing and hearing me. When we are together, and I feel disconnected or want closeness, I will let you know.
> I will rub your hand or reach out or move close to get you

off stride. Or I'll put my hand in your pocket, or maybe we can have a "code phrase": "Would you warm my hands, please?"—with a wink! But I will let you know.

Key phrase here: This next statement is the objective of every conflict resolution. The sole outcome that means anything or will make any difference in the relationship is:

Are you in *agreement* with me on this . . .?

That's it. That is how resolution works. Address the issue. Process the experience. Then come to a resolution that states your *agreement*. This section adds an element to your APR model. Conflict resolution now includes the *most critical* component of this skill. The "gravity" for you is "what's next" in the discussion . . .

Make and Keep Agreements

The conclusion of any healthy conflict resolution is identifying an "action" that is a preventative measure if this issue surfaces in the future. That action is an "agreement." You and your partner are confirming your commitment to the relationship.

> ### FACT:
> **The success of your relationship depends on you and your partner making and keeping agreements.**

The success of the relationship happens when agreements *are kept*. Conflict resolution with your agreement is what connects *all* the dots with regard to relationships.

When you embark on a journey to create a romantic love relationship, I hope the importance of knowing and sharing your preferences from the start has been made abundantly clear. Additionally, a critical part of the process of sharing preferences is to confirm agreements of understanding about preferences. It is mandatory! It is mutual as well; you get theirs, and they get yours.

The confirmation of preferences is verbal, and it is incumbent upon *you* to ask or validate their confirmation. In the beginning, this is done in a somewhat casual but purposeful manner. For instance, when you share your preferences, you query your prospect about their perspective. Their answer *tells you* if they are aligned with you or not. That's critical.

You must be *absolutely vigilant* about stating your nonnegotiable preferences. If you fail to do so, the probability that your unstated nonnegotiable preference will surface as an issue is virtually guaranteed! It is almost 100 percent certain to become an issue. You have not told them, so how would they know your preferences? ESP? In the history of the universe, ESP has been the assumed strategy in countless billions of failed relationships. When reading the obituary of a relationship that died prematurely, before "death [did] they part," miscommunication of preferences using the ESP approach sounds like this:

- "I thought you knew *without me having to tell you*," or
- "You *should have* known!" or
- "*If* you really loved me, you *would have* known!"

Those statements are the ESP strategy being verbalized. Notice the "tense" is clearly *after the fact.*

No. Not being aware of *your* preferences is not *their* fault. If you did not clearly state your preferences, how could this be their problem? It's not, and it's OK. Maybe you weren't aware of the importance of communicating your preferences clearly. You did not know the importance of getting a confirmation after you shared them. If you have assumed the ESP strategy in the past, the suggestion here is not to make that "Mythstake" going forward. In other words, drop the ESP assumption. Immediately.

Issues and conflicts in relationships that are not related to "heart versus ego," preferences, and boundaries, typically arise in the areas of kids, family, money, and sex. Your task is getting agreements on these *well before you make any commitment* to a relationship. *Period.* There is no exception to this rule. It's fixed. It's in stone. There is no debate.

You state your preferences to a prospect. Your work is to confirm their alignment with you (literally). You can do this with a simple statement/ question constructed like these examples:

> So, we are in agreement on having kids before I am thirty?"

Or

> So, we agree: I will work and take care of groceries, insurance,
> gas, and travel. You will take care of everything else: the house
> and the car payments, and so on.

Then you state the action step, which is a critical part of your agreement:

> And *if something changes, we agree* to discuss any changes, and
> we agree we will *not* make any unilateral decisions before we
> talk about things, *right?*

These examples explain how agreements are created *and* confirmed during the romance phase *before* any commitments. You can probably look at your past relationships and understand the importance in the bright light of your personal experience. Agreements determine a great deal about the success of the relationship—100 percent of the success. An agreement not kept and gone unresolved is guaranteed to build into resentment over time.

Here is the other aspect about unaddressed, unprocessed, unresolved issues and broken agreements: Left in this state of disrepair, they are the act of "selling out." Only through resolving issues by making and keeping agreements does any relationship have a chance to deliver the love your heart desires. That is the "gravity."

In romantic love relationships, the elements that must be present to create an agreement are the following:

- **Two people are aligned on a single outcome, purpose, direction, or activity.**
- **Each party takes responsibility for and is accountable to the "other" for executing their individual actions or tasks required to ensure the outcome of the agreement.**
- **They are individually committed to holding to, completing, or accomplishing their responsibility, so they experience the shared goal or outcome as partners.**

Is there a shorter way to say this? Sure!
Agreements are:

- **When two people in a relationship discuss an issue, make an agreement, and commit to do it differently in the future and *then do it*.**
- **People make promises together, and they keep their promises.**
- **People do what they say they are going to do.**

The implication of agreements is critical for the partners to have a chance at a successful relationship. It eliminates a lot of what happens without them. One partner doesn't randomly think about "sumpthin'." Then, without talking to the "other sum'body," goes off and does that "sumpthin'." One partner doesn't unilaterally conclude one morning that they are going do sumpthin' because: "It's my gol'darn right to do what I want." Or because one day they decided, all by their lonesome, "It's my money, and I'll damn well do with it what I please." Or in a moment of pure self-centered N-like unconsciousness realize: "After trying on all six pair, they *all* went with my new outfit. Screw the agreement about a budget, I bought them *all*." We are way down the road on which part of their self is assisting these "sum'bodies" in each of those situations, right? What is at the core of one partner making unilateral choices in the face of an agreement between partners that they will *not* make them? *Hint:* it starts with the letter *e.*

In summary, what is the key element to keep in mind with respect to agreements and healthy relationships (which is what you are attempting to create) is the following:

Partners make agreements.
Healthy partners *keep* the agreements they make.

As noted at the beginning of this chapter, the elements of healthy relating are progressive; they layer in together into a single tapestry. The concept of agreements, as shown by those examples, bring into focus another critical aspect of healthy relationships . . .

Have No Hierarchies

There is no hierarchy in a healthy relationship. One partner is not "better than," "more than," "worth more," and so on. One partner does not "just decide to do [something]" because "I make more money than you, so it's my right." These cannot even fit in a description of "healthy."

A "healthy relationship between two healthy partners" necessarily implies the following for both: Healthy people love their selves, exactly where they are. They are complete and whole. They possess all the love they need, in the manner they needed it. They have nothing that is in deficit. They don't "need someone." They can sustain their life with their means. Where they struggle, they have their resources and skills to figure it out.

When *two* healthy people come together, they walk into the relationship whole *and* choosing to love the "other":

- "Just the way they are,"
- "In exactly the place they are,"
- "Given all the circumstances of their past and family,"

- "Even though they snore at night and tell terrible 'knock knock' jokes . . ." Because?

That is "how it is" when you love a human being, and they choose to love you. What does this have to do with relationships? In a healthy relationship:

Two independent, healthy people come together as equals.

Their agreement is that each has an equal voice. There is no hierarchy. They have equal value. They *add* love to the other, and together they create the relationship. There is no "power struggle" in the world of healthy relationships. Salaries may be unequal. Titles may be different on the "corporate ladder." These are irrelevant. Why? Refer back to the definition of love versus ego. What do you find?

- Love doesn't "compare." Ego compares.
- Love doesn't "make me right and you wrong."
- Love doesn't make a "less than I am" in this relationship.

Choosing "to love" eliminates these, because by giving *acceptance*, partners choose to forgo hierarchies, if for no simpler reason than giving acceptance means acknowledging that we are all different—not better, not worse, not "more than," not "less than"—*just different*. In a healthy relationship, you are "different *together*."

Set these elements side by side, you find a healthy partner, you make agreements, and there are no hierarchies. Making agreements and having no hierarchies implies another critical aspect, too . . .

Do Not Make Unilateral Decisions

When the partners are operating off the same page of "agreements," they make no unilateral decisions that affect the relationship or impact the other partner. That makes sense, doesn't it? This one needs some careful scrutiny, however, because it's a very large "net," which covers all the critical decisions in a relationship. Decisions such as? Time commitments around vacations, holidays, and travel; decisions about money, debt, credit, spending, savings and retirement funds; decisions about having kids, raising them, schooling, discipline, spiritual influences, and more. And the one most people do not think about in the realm of unilateral decisions: Fidelity? It's not the sex act of infidelity that is the issue. The issue is one partner deciding to make a unilateral decision and choose "infidelity." That is the issue. It's actually *two* issues; the other being your agreement to be exclusive with regard to sexual intimacy. There is an issue of the broken agreement *and* the unilateral decision (which impacted the "other" and the relationship).

That last one probably threw you for a loop. But it shouldn't, because cheating is by its very nature a "unilateral" decision. Think about the definition of a unilateral decision again, more closely this time. Infidelity "impacts the other partner." That is a bit of an understatement, which is not intended to soften the blow but rather to provide a dispassionate context from which to view infidelity. What is it really?

Infidelity is a relationship IED[21] going off under the couple's house!

Any individual who decides to have an affair *is* making a unilateral decision. That violates two aspects of the relationship's foundational premises: their agreement and the concept of no unilateral decisions that damage the "other." When the autopsy is performed on dead relationships, *unilateral decisions* about infidelity is number 2, behind unilateral decisions about money.

When taken as a whole, the concept that partners will make "no unilateral decisions that affect the relationship or impact the other partner" is a very powerful statement. It is an even more powerful "commitment." In combination with "agreements" and "no hierarchies," it shines a particularly sobering light on romantic love relationships.

---

21 Instant Emotion Devastation.

That is the "gravity" referred to earlier. It puts "commitment" in a much brighter light. Where is all of this heading?

No Agreements = No Commitment

Simple. If two people come together but do not create agreements about how they will operate together as equals in partnership and if they do not keep their agreements, *they do not have a committed relationship. Period.*

The math is even simpler:

No agreements = No commitment

No commitment to agreements =
***not* a committed relationship**

No commitment to keeping agreements means that there is no commitment. It does not exist. Whatever the arrangement is, it is not a relationship that accommodates two independent people operating interdependently as equals and each having an equal voice.

What it defines is a relationship that requires one partner "giving up" essential parts of their true self as a "condition" to be with the other partner in a relationship. Where have you read that statement before? That sentence frames up precisely what it means to "sell out." So, we are clear here: That describes exactly how "selling out" occurs in a relationship (in all relationships).

Agreements make healthy relationships work. Agreements honor two people who stand on either side of the love they share *between them.* They hold love between their two independent selves. Love exists "between them." "Stuff happens." Conflicts happen between hearts and egos. The conflict moves these two *away from the love they share.* When conflict happens (and it will), they have a choice. Either they choose to address the issue that moved them away from love, or they do not.

When executed in a healthy manner, authentic, vulnerable conflict resolution is guaranteed to move them back toward love.

Healthy conflict resolution produces *agreements*, which make amends and renews their commitment(s). It is their *commitment to keeping agreements* that keeps the relationship focused on growing the love the two partners share.

How does this all fit together—these new elements of agreements, unilateral decisions, hierarchies, and so forth? With these new thoughts about an authentically committed relationship, let's recall the example we were working through about your preference for affection . . . but . . .

Let's add a dose of cold hard reality into the mix.

After you addressed your issue regarding the affection that has "gone missing," you hit Pause and put "the ball" squarely in their court. Let's take a left turn here and ask this: What would be your reaction now if you heard the following from your partner?

> You know what? Back then, I was giving you what you wanted when we were just starting out. But I like my space. I don't want to be close like you like to be all the time. It's like we have to be joined at the hip.
>
> Yes, there are times when we have sex, it's OK to snuggle and all, but mostly I just want to fall asleep. You are welcome to try to cuddle or snuggle if I'm asleep, though. Does that work? Or is that not good enough?
>
> Also, I didn't say anything before, but—wow—I must tell you: Recently there have been a couple of times I have been very uncomfortable holding your hand or having you right on top of me. When we were out with my friends, and then last weekend, when we are waiting in line for that party . . . Geez,

sometimes all that handholding and arms-wrapped-up thing
is downright embarrassing!!

Reality? Yes. That is their *truth.* And it definitely falls into the category of "good *for you* to know"! Have you ever experienced being on the receiving end of a cozy conversation gem like this? Have you ever thought you had one relationship and then six months or two years or ten years later . . . you realize you didn't? Do you realize today that what you have is another relationship . . . completely different from the one back there, "once upon a time"?

Let's hit the Pause button and ask, simply: Does that statement they made resolve anything? No. What that statement does is provide the tailor-made, perfect example of a *red flag warning.*

Upon hearing them "share a bit more deeply about their self," it would be a fabulously sensible time to contemplate their answer in the context of every nonnegotiable preference you have on your list. Furthermore, you would do well to take a complete inventory of your preferences, to see which ones you know for certain you have an agreement on with this person.

And here's the key: It would be advisable to take these actions sooner rather than later. Especially if you have experienced their actions as being one way early on and now they are being a different way.

Specifically, a red flag is raised:

- when their actions were aligned with their words for a period of time,

but now

- Their actions are *not* aligned with their words.

Adding these two together leads to only one conclusion:

- Their commitment to your agreements regarding your preferences and how you want to be loved in relationships have *not* been kept.

This vignette represents one of the most common ways a partner makes unilateral decisions, changes agreements, creates a hierarchy, and dissolves their integrity with you. When these actions and choices are combined, as they often are, they put your relationship in jeopardy. Any other conclusion reflects *your choice* to obfuscate "truth."

The purpose here is to focus your awareness on the truth. Failure to acknowledge the truth is a self-inflicted wound, which you are choosing to do to your self. "What happened before" is "*what is happening now.*" Again!

The truth cannot hide behind "I didn't know!"—as may have been the case in the past. Now you *do* know.

Remember reading when someone made this comment?

> Oh gosh! You are being so dramatic! Holding hands is not
> that big of a deal. Not really!

I believe this brings up a very salient point:

**How, exactly, are you going to experience love
in your romantic love relationship
if your partner does not honor their commitment to
love you the way you have indicated you want to be loved?**

Dramatic? No. This entire micro-section is intended to be a warning.

Your ability to see and hear red flags requires all your resources, your expertise, and your tools of healthy relating. You know what "healthy" and love is, and you know about your preferences, about agreements, about actions matching words, and about the importance of addressing, processing, and resolving conflicts and making agreements. These are the cornerstones of how you *create and maintain* your romantic love relationship. If any of these are missing, what you have is *something different from* a healthy romantic love relationship.

When you are with someone who makes no agreements, makes unilateral decisions, and maintains hierarchies, you have a partner, yes. You have a partner whom you can have fun with, have some good laughs with. Maybe you can do some traveling together, engage in scintillating dinner conversations together with interesting world traveler mutual friends, and you can see a movie or two together. Hopefully, the sex is off the charts just as you imagined it would be back when your mating instinct was mostly all you thought about . . . for weeks, since you figured you had found "the One"! But as far as a committed healthy romantic love relationship . . . No. That is not what you have. Period.

Before you thumb to the back to find my email address and "share your thoughts" because you disagree or are mad or confused or angry because my direct style has offended you or someone you know, or because you believe I am being judgmental (which is absolutely the truth) . . . let me finish the thought here.

Sure, you *do* have a relationship! In fact, the beauty in this whole scenario is *you get to choose!* You can choose whatever kind of relationship you want to create and with whomever you wish. The focus of this conversation has been and continues to be "creating and maintaining a *healthy* relationship." Maybe there will be a forthcoming book on "how to have a fabulous date-mate-procreate relationship with no commitments," but that is not this work. This exercise is focused on navigating you to achieve the "end," called a healthy romantic love relationship.

So, let's be a bit more precise. You can choose to create a dinner, movie, and sex relationship. Absolutely! In fact, most of those people labeled "Undatables"? *They* would *strongly prefer* the dinner, movie, and sex relationship with you. That is *exactly* the relationship they hope you choose to have with them. This type of relationship matches their preferences and how they would prefer to operate in relationships. They would much rather be committed to date-mate-procreate, and if it doesn't work out, no biggie.

Let me ask you: Have you ever met "the One," who after three dates morphed into one of the Undatables? Then you wanted to wish them well and you attempted to move on, but they were relentless about contacting you with bent-knee confessions: "I've changed." Or "I'll do anything you want to make it work." Or "Just give me some more time . . ." Have you ever experienced the "never ending" undatable partner?

Question: In your opinion, did they fall out of bed, hit their head, and decide to get on the road to becoming healthy? Automagically? Overnight? *Or*, do you think they would *really* prefer a dinner, movie, and sex relationship with you that doesn't require that they change or make commitments or keep them?

Hold your answer . . . We'll pick that question up in the next chapter, after these next few paragraphs, which finish the conversation about creating a *healthy* relationship.

Back to the example of your preference for affection:

Recall that we left off just after the about-not-to-be-a-prospect delivered a red-flag warning.

You offered a resolution to your affection issue, and they responded. They don't like affection. They were showing you affection just to appease you. They were not being their authentic self in the beginning. Their actions were, in fact, disingenuous and were intended to mislead you. They were going to tell you whatever you needed to hear early on. It is not a reach to conclude that their intent was mainly focused on the shortest route to the bedroom. Who knows? But, is it safe to conclude this is not a romantic love relationship prospect? By my calcs, yes, a very safe bet.

Your relationship, and *every* relationship endeavor that began with the intention to be a long-term romantic love relationship that reaches this impasse where their true self is revealed, is *over*. You were diligent about stating your preferences, communicating your boundaries, and making *your actions* match your words. You wanted and needed to make an agreement to move the relationship forward *before* you were willing to make a commitment. Now you have more information. Critical information *for you*. There is no commitment. You have no agreement. This is "The End." There is no "what's next." They showed you everything you needed to know. They have no intention to love you in the way you want. They have no skills to make agreements. In their authentic presentation of their true self, they have *told you* they have no interest in evolving their relating skills and becoming healthy, which is another one of your nonnegotiable requirements.

We picked up the conversation after the truth was revealed. It is time for this relationship to move into your past (good news). This partner, and this "potential" relationship, has now landed in the category of an unworkable relationship.

Chapter 7.

Unworkable Relationships

The fact that the circumstances and this prospect ended up being unworkable is OK. It happens when people reveal who they really are over time. *They will always show their true self!!* These are reminders about our humanity and the fact that we do not know what the future holds and, thus, "we all make mistakes." Because? "Something happened" that you didn't expect. Of course, you're human, and that's life. This conclusion applies to your relationship life—in significant ways, too!

Certainly, you know you do not have ESP. That is a given. But something happens, something changes, someone acts a certain way—all unexpected—and the results are "new circumstances." Life changes, and "new circumstances" is how life happens every day! The aspect of "new" that we are concerned with are when these "new circumstances" have negatively affected you and your relationship. Specifically, when you realize the possibility of creating a relationship is lost. Acknowledging this is hard. You've invested time and self to create something, and your hopes are dashed. Acceptance is your only healthy option. Yes! *That* acceptance; Love.

Even when you are at the top of your relating game, no matter your diligence, no matter your caution, no matter how well you maintain your awareness and how clear you are in communicating your boundaries and preferences, no matter how well you have refined your self to become healthy—even with all of this in place—the truth is that sometimes "something happens." At that point, the relationship becomes *unworkable.* As sad as it is when it happens, earlier is better! Life is short!

You had no way to know if this "one" was "*the* One" unless you took a risk to find out. You did. You made a fabulous connection. Everything seemed as though it was working. They had some relating skills, had stepped up on occasion, together you worked through a few issues, and it seemed like a "fit." You may have chosen to venture into sexual intimacy, which deepened your connection.

But after a period of time, the truth was revealed, which was that something was "off." You were cautious, but to find love and create a romantic love relationship, you had to take some risks. So, you pressed on a bit further. *But* today you are different, because *you steadfastly refuse to "sell out" on your self!*

This time, when you realized something was off *before you made a commitment,* you made the healthy choice to accept the "ending." In other words, "accept the ending" means "choose to love your self." That, my friend, *is* good news. And, it's OK. There are "plenty of fish," so it's highly likely you'll meet another one who may be "the One" after all. When you do, you'll take some risks to find out again. That's life.

But with this particular partner, the relationship has become "unworkable." There is nothing more you or they can do. No one is to blame. Certainly, there is no guilt, because you both "gave it your best." You gave them love in abundance. You received all the love they shared back. The truth is, however, even though so many things worked, felt comfortable, and were things you cherished about them, some vitally *important things* were *missing* for you. The relationship did not—and, you realized, was not going to—satisfy your deepest needs and wishes. You cannot change the circumstances. You cannot change your partner, either. The details of the events are irrelevant at this point. This relationship cannot develop any further. When you see the truth, your response is to acknowledge it, act with integrity, and let the relationship go.

Yes!! Sure, you could probably "give up" a "few things." With some elementary-grade rationalization magic, you could make whatever you give up sound like "Oh gosh, it's not that big of a deal . . . really." I call BS. That is a lie. There would be a cost, and it's a heavy toll. What you would be giving up *are* your preferences. "I want to be loved this way; you can't or won't, but it's OK, it's not that big of a deal!" The unique way you want to be loved is not a Big Deal now? I beg to differ.

You know the name of "the cost"; it's called "selling out." Maybe "selling out" was the option you chose in one of your past relationships. That relationship was *also* "unworkable," but you thought you could make it work; all you had to do was just "sell out" a bit of your self to make it work. If this is your experience, you know the outcome when you sell out. You are also very aware of what "the cost" feels like, in your heart and in your soul. Selling out is not a healthy choice or option.

When relationships are unworkable, it doesn't make "The End" any easier. Unworkable endings are hard, too. There is usually an abundance of sadness. Until the circumstances became unworkable, you held on to the hope this person was a fit. You began to imagine a future—what life would look like if the relationship could work. The journey for you would be to experience the love your heart desires and then sharing that experience together.

That is what you have been aiming for. That is what healthy romantic love is all about, after all!! The dream faded with the reality that the circumstances had changed. The dream finally faded out of sight. It's natural that this "ending," like all endings, delivers its final address in the sadness from losing a hope and dream. There are tears. There are long days where time is consumed by looking at the dream through tearful eyes as it vanishes from you like a cloud drifting over hot desert sands. Slowly you watch it disappear; you can't see it any longer . . . all you know is it's gone. You let it go and move on, but you must take care of your business.

Loving "from a Distance"

When circumstances change, the healthy choice is to let the relationship go. The key to ending an unworkable relationship is choosing "to love." Here we are adding another piece to your growing mix of relationship skills. The ending needs to end with the choice "to love," but you cannot love them "close," in the closely connected manner of a true romantic love relationship. Here, we add "love from a distance" to your skills. The key component is "from a distance," which has a wide variety of applications. Many times in your life you will be choosing to "love from a distance," because "circumstances" exist that make it impossible to love someone "up close." While your focus here needs to be on an "ending" with an individual with whom you cannot maintain a healthy, committed romantic love relationship, there are individuals—such as parents, siblings, other family members, and coworkers—whom *you must also* "love from a distance."

In both instances, this is the choice you make because loving *them* closely requires you to give up some piece of you and to *not* love your self. What you would be giving up would be boundaries, preferences, healthy choices, and so on. We'll go over these later.

In the matter of this partner prospect, however, recall the point earlier:

Healthy people create healthy relationships.

Although you did your best to select a reliable companion, it turned out they didn't have all the skills needed, and the "alignment" of your preferences and theirs was slightly off. It happens. Again, the circumstances are irrelevant. What is relevant is that you did your best. You stepped into the relationship living from your heart, with all your refined, healthy skills; you listened, and you did your best to resolve conflict and make agreements. Unfortunately, despite your best efforts, the actions and words of ego continued to surface. One item to note here, however, is that there is no place for blame or shame. Maybe some of the ego was yours, and perhaps some was the other person's. The important point is "what happened," with the knowledge you gained about them, about your self, and about the circumstances that changed, describes the unworkable nature of this relationship "to a *T*."

Now it's over, because you are not needy, nor do you have to be attached to someone in unhealthy ways in order to experience love. That is not you. Once a relationship becomes unworkable, you choose "The End," *because* you love your self. "The End" for you means that you "resolve" the ending in a healthy way:

> **You choose "to love," *and*
> you choose to "love them from a distance."**

It is important to note your love *does not* change, neither about them *nor* about *you*.

You are **attentive** both to your self by choosing not to sell out and to them by realizing that their needs and wants are different, not aligned with yours. You grant full **acceptance** to them "just the way they are." That acceptance still stands. There were many aspects of their true self you found connection with, *and* there were some you didn't; these latter aspects are likely those that contributed to the relationship becoming unworkable. It happens. It's OK. You **appreciate** their gifts and talents; their worth as a human is unchanged. They are just as uniquely valuable *today* as they were the day *before* they stepped into your world. They have their own circumstances and challenges. You grant love by **allowing** them to be OK the way they are and where they are on their own personal journey. These are the ways you love—and in this instance, the way you love them "from a distance."

What about the matter of **affection**, the remaining one of the five A's? You may ask, "How can I give them affection?" Certainly, it is possible that you can grant affection, but it's important to look closely at the definition: "being respectful, in the presence of an 'other.'" This one is tricky, especially if you have been sexually intimate.

You learned that sexual intimacy creates a "bond," and this is something that you both experienced. If you have chosen to end the relationship, and this was met with protestations on their part, it's likely that "bond" is present for them *in your presence*. Being *in their presence* or spending time together cannot require that you "sell out" to be in their presence. "Selling out," in this instance, would mean changing your boundaries as the only way you could be near them. What would that look like? If you met for coffee or dinner, they *or you* would need to be affectionate *just like before*. But, for you, you must acknowledge the (often painful) truth that the relationship is over, and you must "love them from a distance." Regarding **affection**, you must be aware of the dynamics as you consider being with them after "The End." It's more like a note of caution, one of our "good to know" items.

When endings happen, it is usually best to maintain a complete disconnect until the "desire" for sexual intimacy has totally evaporated. Those high-octane chemicals of sex drugs are a "high," and your body "knows" the experience. This can be a very strong pull to experience the wonderful "affection" that the two of you had shared. It's best to maintain a healthy distance until the drive of those sex drugs has completely dissipated. Understand that this may take some time, too. Earlier it was pointed out that the "mating chemistry" takes between six months and two years to dissipate. That is the case with endings as well. Once the drive *in you and in them* has disappeared, you are fully capable of being in their presence *if* by being in their presence, you respect your self. In the end, the fact remains: The unworkable nature of the relationship *requires you* to love them "from a distance." In this regard, you grant them all of the five A's—but from a distance.

Reconciling Your Self Back to Love

Regarding the restoration of your self: Healthy people handle endings by "reconciling the relationship back to love." This reconciliation is the same process as conflict resolution. You address, process, and resolve the ending, grieving the loss you experience and any sadness that surfaces. You grant your self Grace and any forgiveness, *and* you grant Grace and forgiveness to them, as well. You resolve to continue on your journey living from your heart and to love your self. *That* never changes. The last piece of reconciliation is the opportunity, as it always is, to "mine the gold." You know this is your work, and since you are "practiced" at this skill, you find that gold for your self. It is there to be found. It may take some time, but if you are introspective about "what happened," the nuggets will shine through. They *always* do.

One last note here before moving on from reconciling. You may not be able to do the APR work on this relationship together. At least not shortly after the "ending." This is not unusual, because there is hurt and sadness that is going to be present. Until these are addressed and processed, a conversation of reconciliation may not be possible. That's OK. Your course of action is to draw on the resources within your self and do this reconciliation work "with your self." Yes, in the same manner that you resolved the issues of *your past* when you were left to process your past without the help of "them." That is where this relationship now sits. They are not "with you," and you must finish this work *for you*. But you are healthy, have done this work . . . and you can do your work on this relationship, too.

Reconciling unworkable relationships and "loving from a distance" brings to the forefront another highly relevant situation. It should be readily apparent that there are a lot of unhealthy people walking around. For the most part, you are not going to be "relating" with them, so they are not really a concern of yours. However, we need to look at situations where you must deal with unhealthy people, because these relationships do impact you. The next section addresses a few of these and highlights some of the skills and practices you will be calling on . . .

Healthy Boundaries with Unhealthy People

The truth is you will be relating with individuals who have not chosen the path to live from the heart, choosing to love. Obviously, standing in a grocery store line or being in a cubicle next to someone is different from being in a relationship with someone. Specifically, we are talking about being in a "relationship" not only with a partner or a spouse, but with a former spouse, parents, children, siblings, and other family members. You are in these relationships *today*.

With these relationships, the sad fact is there are circumstances that surface that make these relationships unworkable as well. These are *often* relationships that you *do not get to choose*. These relationships are "there"; they are *your life*. The truth, which you know already, is many of these people may not be healthy. (*Wow! . . . What an understatement, huh!!*)

Inside the Vortex

As often happens when issues surface with partners, spouses, former spouses, parents, children, siblings, and other family members, they do not get resolved. In fact, with family, the issues may lie dormant for years. That happens a lot with family, in fact. Typically, the "default choice" of all those involved is to "handle the issue" simply by ignoring it completely. In other words, their default way to "handle the issue" is by *not handling* the issue. Somewhere, somehow, there is a fantasy belief that the issue(s) will "simply disappear." You know better. The fact of the matter is:

> **Unresolved issues from the past
> are unresolved in the present.**

What you know is that family conflicts can be particularly nasty. The conversations are highly charged. Often, they are loaded with words of shame, blame, and guilt—lots of ego and not much heart.

Narcissistic parents are noteworthy cases. Even after you have moved into your thirties or forties, they continue to come "downhill" just as they have always done. It is of no consequence to them when they violate your personal boundaries or the boundaries of your home or your children or your spouse. They interject their selfish demands at their whim. They engage their well-refined passive/aggressive nature on you by manipulating, controlling, dismissing, comparing, critiquing, judging, and discounting. You consistently find your self "on edge" because you know their next words could send any conversation sliding sideways into the abyss. The aftermath is that you lie shattered in the abyss, and they continue moving on like a wrecking ball swinging in darkness; being completely oblivious is their true nature. "All that" isn't love!

Even the healthiest adult has difficulty keeping their "N" parent or in-laws at arm's length. When you choose to stand up and defend your self . . . things usually get worse. There is no room for you "to choose," even though you are plausibly the healthiest person in *their* life. You have no room to explain or discuss your choices or actions. With your resistance to being subservient to their demands, manipulations, and behaviors, their attacks escalate. It seems impossible to disengage and disconnect from the dark forces at work here. It is possible, however, and that is the subject addressed in this section.

Conflicts with former spouses can be highly charged, too. These often carry an "extra layer" of anger attached to the conversations. This extra layer is from the unresolved pain from "the ending" or from "what happened" that caused the ending. The words are "aimed" at you, and they come at you "downhill." Their target is about four and a half inches below your left shoulder, about three inches on the left side of your rib cage, and about an inch and a half behind your breast. These daggers are intended to inflict deep wounds to your heart. Being where you are today, you immediately recognize the "usual suspects": the *criticizing* decisions, the *judgments* of "not good enough," the charge of "worthless," and unreasonable or strict *demands*. They want *control* of your time, money, kids, shared bills, child support, and vacation schedules, and just about every other aspect of ego can be thrown your direction. It may seem as though there is simply nothing you can do but "take it." Survive it. But not so fast, my friend.

At this point, the question that needs to be investigated is:

> **Question:** Is there a conversation you can generate that will disengage and disconnect *you* from their darkness? Is there something you can say that will stop the madness?
>
> **Answer:** Yes.

Take out your Big Chief tablet. We are adding to your skills with . . .

A Healthy Model for Disengaging and Disconnecting

Did you notice that those conflicts are all the same old battle between heart and ego? When one side is totally committed to living from their ego, your healthy options are reduced significantly. Conflict resolution, which reconciles the relationship back to love, is nearly, if not totally, impossible. If that were an option, then you would use it. The dynamics have not ever changed. If their intractable positions and consistently negative conversation were malleable, a resolution would have shown up a long time ago. There would have been an "opening," which you would have sensed because you are healthy and aware. That is what you do.

You actively listen for "heart," choosing "to love" in all conversations. But with these close relationships where heart is missing, your option for healthy conflict resolution is "off the table." The boundaries between healthy people, "where you end and they begin," do not exist. But you love your *self*, and this love, in the rest of your natural-born life, is nonnegotiable. To reestablish your self means that your only choice in these relationships, which you did not get to choose, is for *you* to disconnect and create distance. The skill you need is the following:

The conversation to disconnect and create distance is how you reset your boundaries.

When you *disconnect*, you are *no longer willing to engage*.

They are *very* intentional about having those "downhill conversations," but this time your reply is: "No, thank you." Their intent is *not* to have a "conversation." They are not interested in your perspective, your opinions, your thoughts, or your point of view. No. They want to talk "at you." You are well aware of how those downhill conversations feel.

This time it is different, however, because *you* are different. You have made your decision not to "just take it." You are choosing "No more." You are unwilling to continue the dynamic. Here is a warning: *Be aware!!!* Disengaging and disconnecting can be tough. You will get a ton of pushback. This is often the case, no matter how healthy you have become.

What makes disengaging and disconnecting so hard? Because the people you are moving away from were at one time very intimately connected with you, and you are changing this dysfunctional dynamic. The difficulty is you may be disengaging from a parent or parents or siblings. There is a very high probability that the relationship has been unhealthy for a very long time. The dynamic you are breaking is the way the relationship has been structured for a long time—for as long as you can remember. The unhealthy way it was "in the past" is the way it is unhealthy "now," in the present. Yes, that means your parent(s) was/were unhealthy "once upon a time," *and*—key point here—*they are still unhealthy today.* It's OK.

Disengaging from a former spouse is difficult as well. You were not as aware or healthy when you were younger. If you or your spouse was unhealthy, your marriage was unhealthy. That is sad, but the good news is that it reached "The End." If the ending was related to a number of issues that were "unresolved," then these have been carried forward with all of those old pains and hurts. That happens. It's OK. You're OK.

Right here, it is an interesting exercise to look back. Ask your self if your parents and former spouse fit the descriptions you learned about in Chapter 6 in the section "Narrow Door of Prospects" and the sections that followed. Were these people N's? Codependents? Victims? (More on "victims" soon.) Were addictions involved? Maybe? This is another "bet the house" moment; the answer is likely "Yes." These people fit into the category of people with whom, knowing what you know today, you would *never choose to have a relationship with*. A couple of things to think about here.

First, it is perfectly OK to acknowledge that "family members" fall into the "less than desirable" category. Obviously, there can't be a "narrow door of parents or family," because you don't get to pick your parents (or siblings or extended family). They are yours. Sorry for the life of inconvenience! But you're not alone, *and* you are OK.

Despite what they may have missed in modeling and installing love, part of your journey is your work to "fill the gaps." Today, you love your self, and, though it would have been ideal for them to have done "their job," you now have the resources to get what you need without them. They made their choice(s), and those are OK. You have overcome those.

Second—and this item is more of an awareness on your part when you are FACED with ego in any of these situations—the most important thing to remember is that they *feed* on *your energy* and *your engagement*. In other words, your response and engagement with them is exactly what they want. That is what they *need* from you. The underlying reasons were discussed in the section on N's, and those characteristics that applied to the "Undatables" in romantic love relationships also apply to family and former spouses—and to those who are married (or in any romantic relationship) as well as those who are very recently divorced or separated. Being aware means that you understand what is happening.

Your healthy response of disengagement and disconnection is the same as when you are putting out a campfire. When oxygen is removed, the fire burns out. Starved of oxygen, every fire eventually dies. Yes, that is your strategy, too. Your new skill is to learn and then practice complete disengagement and disconnection from these unhealthy conversations.

The conversation of this strategy is provided in the following narrative. You need to have it in your healthy relating tool kit. Learn this model, and then begin to formulate it in your own words, speaking your voice, for your circumstances. For example, if you recognize that your ex has many traits of a narcissist, you are encouraged to fill in the details with a conversation you have had with them from the past.

For instance, say the conversation with your ex is where to send your daughter to high school. From your conversations about this, the agreement you have made is clear. He said, "You pick the school," and he told you to let him know before any enrollment paperwork is submitted. Dutifully, you have done the research, and now you are following up. Last night you sent him an email with the details of your research and your recommendation.

This morning you are traveling for business, you land, and your voice mailbox is full: "No longer accepting messages." He has left you twenty-one voice mails. He also sent you thirty text messages. All in just two hours while you were in the air. Your eighteen-year marriage ended four years ago, so this is not your first rodeo. You have a very good idea what's coming. So, you check the most recent message:

What on earth are you thinking? You are probably not thinking, which is typical. There is no way I will agree to send Chelsea to Central High. Call me ASAP because I have some things to say. That is the worst choice you could have ever made. I would rather pay you money to stay home and home-school her than send her off to that drug and sex haven.

This must be one the stupidest ideas you have ever had, and I have a long laundry list of your stupid ideas and decisions.

I knew you couldn't be trusted to handle one simple task. Just like everything else, now *I* am going to have to get all the options, interview all the principals, check the academics. . . . Why didn't you just say "I don't know what I'm doing" when we talked about this the first time? Then I would have known you couldn't get this one small, really simple task done and done right. I would have just handled it, like always, and I could have gotten it done right!!!!

As you slowly make your way downtown from the back of the cab, you delete the other twenty voice mails one by one. No need to waste any time listening to more of "that." You glance at the first text message. The opening line is:

WOW, where are you coming from? How dare you think . . .?

No need to read any more, so you delete the text. Then:

delete, delete, delete, delete, delete, delete, delete, . . .

you hit delete twenty-nine more times.

On cue, at 10:55 a.m., as you about to walk into your meeting, your purse is buzzing. You pick up your phone and see his name. He knew you had an 11:00 meeting. Naturally, he timed his call for five minutes before it started. His goal is to get under your skin right before you walk in to close this thirty-million-dollar real estate deal you have been working on for a year and a half. This is not a new tactic either. The best-case scenario for him is for you to not succeed, and then he will feel vindicated about his accusations.

With regard to the disengagement and disconnection conversation, where you are at this exact second is exactly where you want to be:

> **This moment is the *inflection point* of *disengagement* and *disconnection* . . .**

There is only one conversation for you to have. The conversation that will *stop the madness.* The singular end game for you is simple: You reset your boundaries firmly and disengage. At this point, it is imperative—no matter how much anger or loathing that may be welling up inside you—that you interject your healthy self into this situation. This is something you may not have done in the past. *This time,* however, you are going to *live from your heart* when you speak.

When you answer his call, your conversation *sounds (exactly) like this* (and will sound like this every time from now until either you die, or he changes):

Hi, John, real quickly, I am busy, but I got your messages and saw your texts. I understand your perspective. I heard you. However, I am not prepared to talk to you about this now. When I am ready to talk about it, I will get back to you. Thank you for calling. I am getting off the phone now since my meeting is starting.

Click!

Call ends.

That is a *very* strategic conversation; it is *crucial for you* to understand the structure. The elements of this conversation are *the* model for disengagement; add them to your skill set. Let's look at what you are doing and the words and phrases you use.

Step 1: You control the conversation from start to finish. You are going to have "a conversation," *but* you are going to be completely disengaged from "hello" to "goodbye." You already had the discussion, and you kept your agreement. You are disengaging. To maintain control of the conversation, you speak continuously and directly. You open the call by acknowledging *him* and indicating that you received his communication:

Hi, John, real quickly, I am busy, but **I got your messages and saw your texts.**

Step 2: You acknowledge that *you heard him.* You are literally going to say, "I heard what you had to say" or "I heard you." Because?

357

You did hear him. He now knows you did, because you *told him* that you heard him. Whether you agree or disagree or have another opinion about whatever he said . . . totally, 100-percent, irrelevant. Your goal is: *Do Not Get Hooked.* This is not a bilateral negotiation, this is not a two-way conversation, this is not, in fact, a discussion. Now, you state, clearly:

I understand your perspective. **I heard you.**

Step 3: You disengage by *disengaging*! First, you do not have time to respond; you have a meeting to attend. Second, you have no intention of replying. You don't need to, and why the hell would you??? What's the truth? He has completely reneged on his agreement. He said it was your decision. You made your decision, you chose, and you let him know. That is exactly what the two of you agreed should happen. For the judge and jury, you kept your end of the agreement. But . . .

He responded by "moving the goalposts." *Then*, digging in his deep bag of downhill tactics, he attacked you . . . with *all of them*. At this moment, you are choosing "not to play." This is the time when you must be resolute about your action. If you choose to engage *or* give in . . .? Yes. *That* is selling out. Selling out to appease his ego is one of the reasons you are not together *now*. This not likely to be the first time you've experienced this behavior. But whether it is the first time or not, you are going to make it clear that from this moment forward his style of communication is unacceptable.

The process of disengaging is withdrawing *your energy*. These tactics will test your resolve. But remember, there is a tremendous *need* for this individual to stay connected to you. That is their goal, and you are simply removing *your* oxygen from *their fire*.

Why? Because when you engage, the connection is maintained. As such, you are feeding all the life and energy required to maintain the relationship. Even as dysfunctional as this relationship *is*, that is exactly what is happening here. In this case, your energy would be your focused **attention** on *them*. Recall, this is precisely what addicts, codependents, and narcissists want and need from you; you are their source of energy. That is their end game. They desperately want (and need) to maintain their attachment to, and bond with, you. You provide energy for them when you are engaged with them. Even in the most dysfunctional and unhealthy relationships, as this one is, your engagement provides the life blood of the "relationship" at this point.

You are going to remove your energy. In doing so, *you are changing the dynamic.* That is your goal. You continue with words of disengagement and disconnection:

I am not prepared to talk to you about this now.

Step 4: You are now disengaged and *you* will choose when the conversation resumes. Your declaration notice of disengagement has been delivered, *and* you have informed them that *you will decide when this discussion starts again.* It is your choice: It may be at some time in the future, or it may be never!! But it is not up to them. They do not get to choose. You do:

When I am ready to talk about it, I will get back to you.

You may not be in control of anything else in your natural-born life, or in this (dysfunctional) relationship, but on this matter? You are 100 percent in total control of the conversation. You have made it perfectly clear. You are in control of this conversation going forward. What they hear is "The conversation will resume on *my terms*." When? That is up to you. . . . *It is completely your decision.* They know the conversation will happen when "you are ready." You may never be ready, but that is *not the point. You* are now disengaged and disconnected.

If this conversation reminded you of when little Chuckie was seven, throwing temper tantrums in his room, making demands, holding his breath, and screaming while you stood at the door locked out of the room . . . Yeah, that conversation . . . is *the same* conversation you are having now. You learned back then. That exercise was called "Parenting 101: Dealing with Children under Eight."

In the exercise here, you are drawing wisdom from "Parenting 401: Dealing with a Forty-Seven-Year-Old Former Spouse Who Is Acting Like a Child under Eight." There isn't that much difference. The difference being when little seven-year-old Chuckie was throwing a fit, he was not throwing flaming word arrows while he was kicking and screaming. That part is different. But, surely, it is not new to you. Regardless, you must be the adult here and handle this situation in an adult manner.

An ego is engaged on the other side. That ego left all those voice messages; that is who is listening to you now on the other end of the phone. What's the "real truth"? There is a broken, wounded, very sad, unlovable child on the other end of the phone. They are stomping their feet, yelling, and demanding that you give them what they want. That is all that is happening. (*Some critics of my work may land with both feet on this synopsis, but I am going to stand by it.*)

They are not six or seven years old, they are forty-seven, and there is 100-percent certainty about what is going on "over there":

- This is not a healthy adult you are dealing with, and
- They are clearly not living from their heart, and
- They are deeply saddened by the loss of your love, and
- Their anger allows them to avoid experiencing their sadness.

One thing for sure is that *you* cannot rescue them from their "state of denial," but you can help your self, your relationship with them, and (maybe) them as well by changing the dynamic and disengaging. This is the best thing you can do for them, by the way.

As you are looking at your empty chair at the meeting table from the hallway just past where the elevator doors opened, your number-one mission and primary goal was: *Stop the madness.* To this end, mission accomplished. You deserve respect and the common decency to be treated like an adult. Someone made you a promise with an agreement. Adults are responsible for keeping their end of the bargain. "You make the choice and let me know," he had said. That was the agreement. You did your due diligence, you shared your decision as per your agreement.

Then what happened? Unilaterally, he decided not to keep his end of the deal.

Does this mean that if circumstances had changed, you are going to be resolute and declare you are unwavering about keeping the deal as is and be intractable in the matter? No. Stuff happens. It would have been perfectly OK to change, *if* there was another conversation, which put another agreement in place. But there was not. He did what he does: He "moved the goalposts" and then attacked. But this time *you* are different. You have communicated that you are refusing to play the game.

That example describes the model of disengagement and disconnection. Learn it. Understand each component, and make the conversation and words in your voice. It's highly likely that you will need to employ this same strategy several more times on this same issue: picking high schools. But this is *also* part of the disengagement process when you extract your self from a dysfunctional relationship. You are living from your heart while this individual continues to operate from their ego. This relationship? Not complicated.

In case you are wondering "when *do* we talk about it?" Answer: Until he gets off the floor, stops screaming, and begins acting like an adult—in other words, until he treats you with respect—you stay disengaged. In other words, until this person decides not to live from his ego, you don't "get back with him on this matter." When he brings up the conversation again, *if* there is no change of attitude, your response needs to be "wash, rinse, and repeat" . . . until something on his end changes. And it may never change. But you are OK with that, because you are loving your self and not selling out. Period.

Now, moving much closer to home. You have a similar situation "at home" with your mother, who is a covert narcissist. This is someone who is a manipulative "victim" in all instances in your life (as opposed to an *overt* narcissist, who tosses hand grenades into your life at will).

Today, she is calling in a panic about your sister's wedding. You have already figured out that you just cannot afford to bring all five of your kids. It is unworkable—with two overseas, one in the state championship soccer match, and two taking their SATs that Saturday. This is her fourth call in four hours, to your office.

You hit Play on your voice mail . . .

> Dear, you simply must bring "my grandbabies." You know how disappointed your sister is going to be if they are not there. Of course, I understand, but I would never have had you miss your aunt's wedding because she was my only sister. . . . Jenny is your only sister, too! There is absolutely no reason you can't get them there. This is a once-in-a-lifetime opportunity. You should be there with your kids . . . so they can see their aunt get married, even though it's the third time around, this time it's different.
>
> You should think about her . . . this is her big day . . . and not your self. She is probably not getting married again; John is such a great catch. I know you had two weddings. Gosh, you almost had another until I put my foot down and kept you from making another mistake.
>
> Everyone is coming. Everyone will be here! What can I possibly say to them . . . why you didn't make it. . . and bring the kids? I am going to be so embarrassed. Do you see what this is doing to me, the family, sissy? I guess you want to be the only one who doesn't bring their whole family. This is very, very disappointing.
>
> Call me! As soon as you get my message! *Kisses!* Love you! Mom!

Is this a conversation that is unfamiliar to you? Congratulations! You have lived a blessed life with very healthy parents, *and* all your BFFs have the largest collection of healthy folks on the planet. Reality for most is different, however. In fact, the number of examples of that parenting style is truly amazing. The manipulative, passive/aggressive, guilt-shame-

and-blame strategy is often the substitute for healthy love and healthy relating.

When a conversation like this one is aimed at you, your strategy is to disengage. Especially if this is a common occurrence—say for the past thirty-five to forty-eight years. The purpose of disconnecting is to reestablish your boundaries. You are setting your expectations for how they will treat you, in a way that is respectful and loving as an adult.

No one has the right to demand or insist or interject that they know what is right or best for you. No parent or in-law knows what the right choices are for you or your family. Not parents or former partners, not your siblings or their spouses—none of them have a say. Your life. You choose. You decide.

The conversation of disengagement with family is like the previous model. When you pick up the phone on the fifth call, which arrives during your lunch break (which is not a coincidence by the way), your conversation goes *exactly* like this:

> Hi, Mother, I got your voice mail. Thank you for letting me know how you feel. I heard what you said. I understand. I am not ready to have a conversation with you about my decision in the matter. When I am ready to talk more, I will be in touch. Right now, I have to go. Thank you for calling.
>
> **Pause.**

Notice the pause here. This is a slightly different ending than the *"click"* that terminated the previous conversation of disconnection. Because this relationship is slightly different, you leave the door open at this point for a more civilized end to the call. Your opening is an invitation for her to acknowledge what you have said *and* for her to confirm that she heard you by saying, "I understand. We'll talk soon. Good-bye, dear." Just a quick heads up: That "Goodbye, dear"? It's *highly* unlikely those are the next words you will hear.

Almost a "blood bank" guarantee that she begins her monologue of disparaging, demeaning, dismissing comments. So you gracefully interrupt:

> Excuse me, Mother. Pardon me. I heard you. I am not comfortable discussing this with you. When I am, I will be in touch. Until then, this is not something that I am interested in talking about at this time. I must get off the phone. I will say, 'Goodbye,' and will be in touch. Goodbye, Mother.
> *Click!*

This time you do not leave the door open for a graceful exit. You end the call. Period. That's all, folks.

These two examples of the disconnection model describe two very unhealthy situations, as the conversations reflected. *However*, the strategy for detachment is your skill to use in *any* conversation in which your heart is FACED by an ego. Those downhill conversation are intended to control, discount, or negate your circumstances or your choices. In both, your energy, which you would have to focus on them by staying engaged, *is their end game.* You are stopping that madness.

One aspect that is important for you to see in these two examples is: These relationships probably have had poor foundations for a very long time. Your conversation of disengagement will be completely different for this "other person." They are going to be saying in their head, "*Wow*, this is not the way our conversations are supposed to go." That is *exactly* your intent. You are changing the dynamic *by disengaging.*

What you are communicating to them is that it is no longer acceptable for *you* to continue the relationship in an unhealthy manner. In the big picture, you are doing your dead-level best to change the dynamic of *all* your relationships into the "healthy relationship" category. Notice how these two examples are so different from a healthy conversation.

With a healthy person, there is compassion for *you*. When you say you have made a decision or do not want to discuss a decision or a choice, they *hear you.* They **accept** your decision. They understand you are healthy and doing your best, given the circumstances you are working with. On the other hand, these two persons are both *unaware*. That puts the responsibility on you to impart the practices of a healthy person *as if you were in conversation with a healthy adult*. In doing so, you are extending an invitation from your heart to them to confront their ego by confirming they understand your circumstances, your choices, and your decision in this matter *about your life*. If they do not respond, then you disengage. It is that simple.

Hopefully, by your disengaging, the dynamic of your healthy response *jars* them from their unloving position, and they make changes. That is ideal. Often, that is what happens. Until that healthy conversation of respect and healthy boundaries happen, though, you are committed to the "conversation of disengagement."

For you and your journey to being healthy and creating and *maintaining healthy relationships*, disengaging and disconnecting is how you maintain your integrity and commitment to love your self. That goal is the same as when you must choose to have a "love them from a distance" conversation, discussed earlier in this chapter.

The difference with these two conversations, though, is that you are establishing your boundaries, *and* you are open to another conversation; a healthy conversation. When you are "related" to someone, such as a family member (or an ex with whom you share parenting), your intention is to maintain a connection but disengage from the unhealthy aspects. Can you see the difference? With family, you are willing and open to additional conversations, but the "bar" for these conversations is being "reset." It is being *raised*. You are setting your boundaries with the expectation that they must be respectful and accepting, that they must speak *with you* from a place of love rather than ego.

By disengaging from unhealthy family members and/or their conversations, your *hope* is that they follow your lead with healthier and more thoughtful discussions in the future. But until such time, you are stopping the unhealthy dynamic by establishing your healthy boundaries. Recall that your "healthy boundaries" are an essential tenet when you love your self. In this case, you present them with model healthy boundaries through the practice of *your* healthy conversations with them. Your words communicate and set the bar. It is a hard edge, too. You are showing them how boundaries live for a healthy person. In this case, the limit you are setting is your intolerance for their unhealthy conversation aimed at you. It doesn't seem like that would be a difficult thing to do, does it? No.

This strategy leaves them with only one option *if their intent is to have a conversation with you.* That option is to love you where you are: pay **attention** to you, **accept** you as whole and complete, **appreciate** your choice to be healthy and make healthy decisions in your life, and **allow** you to be OK in the situation you are in.

For some readers, this "crisp and blunt-force" approach to handling conversations with family may be off-putting. Yes, conversations with family members with whom you have been in unhealthy relationships for a long time can be rather delicate *and* difficult. This is completely understandable. But there is a way to extract your self from their ego, and figuring it out is your work. The model for disengagement and disconnection you now have in your arsenal. It is up to you to do your work and apply it to your situations. The end result is either you will love your self and have healthy conversations with those close to you, or you will love your self and love them from a distance. Both choices are in your best interest.

(Rather than leave you in a quandary here, if you would like to discuss a situation that you are dealing with, feel free to contact me directly: spencer.wendt@gmail.com.)

Earlier we touched on a discussion about the "dinner, movie, and sex" relationship. Let's pick this up again . . .

Chapter 8.

Sex: The Drug of Choice

Let's say you have considered where you are and have decided, for now, a "dinner, movie, and sex" relationship works for you. You were intentional about creating a healthy romantic love relationship, but for now you choose "Relationship Lite." No investment of your heart, just "enjoy" a good time and "have an uncomplicated relationship without all the drama!" You are aware and determined that a person you've met is *not* a romantic love prospect. However, they seem to enjoy life, have fun, have a positive outlook, and are intelligent. Not only that, but your personalities are well matched, and there is a heavy dose of "that chemistry" between you . . . so why not enjoy the relationship you can have without all the entanglements of "forever after" expectations?

This relationship is going to be simple, with the low-key, fun dinners, a nice bottle of wine, cuddled up watching a movie, and then exquisitely hot, passionate sex. Three-day weekends in Vegas, nice dinner, some drinks, and more exquisitely hot, passionate sex. A four-day cruise, where you can enjoy the buffet and sunset on the Promenade Deck and then "dessert" in Cabin B1328.

After some period of time, what you notice is the intensity of mating chemistry is getting stronger. In fact, it suddenly seems to have overtaken you. The sexual intimacy is completely different. It's way beyond anything you have ever experienced in past relationships. Literally, you wake up thinking about it, you shower thinking about it, then you drive to work and handle four meetings back to back, but every free moment is consumed with thoughts of the next deliciously intimate play time with this person. You get a text, and your mind drifts away: "Play!" You hear a quick "How are you doing today?" voice message. It happens again. They call and ask, "Would you like to have dinner?" The first thought that streams through your brain is "Yes, dinner then let's play!" You answer "Sure! What time shall I be ready?" [*"So, we can enjoy some fabulously passionate sex!" you mutter to your self!*]

Choosing a "lite" relationship is A-OK. You're healthy, and you know what you are doing. You know who they are and their relating skills. The appealing aspect of is this relationship is that it doesn't carry the heavy weight of expectations of "forever after." It is fun. No big commitments. You can stop anytime, no hard feelings. After all, this relationship is about having a good time without all the entrapments of bonding and attachment. You know what you are doing. You are making a choice. That works.

Things are happening here, however, which you need to be aware of. It's not really a skill or tool, but it is important—another one of those "good to know" items (which are piling up). Let's bring Helen Fisher back for this next part.

In Fisher's "chemistry" work, she identified how hormones and chemistry of humans help to define personality types.[21] She also uncovered some other interesting items about "chemistry" and your brain. This is the "good to know" part of the discussion. You may want to take notes.

Remember when your dreamboat walked into Starbucks, and "suddenly" you felt "overwhelmed"? You learned that this was strictly your natural animal-mating chemistry unleashed into your system. Where did this come from? It came from the part of your brain over which you have no real control or say in "how it operates." System 1, which is on autopilot, "responds" or "reacts" to cues that are happening all around you. System 2 is your "cognitive brain," which you must actively engage. System 2 figures stuff out; it thinks about questions, predicaments, choices, weight options, comparing and contrasting, and so on. That is the different between the two: One reacts, and one contemplates.

Two elements of the "chemistry" of "attraction" that are cued by System 1 are the hormones testosterone and estrogen. When mating is triggered, System 1 releases them into your system, and they begin surging throughout your body. They are engaging your mating instincts. *But* the mating chemicals also do their work to temporarily suspend System 2, your "thinking brain." Yes, your "thinking brain" is restricted from *thinking*. It's true. You are being cued to "mate" and *not* think too much about it. "Just do it"! (*You are welcome to deep-dive the science here in case you are interested; there are links in Appendix E to Fisher's research.*)

Although the mix of mating chemicals is intense and pleasurable, they act to inhibit, restrict, or disable your decision-making processes. In other words, your mating instincts are turned on; your body is operating on "autopilot" to "mate." At the same time, your ability to think and reason is being numbed, *turned off*; your capacity to measure a partner's words, actions, and behaviors are significantly diminished. The "feel good" overrides any desire or need you may have (previously) had to evaluate their words, action or their true self. That is the "good to know" part for you to take in, and it is an important concept, which will be referred to again in a moment.

What about other aspects of the chemistry of sex?

The Real Sexual Chemistry

When your body experiences an orgasm, there is another flood of chemicals released into the system. One of the hormones is oxytocin, commonly referred to as the "cuddle hormone" or the "love hormone," which promotes bonding and physical connection. It is also released when a mother is nursing, and when her skin touches the skin of her baby. This same "chemical" is released into the bloodstream during mating activities and when there is intimate affection (skin-touching-skin contact) such as holding hands, hands on thighs, massaging of the neck, back, or arms, putting your arm around each other, or cuddling on the sofa. The nervous system is stimulated.

In summary, this "sex hormone" stimulates your desire to bond and have *more* physical contact. For women, that drive is the same desire to bond and create a relationship as they experienced with the birthing and feeding of their child. The more a baby nurses, the more bonding chemicals are released. These bonding agents enhance and deepen the mother's desire for connection. Every time the baby nurses, the mother is stimulated (that is, driven) to connect even more closely with the child. That is *how* the child first experiences affection (in other words, physical bonding with the mother). That is "what happens."

What does it all that mean?

All that . . . is the "*real*" chemistry of sex.

The "real" chemistry of sex puts a slightly different light on the relationship being discussed here. First, let's look into the context underlying "Relationship Lite," or the "dinner, movie, and sex" relationship adventure.

When you have sexual intimacy with your "dinner, movie, and sex" partner, every time you make physical contact, engage in sexual play, or have an orgasm, those "bonding" chemicals flood your system. It's not up to you, it just happens. The oxytocin is driving your systems to "create a connection" and "form a bond" with this person. It doesn't matter that System 2 rationalized that "Relationship Lite" was going to be all about being relaxed and fun, with no attachments or bonding. System 2 told you your partner didn't have the skills to deal with issues that *will surface* in *all* romantic love relationships. In fact, you chose this person for the "dinner, movie, and sex" relationship *precisely to avoid* such "weighty entrapments" as attachment and bonding and having to negotiate through conflict resolution.

Whether you wanted to or not, "systems" that you do not control are driving you to "pair bond" with this person. All you wanted was the fun and the great sex, but the precise end you *didn't* want to happen is happening automagically. In this matter, your intentions and your partner's state of "healthy" is irrelevant. Your drive to bond with them is happening because the natural "drugs" of the human animal are coursing through your system and you *have no control over their impact on your self.*

The "bonding agents" in your system are pushing you to create a physical, mental, and emotional attachment. The high you are getting is a dopamine high; it's *almost* as though you had a substance addiction issue. Why? Because *you are* having an "addiction-like" issue. These are the same chemicals associated with the experience of a substance addiction, and they are constantly (orgasm after orgasm) being released into your system; these chemicals are driving bonding, connection, and more sexual intimacy. The dopamine high, and the soothing comfort of the oxytocin—this is your experience, and, of course, you want more of this "high."

Despite your noble effort to maintain distance and separation, your "systems" are "pushing you" to form a close bond with this person. That is exactly what those chemicals are designed to do. You want to experience more of the high. How do you get the high? You must have more contact. More touching. More intimate play. More orgasms. The more you have, the more you want. Almost all of this is beyond your ability to control or change. It's just the way the human animal, *you*, are wired.

Second is a cautionary note about if and when "The End" arrives. The ending of a "dinner, movie, and sex" relationship can be just as difficult as disconnecting from a romantic love relationship—*even though* you actively chose *not* to invest your heart and were *committed* to keeping your distance, emotionally and intimately. Because of the chemicals involved, your ability to keep your distance and keep your heart *out of play* is a nearly insurmountable challenge. How so?

For a particularly healthy individual, who has actively chosen to "love their self," there may be a dilemma in this type of relationship. When you love your self, you **allow** your self to experience all your circumstance, all of your emotions and feelings. To keep your heart *out of play* in a "dinner, movie, and sex" relationship requires that you *suppress*, or *deny* or *dismiss*, the feeling that the hormones are signaling you to feel, the feeling that is your internal "push" to bond. The hormones are being released, a situation over which *you* have no control. That is what happens when you have intimate sex play.

As such, your opting for a "Relationship Lite" is OK, but it requires that you **not allow** your self to experience the feelings of connection and bonding. Unfortunately, the fact is your "systems" are engaged and are prewired to make the connection. The only way *not* to connect is to suppress the feelings that are being generated and over which you have no say.

It is my opinion that this presents a conundrum for you if you have chosen to love your self. Entertaining thoughts about "just enjoying the relationship" on a superficial level by "choosing" to avoid making a romantic love connection is, at best, egregiously naïve.

The paradox with this relationship is as follows:

> **Choosing a "dinner, movie, and sex" relationship**
> **to avoid the messy issues of bonding and romantic attachment**
> ***contradicts natural processes***
> **over which logic exercises *no* control,**
> **and these processes are working overtime**
> **to *create* bonding and attachment.**

In my book, that is a heavy dilemma. In short, your "logic" is fighting against the natural chemistry of your body. You believe you can override the effects of the real chemistry, but the "high" you enjoy is the high from chemicals, which function to *promote* bonding. You don't get to choose here. That chemical rush (to bond) happens every time you experience an orgasm. Whether you want it to be happening or not, your body is being flooded with bonding agents.

That begs a rather interesting question: Is it relevant or not? I think your being aware of what is happening is necessary. When you know the truth about what is happening and the possible outcomes, then you make decisions based on "being aware."

Finally, the complete picture of real chemistry puts a solid foundation under the concept of "chemistry." The intent here is to show that it is much more involved than just attraction and mating. It is possible that the complete story of chemistry can be helpful when you are figuring out "what happened" in relationships that did not work. I believe this is especially true if you are attempting to deconstruct a relationship or marriage with an N. It is also worth considering if you stayed in a codependent relationship for years longer than anyone thought was possible, given those circumstances. Part of the reasoning behind the choices and behaviors before, during, and after a relationship with that category of partner prospect is very likely associated with the chemistry of the human body and chemicals over which you had no control. How so?

In the beginning of each of these relationships, both parties were being driven to "mate" by the presence of testosterone and estrogen. As mating chemicals were released, the thinking brain was "impaired." Literally. The "red flags" were missed because what was happening didn't register. Remember, System 2 is being dulled—turned off. You were probably not thinking when your partner snapped at a waiter or was so abrupt with you on the second date. Those were "red flags," but your logic and reasoning were in a temporary state of suspended animation. If you did catch it, you probably rationalized it away for the next "payoff," which was to re-experience the chemical "high."

The voice of reason in your head (System 2) dismissed red flags by saying such things as "That's not *that* big an issue! Let's have more sex!" Or perhaps your rationalization was "Gosh, he's so wonderful. I am just making stuff up!" No, it *was* an "issue." Looking back, what happened is you didn't pay attention to your self *or* your preferences. Why? Your ability to think through what was happening was impaired. Causing you to let some things slide here and there. Over time, these "things" you "let slide" were the essence of your true self—such as your healthy boundaries or your preferences, which were stepped on and violated, but you dismissed these "minor issues." Selling out? Yes. But you were not aware.

Going back to that statement "Wow! What was I thinking . . .?" That's correct: You *weren't* thinking. . . . Now you know why! You literally had an impaired capacity to make a healthy assessment of words and actions! Your capacity to "think" wasn't available. It's OK. Back then, you didn't completely understand the effects of the "real" chemistry and how they affected your capacity to make choices and decisions. It just "felt so good." Yeah, it did. Now you know why . . . and the cost.

Looking back, you now understand the universe wasn't doing you "favors" on your journey to pick the "right partner" when your mating instincts were triggered by the N or the codependent prospect. In fact, it was conspiring to make your circumstances *more* difficult. After you experienced the sweet elixir of mating drugs from this incredible attraction that impaired your thinking, *then* you started having sex.

Now you were getting a "high" from making a sweet, yummylicious (made-up word) sexual connection (oxytocin/dopamine). You concluded, "Wow, I feel *so* 'comfortable'" and "I feel so connected" and "It just feels right!" Yes, the feelings were so good, you felt like you had been given a drug. Yeah, you *had* been given a drug. And, just like those people with addictions, after four or five sexual encounters, you were "hooked." It is no mystery that you wanted "more of 'that.'" The ecstasy of orgasms is drug-induced; that alone makes it hard to resist any thought of disconnection. *No way* were you giving that up . . . even though the N or the codependent seemed like such a "good fit."

With this information, the hope is that it is easier to understand "what happened." It's possible you could have made different choices had you known a bit of Helen Fisher's work and had the awareness you have now. But this conversation is not about the past. You're interested in "what's next" . . .

So here is the good news!

First, about those past relationships, with your new perspective or insight about chemistry, "what happened" may start to make more sense. And, yes, it's OK. When you embark on your next adventure to find a romantic love relationship and experience sexual intimacy, you know *a lot* is going on. You do not have much if any say-so regarding the chemistry of attraction and mating. Nor is there much you can do about the chemicals of ecstasy and bonding when you enjoy sex; they *are* the "enjoy" part of sex! On this front, now you are aware. Go ahead, soak in all the yummy goodness brought on by a "new flame"!!! That burning attraction is a *significant part* of "romance." You want to *soak it all in.* It's the deliciously intoxicating stuff of romance. Hold on to your attraction.

Second, today you *are* thinking clearly, and hopefully "what happened" with the N or the codependent or the "bad fit" relationship looks different. As those years passed—three, then ten, or may twenty-four years later—the cloud from the mating chems eventually did leave your system. Thinking clearly, you began to reason and evaluate your partner's behaviors. You realized the truth about selling out your preferences and how your boundaries changed. Your clarity also improved as the frequency of sex dissipated. Those thoughts about sex went from every morning, noon, and night to once in a full moon. The high from the pleasure drugs went from a nearly addictive state to barely registering in your system. The constant pull to bond slowly lost its grip. Knowing you connected with a person who was unable to reciprocate the love that you were pouring in, you realize that the "connection" did not extend much beyond the lust and attraction. Your preferences were misaligned. Your desire and capacity for intimacy and vulnerability was not shared or reciprocated. Distance felt much better than closeness. Then, once everything became clear, the relationship came to "The End."

If that last "ending" was where your journey to become aware and to become healthy started, that is very good news!! Gaining a deeper understanding about the "That Chemistry" Mythstake should go a long way in helping you navigate your way through the romance phase of creating a relationship. Add in your awareness about the critical nature of conflict resolution, how it happens and *that* it happens *before* commitment, and you have just about everything you need . . .

There are a couple of more things that need to be added to the mix, though. These I would like to bring to your attention in Chapter 9.

Chapter 9.

ATTACHMENT STYLES

THE NEXT TWO ITEMS YOU need to address on your road to "being healthy" are "attachment styles" and "Chem-*patibility.*" Attachment styles and chem-*patibility* are critical components in healthy relationships. The more you know about them, the better.

First, this chapter is a general information outline on attachment styles. Like the chemistry of personality, attachments are "measurable," and this subject has been exhaustively researched and documented

There are several links in Appendix E that provide background information and reference material about attachment styles. One link takes you to an attachment style survey. I suggest you take the survey to understand your attachment style—if for no other reason than for your knowledge and awareness about your self. After you understand the nature of attachments, even from the fifty-thousand-foot perspective, you will recognize that there is some serious value in having any "live" prospect take the survey as well. Not that your relationship depends on it . . . but it is in the "very, very good to know" category. The following paragraphs provide that "quick, high-level" overview.

In the same way that everyone has a personality type, they also have an attachment style. Your attachment style, like your personality type, is just you. There is no good or bad, right or wrong, better or worse. Your attachment style is *your* attachment style. It is *really good to know* about the attachment style of any prospect you might be considering as a partner candidate.

Attachment style is not the only factor in a relationship's success or failure. The chem-*patibility* of two partners can also heavily influence the outcome of the relationship. There is a slight difference between the two, however.

While the modeling of love and relationships happens during early childhood, key pieces of your personality type, the chemistry part of chem-*patibility* (which is somewhat fixed), were put in place before you were born. Your genetics are a huge piece of this "chemical makeup" that determines your personality type, according to Fisher. Chemistry then is not like an oil change, where you have the option to replace regular 10W-40 motor oil and upgrade to a "synthetic blend." No. Your primary (dominant) and secondary hormonal chemistry is rather fixed; when you pop out, you have "your" unique chemical cocktail, pretty much for life.

On the other hand, your attachment style is "imprinted" after you are born. It is most often shaped by your caregivers. Their interactions with you heavily influence your attachment style. However, your attachment style can shift and change as you go through life. In fact, studies have shown that your attachment style can change from partner to partner and from relationship to relationship. Therefore, the person you are with in a relationship impacts your attachment style, in *that* relationship. But in your next relationship with a different person with a different personality and a different attachment style, your attachment style may change also. My intent here is to acquaint you with these concepts. To give you some resources and information that you can investigate more thoroughly.

In this regard, John Bowlby[22] and Mary Ainsworth[23] are two huge contributors in the field of attachment research. In the 1980s, Cindy Hazan and Phillip Shaver applied these concepts to romantic relationships.[24] Their work led to one of the more impressive recent contributions to the field, which came from Robert. W. Firestone and his daughter, Lisa Firestone, PhD.[25]

The following is a very concise descriptive summary of four attachment styles. This excerpt is taken from an article authored by Lisa Firestone and published in *Psychology Today*. Firestone writes:[26]

Secure Attachment – Securely attached adults tend to be more satisfied in their relationships. Children with a secure attachment see their parent as a secure base from which they can venture out and independently explore the world. A secure adult has a similar relationship with their romantic partner, feeling secure and connected while allowing themselves and their partner to move freely.

Secure adults offer support when their partner feels distressed. They also go to their partner for comfort when they themselves feel troubled. Their relationship tends to be honest, open and equal, with both people feeling independent, yet loving toward each other. Securely attached couples don't tend to engage in what my father, psychologist Robert Firestone, describes as a "Fantasy Bond," an illusion of connection that provides a false sense of safety.[27] In a fantasy bond, a couple foregoes real acts of love for a more routine, emotionally cut-off form of relating.

Anxious-Preoccupied Attachment – Unlike securely attached couples, people with an anxious attachment tend to be desperate to form a fantasy bond. Instead of feeling real love or trust toward their partner, they often feel emotional hunger. They're frequently looking to their partner to rescue or complete them. Although they're seeking a sense of safety and security by clinging to their partner, they take actions that push their partner away.

Even though anxiously attached individuals act desperate or insecure, more often than not, their behavior exacerbates their own fears. When they feel unsure of their partner's feelings and unsafe in their relationship, they often become clingy, demanding or possessive toward their partner. They may also interpret independent actions by their partner as affirmation of their fears. For example, if their partner starts socializing more with friends, they may think, "See? He doesn't really love me. This means he is going to leave me. I was right not to trust him."

Dismissive-Avoidant Attachment – People with a dismissive-avoidant attachment have the tendency to emotionally distance themselves from their partner. They may seek isolation and feel "pseudo-independent," taking on the role of parenting themselves. They often come off as focused on themselves and may be overly attending to their creature comforts. . . .

[P]eople with a dismissive-avoidant attachment tend to lead more inward lives, both denying the importance of loved ones and detaching easily from them. They are often psychologically defended and have the ability to shut down emotionally. Even in heated or emotional situations, they are able to turn off their feelings and not react. For example, if their partner is distressed and threatens to leave them, they would respond by saying, "I don't care."

Fearful-Avoidant Attachment – A person with a fearful-avoidant attachment lives in an ambivalent state, in which they are afraid of being both too close to or too distant from others. They attempt to keep their feelings at bay but are unable to. They can't just avoid their anxiety or run away from their feelings. Instead, they are overwhelmed by their reactions and often experience emotional storms. They tend to be mixed up or unpredictable in their moods. They see their relationships from the working model that you need to go toward others to get your needs met, but if you get close to others, they will hurt you. In other words, the person they want to go to for safety is the same individual they are frightened to be close to. As a result, they have no organized strategy for getting their needs met by others.

As adults, these individuals tend to find themselves in rocky or dramatic relationships, with many highs and lows. They often have fears of being abandoned but also struggle with being intimate. They may cling to their partner when they feel rejected, then feel trapped when they are close. Oftentimes, the timing seems to be off between them and their partner. A person with fearful-avoidant attachment may even wind up in an abusive relationship.

What is the real value in knowing your attachment style? The big takeaway is the insight you gain that may help diagnose and resolve issues that surface in your relationship. How so?

You developed your original attachment style as a child, but that doesn't necessarily define your attachment or the way you relate as an adult. For instance, say you find your self wary about getting close to and being emotionally connected with a partner. The underlying reason may be found by examining your behavior in the context of the four attachment styles. The work you have done to understand your caregivers' modeling and installation of love provides you with fabulous insight into how you "operate" in your relationships. When you use your model of conflict resolution with your partner, how the resolution process evolves is impacted by both your and your partner's modeling (from the past) and each of your attachment styles.

For instance, when an issue surfaces and you notice a pattern that reveals one of you "creating distance," it might be beneficial to see this reaction in the context of each of your attachment styles. This underscores the reason for both you and your partner to complete the attachment style survey. At the end of the day, you will gain more insight about your self and they about their self. In my opinion, for any two partners intent on creating a healthy love relationship, this information is good to know.

Since you are always engaged in becoming healthier personally, being aware of your attachment style means that in your relationships you can always be working toward forming more "secure attachments." This work translates into becoming healthier as a relationship partner.

One aspect of attachment styles needs to be clearly stated. You are "OK" with whichever attachment style you have—secure, anxious-preoccupied, dismissive-avoidant, or fearful-avoidant.

You can have a fabulous relationship regardless of your attachment style. To accomplish this, however, requires communication and vulnerability. When you pick a healthy partner, you have a partner who "accepts" you the way you are without judgment or the need to change you. The beauty of this is that when you find your self *being anxious* in a situation, *you* bring this into the conversation with your partner, because you trust that their love for you (acceptance, allowance) will grant you the room to be OK where you are (allowance). When this anxiety is "addressed, processed, and resolved," it is highly likely that the anxiety you experience in this moment, as well as in the future, is reduced.

Much like how you heal your heart by addressing your past, when an issue is triggered that is related to your attachment style, you use your APR tools, addressing and processing the event with your partner. When issues are related to one of the characteristics of one of the four attachment styles—such as being anxious or wanting to create distance—using the APR requires a measure of vulnerability and intimacy. The resolution culminates with an agreement and ultimately returns you to love, where you are "closer and more connected." In this instance, part of that "deeper connection" is a deepening of your "trust" as a result of your willingness to be vulnerable, and to learn being vulnerable with this partner is a safe, comfortable experience. The "end game" of processing and resolving is that over time, you are moving away from "where you started" with an anxious attachment style and moving in the direction of being more securely attached—that is, you trust that you can share your vulnerability with your partner and that they will respond by *loving from their heart*. That would be a fabulous outcome and, in fact, is the nature of relationships in which the experience of love between the partners is greater over time. What would it look like if you were . . .

Moving toward "Secure"

For example, say your anxious style was a result of caregiver abandonment issues that influenced how they raised you—their modeling and installation of love. Look at the difference in the thoughts and reactions to a few examples that show two different styles.

Securely attached people are at ease with "coming and going." People in your life are always moving toward you and away from you. This happens regularly. They travel, go to work, have emergencies, plan to visit. Comings and goings are the experience of life. It's OK. There is no upset, because comings and goings happen in life and with people in relationships. But for certain attachment styles, regular comings and goings are "not regular." How can that be?

Consider this example of when one partner announces their intent to take a weekend out of town. For this fairly normal event, a securely attached partner responds:

> Oh, you want to visit your friend in LA for the weekend?
> Have a safe trip! Let me know when you land.

When watching a movie together and learning of their partner's intent to head home afterward rather than sleeping over, a secure partner responds by saying:

> OK, you are planning to spend the night at your place tonight.
> That works!! We have been together for a week, and I need to
> take care of some things around my house. I love you. We'll
> talk soon!

In both instances, the comings and goings of life are uneventful. There is neither upset nor fret. However, this is not the case when an anxiously attached person hears these words. In the following example, the insecurely attached person shows that her abandonment issues are triggered when she replies with:

> Oh *no*! What do you mean you are leaving me?! Why would
> you think about leaving me? I do not want you to go!!!

That is how it sounds when comings and goings are *not* OK. This anxiously attached person *believes* that her partner is "leaving" her. She is experiencing the same feelings that were embedded from "early on." Her childhood abandonment has been triggered from how she experienced "love" and how the people who "loved" her acted when she was a child. How did this look, and how did the caretakers act?

Her father was an N. He was never someone she could rely on consistently. He left for weeks at a time. Played "Disneyland Dad" when he did show up. He modeled a constant, unpredictable relating style. Everything was always changing, with unstable relationship models. He modeled "unpredictability" or "instability." Maybe he always showing up with a new girlfriend, maybe drunk; perhaps he showed up unannounced at school, maybe with different "girlfriends" on the same day. Or he was supposed to pick up after school and never showed up. He was flush with cash one month, and five months later he was pawning the sofa, so they could eat. Then he would disappear. He always had a "Big Deal" that he was "working on," which he wanted to "tell" her about, which mostly didn't come through and never happened.

With all that trauma of being left, of not having a father (male role model) she could count on early on, in this moment when her partner speaks of "spending the night at his place," all the early trauma of instability is being reminisced at this moment. In the words "I'm leaving . . ." what she hears is a factual statement: "I am leaving you!!!" This is the childhood trauma crying out from her deepest inner self. That childhood wound is "screaming" the pain of that childhood experience.

If this partnership were between two unhealthy adults, this abandonment event would likely escalate. He would respond, "What do you mean I'm leaving? I'm not leaving. Don't accuse me of something!" The escalation is fueled when her response is "Yes, you are." The communication spiral has already started into the abyss. This is an example of an abandonment issue from the past that has not been resolved. Unresolved issues from the past surface in intimate relationships. It's guaranteed. The only question is when will they show up? Then, how will they be handled . . . in a healthy manner or in an unhealthy manner?

In a healthy relationship, this "event" would be addressed, processed, and resolved between the partners. A healthy person who *knows* they have an anxious, insecure attachment style would "hear *their* abandonment being spoken" in *their partner's words*. They could have translated their partner's words "I'm leaving" through their filter of the abandonment, and it would have sounded more like an alarm: "Oh no, *you* are leaving me!" Being healthy and aware, however, their inner response would be something that acknowledges all that is happening in the moment:

> Ahhh, I know he loves me, he's not *actually* leaving me.
> He's heading out, and when he's finished taking care of that
> business, he will return. He is coming back to me!

That is awareness. That is a healthy adult addressing, processing, and resolving *their* anxious state . . . back to love.

This same circumstance could be addressed between the partners, too. The address portion could be initiated by either partner, with the processing of those anxious feelings of abandonment, which were an old wound bring triggered. The resolution between these two is confirmation of their connection, with reassurance about the love they share. The agreement here will be one of "awareness." When another event occurs, such as "I am heading to my house," the anxious partner will respond with "Be careful. I'll see you soon. I love you!!"

Over the course of their relationship, as the partners handle these events with APR, the sense of "being abandoned" dissipates and maybe even goes away completely—completely resolved. The person with the abandonment issue is *becoming* OK with the regular everyday comings and goings of life.

Attachment styles can morph and change over time. Healthy people in healthy relationships lay the groundwork for this to happen. They possess the awareness and skills to handle issues or events. They resolve these and move closer (rather than further apart). With authentic communication and diligent practice, moving toward a secure attachment style is possible regardless of the "starting point."

Which brings us closer to the end . . .

Chem-*patibility*

On to Chapter 10, right . . .? No. We're taking a pause for a commercial break. I imagine you are sitting there in this overwhelming euphoric state, being so incredibly captivated by the work, having seen so many new and exciting (and downright scary) aspects of your self and other people (including, finally, a way to deal with your mother-in-law next Thanksgiving . . .), and even before you are finished with the book, you have already recommended it to eleven of your BFFs who are *all* in train wreck relationships . . . you cannot wait to get to Chapter 10!

But you flipped the page, and "whoop, der it iz" . . .

Another made-up word: **"chem-*patibility*."**

At some point, I realized the "chemistry of sex" (Chapter 8) had suffered enough on these pages. But, in reviewing the content, I noticed the number of references to "healthy chemistry." Then, I had an "ahh-ha" moment. What hit me was: "That's it! Chemistry *with* compatibility!"

Of course, those steamy-hot mating drugs are a serious "must have" for most of us. But what about the long term? What about creating and maintaining a healthy relationship? We already know that "hot sex" balloon is going to cool off eventually. We also know you need all the skills and awareness we have added about your self and any prospects, and these must be present in a relationship.

Time to add to your toolbox:

> **Healthy relationships are built on chem-*patibility*, the chemistry of compatibility.**

Chem-*patibility* is the Holy Grail! Chem-*patibility* describes the process and melding together of all these parts and pieces we have covered in this work. How so?

To put chem-*patibility* in perspective for relationships, I've chosen the analogy of "winding the watch" by the watchmaker. The master craftsman begins with the parts and pieces laid out on the workbench. Slowly and methodically, he assembles the gears, springs, spindles, jewels, balance wheels, and other essential parts. ***Note:*** *All the parts must be installed, or the watch won't keep time!*

Once the internal components are in place, the watchmaker fastens them in the case and adds the face, the minute and hour hands, and, at last, the bezel: the glass enclosure. Everything is complete . . . ready for the final step. He "winds the watch."

Until the moment he spins the crown the first time, the truth is that all these parts and pieces are just a collection of random metal and plastic. When the watchmaker winds the watch, though, that is when he knows all the elements are in their proper place. Will the time piece keep accurate time? Maybe it will take a few adjustments. Maybe it will take a week or month. But through tweaking, seeing the results, tweaking some more, eventually it will keep accurate time. Perfect time? Nothing on Earth is perfect, so that is an unreasonable (in other words, ego) expectation. I hope you get my point here.

Chem-*patibility* is like "winding the watch." Here's the way I would like you to see your self and this work. Our conversation opened with a look at biases, Mythstakes, truth, and a description of my target audience. The foundation of your "self" was laid with the "love your self" essentials: love, ego, choices, etc. Some of these elements were an in-depth discussion about to love or not to love, the language of ego, preferences, and boundaries. Next, you added some skills: conflict resolution, agreements, how to "love them from a distance," and the conversation of disengagement. Finally, the relationship essentials of prospects, partner selection, undatable people, unworkable relationships, the real chemistry of sex, and attachment styles were put into the mix.

When these elements come together, when the chemistry of attraction is there, when the date-me–mate-me chemistry is off the charts, when both parties are aware of their self, love, their models, and their work, and when they both have some or all the healthy relating skills *and* a solid connection from their shared interests and values, this is what chem-*patibility* looks like between partners.

That is what you have been preparing your self to find and honing your skills to maintain. Am I suggesting that simply finding "the Holy Grail," chem-*patibility,* is the "end game"? What about the "happily ever after" part?

Chem-*patibility* is both your destination and your point of departure. From what you know today is you "love your self," which means your self "where you are today." In other words, in the circumstances of your life today, you have the capacity to experience love *with your self.* In the place where you are today, there is contentment, joy, and challenges, and you have the resources to handle all *your life.* At the same time, where you are today, you have a much broader perspective of the journey to experience the *love your heart desires* with an "other."

You are still holding on to the hope; that has not changed or diminished. I contend you are holding that hope with a much more comfortable and more confident "grip" than when you opened this book. There is an excitement you have because you know you have done a hellova lot of work looking at your self and your relationships and seeing both the aspects of your self that were fabulous and the areas where you needed to do "your work." And you've done it!

Chem-*patibility*? Yes. You are the watchmaker. You have taken inventory of all the components, you know what they are, how they fit together. . . . You are ready to wind the watch; you are ready to get in the game. This time with your eyes wide open!

One last word on chem-*patibility*. Even when everything seems perfect, all the elements and aspects of being healthy are in place, sometimes relationships don't work. It's not a fit. It happens. There is no fault or blame. That's how life goes sometimes. When "The End" comes, both people walk away with the experiences they shared, both the good times and the challenges, and they mine the gold, which is theirs to keep and learn from this relationship. The return to love. Love is the "always" experience of your life.

This section on the chemistry of compatibility, chem-*patibility*, has been focused on wiring the elements of attraction that are mostly out of your control to the decision-making aspects of your creating a healthy relationship.

I am not sure there is a moment when one could claim to have it "all wired together." Certainly, I can't make such a claim. But, as you can see, there are some critical parts to the puzzle, and there are some parts that without a clear understanding can lead to mistakes. That is all "good to know" and will be beneficial for you going forward. (*You can always tuck the book under your arm or in your purse and refer to it on your trip to the powder room on that "first date."*)

And, now . . . we have come to "The End"!

The final chapter . . .

Chapter 10.

Standing Where the Road Divides

The "puzzle of you" is complete. The last few critical elements or dimensions of healthy relationships are now in place. These perspectives of love, ego, selling out, boundaries, conversations of connection, distancing, APR, and the skills of healthy relating are now "your practice." If you concluded that "your practice" has become "your work," you are correct. Practicing these skills is "your *ongoing* work."

In these pages, you have explored "what happened." You have gathered your self and reconciled most of what happened. You understand the parts you have and have not resolved. They are the "work" that lies ahead. Today, you can do your work because you know how! You have already done a helluva lot just to get here!

You are more comfortable with "who am I." You love your self, just the way you are. You are complete and whole, and there is nothing "missing." You are valuable, and you know that inside is your true self. You won't always be comfortable, but it's OK to be uncomfortable. It's OK to be in any season of your life; you can handle the circumstance of life. You are in need of no one. You are OK being "with your self"; if you are with someone, it is because you "choose to be" versus "need to be."

Today, you have love in abundance. You can give, grant, portion out love—anywhere, anytime, to anyone. It's your choice. You have the freedom to choose. You have an infinite supply. You know where sadness does its the best work: healing your heart and making you whole again, restoring. Some wounds are healed, but those scars remain. You know Grace, and you give forgiveness to your self and others. They are not perfect either. You grant these to your self and to others so that you can focus your time, your attention, and your love on "what's next"; in the future is where you can and will experience more love—the purpose for your being.

You have fine-tuned your listening, and you measure your words. You do your best to "choose" words and actions that add love—in your life and in your self. You bristle when you hear any choice that is "not to love" . . . in your self and in others. You know what work must be done to restore love and heal hearts, wounds, pain, and suffering when these have been inflicted by the choice not to love. These things live as "your awareness"—both your conscious thoughts and what lies unseen just below the surface.

You are choosing "healthy." You are choosing healthy relationships. In this matter, the universe of prospects has been identified and narrowed . . . significantly. You know the language of love and ego *before* you meet a prospective partner. There are healthy adult candidates, and then there are "all the rest." These you must *still* love, but today you know how: You can "love them from a distance." You have the facilities to determine a prospect's "state of being" (healthy . . . or not). The "chemistry" that surfaces so strongly in the beginning you know is primal attraction and mating instincts. Somewhere in the "unconscious" realm of your being, you are fully primed to experience passionate sexual intimacy with this person. It feels as if you are "high" because it's a fact: You are!

But you are aware that chem-*patibility*, the "chemistry of compatibility," is the foundation of a relationship. You know your preferences and which ones are nonnegotiable. You are patient in learning about theirs and sharing yours. The boundaries you set and communicate are respected and honored. When they are not, you notice . . . and you do not sell out. Chem-*patibility is the foundation* that offers you the opportunity to experience "the love your heart desires" . . . which is the destination of your journey.

With "what happened" and "who am I" addressed, you arrive at the "final question" . . .

"What's Next?"

At this moment, "what's next" is that you are standing "where the road divides" on your journey.

Perched atop a hill that has consumed your lifetime, you are looking into the future, because that is "what is next." But on the hill where you are now standing, the view is slightly different.

In one direction is a road that seems all too familiar. You have taken this road before. You remember the pavement; it is old and cracked. The shoulders are unkempt and overgrown. As the road winds away into the valley, you notice that it narrows. The trees are overgrown. They are older now, with thick, heavy branches, weathered and bent by storms. The streambeds in the valley are dry. You wonder, "Were these streams ever full?" You call to your memory and find nothing.

Your eyes strain to see the horizon. The road barely the width of a thread passes behind a grassy hill in the distance. All you can make out on the horizon is the hill blending into the sky. "Is *this* the same road I've been on before?" You notice that clouds are gathering on the horizon. These you can see clearly now. Where this road leads, what lies beyond those hills, there is certainty: A storm is raging in the distance. That too seems very familiar . . .

You pause . . . and turn.

Facing the other road, you wonder, "Is this what's next?"

As your eyes follow this road, one thing is certain: This road is new. It is unlike any you have traveled before. The pavement is fresh. As it leads away, you notice the stark contrast. There are long swells of open roadway through lush, green meadows as it traverses up to the crest of the hill. Yes, there are a few turns but none appear to twist sharply. Then you notice the road passes out of sight beyond the edge of this first hill. You wonder, "Is there an open valley beyond the crest of the hill?" Obviously, there is, because what you can see beyond the crest is the gentle slope of a second hill. As it rises in the distance, you fix your gaze and can barely make out the thin thread of this road as it continues, weaving its way up the second hill. In fact, you see the road all the way to the top; then just as with the first hill, it passes over the crest of the next one. You ponder for a moment.

This road seems different. It appears to hold more possibility. The unknown is comfortable and inviting. The faraway hills the road climbs to are green and lush as far as you can see. "Is this the way?" Of course, you don't know. But where this road leads has one difference from the road you seem to know so well. This direction takes you to open spaces, under clear, blue, cloudless skies. The sun warms this path from where you are standing until it disappears way in the distance.

"The new road with its possibility and promise? I choose this new direction." And why not? This new path, unlike the more familiar one, feels like the journey you always dreamed of taking. You gather your self and step onto the new road. Into this wide expanse of open space under the warmth of the sun . . . you step off with renewed hope, eager with anticipation.

All Roads Lead to Somewhere

That is how life and relationships work, I think. I speak the following words to you wherever you find your self at this moment. Yes, *you*, sitting over there in an airport, a coffee shop, or nestled in your bed before turning in. The universe knew well in advance of our encounter. Yes, I am 100-percent certain that is how life works, too. Remember, you passed a lot of books before you picked mine. I have some closing thoughts to share.

In relationships, you may often have chosen to follow the familiar road. The one you have taken before. It always delivers the thrills of attraction and passion of a new connection. However, there is a cost when you invest your heart in people and relationships that cannot return your love "in kind." The "in kind" measure is the love that satisfies your heart's desire. My goal is for you to avoid the people and relationships that bring the certainty of painful endings: heartbreak and heartache.

My hope is that you can see your self in the light of love, and that your view of the people you choose for your intimate relationships is now different. Holding this new perspective, you envision life as having unlimited possibilities for your self to experience love in your life and future. Today, over there, wherever you are, every skill to manifest the love you want in "your life" is in your possession. Because you are aware, hopefully this work and these pages have made choosing "the old, familiar" path exponentially more challenging. Why? You know the truth.

That is a new journey. Relationships with possibilities do not require giving up anything. Being aware allows you the freedom to enjoy the anticipation and to experience the passion. It's OK to lavish your self in the "high" of attraction. It feels fabulous to experience the ecstasy of passionate lovemaking and the beginning of a romantic connection! But this time is different. *The relationship* is about being healthy and being aware. No matter the "high," and the dreamy experience of *this* connection, you remain vigilant about communicating "what matters" *to you*; these are your preferences, boundaries, and deepest needs and wishes.

On this "road" you hold the intensity of your attraction, but today you have a genuine curiosity and sincere desire to know about "the One" you have newly discovered. What is the possibility that you will experience the love your heart desires? You want to know:
- "Are they able meet me where I am"?
- "Do they have the capacity and ability to love?"

- "Do they have the skills, the awareness, and the practices?"
- "Do they have the desire to share this journey, side by side?"
- "Do they express a commitment to do their work?"
- "Can they join me as an equal?"
- "Will they expose their true self, authentically and vulnerably?"
- "Will they enter into agreements that honor each of us?"
- "Will we align and accept our individual preferences?"
- "Will we share a love that brings us closer together?"
- "Are they committed to resolve issues and thereby strengthen our connection?"

Is this the romantic love relationship where finally the dream meets reality, where the full measure of a healthy intimate romantic love relationship happens for you?

Is this "the One"?

You are aware . . . You choose!

Epilogue: Afterthoughts and Considerations

We are done!! But true confession: I didn't tell the truth!!

Geeeez!!! Relationships are complicated!! They seem like they are the hardest thing on Earth to understand, much less "get right" and make work!! I think the problem is because of all the volume of information and different perspectives. At the end of the day, the complication of relationships resolve out to the last two words that closed out Chapter 10:

You choose!

Why is that so? I think it's because we are human. We can have all the evidence in the world that one particular choice brings a result we don't want . . . yet we will still make that our choice. We know the outcome, or at least we have a very good sense of it, yet we go against what we "know." That's a pretty good summary of the human experience. We are "experiential learners." We learn by doing . . . and we pay a boatload of dumb tax.

When I was about eight years old, I was standing next to my mother at the kitchen stove. We had a new house and brand-new appliances. Out was the gas range, and the new one had this heating element that was a coil of thick flat wire. When the coil heated up to red hot, the pan was placed directly on top of it. How cool was that "new invention"! (this was 1963). One day, shortly after we moved in, standing with my mother while she was starting dinner, I decided to flip the dial to "Max." I watched in amazement as the wire came to life with its dark red glow. I could feel the heat drifting over my face as I looked down. To my utter amazement, I asked my self, "I wonder how hot that is . . ." I was totally aware: It was very hot. It could boil water!!! I knew the answer.

Then I watched my self as I placed my *entire* palm on the coil.

As you can imagine over the next month or so, every time I glanced down at that really neat-looking circular burn on my hand, I knew. I knew exactly "how hot that was." It's damn hot. It will burn your skin off. No one would *choose* to touch it. In my case, that insight needs to be modified slightly to read "touch it . . . *again.*"

You know what? I never touched it again. I knew how hot it was. No one had to tell me. The truth is, hell, I knew it was damn hot *before* I touched it the first time.

Something funny happened over the course of my life: I had kids. Two to be exact (you already knew that, too).

Want to know something else? They never touched the stove's burner. Ever. They never needed to "sample the facts" or "test the concept" for their selves. They didn't need to. I had already conducted all the tests necessary and had passed the information on to them. "Dumb tax"—remember that phrase? I saved them some dumb tax regarding ranges, burns, heat, temperature, the impact of heat on skin, healing periods for skin regeneration, and other trivial bits of knowledge in this inconsequential realm of life. I shared my experience with them, and they listened!!

Unfortunately, my experience and education about people and relationships have been mostly "experiential" learning processes (that is, "dumb tax"). I have "touched the burner" a *bunch* of times. Lord, some of the relationships I have been in and some of the choices I have made have been train wrecks of epic proportion. My only regret is that, as my personal train wrecks were coming off the tracks, YouTube was not yet around. Shoot, I would have recorded every moment and would be a zillionaire because my "YouTube channel" would have been a runaway box office hit. *The Train Wreck Survivor* would have been a very appropriate title.

I have talked to my kids *a lot* about my train wrecks. In a way that was much different from the way my parents spoke to me during the thirty-year slow-motion train wreck they modeled for me. I chose to share what I learned, because I wanted my kids to know what it was like to "touch the stove's burner" without their needing to put their palm down to learn the lesson. My hope was that they would listen.

Yes, I have shared my entire life story. The pain of two divorces, which were heartbreakers. The humbling experience of losing everything . . . twice. Considering that I am a man, rest assured that the experience of having only fourteen cents in the bank, with a one-and-a-half-year-old child, with no job, living in a new city, with no lifeline of family or friends was *the* lowest point of being worthless that I ever experienced. Slather on a couple of decades of solid "Catholic Guilt" . . . well, you get the picture. My kids have seen me experience sadness with tears; I made sure they would, because as a kid, I never saw such a thing. I missed something there, too. I missed knowing the experience of *experiencing* real emotions. I wasn't going to let my kids grow up "missing" that experience. There is a lot of "life" in those tears!!

Life is meant to be lived, fully, all of it. An authentic life is living:

a *"Life Of Vulnerable Experiences"*

That life is "the life" I want my kids to know. It is something that I want for you, too. Experiencing a life of love, while paying as little dumb tax as possible. Sure, everyone will pay some, of course. The possibility you can avoid some of the potholes, however, and gain some valuable insights about your self, relationships, and life—that is a large part of my motivation for sharing all of this with you. It is my motivation for doing counseling as well.

I attended Gateway Community Church in northwest Austin before moving to Colorado. Several years ago, Gateway offered a series for men. I don't remember that much about the workshop, but the title stuck with me. Mainly because of the vivid truth it spoke about life. They produced a T-shirt for the series. On the front, it read: "Story Has Power." On the back was written three words of exceptionally insightful wisdom: "Tell Your Story."

Story Has Power: Tell Your Story

Truth, spoken in six words. The depth of this truth is quite profound, since it relates to what we are doing here: being healthy, dealing with the past, love, relationships.

Sometimes you are unable to see the truth when you stand, alone, in front of the mirror. But when others stand in front of you, they can see you clearly. With a lot of love, they can reflect the truth to you about what they see. You need the truth. You need to see what you cannot see alone.

They see both sides of you . . . your heart and your love and the "other side" of you: ego. Sometimes your truth is found in the life and experiences of others: the story. Story Has Power . . .

Meet Kaylee. "Once Upon a Time" . . .

> Kaylee grew up the youngest of three children; the two older ones were brothers. Cut to the chase: Her mother was a "overt narcissist" who had probably wanted a third boy. Her father "wore the pants"—but not really. The mother was in control, and "Dad just kept the peace by going along to get along." Maybe it was the way it was supposed to be, since Kaylee's mother's side of the family owned property, and most of the wealth in this marriage was from inheritance. The boys were into sports; the younger son was a star, and the older one . . . well, he was never quite all that. Eventually, the older boy became an all-star addict, skilled at drinking and being irresponsible.

When Kaylee was an early teen, her parents left on Friday to spend the weekend watching the younger son play college football. They put her on the bus to go to her grandmother's house, headed out of town, and didn't return till Sunday. Sometimes late Sunday evening. Kaylee was instructed to go to Grandma's house and spend the weekend. But it wasn't so Gram could watch over her. It was because Gram was nearly an invalid and needed 24/7 attention. Kaylee, at fourteen, was in charge of the personal care of her invalid eighty-five-plus-year-old grandmother. Everything. Food. Cooking. Cleaning. Bedpans. Diapers. Water. Bathing. Yes. Fourteen years old.

She survived, moving through high school above average and graduating from college. The summer after graduation, she met Jim. A business school grad, heading into the master's program, with big dreams and aspirations. A collegiate championship caliber sailor, he was competing in the Olympics in two years—something called the J/80 class.

Kaylee's story picks up twenty years later, with two middle school sons and a fourteen-year-old daughter. The divorce papers were finalized, and it was time for her to start a new life. However, counseling was the first piece of business.

The marriage was the only intimate relationship Kaylee had ever had. A virgin going in, and angry coming out. But the anger had always been there, under the surface. Her mother's focus on the boys had rendered her invisible. She had been the eye of her Daddy's eye, but he was emotionally disconnected, under the thumb of a controlling, self-centered wife. Her brothers had teased and taunted her most of her childhood. At one point, when they were playing a prank on her, they realized how much "fun" they could have if they put a snake in the back of a horse stall and tossed her in . . . she was deathly afraid of snakes. The result scarred her for life.

Her marriage went from bad to worse, starting with the honeymoon. Since she was a virgin, that first night was supposed to be blissful and erotic. But in the early stages of that first experience of making love, the pillow pushed the candle into the curtains, and they were barely dressed and out the door when security arrived, followed shortly by the fire marshal and a four-man crew. By the second year in, their marriage was a rote habitual journey. He went to work, she managed the house, and they took some trips . . . so, he could practice sailing. Which was OK, because he was making serious money, so she was not left lounging poolside at a Motel 6. The resorts were "Four Season" class, and the food and drinks were even better. The sex was "no season," however. Twice a month, Saturday morning, 6:00 a.m. It produced three kids and zero orgasms. And that was in the first ten years. The last ten they slept in separate bedrooms but kept the same "maintenance" plan for "pleasure." Now the anger and resentment were about to be unleashed. The screaming and rage were epic battles. Sometimes she walked out, and sometimes he did. The final straw was when she was locked in a coat closet when he left for work and was let out when he returned late in the afternoon. Finally, they had had enough. The papers were filed, and the ink was dried.

Meet Mikala. "Once Upon a Time" . . .

Mikala's earliest memories were of her sitting on the sofa with her younger sister and her little brother watching Saturday morning cartoons. She was ten or eleven, her sister was eight, and her brother was six. She had already made breakfast and was wondering how she was going to entertain them that day. Her father was in the bedroom with his girlfriend; the two of them were laughing, enjoying a morning mimosa, and "playing" together. Where was the mom? Mikala didn't know. Dad had said a couple of years back that she was leaving, and then . . . *poof!* she was gone.

Yes, they did see her from time to time. But it was not like a regular "divorce" schedule. They might go for a week or two and then not see her for a week or ten days. When they did visit, she rarely left her bedroom. She was pretty much disconnected from her self, her heart, and her children. Her parenting model? There wasn't any, really. There was certainly no conversation about life or about handling life. Vacant. One "memorable Saturday," about 6:00 p.m., they were hungry after going through the last of the peanut butter, jam, and bread, with a few remnants in the bottom of a chip bag. Mikala asked her mom, "What's for dinner?" Her mother replied, "There is a frozen chicken in the freezer." That became a family joke. The kind of banter the whole family smiles and gives a forced chuckle about, because inside, the sadness and pain are still there every time one of them tries, just one more time, to find a bit of humor in the tragedy of this dark part of the family history.

Mikala found solace finally when she joined a youth group at a local church. The people were real, and they cared about her. They talked about life and God, and it felt like home. When summer rolled around, she signed up for the summer camp, and all spring she looked forward to that week. The day finally arrived, and the buses were loading and leaving around noon. She came early, too, so she could pick her seat, way back in the very last row. Plenty of room to stretch out and maybe even sleep on the four-hour trip. When the bus was full, the last person on was the youth group leader. He was about eighteen or nineteen, and while she barely knew him, they had greeted each other and had shared some small talk before the Wednesday evening meetings. He moved down the aisle and claimed the last seat on the bus, next to Mikala. Before the bus left the city limits, John had made his self uncomfortably close to Mikala. Soon, she felt his hand moving from the outside of her thigh, to where it was never supposed to be. She was frozen. Whatever trust about men and church and God she had harbored vanished by the time she returned home that next Saturday morning. She never told a soul.

She managed her pain through high school and escaped her life back there when she entered college. She wanted to get closure on her old life and figure things out. She studied psychology. What was wrong with them? What was it about me? Why was my mother disconnected? Her junior year, she walked into her Psych 410 class, and seated at the front was Mr. Clark. She guessed he was about thirty-five, a doctorate student, getting his teaching requirements finished by teaching this course. While she knew she did not want to feel what she was feeling, she wanted to know this man. In less than a week, she had made her way to his office and signed up for his weekly Wednesday night "open discussion" forum. It was a small group, which met as his house, located just off campus. The seven students who showed up were regulars. Starting at 6:30 with a few snacks and beer or wine, the group lasted until 10:00 p.m. The conversations were "free form," "anything goes," which meant that at some time nearly every Wednesday evening, the topic landed on sex. It was totally uncomfortable for Mikala, but not wanting to reveal her secrets, she played right along. And Mr. Clark noticed her cautiously enthusiastic responses.

When the sixth weekly evening came and went, Mikala decided to invite her self to clean up after the session was over.

She said, "I felt something 'was there' between us." She could not explain it. "There was this overpowering connection I felt all over my body, and it was so intense . . ." When the last dish was dry and the trash was all neatly bagged, the moment had arrived. It was she and Mr. Clark in his kitchen, alone. That night the affair started. The sex was hot and exciting and passionate. It was nearly five weeks of lovemaking—at lunch, before breakfast, late at night, and after every session. Then he broke the news. Mikala learned that Mr. Clark's wife was on sabbatical in England. She was finished with her doctorate research and would be returning "next weekend." Devastation? Heartbreak? Trust broken? Heartache? She carefully stuffed it all away.

She did what she knew well. She took the pain and heartache, sealed it in an unbreakable, impenetrable container, and buried it deep in her soul. After getting her master's, she left for the West Coast to "start anew." The only problem with starting "anew," of course, is that all those unresolved issues, all those hurts, and pains, don't get left behind. Also, not left behind are the patterns of relationships and the unhealthy choices, which are the unsuccessful attempts to "fix what is broken."

Finding a new life on the West Coast meant getting involved with a work life and making connections to establish a social circle. Work took care of itself. The master's degree landed a psych job with supervision, which was ultimately the launch point for a twenty-plus-year private practice. But the social side of her life took some serious work. Sure enough, an upcoming seminar in LA on some random psych topic set the stage for meeting "Will."

Will was a nine at a prestigious East Coast university. He was also there for the weekend and was single, but he was fifteen years Mikala's senior. But, wow, intelligent, funny, outgoing—and for a forty-two-year-old guy, he was "ripped." She was committed to "take it slow" this time. Over the next couple of months, he visited her, and she flew back there. Her course was charted, however. The sex was not great, and as it turned out, Will was not outgoing at all. It turned out that he was a "rocket scientist"; that is, he was smart and extraordinarily introverted. Mostly he was quiet, composed when they were together. He never expressed too much emotion and surely never expressed any rage or anger. He was very attentive and enjoyed their conversations and thoughts about life. He seemed interested. These were things he was not that familiar with, but they were her life, so it became his interest, too. But despite her cooing and pleading and cajoling and other miscellaneous attempts to lure him out to live there, he was not moving west. He was comfortably settled in where he was and would stay that way, with or without her. But "I love you," she said. For her, this new, rather odd relationship was safe, balanced, and steady—items that she did not know existed coming from a male or concerning love, another experience she did not know well.

Barely established on the West Coast, she up and moved. The first three years brought on a child, her setting up a new practice, and the big surprise. They bought near downtown, but he was taking a "short-term" fellowship position at a college nearly four hours away. He would be commuting—leaving Monday at dawn and returning late Thursday night. Resolute, she convinced her self she could "handle it."

The "it" part that she had convinced her self she could "handle" included starting a business, dealing with the emotional trauma and drama of eight to ten clients per day, commuting home, and caring for a newborn as a single parent four days a week. Yes, the grinding-metal sound you hear? It is the full-spectrum Dolby sound profile of the train leaving the tracks—in 3D, wide-screen, slow motion.

A year in, deep in a nor'east December, a foot of snow was on the ground, and the city was shutting down. Mikala had already talked with the nanny, who was able to watch the baby if Mikala needed to stay in town, which was what she needed. As she closed around five, the other "new psych" in the building was boarding the elevator, whose door he dutifully held open for her. They met two weeks prior at the building's holiday open house. He was charming, funny, and also married. The elevator door opened to reveal a foot of snow on the sidewalk; no one was going anywhere. Now the only question was the one he posed: "Would you like to have dinner? It looks like we're snowed in . . ." Dinner was preceded by several glasses of wine and ended with a discussion along the lines of "Hope your sofa is comfortable. Looks like you and I will you be spending the night!" Her office was sparse, but he had spent many nights in his office on a pull-out sofa bed when he was too tired to make the one-hour commute to his three-bedroom condo in the "burbs." Another two or three glasses of wine were not a good idea. When he pushed the door open to his office, they "met" very comfortably in the threshold. This time the affair lasted nearly a year, and it was not hard to figure out the logistics, because everything was in place . . . just like it was that first night.

Where was Mikala's marriage at this point? Remember the grinding-metal sound? The second child was on the way. The short-term fellowship turned into a full-time position, with the possibility of tenure. Sex and romance were gone. Will was perfectly happy. Nothing had changed on his end. But at this point in her life, Mikala was bursting at the seams. The times her heart had been crushed, used, abused, manipulated, and thrown away were countless. The times she screamed out for connection, for love, for intimacy, for a relationship, for romance . . . had all fallen short. Her skills at covering up were worthy of an Oscar nomination. No one knew. Not her friends. Not her family. Certainly not her mother, and definitely not her father. But it was time to leave it behind again and start "anew."

She remembers dialing her father's cell number. He answered her call as though the gap of four years since she had called him to wish him a happy birthday was just yesterday. Could he pick her and the kids up at the airport? "Yes!!" Could they stay at his place? (After all, his business was exploding, and he was rolling in money.) "Of course, you can stay with us." Us? She didn't know he had remarried, but now she inquired. Would "Sasha" mind her and the two kids staying for a week? "Of course, she won't mind. Stay as long as you would like." Maybe this was the chance to finally reconnect with Dad; she entertained this thought once again.

On the trip from the airport, he had one meeting, which might take forty-five minutes, an hour max. He suggested they pick up some lunch and he would drop them off at the park, where she and the kids could wind down. Of course, that would work. The kids would have a chance to run around after the four-hour westbound flight. He waved bye, with a neatly tagged "See you in about an hour." That was shortly after noon. Then 1:00 p.m. became 3:00, and 3:30 became 5:00, which turned into 5:30. No call. No text. Nothing. Livid, panicked, alone, frustrated, despondent, angry, bitterly sad. . . . The abandonment of her childhood crashed down all at once in one afternoon in the park.

Four years later, divorced, with two kids and a mortgage, she was once again restarting life: a single mother, a new city, with no husband, and with a heart encased in a steel shell, never to be put at risk again. Even with all the skills of a twenty-year counselor, working with hundreds of folks with the same pains and wounds and trauma she had, she had never ventured down the path of addressing, processing, and resolving her life of hurt and suffering. She never grieved the losses and Graced her self with forgiveness. And she never shared intimacy, trust, or genuine connection with a man. She never experienced the one thing she had been longing for her entire life: the love her heart desired.

Does story have power? I believe it does. The power is not in the story about "what happened," however. Reflecting on that usually does bring a dose of sadness. The "life" part of the story rips at your gut. You can feel the agony of the protagonists in the story of what "they" lost. Perhaps their heartache or the weight on their chest is something *you* "know." The power is in the "learning" you take with you. Those lessons are hard-earned, which makes them priceless.

With the "power of story" told, we are finished. My sense is that more stories are not relevant. "What's next" for you is, though. I have enjoyed being on this journey with you. I don't know where you started or the circumstances of your life; nevertheless, I am convinced what is right about "life" and "you" is this:

> **By the power of Love,**
> **which has been granted to you,**
> **as a gift of Grace from God of the universe,**
> **and placed in your heart by His will,**
> **you have everything you need**
> **to experience Heaven on Earth.**

That is not my promise, nor are those my words. Those are His promises. He will do what He said He was going to do and keep the promises He said He would keep. I choose faith.

I choose L.O.V.E.

Appendix A.

About God and Me: *Continued*

God is Love.
Connect the dots.

I LEFT THIS CONVERSATION EARLIER. In fact, well before we started our relationship conversation, I shared the following statement:

I believe in God. I do. One hundred percent.

God is. I have not one doubt in my mind—except when I do have doubts. I'm human. I have my doubts occasionally. I can live with doubt. But in my core, I also have faith: a belief in what is not seen or cannot be known . . . which brings us to God.

I did my best to figure out what I was "seeing" about God. And to know what I could "know" or learn or even understand as it relates to the discussion of God. Maybe you have stood in my shoes; perhaps you have not. Whichever is the case for you, here are some of my thoughts that have contributed to my perspective on God and its impact on relationships.

Concerning "God," what I can "see" is damn convincing. I look at the mountains, stargazer lilies, golden retrievers, my kids, a fly-fishing stream in the middle of nowhere, a speckled trout, the ocean, a humpback whale doing a back flip, the way clouds form and move, the mysteries of Earth (such as wind or smells), the stars, the big blue sky, the endless expanse of the universe at night . . . yeah, I believe God is. One hundred percent. Behind all the billboards and houses and skyscrapers and lights . . . it's all there. Everything He created is there to see. I used to "not" see it. Now I look for it. Every day. Everywhere.

I think about God . . . *a lot*.

When I was still "a bit unsure," I thought about it logically, too . . . since that is what we do as humans; we attempt to make sense of that which is beyond our grasp intellectually! We live in a world where some humans *believe* it is within the human capacity to create, from scratch, a stargazer lily . . . *from scratch, mind you!!!* That's kind of funny when you think about it (no ego involved here . . . Right!!!).

My request is simple: "Make one, then!!" [Pause . . . silence]. Uh-huh.

Humans are a funny lot.

Just as important as what I can "see" is that "Big Book." Yes, the all-time bestselling, most-printed, most-read, most-controversial Book. The one that outlines the life story of a Man who walked on water, who brought a dead man back to life, who turned water into wine for a party, and more. Then He told His good friends what must have sounded like a crazy tale; He told them of His death, and *then*, in what would be the most incredible Miracle in the history of the universe, after dying, He said He would *join them for dinner*. Then, exactly as He said He would, it *all* happened. He died. He came back to those with whom He had spoken that promise. . . . He joined them for a little celebration dinner!!! It was *crazy*! He blew their minds.

Life on Earth has never been the same.

How could it be? He's the only one, ever, to pull it off. Impossible, right? Yeah, for any human, totally improbable. But when you take out the fact that this feat (along with the other three just listed) is beyond the capacity of any human, then God makes sense. God exists. If God took the form of human, He could pull it off. The logical side of my brain wanted to figure exactly how unique were these feats by this one Man.

I did a little math exercise to determine if this Man and these feats were "that special." Here's my reasoning . . .

Over the course of human history, about 108,000,000,000 people have set foot on this planet. Yes, that is 108 *billion*. I wanted to know what the odds are that only *one* person, ever, in history, would walk on water, turn water into wine, raise the dead, and *then* be killed and come back to life. Look at that list of four items again. Forget doing all four? Let's make it simpler and just pick doing *just one*!

What are the chances that one human being out of 108,000,000,000 has ever accomplished *just one* of those four events? Another way to look at it is to ask the question: Has there ever been another documented case for any human in the history of the planet to accomplish any *single one* of the four events listed? No. So, for me, *four* is beyond *epic!!!*

The chances that not a *single* human out of 108,000,000,000 has ever accomplished *one of those feats* would be the same odds of me being struck by lightning 8,000 times *in all your* years on Earth. The odds of you or me or anyone being struck by lightning a thousand times in their life are better than the odds of a single human out of 108,000,000,000 ever accomplishing just one of those feats. Four is out of the question, then. The fact that not one human out of 108 billion has ever performed even one, but this one Man did all four in thirty-three years? That must give even the most cynically skeptical person reason for pause and contemplation. Seriously.

Some 108 billion humans have lived an average of forty years, which is 14,610 days per human, which renders a total of 1,577,880,000,000,000 (just shy of *1.6 quadrillion*) days. In any *one* of those 1.6 quadrillion days has one person done a single one of these . . . Miracles? I think the term *Miracles* is "appropriate." Seriously.

My intention for sharing this is *not* to convince you. I am sharing my thinking as I was trying to make sense of life and my purpose and God. That is what I put together. Some readers may challenge the math, or the numbers, or the logic. That makes sense; divide it all by 1,000,000 if that makes the error rate something that becomes digestible. Cut the hit rate on comparative lightning strikes by 1,000. I am OK with whatever makes any reader more comfortable. The need to rein in the math is entirely understandable. It's not necessary, though. Everyone already knows the truth. It's been done exactly once. And when it happened . . . it changed the world forever.

I thought it was important to bring these two items, God and the Bible, into focus, so you understand my perspective and my reasoning.

It is my experience and thinking, which provides the foundation for what is shared in this book. What I think of this work is more like a "compilation" of some smart folks. That is why, throughout these pages, I provided you with my references and sources—including my favorite authors, scholars, and spiritual thought leaders. Some of these are leaders in behavior and human psychology. Some of them have produced works on the science side of social studies. And, as I just stated, there is God and the Bible.

God is Love.

Connect the dots.

<h1 style="text-align:center">Appendix B.</h1>

Example: Finding Your Unique Love Requirements

I THOUGHT I WOULD ADD one last item to the conversation concerning skills and awareness. Earlier I mentioned figuring out "the attraction," which is of "you" to "them" and of "them" to "you." That is two sides of the same coin, and—no surprise here—the coin is love.

It's a good idea to know how you want to be loved uniquely. The tool you use to do that is David Richo's 5A model. Think about each one of the A's as a bucket. You have five buckets. How you experience love is how much of each A you want from your partner. That is your "unique love need." Your partner's task is to keep your buckets filled at the level where you are "good to go" (in other words, you are being loved the way you want and need). Once you know the unique way you want to experience love, then you know how much of each of the five A's you need or desire from your partner. That is the essence of the giving and receiving parts of relationships.

Since I know my self better than anyone else does, and I have done a fair amount of my work, it makes sense that I share my buckets. That will model how you do the exercise. Each of the following is my perspective on how I want/need love in my relationship:

- **My attention bucket?** I want my attention bucket way over half, maybe two-thirds, full. I have lots of things I like to do that keep me busy, so I pay a lot of attention to my self. Although I am good

415

being "with my self," I prefer being "with someone," too. Not a "must have," but it is a sure "nice to have." I don't need or want smothering attention. If someone is smothering me, that is not loving me the way I want or like. It may be what others need, but smothering is not for me. I have a life over here, and I am content, so what I want is someone who complements my contentment, who loves me with the attention I prefer (recall that "preferences" was on our "Big List" of elements; make a note of yours as you read through mine).

- **My acceptance bucket?** How do I want someone to love me on this one? One hundred percent. The same way I accept my self: "just the way I am." All the stuff that works, as well as the stuff that doesn't work—it's all connected; it comes as a package. For example, I accept the fact that I am pretty funny . . . and sometimes tell some ill-timed, poorly delivered, fall-flat-on-their-face jokes and pranks. I have a propensity to talk with everyone; I want to know them, or at least enjoy their company at the moment. And mostly, the people I meet engage, but some are offended. They are not open to talking; they don't want to speak . . . but I accept I am this way; it's my preference. Yeah, I have a few boundary issues, and I am working on them. I accept my outgoing nature. That may be something someone else does not accept. I get it. It's OK. If someone can't accept all of me, it is a red flag. Eject. I am good with this, because I accept others 100 percent. Does it take work sometimes? Hell, yeah! But they are how God made them, so who am I to judge? (I'm not God). If they are "good enough" for Him, they are good enough for me. It could be that I choose to "love them from a distance," but that is OK, too. Sometimes these are the circumstances, and we must love some people from a distance.
- **My appreciation bucket?** One hundred percent. I am valuable; I have a unique set of gifts, skills, and talents. I am good enough. By the way, being a reformed Catholic, I did not always see my

self this way. For fifty years, I mostly knew and focused on the parts of me that were "not good enough." That is not me today. I am valuable. I want to give and receive this appreciation from anyone with whom I am in a long-term relationship or have a connected relationship. I am not that concerned with (nor do I care if) others whom I am not connected to value me; that does not impact my life nor how I hold my self or love my self. I love my self and appreciate who I am. I expect 100 percent from my "other," because I can and will give this. It is something I have "about me," and I can give it to others . . . to significant others.

- **My affection bucket?** This one is easy: "Fill it to the brim." In other words, I want to experience generous amounts of tender love. I prefer holding hands, a midday romantic text, snuggling at movies, and a kiss in public—all are perfectly acceptable, not to the point of hearing "Get a room" from some prude behind me in line, though. I like to touch. I want this to be something that is shared and reciprocated with my significant other. Hopefully, the "other" who is attracted to me shares this "filled-to-the-brim" bucket also.

- **My allowance bucket?** One hundred percent. If you took in my story, then you know about me. I have experienced many times being "stuck" or "being in a season of struggle." That pretty much describes the path I have taken to share all these thoughts with you. Some experiences in my life have been a b!tch! But I have experienced these fully, and I allow my self to be OK where I am in any particular season of my life. I have the capacity to grant allowance to others, and this is a "must have" element for my relationships. How could someone *not* grant another allowance? Whenever allowance is missing, the situation is directly related to FACED: expectations, arrogance, condescension, and more.

The foregoing exercise is for you to figure out your preferences in this same manner. Once you have this clearly defined, it will be much easier to communicate as well as measure how you are doing in any relationship. The measure is always to be "loved according to your heart's desire."

Appendix C.

FANTASY BOND: RELATIONSHIP WITHOUT RISK

ONE ADDITIONAL THOUGHT ABOUT ATTACHMENT theory. A fabulous read by Robert Firestone extends the discussion in a rather interesting direction:[28] Some "love" relationships have very few elements of "romance" present *in the relationship*. It is as if all the romance, the attraction, the passion—all the steamy, dreamy aspects of romance—have been muted or are just flat missing. These relationships are attachment and bonding arrangements that are about "function"; the tie is based on routines, responsibilities, and roles.

In these fantasy bond connections, the "feeling" aspect of romantic love is missing. The relationship relies on "execution" of tasks and responsibilities. In other words, these partners have definitive agreements, and they are committed . . . to keeping their agreements. How important is this feature for this partnership?

The participants who share this bonding are likely doing so as a *defense against* separation anxiety, fear of intimacy, insecurities about self-worth, and other similar perspectives about their true self. They can accommodate their need to keep an emotional distance while not experiencing loneliness.

What an oddly beautiful arrangement (yes, judgment). This pair is "in a relationship," which alleviates both of their simultaneously held dominant fears—the fear of intimacy and the fear of loneliness. The arrangement is ideal! . . . for them. And for you *if it is your choice!*

Appendix D.

Plutchik's "Wheel of Emotions"

The following graphic represents Robert Plutchik's model of emotions.[29] As noted earlier, Plutchik's work doubles the number of "base" emotions that are in David Richo's "SAFE" model: sadness, anger, fear, and exuberance (or ecstasy).[30] Each model has the same "polarities"; fear lies opposite anger, and sadness is opposite joy (or ecstasy).

One extremely valuable aspect of Plutchik's wheel is that it shows the layers and depth of various emotions. Many more dimensions exist when these are combined. For "your work," Plutchik's effort falls into the "good to know" realm.

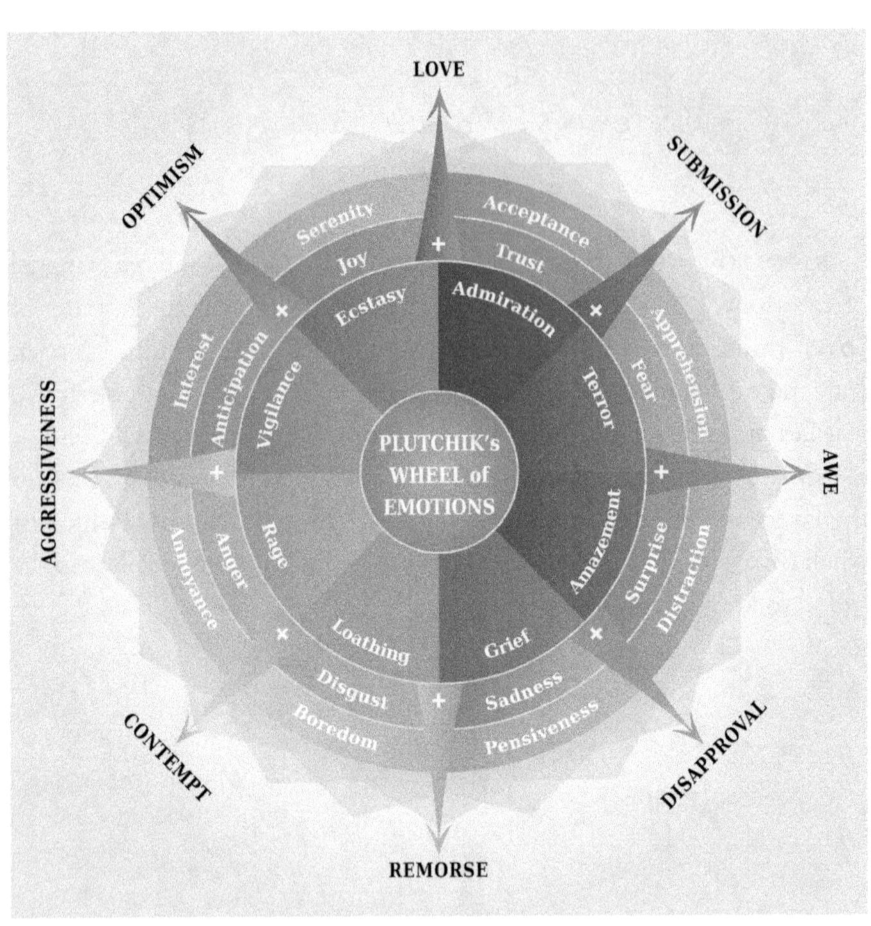

LOVE
OPTIMISM
SUBMISSION
AGGRESSIVENESS
AWE
CONTEMPT
DISAPPROVAL
REMORSE
Serenity
Acceptance
Joy
Trust
Ecstasy
Admiration
Interest
Anticipation
Vigilance
Apprehension
Fear
Terror
PLUTCHIK's WHEEL of EMOTIONS
Amazement
Surprise
Distraction
Rage
Anger
Annoyance
Loathing
Grief
Disgust
Sadness
Boredom
Pensiveness

Appendix E:

SURVEY RESOURCES

THE FOLLOWING ITEMS ARE EXCELLENT resources from both a personal and relationship perspective. Attachment styles and chemistry have been covered extensively throughout the book. Though it might have been more impactful if you had taken the surveys first, so your understanding of these concepts would be experiential—that is, your personal experience—I have provided them here in an appendix because I didn't want them to be a distraction in the main text.

How do you apply these resources in your life? Initially, I suggest that you take the surveys to create a benchmark your self. Maybe you have taken one or more of these surveys in the past, maybe not. Take them again. The idea is to put a stake in the ground "today" with respect to your self. One thing is certain: You are different today than you were before you plopped down your credit card for this book. So, on that note, enjoy the surveys.

Attachment Styles

Chapter 9 presents a short summary discussion from an article authored by Lisa Firestone and her work on attachment styles. The summary provides a solid foundation for understanding each of the four attachment styles that were first brought to light by John Bowlby[31] and Mary

Ainsworth.32 If you are interested in additional reading, I suggest a Google-search for "attachment styles." For our purposes here, the foundation is set, and next is to determine your attachment style. Remember, attachment styles can evolve and change—over time and with different partners and relationships. Now let's benchmark your attachment style . . . today.

Attachment-Style Lite

The following two survey recommendations I have labeled as "attachment-style lite":

- https://psychcentral.com/quizzes/romancequiz.htm
- http://www.attachedthebook.com/compatibility-quiz/

The surveys present a nice overview of each attachment style with some cursory comments about its characteristics and behaviors. While they help you focus and know your self, these are not research-grade works.

Relationship Structures

The following link leads to a website created R. Chris Fraley, a very prominent researcher in the field of attachment-style studies:

- http://www.yourpersonality.net/relstructures/

Fraley has a vast store of work product that can be found on the Web. His survey is the one I prefer to use when working with clients. It is a bit longer, but the commentary is in-depth and more detailed than the two "lite" versions listed earlier.

Personality Assessor

I am also including the following link, which incorporates your relating style with partner, parents, and close intimate friendships:

- http://www.personalityassessor.com/attachment-styles/

This discussion ties into previous chapters about the critical nature of your caregiver's role in modeling love and healthy relationships. Their impact is often revealed from this attachment-style survey.

Helen Fisher's Anatomy of Love

With four hundred pages in, you know my appreciation for Helen Fisher and her work. Note that the clear majority—and the most significant portion—of her contributions to the study of brain chemistry and romantic love came well before she was engaged to do work for the website chemistry.com. It would be a mistake discount the relevance of her work based on a value judgment regarding this website. In fact, the reason chemistry.com chose to base their personality-matching algorithms on Fisher's work was precisely the relevance and accuracy of her findings. Remember, her work covers nearly three decades and was in process before the Internet became a public utility.

Fisher's current Web presence can be found at the follow URL:

* https://theanatomyoflove.com

For a "primer" to understand Fisher and her work, I refer you to two video links that are short and that provide a great foundation for you. Fisher's first and now famous TED Talk, "The Brain in Love," thrust her into the media spotlight as the expert on the chemistry of love:

* https://www.youtube.com/watch?v=OYfoGTIG7pY

The second video segment, "Why People Fall in Love," dives right into her work on romantic love:

* https://www.youtube.com/watch?v=aoKbMPyBwF8

What is your personality profile? Whom are you most compatible with? What personality are you likely to have tension with? To find out, take the following survey, "Helen Fisher's Personality Test"!

* https://theanatomyoflove.com/relationship-quizzes/helen-fishers-personality-test/

I recommend that you spend some time on her website. She offers a lot of information regarding the subject of "love." Her video library is extensive. Are you contemplating another big bowl of popcorn and your fourteenth view of *The Notebook*? I suggest instead that you fire up a few of Fisher's videos. Just a thought!

REFERENCES

Aron, Elaine N. *The Highly Sensitive Person in Love: Understanding and Managing Relationships When the World Overwhelms You.* New York: Harmony Books, 2016.

Arterburn, Stephen. *The Secrets Men Keep: How Men Make Life and Love Tougher Than It Has to Be.* Nashville, TN: Thomas Nelson, 2006.

Brach, Tara. *Radical Acceptance: Embracing Your Life with the Heart of a Buddha.* New York: Bantam Dell, 2003.

Breuning, Loretta Graziano. *Meet Your Happy Chemicals: Dopamine, Endorphin, Oxytocin, Serotonin.* North Charleston, SC: CreateSpace, 2012.

Brizendine, Louann. *The Female Brain.* New York: Random House (Broadway Books), 2007.

Brogaard, Berit. *On Romantic Love: Simple Truths about a Complex Emotion.* New York: Oxford University Press, 2015.

Brown, Brené. *Daring Greatly: How the Courage to Be Vulnerable Transforms the Way We Live, Love, Parent, and Lead.* New York: Avery, 2012.

———. *The Gifts of Imperfection: Let Go of Who You Think You're Supposed to Be and Embrace Who You Are.* Center City, MN: Hazelden, 2010.

Brown, Byron. *Soul without Shame: A Guide to Liberating Yourself from the Judge Within.* Boston: Shambhala Publications, 1999.

Burton, Neel. *Heaven and Hell: The Psychology of the Emotions.* Oxford, UK: Acheron Press, 2015.

Campbell, Susan. *Truth in Dating: Finding Love by Getting Real.* Tiburon, CA: New World Library, 2004.

Carter, Steven, and Julia Sokol. *Help! I'm in Love with a Narcissist.* Lanham, MD: Rowman & Littlefield (M. Evans), 2005.

Chopra, Deepak, and Marianne Williamson. *The Shadow Effect: Illuminating the Hidden Power of Your True Self.* New York: HarperCollins, 2010.

Cloud, Henry, and John Townsend. *Boundaries: When to Say YES, When to Say NO—To Take Control of Your Life.* Grand Rapids, MI: Zondervan, 1992.

Cori, Jasmin Lee. *The Emotionally Absent Mother: A Guide to Self-Healing and Getting the Love You Missed.* New York: The Experiment, 2010.

Crabb, Lawrence J. *Connecting.* Nashville, TN: Thomas Nelson, 1997.

———. *Men & Women: Enjoying the Difference.* Grand Rapids, MI: Zondervan, 1991.

———. *Understanding Who You Are: What Your Relationships Tell You about Yourself.* Colorado Springs, CO: NavPress, 1997.

Csikszentmihalyi, Mihaly. *The Evolving Self: A Psychology for the Third Millennium.* New York: HarperCollins, 1994.

Dean, Ruthie, and Michael Dean. *Real Men Don't Text: A New Approach to Dating.* Carol Stream, IL: Tyndale House, 2013.

DeMoss, Nancy Leigh, and Dannah Gresh. *Lies Young Women Believe: And the Truth That Sets Them Free.* Chicago: Moody Publishers, 2008.

Edwards, Aleta. *Fear of the Abyss: Healing the Wounds of Shame and Perfectionism.* Otto, NC: Red Hill Press, 2016.

Firestone, Robert W. *The Fantasy Bond: Structure of Psychological Defenses.* Santa Barbara, CA: Glendon Association, 1987.

———. *Fear of Intimacy.* Washington, DC: American Psychological Association, 1999.

Fisher, Helen. *Why Him? Why Her? How to Find and Keep Lasting Love.* New York: Henry Holt, 2009.

———. *Why We Love: The Nature and Chemistry of Romantic Love.* New York: Henry Holt, 2004.

Forward, Susan, and Craig Buck. *Obsessive Love: When It Hurts Too Much to Let Go.* New York: Bantam Books, 2002.

Forward, Susan, and Donna Frazier. *Emotional Blackmail: When the People in Your Life Use Fear, Obligation, and Guilt to Manipulate You.* New York: HarperCollins, 1998.

Friesen, James G., and E. James Wilder. *The Life Model: Living from the Heart Jesus Gave You.* East Peoria, IL: Shepherd's House, 2000.

Fromm, Erich. *The Art of Loving.* New York: HarperCollins, 2006.

Fromme, Allan. *The Ability to Love.* Chatsworth, CA: Wilshire Book Co., 1992.

Fruzzetti, Alan E. *The High-Conflict Couple: A Dialectical Behavior Therapy Guide to Finding Peace, Intimacy, and Validation.* Oakland, CA: New Harbinger Publications, 2006.

Gottman, John. *The Relationship Cure: A 5-Step Guide to Strengthening Your Marriage, Family, and Friendships.* New York: Three Rivers Press, 2001.

Hart, Thomas M. *The Art of Christian Listening.* Mahwah, NJ: Paulist Press, 1999.

Hindy, Carl G., and J. Conrad Schwarz. *If This Is Love, Why Do I Feel So Insecure?* New York: Atlantic Monthly Press, 1989.

Horney, Karen. *Our Inner Conflicts: A Constructive Theory of Neurosis.* New York: W. W. Norton, 1992.

———. *Self-Analysis.* New York: W. W. Norton, 1968, 1994.

Hotchkiss, Sandy. *Why Is It Always about You? The Seven Deadly Sins of Narcissism.* New York: Simon & Schuster (Free Press), 2003.

Johnson, Sue. *Hold Me Tight: Seven Conversations for a Lifetime of Love.* New York: Little, Brown, 2008.

Kahneman, Daniel. *Thinking, Fast and Slow.* New York: Farrar, Straus and Giroux, 2011.

Krummel, Richard P. *Fear, Control, and Letting Go: How Psychological Principles and Spiritual Faith Can Help Us Recover from Our Fears.* Bloomington, IN: WestBow Press, 2013.

Langer, Ellen J. *Mindfulness*. New York: Perseus Books (Da Capo Press; a Merloyd Lawrence Book), 1990.

Lerner, Rokelle. *The Object of My Affection Is in My Reflection: Narcissists and Their Relationships*. Deerfield Beach, FL: Health Communications, 2009.

Levine, Amir, and Rachel Heller. *Attached: The New Science of Adult Attachment and How It Can Help You Find—and Keep–Love*. New York: Jeremy P. Tarcher/Penguin, 2010.

Lewis, C. S. *The Four Loves*. New York: HarperCollins, 1960.

Lowen, Alexander. *Narcissism: Denial of the True Self*. New York: Simon & Schuster (Touchstone), 2004.

Malone, Thomas Patrick. *The Art of Intimacy*. Upper Saddle River, NJ: Prentice Hall, 1989.

McNally, Tom. *The Complete Book of Fly Fishing*. 2nd ed. Camden, ME: International Marine/Ragged Mountain Press, 1997.

Mellody, Pia, and Andrea Wells Miller. *Facing Codependence: What It Is, Where It Comes from, How It Sabotages Our Lives*. New York: HarperCollins, 2003.

———. *Facing Love Addiction: Giving Yourself the Power to Change the Way You Love*. New York: HarperCollins, 2003.

Mikulincer, Mario, and Gail S. Goodman, *Dynamics of Romantic Love: Attachment, Caregiving, and Sex*. New York: Guilford Press, 2006.

Mollen, Jenny. *I Like You Just the Way I Am: Stories About Me and Some Other People*. New York: St. Martin's Press, 2014.

Northrup, Chrisanna, and Pepper Schwartz. *The Normal Bar: The Surprising Secrets of Happy Couples and What They Reveal about Creating a New Normal in Your Relationship*. New York: Harmony Books, 2013.

Olsen, David C. *The Spiritual Work of Marriage*. New York: Taylor & Francis, 2008.

Parkes, Colin M. *Place of Attachment*. New York: Basic Books, 1982.

Phillips, Lisa A. *Unrequited: Women and Romantic Obsession.* New York: HarperCollins, 2015.

Putnam, Robert D. *Bowling Alone: The Collapse and Revival of American Community.* New York: Simon & Schuster, 2000.

Richo, David. *Daring to Trust: Opening Ourselves to Real Love and Intimacy.* Boston: Shambhala Publications, 2011.

———. *The Five Things We Cannot Change: And the Happiness We Find by Embracing Them.* Boston: Shambhala Publications, 2005.

———. *How to Be an Adult in Relationships: The Five Keys to Mindful Loving.* Boston: Shambhala Publications, 2002.

———. *When Love Meets Fear: Becoming Defense-less and Resource-full.* New York: Paulist Press, 1997.

———. *When the Past Is Present: Healing the Emotional Wounds That Sabotage Our Relationships.* Boston: Shambhala Publications, 2008.

Scarf, Maggie. *Intimate Partners: Patterns in Love and Marriage.* New York: Random House, 1987.

Shapiro, Francine. *Getting Past Your Past: Take Control of Your Life with Self-Help Techniques from EMDR Therapy.* New York: Rodale, 2012.

Siegel, Daniel J. *The Developing Mind: How Relationships and the Brain Interact to Shape Who We Are.* 2nd ed. New York: Guilford Press, 2012.

Smalley, Gary. *The DNA of Relationships.* Carol Stream, IL: Tyndale House, 2007.

Storr, Anthony. *Solitude: A Return to the Self.* New York: Ballantine, 1988.

Taleb, Nassim Nicholas. *Antifragile: Things That Gain from Disorder.* New York: Random House, 2012.

Tannen, Deborah. *That's Not What I Meant! How Conversational Style Makes or Breaks Relationships.* New York: HarperCollins, 2011.

Tatkin, Stan. *Wired for Love: How Understanding Your Partner's Brain and Attachment Style Can Help You Defuse Conflict and Build a Secure Relationship.* Oakland, CA: New Harbinger Publications, 2011.

Warren, Rick. *The Purpose Driven Life: What on Earth Am I Here For?* Grand Rapids, MI: Zondervan, 2002.

Weber, Jill P. *Having Sex, Wanting Intimacy: Why Women Settle for One-Sided Relationships.* Lanham, MD: Rowman & Littlefield, 2013.

Welwood, John. *Perfect Love, Imperfect Relationships: Healing the Wound of the Heart.* Boston: Shambhala Publications, 2007.

Whitfield, Charles L. *Co-Dependence:* Deerfield Beach, FL: Health Communications, 1991.

———. Deerfield Beach, FL: Health Communications, 1987.

Wile, Daniel B. *After the Honeymoon: How Conflict Can Improve Your Relationship.* New York: John Wiley and Sons, 1988 (rev. 2008).

Zahl, Paul F. M. *Grace in Practice: A Theology of Everyday Life.* Grand Rapids, MI: Eerdmans Publishing, 2007.

Zayn, Cynthia, and M. S. Kevin Dibble. *Narcissistic Lovers: How to Cope, Recover and Move On.* Far Hills, NJ: New Horizon Press, 2007.

Notes

This Work: Overview

1   *Thinking, Fast and Slow* (New York: Farrar, Straus and Giroux, 2011).

Chapter 1

2   See, for example, their "Prospect Theory: An Analysis under Risk," *Econometrica* 47, no. 2 (March 1979), 263–92, doi: 10.2307/1914185.

3   (New York: Henry Holt, 2009).

4   Melanie Gorman (host), "Marriages Fail and Some Survive," *The Anatomy of Love: Know Thy Brain, Know Thy Self, Know Thy Partner* (*Sex, Marriage, Dating, Love: The Experts*, 2:43) https://theanatomyoflove.com/blog/videos/marriages-fail-survive/.

Chapter 2

5   C. S. Lewis, The Four Loves (New York: Harcourt, Brace, Jovanovich, 1960), 169–70.

Chapter 3

6   Gary Chapman, *The Five Love Languages: How to Express Heartfelt Commitment to Your Mate* (Chicago: Northfield Publishing, 1995).

7   Kahneman, *Thinking, Fast and Slow.*

8   New International Version.

9   *Mere Christianity* (London: Geoffrey Bles, 1952).

10   *How to Be an Adult in Relationships: The Five Keys to Mindful Loving* (Boston and London: Shambhala, 2002).

Chapter 4

11   Revised Standard Version.

12   Brené Brown, *Daring Greatly: How the Courage to Be Vulnerable Transforms the Way We Live, Love, Parent, and Lead* (New York: Penguin, 2012), pp. 9–10.

13   Brown, "The Power of Vulnerability," TED Talk, June 2010, https://www.ted.com/talks/brene_brown_on_vulnerability#t-187198, time mark 3:19.

14   New Living Translation.

15   David Richo, *The Five Things We Cannot Change . . . and the Happiness We Find by Embracing Them* (Boston: Shambhala, 2010).

16   Ibid.

Chapter 5

17   Robert Plutchik, "The Nature of Emotions," *American Scientist*, July 16, 2001.

18   Richo, *The Five Things We Cannot Change*, p. 120.

Chapter 6

19   Richo, *How Relationships Work* (workshop lecture), https://davericho.com/cds-of-live-classes-by-david-richo/

20   New International Version.

Chapter 8

21   *Why We Love: The Nature and Chemistry of Romantic Love* (New York: Henry Holt and Company, 2004), and "Why We Love, Why We Cheat," *TED Ideas Worth Spreading*, February 2006, https://www.ted.com/talks/helen_fisher_tells_us_why_we_love_cheat

Chapter 9

22   J. Bowlby, *Attachment and Loss, Vol. 1: Attachment* (New York: Basic Books, 1969); *Attachment, Vol. 2: Separation* (New York: Basic Books, 1973); and *Attachment and Loss, Vol. 3: Loss, Sadness and Depression* (New York: Basic Books, 1980).

23   M.D.S. Ainsworth, "Attachment: Retrospect and Prospect," in *The Place of Attachment in Human Behavior*, ed. C. M. Parkes and J. Stevenson-Hinde (New York: Basic Books, 1982), 3–30; and "Attachments beyond Infancy," *American Psychologist* 44 (1989), 709–716.

24   Cindy Hazan and Phillip R. Shaver, "Attachment as an Organizational Framework for Research on Close Relationships, *Psychological Inquiry* 5 (no. 1, 1994), 1–22, http://www.psy.miami.edu/faculty/dmessinger/c_c/rsrcs/rdgs/attach/hazanandshaver.pdf

25   Robert W. Firestone, Lisa Firestone, and Joyce Catlett, *Conquer Your Critical Inner Voice: A Revolutionary Program to Counter Negative Thoughts and Live Free from Imagined Limitations* (Oakland, CA: New Harbinger Publications, 2002).

26   Lisa Firestone, "How Your Attachment Style Impacts Your Relationship," *Psychology Today*, July 30, 2013, https://www.psychologytoday.com/blog/compassion-matters/201307/how-your-attachment-style-impacts-your-relationship

27   Robert W. Firestone, *The Fantasy Bond: Structure of Psychological Defenses* (New York: Human Sciences Press/Insight Books, 1985).

Appendix C

28   Ibid.

Appendix D

29   Plutchik, "The Nature of Emotions."

30   Richo, *The Five Things We Cannot Change*, p. 120.

Appendix E

31   Bowlby, *Attachment and Loss, Vol. 1*; *Attachment, Vol. 2*; and *Attachment and Loss, Vol. 3*.

32   Ainsworth, "Attachment: Retrospect and Prospect," and "Attachments beyond Infancy."